Studies in Latin American Ethnohistory & Archaeology

Joyce Marcus
General Editor

Volume I *A Fuego y Sangre: Early Zapotec Imperialism in the Cuicatlán Cañada, Oaxaca*, by Elsa Redmond, Memoirs of the Museum of Anthropology, University of Michigan, No. 16. 1983.

Volume II *Irrigation and the Cuicatec Ecosystem: A Study of Agriculture and Civilization in North Central Oaxaca*, by Joseph W. Hopkins, Memoirs of the Museum of Anthropology, University of Michigan, No. 17. 1984.

Volume III *Aztec City-States*, by Mary G. Hodge, Memoirs of the Museum of Anthropology, University of Michigan, No. 18. 1984.

Volume IV *Conflicts over Coca Fields in Sixteenth-Century Peru*, by María Rostworowski de Diez Canseco, Memoirs of the Museum of Anthropology, University of Michigan, No. 21. 1988.

Volume V *Tribal and Chiefly Warfare in South America*, by Elsa Redmond, Memoirs of the Museum of Anthropology, University of Michigan, No. 28. 1994.

Volume VI *Imperial Transformations in Sixteenth-Century Yucay, Peru*, transcribed and edited by R. Alan Covey and Donato Amado González, Memoirs of the Museum of Anthropology, University of Michigan, No. 44. 2008.

Volume VII *Domestic Life in Prehispanic Capitals: A Study of Specialization, Hierarchy, and Ethnicity*, edited by Linda R. Manzanilla and Claude Chapdelaine, Memoirs of the Museum of Anthropology, University of Michigan, No. 46. 2009.

Volume VIII *Yuthu: Community and Ritual in an Early Andean Village*, by Allison R. Davis, Memoirs of the Museum of Anthropology, University of Michigan, No. 50. 2011.

Memoirs of the Museum of Anthropology
University of Michigan
Number 50

Studies in Latin American Ethnohistory & Archaeology
Joyce Marcus, General Editor

Volume VIII

Yuthu

Community and Ritual in an Early Andean Village

Allison R. Davis

Ann Arbor, Michigan
2011

©2011 by the Regents of the University of Michigan
The Museum of Anthropology
All rights reserved

Printed in the United States of America
ISBN 978-0-915703-77-7

Cover design by Katherine Clahassey

The University of Michigan Museum of Anthropology currently publishes two monograph series, Anthropological Papers and Memoirs, as well as an electronic series in CD-ROM form. For a complete catalog, write to Museum of Anthropology Publications, 4013 Museums Building, 1109 Geddes Avenue, Ann Arbor, MI 48109-1079, or see www.lsa.umich.edu/umma/publications

Library of Congress Cataloging-in-Publication Data

Davis, Allison R., 1978-
 Yuthu : community and ritual in an early Andean village / Allison R. Davis.
    p. cm. -- (Memoirs of the museum of anthropology, University of Michigan ; number 50) (Studies in Latin American ethnohistory & archaeology)
 Includes bibliographical references and index.
 ISBN 978-0-915703-77-7 (alk. paper)
1. Indians of South America--Peru--Cuzco Region--Antiquities. 2. Social archaeology--Peru--Cuzco Region. 3. Excavations (Archaeology)--Peru--Cuzco Region. 4. Cuzco Region (Peru)--Antiquities. I. Title.
 F3429.1.C9D38 2011
 985'.37--dc23
                          2011041142

The paper used in this publication meets the requirements of the ANSI Standard Z39.48-1984 (Permanence of Paper)

Contents

LIST OF ILLUSTRATIONS	*vii*
LIST OF TABLES	*ix*
AN EARLY VILLAGE IN THE INKA HEARTLAND, *by Joyce Marcus*	*xi*
ACKNOWLEDGMENTS	*xix*

CHAPTER 1. INTRODUCTION — *1*
- The Formative Period and the Origins of Inherited Rank and Multi-Settlement Polities — *1*
- The Shortcomings of Focusing Only on Comparative Questions — *4*
- The Archaeology of Community — *5*
- The Cultural and Historical Particularities of Andean Communities — *8*
- Community Study of Yuthu, an Early Andean Village — *10*

CHAPTER 2. ACTIVITIES AT YUTHU — *13*
- Activities That Shaped the Annual Cycle — *13*
- Daily Activities in the Village — *20*
- Periodic Activities in and around the Village — *25*
- Discussion — *40*

CHAPTER 3. THE SPACES OF DAILY LIFE — *41*
- Archaeological Deposits in the Northern Sector — *41*
- Discussion of the Deposits and Features in the Northern Sector — *91*
- Domestic Architecture at Yuthu in a Regional Perspective — *92*
- Domestic Ritual — *92*

CHAPTER 4. CEREMONIAL LIFE AT YUTHU — *93*
- Archaeological Deposits in the Southern Sector — *94*
- Discussion of the Deposits and Features in the Southern Sector — *133*
- What Accounts for the Differences between the Northern and Southern Sectors? — *133*
- Activities in the Northern and Southern Sectors — *136*
- Ceremonial Architecture at Yuthu in a Regional Perspective — *139*
- Ceremonial and Domestic Spaces — *141*

CHAPTER 5. GROUP IDENTITY, THE SACRED SYSTEM, AND POLITICS   143
    Andean Social Groups   143
    Ancestor Veneration and Sacred Landscapes before the Inka   147

CHAPTER 6. CONCLUSIONS   155
    The Emergence of Inherited Rank in Cusco   158
    The Role of Social Institutions in the Emergence of Multi-Village Polities   158
    Implications for Comparative Study of Early Villages   159
    Concluding Remarks   159

APPENDIX: RADIOCARBON DATE CALIBRATION   161
GLOSSARY (QUECHUA AND SPANISH)   163
BIBLIOGRAPHY   165
INDEX   177
COLOR PLATES   181

ILLUSTRATIONS

Figures

1.1. Map of Peru showing Yuthu and other nearby Formative period sites, *2*
1.2. Excavations in the Southern and Northern Sectors at Yuthu, *3*
1.3. View of Wimpillay and Muyu Orqo, *6*
1.4. Landscape view in the province of Paruro, just south of the modern city of Cusco, *9*

2.1. Crops grown at Yuthu, *14*
2.2. Faunal remains at Yuthu, *15*
2.3. Camelid species and size classifications at Yuthu, *17*
2.4. Age profile of camelids at Yuthu, *17*
2.5. Resource zones available to sites in the Xaquixaguana Plain survey area, *18*
2.6. Locations of the largest Formative sites and early planting zones in the Sacred Valley, *19*
2.7. Labor schedule for planting and harvesting major crops, *20*
2.8. Modern example of small grinding stone, *21*
2.9. Objects used for personal adornment, *23*
2.10. Cranial modification at Yuthu, *24*
2.11. Wild species that were hunted or trapped, *27*
2.12. Wild plants collected at Yuthu, *27*
2.13. Examples of bone tools from Yuthu, *28*
2.14. Pottery forms at Yuthu, *30*
2.15. Chanapata sub-styles identified at Yuthu, *31*
2.16. Raw materials for chipped stone by count and weight, *32*
2.17. Examples of Formative period projectile points found at Yuthu, *32*
2.18. Skeletal trauma observed in men, women, and children, *34*
2.19. Four types of burial practiced at Yuthu, *36*
2.20. The old road to Maras and Urubamba, the limit of both sectors, *39*

3.1. The stratigraphy of Unit D, *42*
3.2. The earliest occupation of Yuthu, *43*
3.3. A cross section of the final excavation of Intrusion M, *44*
3.4. Intrusion M was filled with five phases of deposits, *45*
3.5. Modern semi-subterranean thatched structure excavated into a hillside, *46*
3.6. Two unique artifacts found on the floor of Intrusion L, *55*
3.7. Burial 20, a secondary burial that included incomplete skeletons of two individuals, *56*
3.8. Burial 21, a secondary interment of two individuals, *57*
3.9. The semicircular floor in the northwest corner, *61*
3.10. Several obsidian tools found in Ashy Intrusion 2, *62*
3.11. The structure in the southeast corner of Unit D, *65*
3.12. An above-ground domestic structure in the southeast corner of Unit D, *66*
3.13. A carved antler found on the first trampled surface of the structure, *67*
3.14. Chipped stone tools found in the ashy intrusion, *70*
3.15. Burial 19, an 11- to 12-year-old child, *74*

3.16. Burial 19, with cranium removed, *74*
3.17. Several chipped stone tools found in Level E-7 of the hearth, *75*
3.18. Worked bone from Level E-7 of the hearth, *75*
3.19. Chipped stone objects from Level E-10 of the hearth, *76*
3.20. Worked bone from Level E-10 of the hearth, *76*
3.21. The final phase of use in Unit D, *82*
3.22 The circular intrusion covered by rocks set in burned soil, *84*
3.23. Four human burials surrounded a small circular stone hearth, *89*
3.24. Burial 16, a 26- to 35-year-old man who had been stored as a mummy, *90*

4.1. The artificial platform in the Southern Sector is a striking feature on the landscape, *94*
4.2. Stratigraphic profiles of Unit A, *95*
4.3. Structure 1, a sunken floor surrounded by a bench, *96*
4.4. Schematic cross section of the western and eastern parts of Structure 1, *97*
4.5. The two parts of the southwestern bench, separated by a drain and retaining wall, *98*
4.6. Burial 12, placed in construction fill of Structure 1, *98*
4.7. Burial 13, incorporated into western section of the bench in Structure 1, *100*
4.8. Photograph of Burial 13, *100*
4.9. Burial 14, in the construction fill of Structure 1, *101*
4.10. Features added after Structure 1 was built, *101*
4.11. Laminar deposits of soil typical of those deposited by water inside Ritual Canal 1, *102*
4.12. A section of Level 2 from the interior of Ritual Canal 1, *103*
4.13. Large semicircular intrusion in front of the intake of Ritual Canals 1 and 2, *107*
4.14. Stone tools from Level D-1 in base of the intrusion, *107*
4.15. Stone-lined cist associated with a white clay floor, *109*
4.16. Chipped stone tools for punching and cutting found in the circular cist, *109*
4.17. A potato illa, *111*
4.18. Canal 3, built after Structure 1, *113*
4.19. Canal 3, a stone-lined channel very similar to Ritual Canals 1 and 2, *114*
4.20. Burial 9, which cut off Canal 3 and symbolically and ritually ended its use life, *115*
4.21. Burial 9, a 1- to 2-year-old child included in Stratum 9, *115*
4.22. Burial 8, a 36- to 45-year-old woman included in the matrix of Stratum 9, *115*
4.23. Burial 10, an 18- to 25-year-old woman included in the matrix of Stratum 9, *116*
4.24. Ritual Canal 2, built to replace Ritual Canal 1, *117*
4.25. Photograph of Ritual Canal 2, which cut off Ritual Canal 1, *118*
4.26. Burial 11, a 2- to 3-year-old child buried in a cavity below Ritual Canal 2, *119*
4.27. The last use of Structure 1 before it was abandoned and buried, *120*
4.28. The mud structure, which had three walls and was open to the southwest, *126*
4.29. The mud structure, *126*

4.30. The final use of Unit A, *127*
4.31. Burial 4, an 18- to 25-year-old man, *128*
4.32. Individuals 6 and 7 in the group burial of children, *129*
4.33. Individual 7, a 1- to 2-year-old child, *129*
4.34. Individual 6, probably killed by a blow to the head, *130*
4.35. Individual 3, stratigraphically highest in the group burial, *131*
4.36. Burial 5, an older woman, *131*
4.37. Burial 2, a man who had unique burial treatment and physical characteristics, *132*
4.38. The final view of excavations in Units A and D, *134*
4.39. Simplified sketch of possible original construction of Structure 1, *135*
4.40. Radiocarbon dates from the Northern and Southern Sectors of Yuthu, *136*

5.1. View of the Southern Sector platform and Cerro Huanacaure, *149*
5.2. Ceremonial architecture and the local landscape, *150*
5.3. The alignment of ritual canals in the Southern Sector with distant glacial peaks, *151*
5.4. Ritual objects found in the Southern Sector, *152*

Color Plates

1. Objects used for personal adornment; bone tools
2. Chanapata sub-styles identified at Yuthu
3. Semi-subterranean structure; obsidian and chipped stone tools; carved antler
4. Views of Southern Sector
5. Stone tools and stone-lined cist, Unit A
6. Ritual Canals 1 and 2
7. Final view of excavations in Units A and D
8. Objects found in Southern Sector

TABLES

4.1. Dimensions of sunken rectangular structures from the southern Andes, *139*
A. Radiocarbon date calibration for samples from Unit A, *161*
B. List of Cusco area Formative period dates, *162*

AN EARLY VILLAGE IN THE INKA HEARTLAND

Joyce Marcus

Scholars who think about Peru usually picture the Inka. Images of their tight-fitting sillar walls, featured at Machu Picchu, Cusco, Saqsayhuaman, Tambo Machay, Q'enko, and Ollantaytambo, grace the postcards that we send home. The rich documentary record left by sixteenth-century writers like Pedro Cieza de León, Garci Diez de San Miguel, Juan Polo de Ondegardo, Pedro Sancho de la Hoz, Juan de Betanzos, Pablo José de Arriaga, Cristóbal de Molina, Francisco de Ávila, and Felipe Guamán Poma de Ayala excites us. The Inka captured the imagination of John Murra, John Rowe, María Rostworowski de Diez Canseco, R. Tom Zuidema, Craig Morris, Franklin Pease, Frank Salomon, Brian Bauer, R. Alan Covey,* and others yet to come.

The crown jewel of the Inka was Cusco, the architectural showcase of their empire, where the Spaniards witnessed feasts, ceremonies, and events at the holiest of shrines, the gilded Qoricancha or "Golden Enclosure" (Bauer 1998, 2004). Cieza de León says that he was "amazed . . . that the whole city of Cusco and its temples were not of solid gold" (1959:156). "This city was full of strange and foreign peoples, for there were Indians from Chile, Pasto, and Cañari, Chachapoyas, Huancas, Colla, and all the other tribes to be found in the provinces . . . each of them established in the place and district set aside for them by the governors of the city" (Cieza de León 1959:148).

So celebrated was the Cusco of Inka times that we sometimes forget how little we know of earlier times in the region. How much did the Inka borrow from their predecessors, and how much did they invent? Did pre-Inka societies conduct rituals at the confluence of two rivers, as the Inka did (Sherbondy 1982)? Did pre-Inka cities have a main plaza divided into two, as the Inka did (Bauer 2004)? Did earlier societies have shadow-casting stones set up to mark the summer and winter solstices (Bauer and Dearborn 1995)? Did they have as accurate a calendar, helping them coordinate an annual round of rituals related to the agricultural cycle (Zuidema 1977)?

---

*References are at the end of this foreword.

Yuthu

Allison Davis' pioneering excavations at the Formative site of Yuthu provide our first data on early village life in the Cusco area. Yuthu lies near the shore of a spring-fed lake, on a high rolling plain at 3600 meters. There Davis examined early households, and evidence for the villagers' subsistence strategies, craft production, and mortuary practices. From her excavations we learn a great deal about daily life and about public rituals, each conducted in a different sector of Yuthu.

An unexpected bonus of Davis' excavations was the discovery that some well-known Inka practices actually had their origin in the early villages of the Cusco region. Before her work at Yuthu, so few early houses and ceremonial structures had been published in detail for the Cusco area that we had much less evidence for understanding sacred versus secular space.

Davis' excavations contribute to our understanding of one of the most important transitions in Andean history—the shift from autonomous egalitarian villages to multi-community polities with hereditary inequality. She is able to link archaeological houses, sites, and multi-site clusters to socially meaningful units such as families, villages, and communities. Davis is also able to combine her excavations with settlement pattern data to develop a regional picture of the Formative period in Cusco. This regional perspective was made possible by her collaboration with R. Alan Covey, director of the Xaquixaguana Plain Archaeological Survey.

This volume is not only the first excavation report on a Formative village in the Cusco area, but also a study that contributes new data on many traditional Andean themes—zonal complementarity, sacred landscapes, community composition, mummies and ancestor veneration, ritual canals and religious rites, and intra-village subdivisions.

Zonal Complementarity

Davis' excavations provide new insights into the way early villages gained access to resources from other environmental zones. Rather than placing colonists in different zones as the Inka did, the early villagers at Yuthu traveled to other zones to procure what they needed. With many environmental zones in close proximity, each with its distinctive products, the people of Yuthu encountered diverse resources as they ascended and descended the mountains.

The villagers occupying ancient Yuthu were similar to the herders and farmers of the twentieth century who also elected to travel to different elevations to carry out complementary subsistence activities. Such a strategy led to communities that were spread out across an altitudinal span of 2500 to 3000 meters (e.g., Brush 1977; Paerregaard 1992). Examples of this pattern include the Uchucmarca Valley and the community of Q'ero, whose compressed zonation and steep gradient allow people to exploit their respective valleys for subsistence items without colonies, migrations, or exchange systems that extend beyond the community's territorial limits (Brush 1977:11). The members of the community of Q'ero, whose lands extend from 2000 to 5000 meters, move from zone to zone to procure desired resources (Webster 1971:174–76).

The Yuthu subsistence strategy, like that of the twentieth century, contrasts with that of the Inka who implemented a "vertical archipelago" strategy in which the Inka could force whole settlements to move to different environmental zones to produce crops the empire wanted.

The diversity of environmental zones in the Andean highlands helps to shape the worldview of the villagers who occupy those lands. Quechua speakers in the Cusco area see the environment as an animate being and regard mountain peaks, springs, and caves as origin places or as living ancestors. Divine beings and ancestors are thought to occupy the snowy summit of the mountain that overlooks their community.

Zonal complementarity is the basic component of the vertical archipelago model developed by John Murra from ethnohistoric documents (Murra 1972, 1980, 1985). Murra speculated that because this sixteenth-century strategy was so widespread and had survived so many political changes, it might extend far back into prehistory; he therefore challenged archaeologists to look into the past and determine the antiquity of the vertical archipelago.

Davis did not set out to identify vertical archipelagos in Formative period Cusco, but she did want to address: (1) the degree to which villagers at Yuthu had access to multiple resource zones; (2) the extent to which they were part of a larger community; and (3) the possibility that they saw themselves as part of a sacred landscape.

The Nature of Andean Sacred Landscapes

In speaking of the *runakuna* or highland Andean people, Catherine Allen (1988:41) says,

Runakuna have an intimate knowledge of their landscape; every wrinkle in the Earth's physiognomy—every hill, knoll, plain, ridge, rock outcrop, or lake—possesses a name and a personality. Every child knows a vast number of these place names before the age of ten, for *Runakuna* orient themselves spatially in terms of landmarks rather than through abstract cardinal points.

Every move made by the *runakuna* is overseen by animate and sacred landmarks. Such watchful places are called *tirakuna*. A high snowy mountain is addressed as *apu* or lord, and the mountains are collectively known as *taytakuna* or fathers. Davis' excavations at Yuthu revealed ritual features whose configuration suggests that similar sacred landscapes existed already in the Formative period. They were a legacy that the Inka inherited rather than created.

Community Composition and Village Layout

Some Andean communities today display dual organization. The community of Tapay in the Colca Valley provides an example. Tapay combines dual principles with quadripartition; herders occupy two sectors at a higher elevation (Puna Grande and Puna Chica), while farmers occupy two sectors at a lower elevation (Hanansaya and Urinsaya). Paerregaard (1992:23) says these four divisions are largely endogamous, with marriage being rare between Hanansaya and Urinsaya and between puna herders and village agriculturalists.

We doubt that this level of formal duality existed in the Formative, yet Yuthu seems to have been divided by a gully into a Northern Sector and a Southern Sector. Davis' excavations show that the Northern Sector was mainly residential, an area where everyday household activities took place. The Southern Sector was the scene of rituals that took place in ceremonial structures built atop a large platform. In comparing the ceremonial architecture at Yuthu with that from other parts of the Andes, Davis is able to link it to one of today's widespread patterns, a long ceremonial tradition that involves ritual canals and rectangular sunken structures. Some of the shared details are striking.

Today's Andean herders sometimes make miniature stone effigies or *illa* depicting llamas or other animals, offering them to supernatural beings to help ensure abundance (e.g., Flannery et al. 1989; Isbell 1978; Reinhard 2007; Rowe 1946). Maize beer and burned offerings may also be placed near irrigation canals to ensure sufficient water for successful plantings. Davis found similar effigies and canal rituals at Yuthu.

Many of today's ritual features are oriented toward sacred places on the landscape. Yuthu's artificial platform, sunken plaza, and canals were similarly aligned with local lakes, mountains, and glacial peaks. These discoveries at Yuthu's Southern Sector allow Davis to establish relationships among religious rites, water-control features, and the sacred landscape.

Mummies and Ancestor Veneration

When the Spaniards arrived in Peru, they were surprised to find that each Inka ruler had been embalmed and stored in his palace. The royal mummies were paraded around in public and put on display in Cusco's main plaza in the order in which they had reigned. Whenever the caretakers brought out a royal mummy, they sang about the deceased's reign and his accomplishments. Because the dead king's wealth and rights to land were passed down to them, both the caretakers and royal descendants were eager to maintain the mummy cult for generations.

Here is how the Spaniard Juan de Betanzos ([1557, part I, chapter 48] 1996:185) described the embalming of Wayna Qhapaq in 1528:

> the nobles who were with him had him opened and took out all his entrails, preparing him so that no damage would be done to him and without breaking any bone. They prepared and dried him in the sun and the air. After he was dried and cured, they dressed him in costly clothes and placed him on an ornate litter well adorned with feathers and gold. When the body was prepared, they sent it to Cuzco.

Each dead Inka was given a human oracle who sat next to the mummy and spoke for him. Needless to say, the Spaniards rounded up as many mummies of rulers as they could and burned them in public ceremonies, hoping to end the continuing veneration by their loyal subjects.

What time depth did such ancestor veneration have in the Cusco region? One of the most exciting finds at Yuthu was Davis' discovery of Formative period mummies. Through careful study, Davis shows that as early as 100 B.C., some individuals were mummified and stored in accessible places so that their descendants could continue to interact with them after their death. She also makes the case that such mummy bundles played an important role in the creation of inequality among the living.

Nearly 1500 years before the rise of the Inka, the occupants of Yuthu made offerings to their mummified ancestors and almost certainly relied on ancestor ritual as one means by which a lineage could establish its rights and privileges.

The Legacy of Yuthu

We should probably not be surprised that the origins of many Inka practices have a long time depth. It was unlikely that complex Late Horizon society could have arisen without making use of all the innovations and institutions developed by its predecessors. What the Inka region lacked until now was concrete evidence from the excavation of early villages.

This excavation report takes a community-wide approach to household organization, subsistence strategies, craft production, and mortuary practices. Davis shows that an Andean ideology in which privileges and access to land were established by ancestors (and confirmed by rituals performed in a sacred landscape) was already present in Cusco's early villages. Her work also suggests that, at least in the case of Yuthu, the vertical archipelago of Inka times had not yet developed. The people of Yuthu established their village in one altitude zone and traveled to nearby zones for specific resources as needed. Davis shows us that the early Andean village was about much more than farming and herding. The early Cusco villages occupied a special place in a sacred landscape, one in which ancestors and mountain spirits played crucial roles.

Bibliography

Allen, Catherine J.
1988   *The Hold Life Has: Coca and Cultural Identity in an Andean Community*. Washington and London: Smithsonian Institution Press.

Arriaga, Pablo José de
1968 [1621]   *The Extirpation of Idolatry in Peru*, translated and edited by L. Clark Keating. Lexington: University of Kentucky Press.

Ávila, Francisco de
1966 [1598]   *Dioses y hombres de Huarochirí*, translated from Quechua by José María Arguedas. Lima: Museo Nacional de la Historia and Instituto de Estudios Peruanos.

Bauer, Brian S.
1998   *The Sacred Landscape of the Inca: The Cuzco Ceque System*. Austin: University of Texas Press.
2004   *Ancient Cuzco: Heartland of the Inca*. Austin: University of Texas Press.

Bauer, Brian S., and David Dearborn
1995   *Astronomy and Empire in the Ancient Andes*. Austin: University of Texas Press.

Betanzos, Juan de
1996 [1557]   *Narrative of the Incas*, translated and edited by Roland Hamilton and Dana Buchanan from the Palma de Mallorca manuscript. Austin: University of Texas Press.

Brush, Stephen B.
1977   *Mountain, Field, and Family: The Economy and Human Ecology of an Andean Valley*. Philadelphia: University of Pennsylvania Press.

Cieza de León, Pedro de
1959 [1553]   *The Incas of Pedro de Cieza de León*, translated by Harriet de Onis, edited by Victor Wolfgang von Hagen. Norman: University of Oklahoma Press.

Covey, R. Alan
2006   *How the Incas Built Their Heartland: State Formation and the Innovation of Imperial Strategies in the Sacred Valley, Peru*. Ann Arbor: University of Michigan Press.

Diez de San Miguel, Garci
1964 [1567]   *Visita hecha a la provincia de Chucuito*. Documentos regionales para la etnohistoria. Lima: Ediciones de la Casa de la Cultura del Perú.

Flannery, Kent V., Joyce Marcus, and Robert G. Reynolds
1989   *The Flocks of the Wamani: A Study of Llama Herders on the Punas of Ayacucho, Peru*. San Diego: Academic Press.

Garcilaso de la Vega, El Inca
1966 [1609] *Royal Commentaries of the Incas and General History of Peru, Parts 1 and 2*, translated by Harold V. Livermore. Austin: University of Texas Press.

Gasparini, Graziano, and Luise Margolies
1980 *Inca Architecture*, translated by Patricia J. Lyon. Bloomington: Indiana University Press.

Guaman Poma de Ayala, Felipe
1956 [1615] *Nueva Crónica y Buen Gobierno*, 3 vols. Lima: Editorial Cultura.

Isbell, Billie Jean
1978 *To Defend Ourselves: Ecology and Ritual in an Andean Village*. Prospect Heights, Illinois: Waveland Press.

Molina, Cristóbal de
1989 [1575] Relación de las Fábulas i Ritos de los Ingas. In *Fábulas y Mitos de los Incas*, edited by Enrique Urbano and Pierre Duviols, pp. 47–134. Crónicas de América series, Historia 16. Madrid, Spain.

Morris, Craig
1972 State settlements in Tawantinsuyu: A strategy of compulsory urbanism. In *Contemporary Archaeology: A Guide to Theory and Contributions*, edited by Mark P. Leone, pp. 393–401. Carbondale, IL: Southern Illinois University Press.
1982 The infrastructure of Inka control in the Peruvian central highlands. In *The Inca and Aztec States, 1400–1800: Anthropology and History*, edited by George A. Collier, Renato I. Rosaldo, and John D. Wirth, pp. 153–71. New York: Academic.
1986 Storage, supply, and redistribution in the economy of the Inka State. In *Anthropological History of Andean Polities*, edited by John V. Murra, Nathan Wachtel, and Jacques Revel, pp. 59–68. New York: Cambridge University Press.

Murra, John V.
1972 El "Control Vertical" de un Máximo de Pisos Ecológicos en la Economía de las Sociedades Andinas. In *Visita de la Provincia de León de Huánuco en 1562*, Tomo II, by Iñigo Ortiz de Zúñiga, edited by John Murra, pp. 427–76. Huánuco: Universidad Nacional Hermilio Valdizán.
1980 *The Economic Organization of the Inca State*. Greenwich, CT: JAI Press.
1985 The limits and limitations of the "vertical archipelago" in the Andes. In *Andean Ecology and Civilization: An Interdisciplinary Perspective on Andean Ecological Complementarity*, edited by Shozo Masuda, Izumi Shimada, and Craig Morris, pp. 15–20. Wenner-Gren Foundation Symposium No. 91. Japan: University of Tokyo Press.

Paerregaard, Karsten
1992 Complementarity and duality: Oppositions between agriculturalists and herders in an Andean village. *Ethnology* 31(1):15–26.

Pease, Franklin
1995 *Las Crónicas y los Andes*. Lima: Pontificia Universidad Católica del Perú.

Polo de Ondegardo, Juan
1916 [1571] *Informaciones Acerca de la Religión y Gobierno de los Incas*. Lima: Sanmarti y Cia.

Reinhard, Johan
2007 *Machu Picchu: Exploring an Ancient Sacred Center*, 4th rev. ed. Los Angeles: Cotsen Institute of Archaeology, UCLA.

Rostworowski de Diez Canseco, María
1970 Los ayarmaca. *Revista del Museo Nacional* 36:58–101.
1999 *History of the Inca Realm*, translated by Harry B. Iceland. Cambridge: Cambridge University Press.

Rowe, John H.
1946 Inca culture at the time of the Spanish Conquest. In *Handbook of South American Indians*, Vol. 2, edited by Julian H. Steward, pp. 183–330. Bureau of American Ethnology Bulletin 143. Washington, D.C.: Smithsonian Institution.

Salomon, Frank, and George Urioste (eds.)
1991 *The Huarochirí Manuscript: A Testament of Ancient and Colonial Andean Religion*. Austin: University of Texas Press.

Sancho de la Hoz, Pedro
1917 [1534] *An Account of the Conquest of Peru*, translated into English by Philip Ainsworth Means. New York: The Cortés Society.

Sherbondy, Jeannette
1982 The Canal Systems of Hanan Cuzco. PhD dissertation, University of Illinois, Urbana.

Webster, Steven
1971 An indigenous Quechua community in exploitation of multiple ecological zones. *Actas y Memorias del XXXIX Congreso Internacional de Americanistas* 3:174–83. Lima, Peru.

Zuidema, R. Tom
1977 The Inca calendar. In *Native American Astronomy*, edited by Anthony F. Aveni, pp. 219–59. Austin: University of Texas Press.

ACKNOWLEDGMENTS

I would like to begin by thanking the scholars who have guided me through this process as mentors and as friends. First, I am indebted to Joyce Marcus for propelling me through each step in the transition from student to project director over the past decade. During this time, we have become friends, and I am most thankful for this. For many years of my life, I was equally likely to see Bruce Mannheim crossing the Plaza de Armas in Cusco or walking along South University in Ann Arbor. In either place, his love for the Andes and his truly four-field approach to anthropology have led to countless discussions that transformed my archaeological research into an anthropological study of Andean life. I could never have begun this project without opportunities and support from Alan Covey. He invited me to work in Cusco as part of the Xaquixaguana Plain Archaeological Survey. From the beginning, he has given me the advice and guidance that was essential for developing a significant and meaningful research project in the Inka heartland. Finally, I would like to thank Kent Flannery for always encouraging me to follow the path of the Michigan-trained archaeologists who came before me. At times it has been difficult, but the story of ancient life I have been able to tell has made the challenges worthwhile.

A large part of this book was written and rewritten while overlooking the green at Brown University while I was a Postdoctoral Fellow at the Artemis A.W. and Martha Sharp Joukowsky Institute for Archaeology & the Ancient World. The excitement at the Institute about shaping the future of archaeology as a discipline was a great force in shaping this book. I would especially like to thank Susan Alcock and John Cherry, as well as Mac Marston, Kevin Fisher and Krysta Ryzewski. I am grateful for the support from Oberlin College as I've finished the last stages of manuscript preparation. I am very indebted to Jill Rheinheimer for guiding each step that brought this manuscript to publication and Kay Clahassey for preparing the images for publication.

During this project, I have developed relationships with archaeological specialists without whom I would not have been able to meet my goal of holistic study of a Formative period village. Valerie Andrushko, at Southern Connecticut State

University, generously carried out all of the human skeletal analyses of the burials from Yuthu. I am indebted to her for every sex, age, or trauma identification in this book. Her ongoing work toward understanding the long-terms changes in human health, violence, and physical stresses in Cusco is changing our understanding of the development of Andean society.

In addition, I am very fortunate to have been able to work with Victor Vásquez Sánchez and Teresa Rosales Tham at ARQUEOBIOS, the *Centro de Investigaciones Arqueobiológicas y Paleoecolócigas Andinas*, in Trujillo, Peru. Their team carried out all identification of faunal and botanical remains recovered at Yuthu. Without their expertise, I would not have been able to incorporate key discussions of subsistence or land use in this study.

One of the best things about working in Cusco is becoming part of the existing community of archaeologists in that historic city. In my lifetime, I will never experience the diversity of fieldwork that a *cusqueño* archaeologist will. Relying on the strengths of each archaeologist that I have worked with has made this project stronger. I am particularly indebted to Carlos M. Delgado Gónzalez, the co-director of the Yuthu Archaeological Project. His broad knowledge of Andean archaeology and experience organizing and directing excavations were invaluable. I am happy that I can count him as a friend. Viky Galiano Blanco is not only a great archaeologist, but also a friend. Her family has embraced me (literally and figuratively), and if it not for them, I would not miss my second home nearly as much as I do.

I would also like to thank the community of Ccollana Chequerec Cruzpata for welcoming me to their village, Brian S. Bauer, Rosa Galiano Blanco, Jorge L. Flores Sánchez, Benjamín Castro Quispe, Megalith Galiano Blanco, Yeshica Amado Galiano, Kylie Quave, Whitney Mihel, Wilbert Rodrigo Rojas, Jorge Silva Sifuentes, Henry Harman Guerra, Alfredo Álvarez, Marcela de Harth, Tod Ehlers, Philip D. Gingerich, Guillermo Salas Carreño, and my mother Becky Baker.

This project has been supported by a Fulbright IIE Fellowship, National Science Foundation Dissertation Improvement Grant No. 0832325, and funding from the University of Michigan including the Margaret Wray French Award, Griffin Award, International Institute Individual Fellowship, and Rackham Research Grant.

Introduction

Cusco, Peru, is best known for the development of the Inka Empire (AD 1300–1600), and each year Machu Picchu and other extraordinary ruins from this late period draw scores of visitors to the ancient capital. Because of the central role of the Inka in contemporary national identity and the economic importance of tourism, most resources for archaeology in Cusco have been invested in the restoration and maintenance of impressive roads, storage facilities, and palaces from later periods. In addition, the chronicles of Inka social and political life (written primarily by Spaniards) have been extensively studied and, until recently, have been the primary evidence used by many Andeanists to build a vision of the past. Obviously, the chronicles have little to say about pre-Inka periods, and the earliest huts and camps do not leave impressive ruins on the landscape that attract tourists. Therefore, very little is known about the people who lived before the Inka.

This study is a first step in building a complete picture of early village life in Cusco 1500 years before the Inka. Prior to this project, no Formative period site in Cusco had been excavated on a large enough scale to reveal houses and community structures. What little we knew from this period was based on systematic survey and small opportunistic excavations (for examples, see Bauer 1999, 2002; Bauer and Jones 2003; Chávez 1977, 1980, 1981a, 1981b, 1982; Hey 1984; Kendall 1976, 1994; McEwan et al. 1995; Mohr 1969; Patterson 1967; Rowe 1943, 1944; Yábar Moreno 1959, 1972, 1982; Zapata 1998).

From 2005 to 2007, I excavated Yuthu, a Formative period village located about 20 km northwest of the modern city of Cusco (Fig. 1.1). The site can be divided into two sectors separated by a small gully. The Southern Sector is a small artificial platform that contains ceremonial structures. In contrast, the Northern Sector consists of domestic structures and activity areas located on the natural slope with very little land modification (Fig. 1.2). The majority of the evidence used in this study comes from 156 m^2 of excavation divided approximately equally between the two sectors. These excavation data are linked to a larger regional picture of the Formative period on the surrounding plain, using settlement pattern data that I helped to collect in 2004–2005 as a crew director with the Xaquixaguana Plain Archaeological Survey (directed by R. Alan Covey). In addition, Andean ethnography and ethnohistory provide a framework for understanding some of the human activities I identified from archaeological materials.

The Formative Period and the Origins of Inherited Rank and Multi-Settlement Polities

Although hard to imagine in today's world of global empires and powerful corporations, societies without institutionalized hierarchy or inherited inequality were some of the most stable and enduring forms of social organization in humanity's past. For example, while the Inka Empire lasted only 300 years, egalitar-

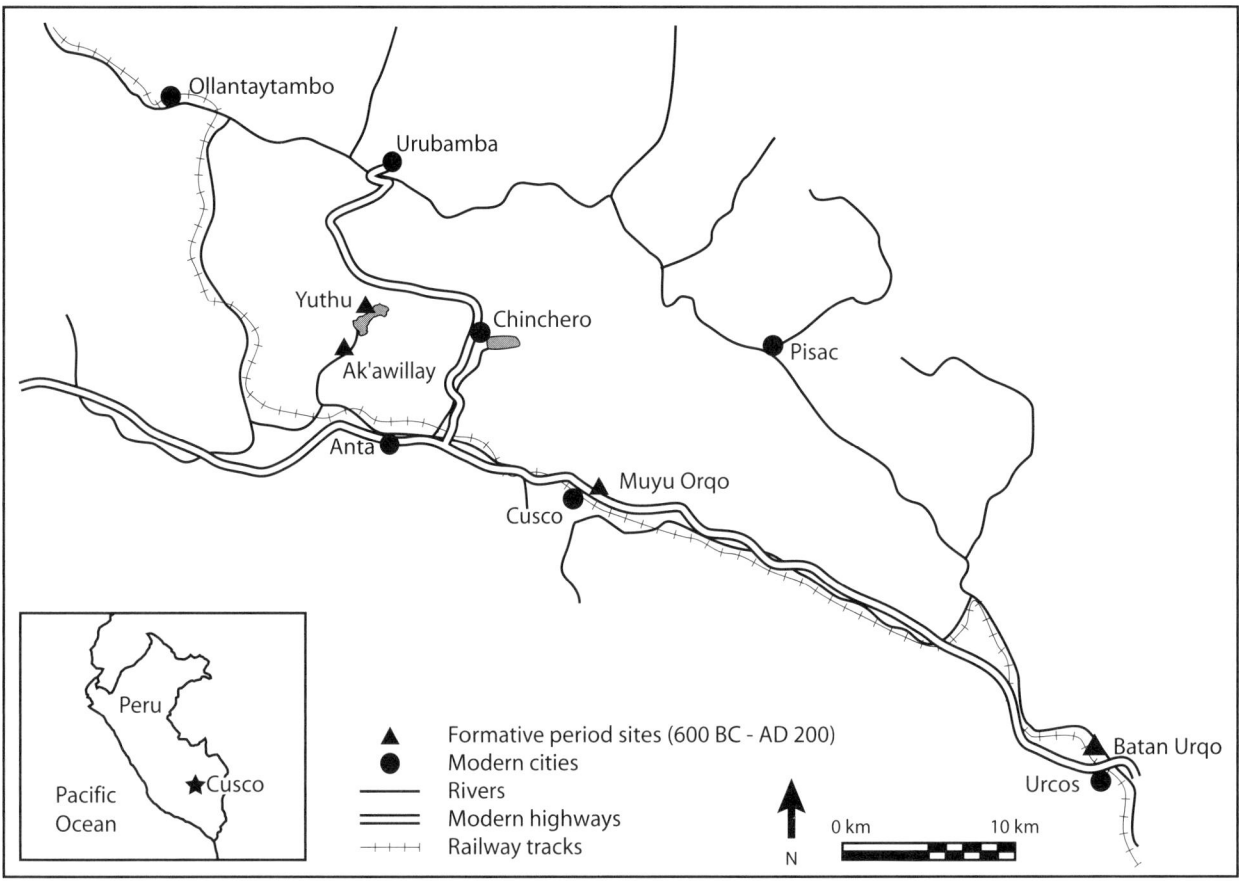

Figure 1.1. Yuthu is a single component Formative period village site northwest of the modern city of Cusco on the shore of Lake Huaypo. It is located on the plain of Anta near the modern towns of Chinchero and Anta.

ian village societies endured around Cusco for as many as 2400 years. Similarly, while ancient Rome flourished for 500 years, tribal Neolithic groups inhabited southern Italy for nearly 3500 years. The endurance of these groups alone makes their study critical to an understanding of any region's history.

One of the most important social and political transitions in human communities worldwide was the shift from autonomous villages organized according to egalitarian principles to multi-community political formations with hereditary inequality. This shift was the critical threshold that made possible the ancient empires, modern nation states, and multinational corporations that followed. In many parts of Latin America, including Mesoamerica and the Andean highlands, the period when this transition took place is called the Formative period. Although the name is shared throughout the area, the specific timing of these transitions varied from region to region according to local history.

Unfortunately, the term *formative* is not a very flattering or suitable adjective to describe one of the most enduring sociopolitical configurations in the history of humanity. How could the early villagers in Cusco—who created and maintained such rich economic, social, political, and ritual lives—be interesting only insofar as they were an ancestral stage in the formation of the Inka Empire? It is true that the social and political changes at this time made the development of the later empire possible; indeed, I have found that some practices known from later Andean states extended back to this time. I hope, however, that this study shows that the villagers of Yuthu are worthy of study independently of the great empire that formed many generations later.

The Formative period in Cusco includes the years from about 2200 BC to AD 200 (following Bauer's 2004 chronology). Previous work suggests that the non-egalitarian multi-village polities probably arose by the end of this period (Bauer 2004; Zapata 1998). Our understanding of that process, however, is in its infancy. To begin to understand the character of sociopolitical organization in any particular place or moment during the Formative period, anthropological archaeologists often ask two distinct questions: (1) did the society have inherited status or rank and (2) did polities include more than one village (following Flan-

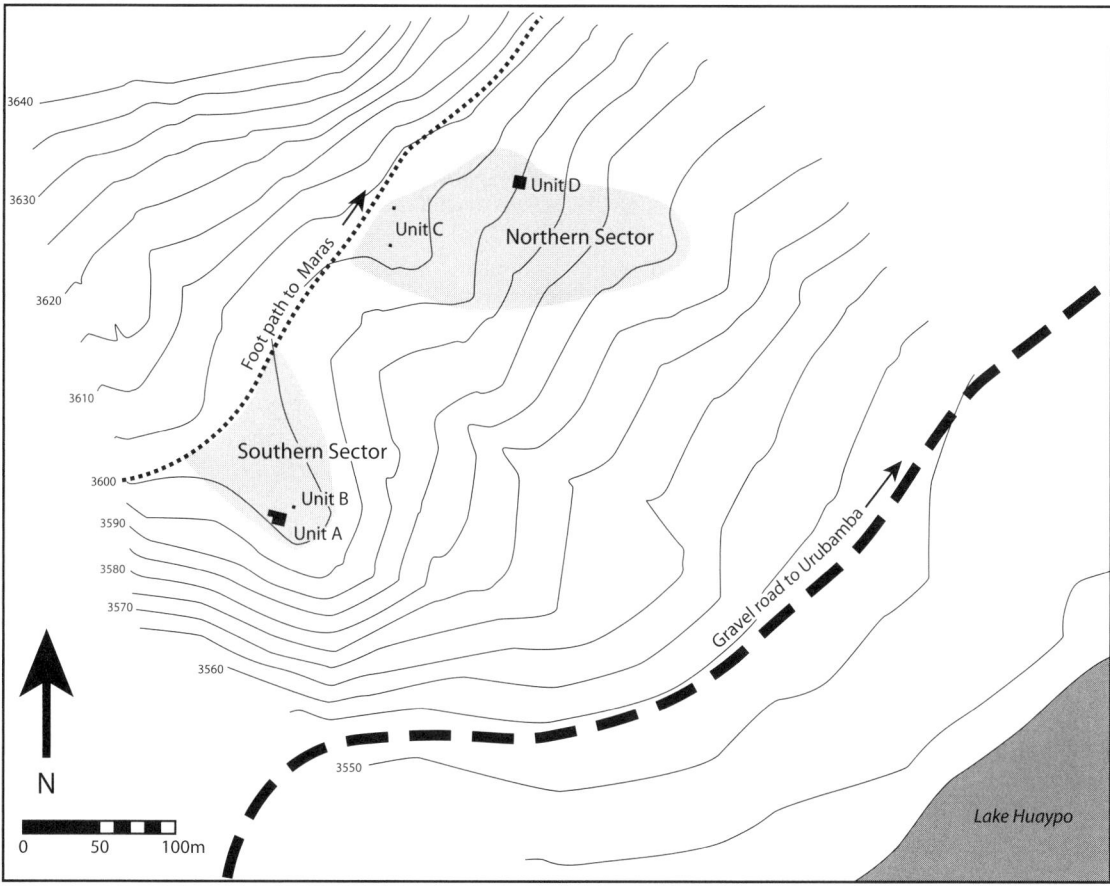

Figure 1.2. Yuthu can be divided into two sectors separated by a small gully. Excavations at the site included 84 m² in the ceremonial Southern Sector (Units A and B) and 72 m² in the domestic Northern Sector (Units C and D).

nery 1995)? This heuristic distinction is useful not only because the two phenomena are distinct, but because the evaluation of each question calls for different kinds of evidence. The general theoretical and methodological approaches to addressing each question, using only archaeological evidence, were well developed primarily by processual archaeologists starting in the 1960s.

Did Society Have Inherited Status or Rank?

Although some kinds of inequality exist in all societies, in groups with inherited rank, status positions beyond those associated with age, sex, or family roles can be passed down across generations (following Berreman 1981). Wason (1994) and Marcus (2008) provide good syntheses of material indications of rank found in the archaeological record. In this short discussion, I highlight only a few.

Because archaeologists recover material things, most prehistoric studies of rank focus on differential access to *goods* that results from having higher or lower status. Commonly, the presence of prestige goods in the graves of only some individuals (e.g., Babić 2005; Binford 1972; O'Shea 1996; Saxe 1970; Song-Nai and Mong-Lyong 1992; Tainter 1977) or in the homes of only some families (e.g., Bermann 1994; Vaughn 2004; Winter and Pires-Ferreira 1976) is considered to be a good indication that a subset of people were of higher rank than others within their community. When high-status burial treatments are given to infants, it is often a sign that status has been inherited since the baby would have been unable to earn prestige in his or her short life. Another common economic indicator of inequality is disparate access to adequate amounts of nutritious foods or access to special high status foods, which can be measured in the human skeleton (Welch and Scarry 1995).

Though it is more difficult to identify archaeologically, the access to or influence over *labor* that disproportionately benefits one or a few families is an equally important consideration when studying the economic effects of rank (Wright 2000). Most often, archaeologists use the presence of one or several houses in a village that are significantly larger, more elaborate, or made of better materials to index unequal access to labor (Coupland 1985; Lesure and Blake 2002). If higher ranking people used their influence to convince others to plant, harvest, or herd on their behalf, it may be much more difficult to identify archaeologically. This point may prove to be particularly troublesome for highland Andean archaeologists because labor was a significant form of tribute for later polities (Murra 1975, 1980; Rowe 1946). Hereditary rank may also carry symbolic, ritual or social benefits that leave no material trace and are, therefore, invisible to archaeologists.

Did Polities Include More Than One Village?

Unlike in autonomous villages, where political decisions are made within each community, in multi-village polities leaders living in one village gain so much influence and power that the social structure is transformed in such a way as to allow one village to assert political control over another. This loss of autonomy is rarely voluntary (Carneiro 1981).

In contrast with studies of rank, it is necessary to have information about more than a single settlement to identify multi-village polities. In the absence of data gathered from decades of excavation, the most common and expedient way to gain information about a region is through systematic survey that identifies all settlements within a large study area. When archaeologists find sites of at least two different size classes within a single region (that is, a settlement hierarchy with two tiers), they often infer that the largest site was the seat of power in a multi-village polity (Bandy 2004; Johnson 1980; Parsons 1972).

Although this is a necessary and productive first step, low temporal resolution means that survey alone cannot reliably identify multi-village polities. Except in special circumstances, no absolute dating methods are suitable for surface artifacts. The time periods used by survey archaeologists are defined by changes in ceramic style that may occur infrequently. As a result, based on survey data alone, it is impossible to determine whether larger sites were contemporary with small sites (see Chap. 2 for further discussion of this problem in Cusco). Even if sites could be shown to be contemporary, size difference may not necessarily mean that the large village controlled the smaller villages. In addition, survey cannot identify social and political institutions that crosscut multiple settlements.

There are other ways to identify multi-village polities when special evidence is available. For example, Marcus (1976) has used hieroglyphic writing to show that lower order sites frequently refer to the site that was the center of power in Maya chiefdoms. In areas where pottery decoration is elaborate, a higher proportion of shared motifs or designs between central and dependent sites has also been used to infer multi-village polities (LeBlanc 1971; Plog 1976). In addition, archaeologists may be able to demonstrate that work gangs from small hamlets provide labor for constructions in the center when materials are also transported. For example, Marcus and Flannery have shown that stones were brought from a small hamlet to the paramount center to build the temple of the chiefly center (Marcus and Flannery 1996).

The Shortcomings of Focusing Only on Comparative Questions

Focusing on these comparative questions has been critiqued for masking local traditions and failing to consider the roles of individuals in change. In anthropological archaeology scholarship outside the central Andes, variation in pre-state societies has long been recognized, and today most of the discussion about the emergence of multi-village polities focuses on the differences between them (Drennan and Peterson 2006; Earle 1987; Feinman and Neitzel 1984; Renfrew 1974). In other parts of the world, variability-focused research builds upon decades of previous work that has provided an important baseline for more detailed and particularistic studies (for example, highland Mexico, the American Southwest, and southeast U.S.). In Cusco, this baseline does not yet exist and we are just beginning to scramble to catch up.

Only in the last thirty years has Cusco scholarship begun to address these two comparative anthropological questions for the Formative period. Beginning with Bauer's 1980s survey work in Paruro (Bauer 1992, 1999), the questions were usually addressed as a small part of larger projects that aimed to understand the long pre-Inka culture history in the region in order to demonstrate that Inka state formation was a long process rather than a single historic event. Because the research interests of scholars doing this kind of work have been primarily in Inka State formation and the Inka Empire, fieldwork designed to investigate issues central to the Formative period has been rare.

As a result, settlement patterns from survey are the largest data set available to address comparative anthropological questions. As the previous section illustrated, however, a large and diverse data set involving excavations at several Formative villages will be necessary to identify either rank or multi-village polities archaeologically. Settlement patterns are only one of many lines of evidence that speak to the presence of multi-village polities and are not at all applicable to the study of inherited rank. Unfortunately, such extensive data are still not available for Cusco or many other parts of the Andean highlands.

As a scholar, I am indebted to and appreciative of the work that has been done before my own entry into Andean studies. Without knowing that Chanapata style pottery was associated with the first settlement hierarchy in Cusco, I could not have chosen a site with any hope that it would provide data on the origins of hereditary inequality or multi-village polities. While this work has provided an important foundation, it relies too heavily on ceramic typologies and surface data.

In a recent summary of the Formative period in the Valley of Cusco, Bauer (2004) described the society of the Middle Formative period (1500–500 BC). This period is known archaeologically from very small excavations at the site of Marcavalle (now buried under Centro Juvenil de Marcavalle, a rehabilitation and detention center for young boys in the modern city of Cusco). Although Marcavalle has a distinct pottery style, no contemporary sites were identified by survey. Either similar pottery was not found during fieldwork or the project did not distinguish the style from other Formative pottery during laboratory analysis. Either way, settlement pattern data are not available for the Middle Formative. Bauer proposed that, during this period, all villages were probably small like Marcavalle, and he asserted that inhabitants lived in undifferentiated villages run by Big Men.

Big Man societies are a type of egalitarian group in which individuals (specifically men) can gain status, prestige, and influence through competition framed in terms of reciprocity (especially of material goods) and through favored distribution to their own factions. These societies are known ethnographically from Melanesia. In this system, increasing competition between ambitious men may lead to a particular type of multi-village polity with hereditary rank in which self-aggrandizing individuals become wealthy and manipulate power through wealth and redistribution of goods (Sahlins 1963; Wiessner 2002).

This model is appealing to archaeologists because political economy, prestige goods, and trade networks are very amenable to archaeological study. Big Man systems are not, however, the only way in which egalitarian villages can be organized. In fact, scholars often remark that egalitarian autonomous village societies are incredibly varied, and that, as a result, the paths to hereditary inequality and the emergence of multi-village polities are multiple and diverse (Marcus 2008; Wiessner 2002). The Big Man society cannot be assumed to be the sociopolitical starting point for the emergence of rank and multi-village polities in the Andean highlands or anywhere else.

In the following phase, the Late Formative period (500 BC–AD 200), Bauer identified a settlement hierarchy of sites with Chanapata-style pottery on the surface. Sites were separated into five size categories, including a single large center. Based on this and the presence of sunken court architecture at the central complex of Wimpillay and Muyu Orqo, a notable round mountain near the modern Cusco airport (Fig. 1.3), and at Batan Urqo, a similarly large and central site outside his survey area, Bauer proposed that parallel processes of chiefdom formation were probably happening in many regions of Cusco. He went on to say, "If this model of the Late Formative Phase is correct, excavations at Wimpillay should find evidence of sumptuary goods, elite burials, and gradients in household status, craft production, and additional public works projects" (Bauer 2004:45).

A multi-settlement polity with those five characteristics is typical of models of chiefdoms that emerge from Big Man societies. Like the Big Man concept, this type of chiefdom is also based on Sahlins' work in the Pacific (Sahlins 1963), but was further articulated in terms of archaeological correlates by processual archaeologists (e.g., Carneiro 1981; Earle 1977; Peebles and Kus 1977). While most of these archaeologists acknowledged that any particular chiefdom may or may not have all the traits of the ideal type, others who applied those models have sometimes ignored this important point in order to try to build a complete picture of a society without sufficient archaeological data.

In that tradition, for both the Middle and Late Formative periods, the sparse available data in Cusco have been paired with typological categories in an effort to create a more complete view of life during the Formative period. This kind of typological reasoning has long been recognized as flawed. No single variable or trait, whether archaeological or cultural, can imply the existence of others (Feinman and Neitzel 1984; Wylie 2002). Despite this, the use of the Big Man model and the corresponding chiefdom model endures among archaeologists trained in anthropological traditions in North America who are committed to understanding long-term processes of cultural change but who do not specialize in the study of pre-state societies.[1]

In some ways, this study is a necessary step back. Even though I have access to many more data than scholars who came before me, at the conclusion of this project I am less confident about when hereditary rank developed and when multi-village polities emerged. And, I am more aware that we need additional excavation data from many more villages. With this in mind, rather than theoretically framing my work in terms of these two sociopolitical transformations, I have chosen to take a more social approach to the study of Yuthu. Rather than identifying *whether or not* the transition to ranked multi-village polities happened, I have focused on identifying particular social and political traditions and institutions at Yuthu from 400 to 100 BC. With that focus, I hope that someday we may understand *how* those important transitions took place.

The Archaeology of Community

The goal of the archaeology of community is to understand a human group living in a particular place and time in a holistic way—incorporating ecology, subsistence, social and political institutions, social identities, and factions. The approach does not require prior knowledge or assumptions about the presence of inherited rank or multi-village polities. Likewise, the success or failure of the project does not depend on answering those questions. Therefore, this approach is well suited to the current project in part because of the lack of previous research in Cusco (discussed above).

Beginning with the publication of *The Archaeology of Communities* (Canuto and Yaeger 2000), many archaeologists have framed their research in terms of "community" (e.g., Janusek 2004; Knapp 2003; Owoc 2005; Peterson and Drennan 2005; Wernke 2007). Discussions often contrast "natural" and "imagined" concepts of community (sensu Isbell 2000), but many fail to make an important distinction. Within a single article or book, the term "community" may be used to refer to both (1) a heuristic type of human group that is desirable for holistic study of human society, and (2) a universally applicable definition of an emically meaningful social group. Although these two conceptions of community are not directly comparable things, they have been contrasted as if they were. In fact, an emically meaningful social group is only one aspect of society that might be studied employing a community approach.

The "natural" community concept is typically attributed to early anthropological and sociological works that outlined meth-

Figure 1.3. A view of Wimpillay and the conspicuous Muyu Orqo, or "round mountain" in Quechua, from the Inka site of Sacsaywaman, visible in the foreground; the tops of houses and buildings in the modern city of Cusco are visible in the valley. The complex of the two archaeological sites was probably the center of a multi-village polity during the later part of the Formative period in the Cusco Valley. Although they both have been sites of excavation and field training for archaeology students from the University of San Antonio Abad of Cusco, little is known about them. Today, they are mostly destroyed by the modern city's expansion. As a result, study of the Formative period in the Valley of Cusco itself would be difficult if not impossible.

odologies for research, including those of Murdock, Redfield, Arensberg, Kimball, and Greer from the 1940s through the 1960s (Arensberg 1954, 1961; Arensberg and Kimball 1965, 1968; Greer 1955; Minar and Greer 1969a; Murdock 1949; Murdock et al. 1945; Redfield 1955). Current discussions summarize the work as having elaborated a definition of a universally recognizable human social unit that was a bounded, homogeneous, slow-changing group that was self-sufficient and based on face-to-face interaction. In truth, the characteristics listed above were criteria for selecting a *place* (usually a small sedentary village) for a certain type of ethnographic study with the aim of understanding a human whole. Early scholars believed that a small community with those characteristics could be a manageable research unit suitable for studying the intersection of society and culture. The creation of such a wish list of desirable traits makes it clear that they did not believe that all communities could be defined in this way. As Isbell points out, however, it is probably true that over time the heuristic type became conflated with the definition of community as a socially meaningful unit (Isbell 2000).

The "natural" community is often contrasted with what is referred to as an "imagined" community. The term has been borrowed from the historian Benedict Anderson (2006), though Knapp rightly points out that the archaeological version is only loosely related (Knapp 2003). Anderson described and theorized the emergence of modern national identities after the fall of religious communities and in conjunction with vernacular language and the technology of the modern printing press. Certainly, his "imagined community" in a strict sense cannot be extended deep into prehistory. When most archaeologists use the term, however, they reduce it to the basic idea that individuals can imagine themselves to be part of a community of people that they will never interact with. This purportedly removes the criteria of face-to-face interaction from the definition of community, replacing it with the notion of perceived group identity and affiliation. This substitution is not valid, however, if scholars recognize that face-to-face interaction was only meant to be a desired characteristic of an ideal heuristic type (see further discussion below).

The adoption of the "imagined" community in anthropological and archaeological study occurred in part as a response to many criticisms of the original concept when perceived as a definition rather than a heuristic type. Substituting a definition based on emic social identity for a heuristic type has transformed discussions of the community approach from elaborations of effective methodology into debates over the proper definition of a particular type of human group. This implicit conversion makes the "natural" and "imagined" community concepts incomparable. From my perspective, "imagined" community is just one kind of group identity that might be studied using a community methodology—though it is certainly an important one.

Nevertheless, scholars who prioritize the study of community identity have incorporated decades of advances in social theory that bring valid critiques of the original method and offer important advances. The new identity-focused conception of the "imagined" community is frequently coupled with practice theory, which refocuses the study of society from units such as "communities" to individuals. The approach draws on concepts like Bourdieu's *habitus*, or the representation of social structure in the schema and sensibilities in the minds of individuals (1972), and Giddens' structuration, which adds a mechanism for change by emphasizing that individuals act within existing structures but also shape them (Giddens 1984).

The original goal of community study was to understand the interrelationship between culture and the social by observing everyday activities and interactions within a "whole." The prospect of achieving this goal is greatly improved by the addition of practice theory as a way to understand the process by which it happens. In addition, structuration introduces change as a potential in every social interaction. To be fair, early anthropologists did recognize that some communities changed, but they naively hoped to be able to select one for study that did not.

For archaeologists, the incorporation of the importance of change (in this case, in terms of the recursive relationship between structure and agency) is an important contribution. Practice theory, however, always presents a special challenge to prehistorians because very few individuals are visible in the archaeological record. Despite that, we understand that the trade networks, subsistence systems, and social identities that we study were created and changed day-to-day by individuals acting within existing frameworks.

Some of the critiques of the original community approach have been misplaced. For example, early anthropologists did not always assume internal homogeneity. In fact, in their seminal texts, many of the most critiqued authors recognized factions within communities (Murdock 1949; Redfield 1955) as well as social distinctions based on class, gender, or age (Redfield 1955). So, rather than being an improvement over the original concept, the inclusion of the study of factions and social groups is an important—but not a new—part of community study.

One of the most commonly critiqued aspects of early anthropological concepts of community has been the definition limited to people who regularly interact face-to-face (but see Yaeger 2000). Certainly, this was a key part of Murdock's definition in the 1940s (Murdock 1949; Murdock et al. 1945). And, many archaeologists continue to advocate this definition because of its perceived straightforward application to archaeological data (Peterson and Drennan 2005). But, even by the 1950s, many anthropologists recognized that their "little communities" were parts of larger ones—which did not involve or require face-to-face interaction (Minar and Greer 1969b; Redfield 1955).

This became particularly apparent as the types of societies that anthropologists studied began to change and anthropologists struggled to transfer community-based participant observation methodology from the supposedly "primitive" societies for which it was developed to societies that they deemed "modern" (Steward 1956), or in other words, as the anthropological objects of studies became more and more culturally similar to the anthropologists themselves. Certainly, by the 1960s, Murdock's face-to-face definition was out of fashion with proponents of the community study method like Arensberg and Kimball, who made a critical comparison stating that "It is in fact as if a zoologist should require of a beehive that it not be one unless he knew every bee to brush wings with every other bee" (1965:47).

Some aspects of the original conception of community method that are particularly useful for archaeological study have received little attention. First, the heuristic community was a sedentary village. In that sense, it was a spatially defined research unit. Archaeologists must link spatial analytic units like houses, sites, and regions to socially meaningful units such as families, moieties, villages, and polities (Marcus 2000). From my perspective, archaeologists may use a village site comprised of many households and supra-household structures as a meaningful unit of analysis whether or not we conceptualize any or all of the nested group identities of people living in the village as being correlated with a single place.

In addition, early anthropologists advocated studying larger institutions as they played out within a small village. With this approach, archaeologists digging a single site can study multiple levels of social identity and a variety of social institutions so long as the associated practices leave material remains in the village being studied. Yaeger (2000) took advantage of this aspect of community study to examine three levels of shared identity in the classic Maya sites of San Lorenzo and Xunantunich in western Belize.

Early scholars advocated choosing a community that was representative of the greater society. In some cases, this was phrased as a self-sufficient community that could provide for all or most of its own needs (Redfield 1955). But in other cases, it was expressed in terms of being representative, complete, and inclusive. This meant that the village had enough people to fill all roles in society, including some specialists (though a specialized community would be undesirable), and including representatives of larger social institutions outside the local village (Arensberg and Kimball 1965). When the functionalist aspects of self-sufficiency and reproducibility are removed, something important is still left. Choosing a community that has a sufficient breadth of households, ritual structures, and other archaeological deposits will lead to a richer understanding of the larger society.

Early methodologies also advocated studying the community as a whole (Steward 1956). Redfield maintained that the community should not be "atomized," but that the investigation of any single aspect will invariably lead a scholar to study another (1955). In his own experience, he set out to study the ecological system of a Maya village, but once he began farming alongside villagers, he found it necessary to study ritual life because it was inseparably tied to subsistence practices. Similarly, Arensberg advocated the study of social questions in vivo, that is, in relationship with all other aspects of behavior, culture, and social structure within a whole. Like Redfield, he believed that a single research question could not be isolated from the whole (Arensberg 1961). Although neither ethnographers nor archaeologists can address all facets of community life in a single study, the integration of multiple facets (such as ecology, social structure, and ritual) will produce a much more complete view of society (e.g., Flannery 1976).

Finally, early community approaches attempted to balance the interests of comparative research and historical particularism. Steward (1956) stated that being historical and comparative were two of the three characteristics of the community approach[2] (see also Redfield 1955). He was concerned that in the 1950s the practice of ethnography in area studies had become too particular and narrowly focused. Balancing the comparative and historical interests of social science continues to challenge scholars today.

Flannery (1995) has recently summarized this tension as it is felt by anthropological archaeologists interested in long-term change. He builds on Spencer's (1990) work to observe that archaeologists can study change in two equally valuable ways: (1) as general social evolution, using cross-cultural types like chiefdoms and states with the goal of being comparative, or (2) as specific social evolution elaborating the unique history of social change in a particular place without appealing to types. Studying only general social evolution undervalues the richness of life and privileges poorly understood universal processes over the roles of local people. In contrast, limiting study to specific social evolution can prevent comparative study of what it means to be human. The rewards and risks of each are significant and must be balanced in anthropological research.

In this study, I employ a modified community approach. While I do not claim that this method will be suitable for all archaeological projects, it is a particularly good approach to study a small village when little is known and great variation is possible. Elements include:

1. The research focuses on a spatially defined unit that is a small village that included a wide selection of structures and activity areas that probably indicate the presence of many different people, activities, and social institutions.

2. The project aims to be holistic and does not isolate a single aspect for study. Of course, the breadth of topics addressed is always limited by the material remains recovered, and the resources available to conduct the study.

3. Particular attention is paid to social factions or other mechanisms that allow, create, or result in change.

4. The spatially defined research unit is used to study any or all of the nested social institutions and group identities to which local people belong.

5. The study attempts to balance historical and comparative inquiry.

The Cultural and Historical Particularities of Andean Communities

Two characteristics of highland Andean communities known from ethnography and ethnohistory have been particularly influential in framing my research questions and my interpretations of the archaeological record. Both are related in some way to the dramatic mountain landscape in and around Cusco (Fig. 1.4). First, I am intrigued by the possibility that the villagers living at Yuthu were part of a spatially dispersed and vertically integrated mountain community. Second, I am interested in the relationship between community identity, territoriality, ancestor veneration, and sacred landscape.

Spatially Dispersed Vertically Integrated Mountain Communities

In the Andes, ethnographically and ethnohistorically known communities were often composed of more than one settlement, with each practicing a special production strategy determined by ecological variations that correspond roughly to elevation (e.g., Bastien 1978; Flannery et al. 1989; Flores Ochoa 1985; Guillet 1981; Murra 1968; Webster 1971, 1972). People living in distant and distinct resource zones often thought of themselves as part of the same community. For example, a single group may have

Figure 1.4. A landscape view in the province of Paruro, just south of the modern city of Cusco. Although this is an exceptionally dramatic example of mountainous terrain, it is easy to see how Andean community identity might be conceptualized in relationship with the surrounding features of a sacred landscape such as these dramatic peaks and river valleys.

some members living in high grasslands grazing llamas, some living a bit lower growing potatoes and grains, and a settlement in a lower zone growing important ritual crops like maize or coca. Similar systems are common in alpine environments around the world. They provide a means to diversify subsistence strategies and manage risk (Goldstein and Messerschmidt 1980; Rhoades and Thompson 1975).

Today, the landscape may be conceptualized as the head, trunk, and foot of both the community and the mountain (Bastien 1978). Or, the high parts of the community may be associated with Indians and demons while the low parts are associated with friendly spirits and "civilized" Spaniards (Fioravanti-Molinié 1982). Although the details vary according to a particular time and place, the important thing to note is that the vertical system is not understood simply in terms of economic necessity, but is tied into a sacred conceptualization of the landscape.

John Murra developed the best-known model of this type of Andean community, "the vertical archipelago," using Spanish census materials and chronicles from a variety of settlements inhabited at the end of Inka rule and the very beginning of Colonial rule from AD 1460 to 1560 (Murra 1968, 1972, 1985a, 1985b). In this model, the community's core settlement was located in the mid-altitude zone. Family members living outside that core zone still considered themselves part of that community—even while living alongside other families who considered themselves members of different core communities. Exchange among kin living in all zones explained the movement of goods between resource zones in the absence of markets. This ethnographic model described a vertically integrated community in terms of both ideology and day-to-day economic reliance.

Murra speculated that because this strategy is so widespread and has endured so many political upheavals, it might extend far back into prehistory, and thus he challenged archaeologists to discover the time-depth of this tradition. In fact, some have identified similar multi-settlement communities exploiting multiple resources in the Late Intermediate period (AD 1000–1450) (Stanish 1989) and the Middle Horizon (AD 600–1000) (Mujica et al. 1983). However, the time-depth of the "vertical archipelago" model has been doubted by some scholars who regard it as a strategy used by the Lupaqa elite to manage tribute demands of Spanish colonial administration (Van Buren 1996). In addition, some archaeologists note that this model has frequently been applied to explain archaeological patterns that could have been produced by other activities such as transhumance or llama caravans of independent merchant traders (Dillehay and Lautaro Núñez 1988).

This study does not aim to identify a "vertical archipelago" in Formative period Cusco. Rather, I independently address two important aspects of a vertically integrated community: (1) the economic integration of multiple resource zones and (2) the conception of community identity larger than a single village.

Group Identity Conceptualized in Terms of Ancestors and the Sacred Landscape

Historical and ethnographic accounts depict agricultural and pastoral communities that understood and described their shared group identity and territorial rights as having been established by ancestors who traveled through subterranean waterways and emerged from springs or lakes to claim a physical and social place for their descendants. These mythical ancestors established group rights for all members of a particular community (Allen 2002; Flannery et al. 1989; Gelles 2000; Gow et al. 1976; Mariño Ferro 1989; Sherbondy 1992). In addition, veneration of real remembered ancestors established political and resource rights for certain families, thus excluding others (Dillehay 2007; Rowe 1946; Salomon 1995; Sherbondy 1992). Invoking ancestors to create a sense of shared identity and exclusive (and often unequal) access to resources is common in many parts of the world (Helms 1998; Liu 1999; McAnany 1995).

Like the vertically integrated mountain community, shared identity—which was conceptualized in terms of ancestors and the landscape—was so widespread in the Andes that it is possible that some version of it existed very early in time. Archaeologists have found evidence of ancestor veneration among several pre-Inka societies, including above-ground mortuary structures in the Late Intermediate period highlands (Isbell 1997) and ongoing manipulation of human remains associated with public architecture outside Cusco in the Formative period (Dulanto 2002a; Hastorf 2003).

This study considers the possible role of ancestors and the sacred landscape in the conception of a particular type of community identity that was related to territoriality and resource rights.

Community Study of Yuthu, an Early Andean Village

Taking these Andean particularities into consideration, the elements of the community approach can be restated in terms that are specifically applicable to the present study.

1. The majority of the data in this study comes from the village of Yuthu, which was neither the largest nor smallest contemporary village. It was large enough to contain several households and it has ceremonial architecture.

2. The study includes a description of the local environment, subsistence practices, craft activities, social identity, ritual practices, and other activities that left material traces at the site and were recovered in 156 m^2 of excavation. Of course, this study cannot be exhaustive. Over time, continued research at Yuthu will improve our holistic understanding of the village.

3. The study considers how rituals of ancestor veneration tied to the landscape allowed large groups to express their shared identity even as they served as a venue for factional competition.

4. Crops and animals available from particular ecological zones are used to determine whether the village might have been part of a spatially segregated vertically integrated community.

5. The specific details of village economy, ritual, and politics at Yuthu are used to discuss general theory on the origins of hereditary inequality and multi-village polities.

As part of the holistic study of Yuthu, Chapter 2 describes the activities that left material traces recovered by excavation from 2005 to 2007. These included activities that shaped the annual cycle and were tied to seasonal environmental variation (such as farming and herding), activities that occurred every day or nearly every day (like cooking and fuel collecting), and other activities that were carried out periodically when necessity or interest arose (such as human burial and stone tool production). This chapter evaluates the evidence for a vertically integrated community as it prepares the reader for the description of excavations presented in Chapters 3 and 4.

Chapter 3 describes the houses and outdoor activity areas in the Northern Sector where everyday life took place. Structures and activities are compared with other examples from the Andes to demonstrate that the organization of domestic life varied greatly at this time. Rituals of integration took place periodically in a distinct space that included ceremonial structures built atop a platform in the Southern Sector. Chapter 4 compares the ceremonial architecture at Yuthu with that from other parts of the Andes to argue that Cusco shared some aspects of a regional ceremonial tradition, including sunken rectangular structures and ritual canals.

Chapter 5 integrates the archaeological evidence from the Southern Sector of Yuthu with anthropological theory and Andean ethnography to argue that the ceremonial structure was used periodically to establish group identity that was tied to the landscape and community-level interaction with the dead. Architectural remodeling of this structure indicates that perceived relationships between the community and the landscape were not static, but shifted over time. Later during the occupation of Yuthu, mummy-focused veneration shifted the focal point of rituals of group identity from the community level to smaller groups within the community, most likely lineages. Access to resources was probably also restructured to run along family lines. Community and lineage-focused veneration of the dead were two potentially conflicting integrative practices that existed alongside each other for some time. This ideological shift was a key transformation in social institutions that may have legitimized the emergence of inherited rank and the development of multi-village polities.

The concluding remarks (Chap. 6) summarize the holistic study of this Andean village. The specific economic, social, ritual, and political practices at Yuthu can help us understand the particularly *cusqueño* context for the emergence of hereditary inequality and multi-village polities.

Notes

1. Bauer is far from being the only scholar who has used the Big Man society as the model of sociopolitical organization in Andean egalitarian villages (see also Stanish 2003).

2. The third characteristic was that the community approach was ethnographic in the sense of studying all components of life by qualitative and, to a lesser extent, quantitative observation as discussed in the previous paragraph.

— 2 —

Activities at Yuthu

To understand past social systems, it is necessary to identify the activities that filled the lives of men, women, and children each day, week, and season. Such activities structure social interactions, even as they are shaped by necessity, expectation, and tradition. As archaeologists, we can identify just the activities that leave behind material traces, and only in exceptional cases do we overcome this limitation and recover data on such important practices as gossiping, singing, and non-violent conflict resolution. Many other facets (like gender relations, violence, and the calendar cycle) can be only partially understood.

In this chapter, I describe those activities that left material traces at Yuthu. These were diverse, ranging from subsistence practices to craft production to ritual activities. Many are not well understood because of fragmentary evidence, and some interpretations remain preliminary. Nevertheless, these descriptions should be considered the first step toward creating a more complete characterization of village life.

The remains of many daily activities were found in and around houses and outdoor activity areas surrounding hearths in the Northern Sector (a domestic area described in Chap. 3). With the exception of some construction methods, few activities that left material traces took place exclusively in the ceremonial Southern Sector (described in Chap. 4). Many ritual practices (such as human burial and bird related rituals) took place throughout the village. When possible, the location of each activity is identified in this chapter, but some activities are described in general terms—pulling together evidence from middens and soil deposited by natural processes. Although artifacts recovered from such contexts can provide valuable information about life during the Formative period, they cannot be used to determine where activities took place—whether in open areas, in fields outside the settlement, or even in another village.

Activities That Shaped the Annual Cycle

To understand the annual cycle at Yuthu, I identified the most important subsistence practices and considered the scheduling and land requirements of each. Prior to this project, little was known about early subsistence practices in Cusco because very little faunal and ethnobotanical research had been carried out. Elsewhere in the Andes, potatoes and other tubers were domesticated by 8000–6000 BC (Pearsall 2008), and common beans were found in the highlands by 8000–7500 BC (Chávez 1980). Gourd, quinoa, squash, coca, lúcuma, and maize were present by 4400–3100 BC, and peppers and achira were introduced by 3100–1750 BC (Rivero Luque 2005). Highland people kept guinea pigs in pens by 5500 BC (deFrance 2007). They managed herds of camelids by 3500 BC (MacNeish 1983; Stahl 2008), and by 2500 BC camelids had been domesticated in the *puna* of Junín (Lavallée et al. 1984; Wheeler Pires-Ferreira et al. 1976).

In Cusco, prior to the Formative period (4400–3100 BC), people exploited undomesticated resources like wild camelids, wild guinea pigs, deer, and birds such as the tinamou (or *yuthu*

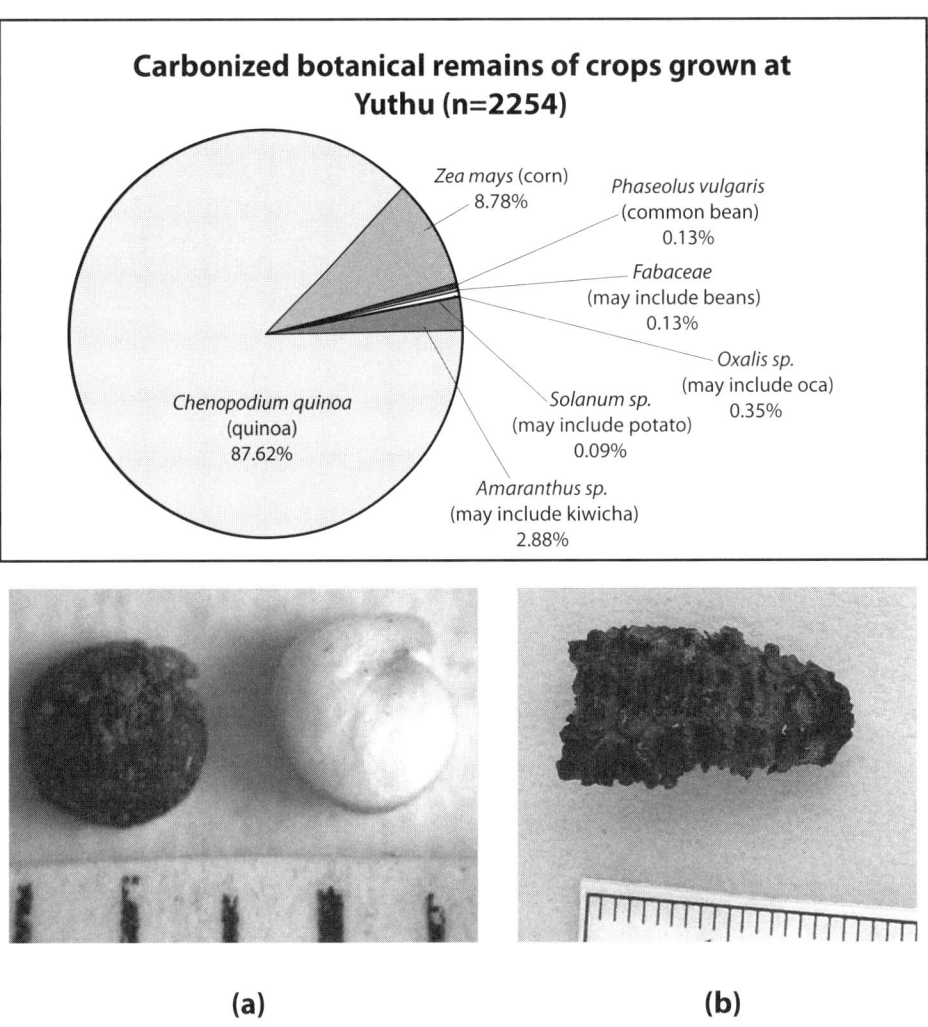

Figure 2.1. Crops grown at Yuthu. Plants recovered from Yuthu were carbonized remains recovered during flotation. Quinoa (*a*) and corn (*b*) were the most common domesticates. There is also some evidence of bean, potato, oca, and kiwicha. Photo (*a*) courtesy of Victor Vásquez Sánchez.

in Quechua) (deFrance 2007). By the Early Formative period (around 1500 BC), camelid herding was an important activity (Chávez 1980; Miller 1979). Villagers kept domesticated guinea pigs, and wild animals were a very minor component of the faunal assemblage (Chávez 1980). Beans were grown by 800 BC and corn by 200 BC (Chávez 1980). A mixed agropastoral subsistence economy had been in place for many generations before people moved to Yuthu. Farming and herding traditions were the most important factors shaping the annual cycle at the village.

Farming

Excavations at Yuthu (400–100 BC) included the first systematic recovery of macro-botanical remains using flotation for the Formative period of Cusco. People at Yuthu relied heavily on domesticated crops; 86.57% of all carbonized plant remains were probably domesticates ($n = 2634$; see Fig. 2.1). The most common crop recovered was quinoa (87.62% of domesticates). Given the high proportion of quinoa recovered and the fact that European grains like wheat and barley are grown around Yuthu today, quinoa farming was probably a local activity.

It is likely that other high-altitude crops were grown locally as well. Although the evidence is scarce because of difficulties in identification and poor preservation, potatoes (*Solanum* sp.) and oca (*Oxalis* sp.) were probably grown in the surrounding area, as they are today. Yuthu is located just above the upper limit for kiwicha (*Amaranthus* sp.) cultivation (3500 masl), but some nearby farm fields might have been adequate for growing this native grain.

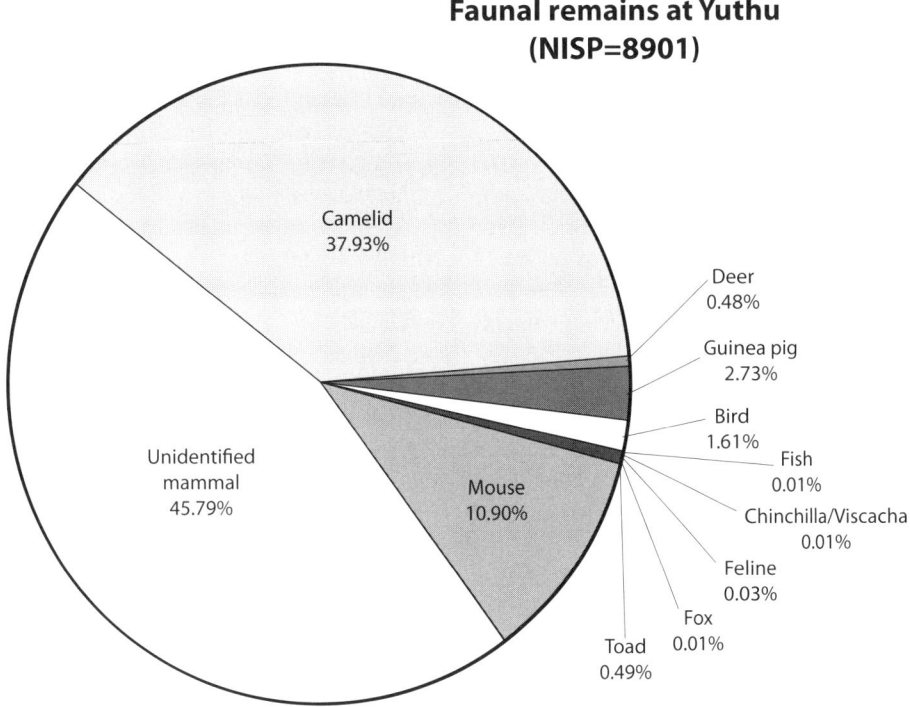

Figure 2.2. Faunal remains at Yuthu. Percentages are based on the number of identified specimens for each species.

Corn was the second most common crop (8.78%). In general, the plain of Anta is too high and too cold to grow corn. Despite this, villagers today in Cruzpata do grow some corn around the edge of Lake Huaypo where ample water and the insulating effect of the lake create a small suitable microenvironment. They all agree, however, that their corn is much smaller and less tasty than that grown in the Sacred Valley, a warm river valley 600 m lower in elevation and only a 4-hour walk from Yuthu. Many families grow some corn for household consumption, but buy the majority from farmers in lower altitude areas.

Settlement surveys show that most of the largest sites on the high plain are located along the natural route from Yuthu to the valley (Davis and Covey 2007). There are no large Formative period sites at lower altitudes. Although I cannot say for sure, it seems likely that villagers at Yuthu may have kept maize fields at lower altitudes about a half-day's walk from the village.

In addition to botanical remains, some farming tools were found at Yuthu. A groundstone biface found resting on the floor of a pit house (Intrusion I; see Chap. 3) might have been the blade of a traditional foot plow called a *chaki taklla*. This tool has a blade that cuts the soil vertically before the plow is used as a lever to turn the soil over. Alternately, it may have been the blade of an agricultural tool in which the blade attaches to the handle at an angle so as to cut the soil horizontally (*allachu*) (Rivero Luque 2005). In addition, we found several broken fragments of doughnut-shaped stones that are attached to a handle and used to break clumps of dirt (*wini* or *warmiq p'ananan*). This tool is used today alongside the *chaki taklla* for secondary preparation of the soil (Rivero Luque 2005). Finally, we found one unmodified deer antler. Ethnographically, deer antlers are used to harvest small tubers (*qachi*) (Rivero Luque 2005). These tools have also been found at the Formative period site of Lukurmata in Bolivia (Bermann 1994).

Herding

Villagers at Yuthu continued a herding tradition that had existed in the area for at least 1000 years (Miller 1979). As was true for Marcavalle, camelid was the most common animal bone identified at Yuthu (37.93% NISP), although this number probably underrepresents the true proportion of camelid bones. Based on size, most of the unidentified mammal bones were probably camelid. Therefore, the true percentage of camelids was probably closer to 80%. Considering that toads and mice (two economically unimportant species) made up 11.38% of the faunal sample, camelids were clearly the most important animals at Yuthu (Fig. 2.2).

Although differentiating camelid species based on skeletal evidence alone is controversial, Vásquez Sánchez and Rosales Tham identified both llamas and alpacas at Yuthu by examining two anterior first phalanges and nine posterior first phalanges using methods developed by Kent (1982, 1988). The phalanges fell into two size groups, but the large and small groups did not correlate neatly with the species classification; some large animals were identified as alpacas, while some small animals were identified as llamas (Fig. 2.3). The same pattern was observed for contemporary herds at Wat'a (about 20 km away) (Vásquez Sánchez and Rosales Tham 2008). Although the sizes of camelid species are known to overlap, Vásquez Sánchez and Rosales Tham suggest that these animals were hybrids. It seems unlikely that villagers purposefully maintained mixed herds because llamas prefer to graze on dry bunch grass while alpacas favor moister plants from highland bogs (Wheeler 1993); nevertheless, hybridization does occur frequently when herds are not managed carefully (Wheeler et al. 1995).

To understand herd maintenance strategies, age was recorded based on the degree of wear on superior and inferior teeth (using methods developed by Puig and Monge 1983; Wheeler 1982). Vásquez Sánchez and Rosales Tham examined 26 animals (MNI). Although both alpacas and llamas were present at Yuthu, all of the aged specimens were probably llamas, based on the presence of enamel on both sides of the mandibular incisors. Only llamas (*Lama glama*) or guanacos (*Lama guanacoe*) have enamel on both sides; alpacas have it on only the labial side.

Most llamas died or were killed as subadults or adults (older than 1 year), the largest subset between 1 and 3 years of age (Fig. 2.4). Many of the older adult llamas had very worn teeth, indicating that they may have been slaughtered when they were no longer able to graze effectively or carry burdens on llama caravans (Vásquez Sánchez and Rosales Tham 2009).

It is difficult to compare this pattern directly with other samples from Cusco—not only because of the small sample size, but also because the only other study that addressed age curves was based on fused vs. unfused bones. It is still worth noting that the attrition curve at Yuthu is unlike that of Marcavalle (a sample that includes Marcavalle and Chanapata period occupations), where Miller (1979) found mostly juvenile animals, possibly selected for their tender meat (51% of the bones were unfused and 30% of the camelids had died by 1 year of age). Nor is the pattern at Yuthu exactly like the one from the Inka period site Qhataq'asallaqta, where most animals were slaughtered only after they had passed their prime as wool sources and caravan pack animals. At that site, 23% of the bones were unfused and only 2% of camelids died by 1 year of age. The pattern at Yuthu seems to be closer to that of the Inka period site, but with the addition of some younger adults that had reached maturity. Perhaps herders at Yuthu prioritized keeping animals for wool and as pack animals, but selected some young (yet mature) llamas to maximize the meat from each animal. Alternatively, they may have slaughtered young males to maintain a desirable sex ratio in the herd and encourage breeding of the best quality animals.

Discussion of Activities That Shaped the Annual Cycle

How was the landscape around Yuthu used to manage herding and agriculture? Three factors affected the annual cycle: (1) seasonal variation in weather, (2) the availability of land that was suitable for farming and herding, and (3) the labor required to maintain each crop or domesticated animal.

Agropastoralists must consider the seasonal fluctuations in rainfall and temperature and the variety and quality of land that is available to them when scheduling many activities. In the Andean highlands, there are two pronounced seasons—the rainy season and dry season. In and around Cusco, this allows only one growing season. Both planting and harvesting crops, at the beginning and end of the growing season respectively, require large amounts of labor. In contrast, herding requires constant management, and although herding practices may change seasonally, there are no periods of intense labor demands.

The Andean practice of exploiting multiple ecological zones can provide flexibility in labor scheduling because planting and harvest seasons can be slightly earlier or later depending on the microclimate. In addition, diverse zones provide rich pasture at different times of the year. The way that societies combine trade, transhumance, and direct exploitation of multiple ecological zones to farm and herd influences how and when subsistence, ritual, and other activities take place throughout the year.

The Xaquixaguana Plain where Yuthu is located includes a large, low, and often rather wet pampa in the southwestern part of the survey region, near the modern city of Anta, and higher rolling hills with two large lakes in the northern part, near Maras. Higher mountains that reach over 4000 masl surround the area to the south and east. Small areas of *puna* are located to the east and northwest. The Sacred Valley borders the northern and western edges of this region; the valley floor is 2800–2900 masl. Large parts of the valley floor are currently used for intensive maize agriculture while the higher plain is used to pasture sheep and to grow grains and tubers (Fig. 2.5).

Today, llamas and alpacas are herded only above 4000 masl in this area, but Flores Ochoa (1982) has suggested that both species were herded as low as 3300 masl in prehispanic times, and that the pampa of Anta was the primary pasture for Inka Cusco. Tribute pressures placed on local people by the Spaniards, who preferred European products, probably resulted in the absence of camelids on the plain today. Therefore, access to the *puna* to maintain herds may not have been important in the Formative period. In fact, no Formative period sites were found in a recent survey of the *puna* east of the Xaquixaguana Plain survey area (R. Alan Covey, pers. comm.).

The low wet plain and the rolling hills around Yuthu provide two distinct types of pastureland. Each may be considered in terms of the distinct requirements for herding alpacas and llamas. Alpacas require constant monitoring and attention. They must be moved between pastures, protected from predators, and supervised during breeding (Webster 1971). Alpacas prefer grasses that grow in wet environments and must often be moved

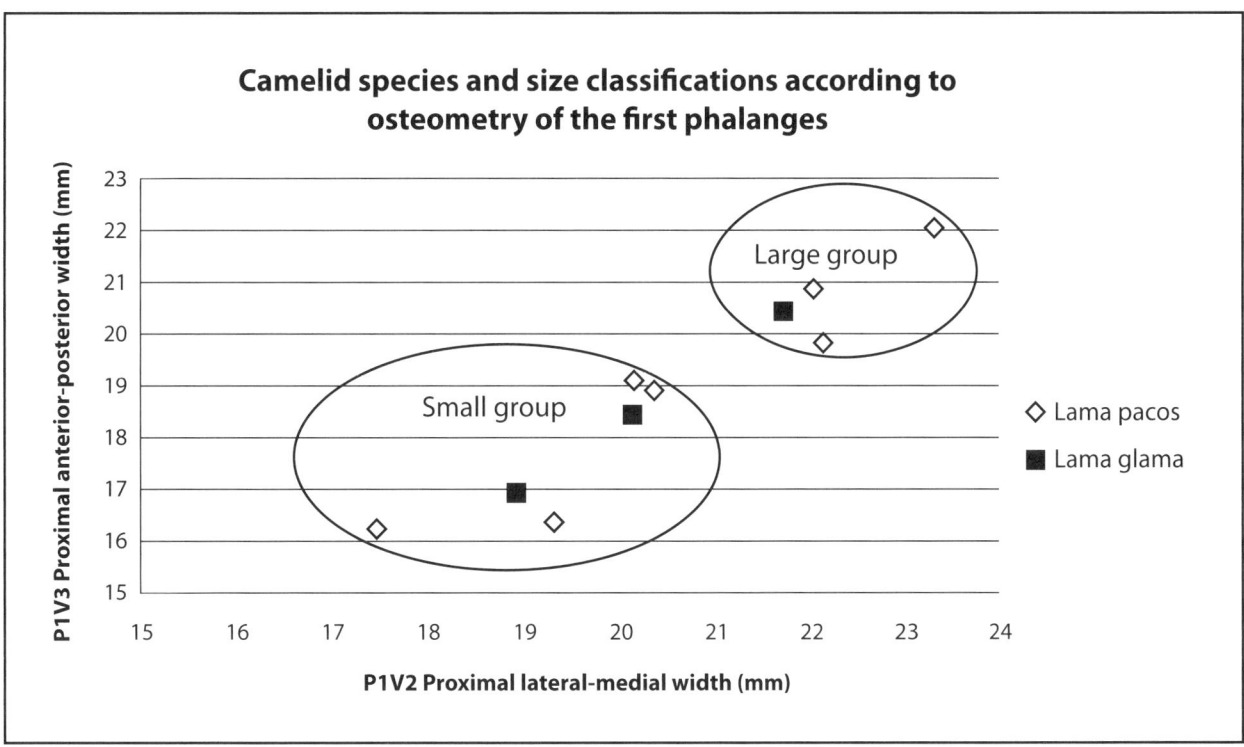

Figure 2.3. Camelid species and size classifications at Yuthu. Note that some phalanges identified as llamas fell in the small group, while some identified as alpacas fell in the large group (redrawn from Vásquez Sánchez and Rosales Tham 2009).

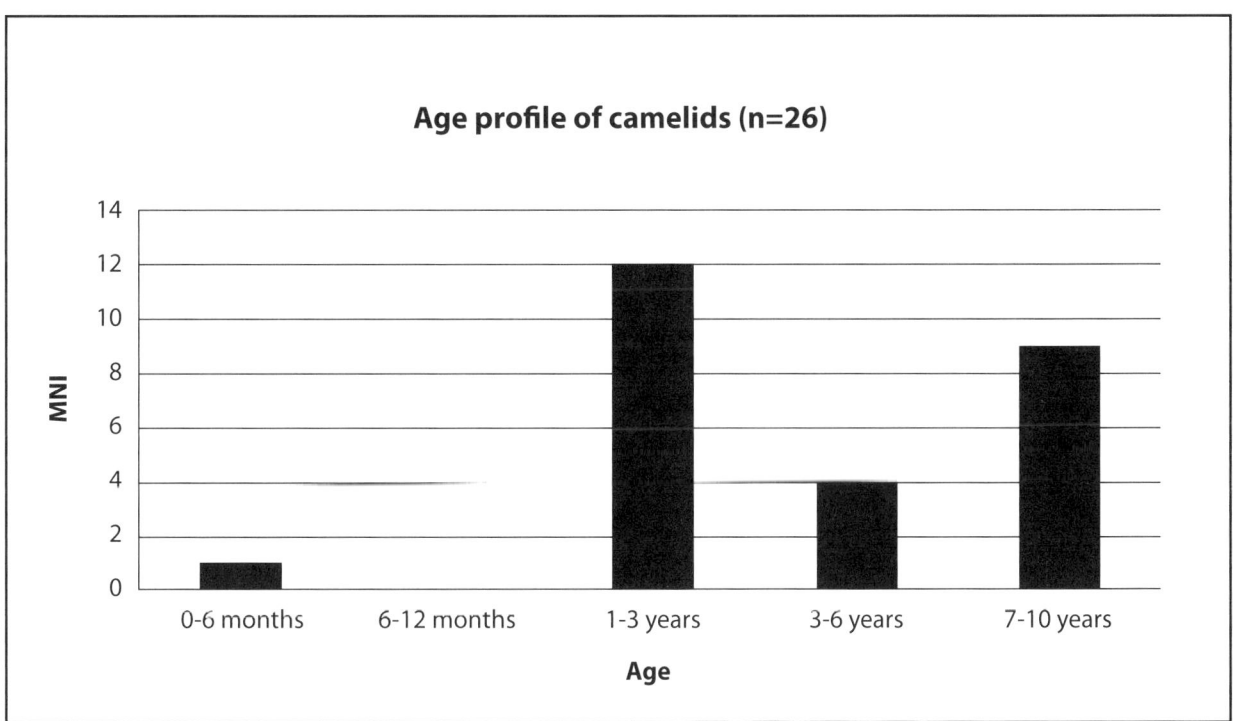

Figure 2.4. Age profile of camelids at Yuthu based on degree of tooth wear. The presence of enamel on both sides of the mandibular incisors indicates that all animals included in this chart were probably llamas. Most llamas were slaughtered or died shortly after reaching maturity or in old age (redrawn from Vásquez Sánchez and Rosales Tham 2009).

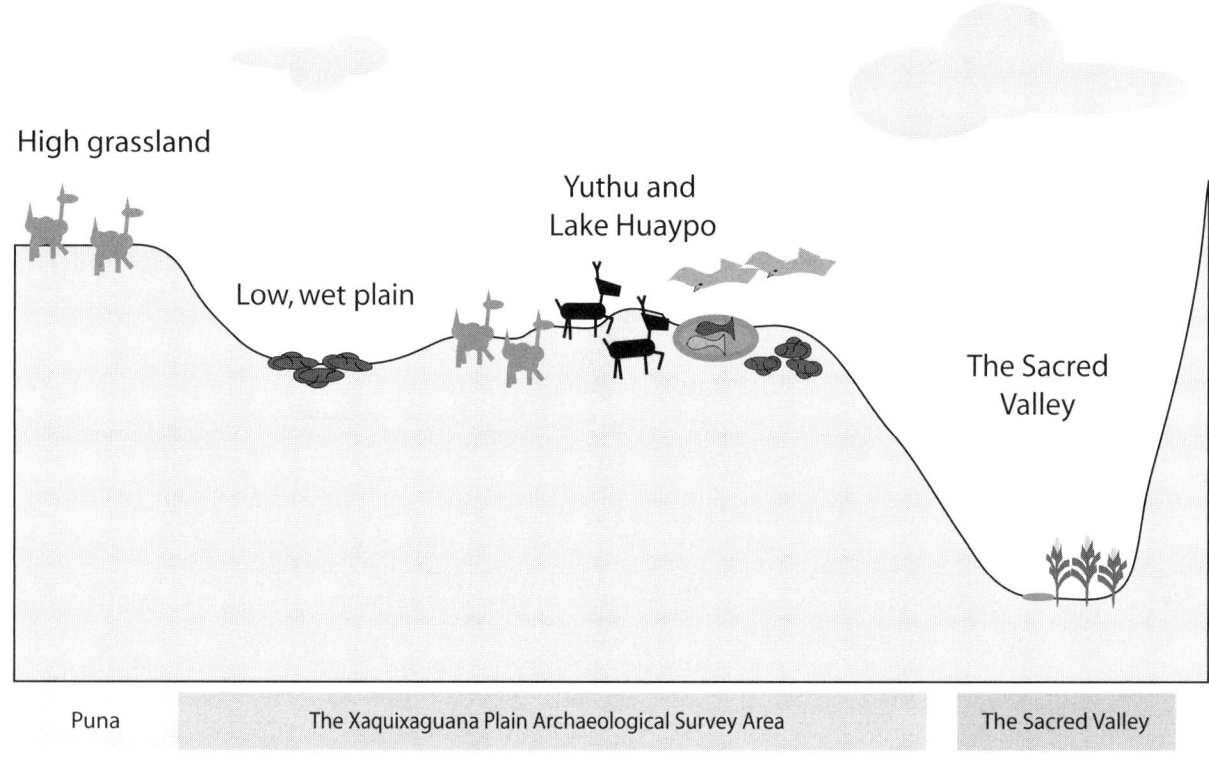

Figure 2.5. The resource zones available to sites in the Xaquixaguana Plain survey area include: a high rolling plain with marshes and lakes, the low warm Sacred Valley, and high grassland puna.

to new grazing areas during the dry season (Bonavia 2008; Flores Ochoa 1979). In contrast, llamas can be herded with less care. They happily graze in a wide variety of pastures and can be left unattended, though they prefer dry pasture (Bonavia 2008; Webster 1971).

Llamas might have preferred the high rolling hills around Maras while alpacas might have been moved from the drier rolling hills during the rainy season to wetter pastures in the marshy areas in the dry season. Unfortunately, faunal data from excavation do not clarify which species was more important. For either species, it would not have been necessary to take herds to the *puna* as long as crowding was not a problem. Depending on the species, camelid herding could have placed constant demands on everyday labor during the Formative period (Webster 1971). But, herding most likely took place close to the village and could have been incorporated with other activities.

Planting, tending, and harvesting crops had to be integrated with herding practices. The proximity of the plain and the nearby valley provide the opportunity to grow diverse crops that are adapted to different climates, which would allow communities to manage risk, be self-sufficient, and have more diverse cuisines. There is an additional advantage to having access to multiple ecological zones. In a single zone, the planting and harvesting seasons for all crops often overlap. As a result, these two periods of intensive agricultural labor can limit production even when land is abundant. Access to fields in multiple zones can allow a family to grow additional crops with different growth cycles or the same crops on an offset agricultural schedule (Zimmerer 1996). As a result, farmers can avoid the labor bottlenecks during planting and harvesting and produce more crops than they would be able to grow in only one zone (Mitchel 1978).

In and around the area today, most crops are grown during the same agricultural cycle, with planting from October to December and harvest in May and June. Some crops, however, are grown on an "early" cycle. For potatoes, this is called *maway* and for corn it is *miskha*. On the high plain, many varieties of potatoes, beans, and native pseudo-cereals can be grown on the normal cycle. Near Maras, however, there is an early potato planting area (Kimura 2000).

Crops like corn that cannot grow on the plain because of the short growing season and risk of frost can be grown in the neighboring Urubamba Valley during the normal cycle. In addition, there are two important early planting zones in the part of the valley that borders the plain (Gade 1975). From Ollantaytambo

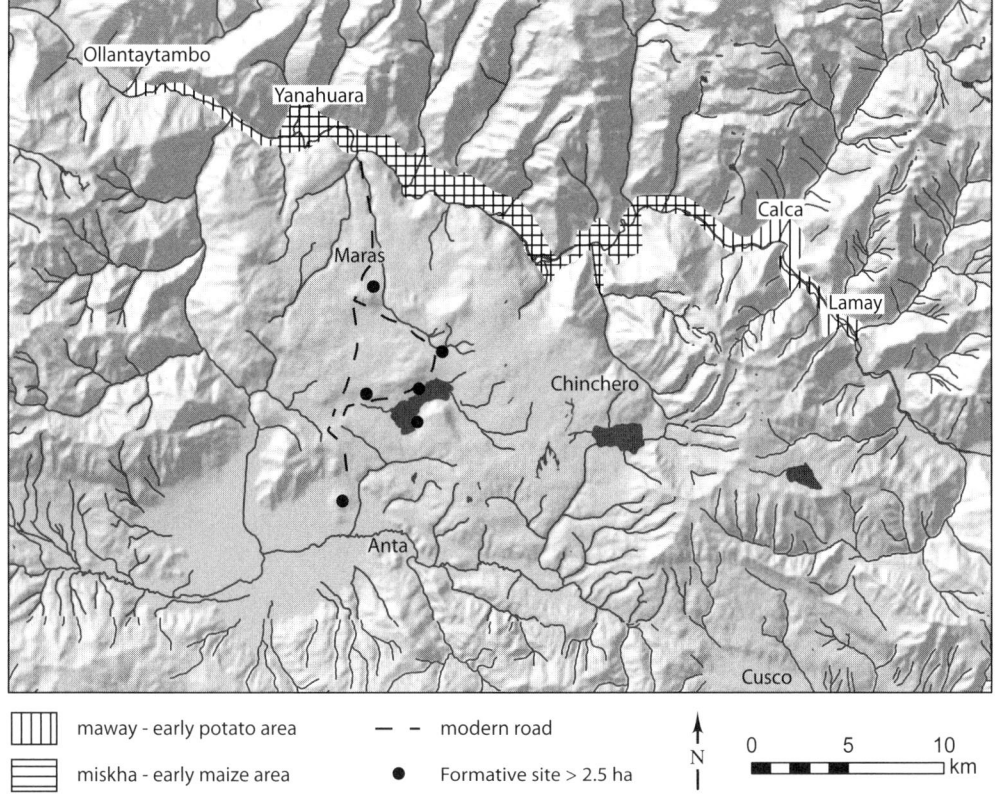

Figure 2.6. Locations of the largest Formative sites and the early planting zones in the Sacred Valley.

to Lamay, potatoes can be planted and harvested early. In addition, the stretch from Yanahuara to just west of Calca is an early corn area (Fig. 2.6).

Archaeological evidence suggests that quinoa and corn were both important parts of the Formative diet. Therefore, the possibility that farmers could have scheduled agricultural labor for these crops in diverse climate zones is intriguing. Today, on the high plain, the main quinoa and potato crops are planted in late September and October and are harvested in June and July. The early corn planting in the valley is in August and harvest is in January and February when little labor is required for crops on the plain. Early potatoes are planted in the valley in June and July and harvested in October and November—the reverse of the normal schedule of crops on the high plain. Early potatoes would not carry the same advantages as early corn in terms of avoiding labor bottlenecks, but they may have been valuable because little fresh food is otherwise available at this time (Fig. 2.7).

Did Formative villagers take advantage of diverse zones to manage labor shortages and increase the diversity of crops that they grew? Did they make distinctions such as "early" and "late" growing areas within the high plain of the survey area? Given that corn was a significant part of the diet for villagers living too high to grow it, how did they obtain this important food? Did each family or village have direct access to multiple ecological zones or were they part of a spatially dispersed and vertically integrated mountain community? To evaluate how Formative period villagers might have incorporated multiple ecological zones, I asked two questions using survey data: (1) is there evidence for different activities at high and low sites? and (2) does the location of sites suggest direct access to multiple zones or a trading relationship between villages on the plain and in the valley?

Based on differences in ceramic forms used for food preparation at sites above and below 3660 masl (roughly above and below the elevation of Yuthu), people divided their landscape into higher and lower zones, and their activities varied accordingly (Davis 2010; Davis and Covey 2007). In addition, the location of the largest sites along a route to the Sacred Valley indicates that both the high plain and the lower valley were important ecological zones (Davis 2010; Davis and Covey 2007). Living in a place with direct access to at least two ecological zones is common in archaeological and ethnographic Andean communities. Most often, settlements are located on the border between the *puna* and the *quechua* (Brush 1976; Flores Ochoa 1985; Perry et al.

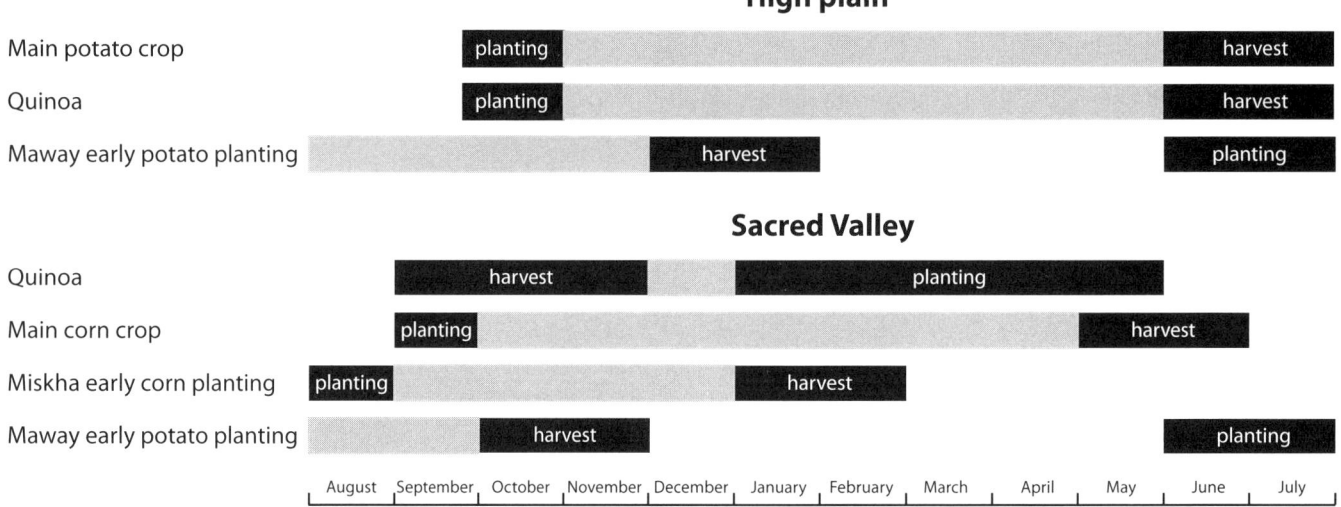

Figure 2.7. Labor schedule for planting and harvesting major crops on the high plain and in the Sacred Valley. By incorporating early planting zones in the valley, agricultural labor can be more evenly spaced throughout the year. Data are taken from Gade (1975), Kimura (2000), and Zimmerer (1996).

2006). In the case of Yuthu, each of these zones is located within a half-day walk from the other.

This kind of configuration has been described as the "compressed type" of Andean ecological zonation (Brush 1976). In modern contexts, when resource areas are so close together, migration and exchange are not necessary to exploit multiple zones. Instead, farmers have direct access to fields in each area (Brush 1976; Flores Ochoa 1985). This seems the most likely scenario for the Formative period on the plain. Direct use of both these zones by villagers living on the high plain would account for the presence of corn in sites on the high plain and could have allowed the same number of people to work more fields by spacing planting and harvesting throughout the year.

Daily Activities in the Village

Even as people scheduled their time around the demands of maintaining herds and fields, there were some activities—such as food preparation and consumption, child care, and clothing choice—that must have taken place every day within the village.

Raising Guinea Pigs

After camelids, the guinea pig (*cuy* in Spanish or *quwi* in Quechua) was the second most common economically useful animal (2.73 % NISP). Ethnoarchaeological studies have shown that guinea pig bones are often underrepresented in archaeological sites because many guinea pigs are eaten outdoors and the discarded bones are consumed by scavengers (Valdez Cárdenas and Valdez 1997). Therefore, it is likely that guinea pig was an even more important part of the diet than the number of recovered bones suggests.

There was no evidence of a special structure to raise *cuy* at Yuthu. This is not surprising considering that in highland houses today most guinea pigs are raised in kitchens, in close range of tossed cooking scraps and the warm hearth. Though an ethnoarchaeological study found that a kitchen that had been used to raise *cuy* for 50 years was swept clean, leaving no evidence for an archaeologist to recover (Valdez Cárdenas and Valdez 1997), I found a guinea pig coprolite in the early levels of occupation debris inside the earlier pit house next to a cooking hearth (Northern Sector, Intrusion M). Therefore, rather than having a special structure for raising guinea pigs, it seems that they were kept inside homes, close to the warm hearth where they were fed and cared for every day.

Grinding

Grinding plant material was an important part of food preparation at Yuthu. It is also possible that animal products—possibly including small dried fish—were ground as well. Grinding stones of many sizes and shapes were common at Yuthu. My experience in many Andean kitchens (as sous-chef or curious observer) has

Figure 2.8. A modern example of a small grinding stone that is oval in shape with a rectangular cross section (Type E). This type of stone is primarily used by rocking it back and forth along its edge against a grinding slab with a slightly concave surface.

led me to believe that no grinding stone has ever been used for a single purpose. Informal interviews with women who helped to excavate Yuthu tend to support this belief. When we found grinding stones, I would often ask, "What would you do with this stone?" The most popular response for the small hand-sized stones (*qulluta*) was simply "I would grind condiments." When pressed further, women could think of many other things to do with the stones. Grinding grains, seeds, and condiments were the most common suggestions, but I have also seen kitchen stones used as hammers and paperweights.

Although it is not possible to determine what was being ground based on the shape and size of stones, the morphology can be used to infer what type of grinding motion was used. Grinding stones were distinguished by two main characteristics: (1) the size of the stone (some stones fit into one hand while two hands would have been necessary to use others; in addition, there were even smaller stones that were held between the fingers) and (2) the motion that produced the grinding surfaces (some stones were pushed back and forth or in a circular motion against a lower surface whereas others were rocked from side to side against the lower surface).

Several hand stones had one or more flat surfaces that were produced by grinding against a flat or slightly concave surface. In addition to flat grinding surfaces, many of these stones had pock marks indicating that they were also used for pounding or hammering. They may have fit in one or two hands. Today, stones similar to these are called *qullutas*. There were stones with curved edges that were rocked side-to-side against a flat or concave surface. These were mostly oval stones with rectangular cross sections that could be used with two hands (Fig. 2.8). Similar rocker grinders are called *tunaw* or *k'utuna* today. There were also pestles for crushing and grinding in a cuplike mortar. Most mortars were very large heavy stones with concave grinding surfaces. There were also some with deep cuplike grinding basins.

Some of the grinding stones found at Yuthu were small enough to be held between the thumb and fingers. It is very difficult to assign specific functions to these stones, but they may have been used to polish or smooth pottery, pulverize pigments, or grind condiments and medicines—in which case they were probably not used every day like the larger food preparation stones. There were also palm-sized mortars that may have served as bases for small grinding tasks.[1]

Gathering Fuel

Gathering fuel for cooking was probably an activity that was carried out every day or nearly every day. *Ambrosia arborescens* (*markhu*) is a woody shrub that grows in the Cusco area. The high proportion of *Ambrosia* sp. in hearths (12.86% in hearths inside houses and 7.07% in outdoor hearths compared with 6.72% overall) indicates that it may have been collected and used for fuel at Yuthu as it is today in nearby Chinchero (Franquemont et al. 1990). Many other kinds of fuel may also have been used. Today, the stalks of quinoa are frequently burned as fuel (Gade 1975), a practice that may partly explain the very high proportion of carbonized quinoa seeds throughout the site. In addition, camelid dung and guinea pig droppings are used today in homes without kerosene stoves (Franquemont et al. 1990). These droppings could be gathered from the kitchen or camelid grazing areas.

Cooking

Cooking took place many times each day. The largest cooking hearths were located in the domestic Northern Sector in open areas outside structures. These hearths were deep pits with sloping walls and were filled with multiple layers of ashy soil and trampled surfaces that accumulated on top of each other (see Chap. 3). These hearths contained the carbonized botanical remains from many possible food species including quinoa, corn, and possibly *kiwicha* (*Amaranthus* sp.), *wakatay* (Asteraceae), and potato (*Solanum* sp.) along with bones from llama, guinea pig, birds (duck, coot, unidentified bird), deer, and unidentified mammals.

Smaller cooking hearths were located inside domestic structures. They had vertical walls and no trampled surfaces. Rather than being filled with accumulating strata of ash, these hearths were filled during use, dug out, and filled again with new ash. They contained carbonized botanical remains from many possible food species including quinoa, corn, wild greens (*Brassica* sp.), and possibly oca (*Oxalis* sp.). They also included camelid, guinea pig, heron, hawk, and unidentified mammal bones.

At present, the samples of botanical and faunal remains are too small to detect significant differences in the species represented in each type of hearth. In contrast, pottery vessel forms in hearths located inside and outside the houses differed in statistically significant ways ($\chi^2 = 47.285$, $df = 4$, $p < .001$). More specifically, cooking and storage vessels were found in differing proportions in these hearths. Restricted vessels with a neck were much more common outside; restricted vessels without a neck were more common in indoor hearths. In contrast, open serving vessels occurred in similar proportions in both areas. This suggests that the kind of cooking done in each context was different, though it is hard to specify in which ways.

Processing and Cooking Camelid Meat

Camelid bones were found throughout Yuthu in hearth and domestic trash contexts. Burning data were collected for camelid bones by Vásquez Sánchez and Rosales Tham (2009). Only 9.73% of the camelid bones that could be identified to skeletal element were burned (NISP = 2385). These included parts of the neck, trunk, limbs, and feet; the head was never burned.

This low proportion of burning is not surprising given that meat is often boiled and served in stews in the Andes, though it may be occasionally roasted. In an ethnoarchaeological study, Miller (1979) found that parts of the head were almost always boiled, never burned. The most frequently burned elements at Yuthu were scapulae, patellae, and third phalanges. Miller mentions that lower limbs may be laid in a fire to singe off all the hair before further butchering. Then, the hoof (including the first and second phalanges) is cut off and set aside to boil. It is possible that a similar cooking technique resulted in the burned phalanges at Yuthu.

Storage and Trash Disposal

In the domestic Northern Sector at Yuthu, there were two kinds of storage features, both consisting of simple pits dug into the soil. The more common storage pit type was shallow with vertical walls and a slightly rounded bottom. When I asked men and women from the village, many said that these pits were similar to potato storage pits that they line with eucalyptus leaves to preserve the potato. These early pits may have been used in a similar way. Although eucalyptus is not native to Peru, Gade (1975) found that in the 1960s peasant farmers used the native species *muña* (*Minthostachys* spp.) to line storage pits in order to prevent potatoes from sprouting upon contact with soil. In addition, *muña* has properties that discourage the growth of fungi, bacteria, and larvae, much like the acidic eucalyptus.

Many pits probably had two stages of use: (1) primary use to store potatoes or other foods and (2) secondary use as trash pits once they were no longer suitable to store food. Overall, these pits contained many carbonized plants (listed here from most to least common): quinoa, corn (seeds and cupules), *Galium* sp., *Ambrosia* sp., and one seed of *Amaranthus*, *Trifolium*, and *Verbena*. In addition to plant remains, these pits contained animal bones (listed here, beginning with the most common): unidentified mammal (small fragments from flotation), field mouse, guinea pig, and llama. Most remains are probably rubbish from the secondary use of the pit.

Intrusion R may be the only pit with evidence of use for both storage and trash disposal. The pit had two layers of soil. The lowest was a ring of burned soil along the sides of the base. Above that, the pit was filled with loose soil mixed with broken pottery, chipped stone, botanical remains, and animal bone. It is possible that villagers burned the stored contents of the pit after it had become infested with pests and could no longer be used. If that were true, the carbonized remains in the lowest layer of soil may be from plants that were actually stored during primary use. These included: *Chenopodium quinoa*, *Galium* sp., *Verbena* sp., and *Ambrosia* sp. Although no potato was recovered, this may be due to the difficulties associated with recovering and identifying tubers.

The second type of storage feature was a deeper pit with straight walls and a very flat base. Carbonized remains recovered from the pit included (from most to least common): quinoa, *Ambrosia*, corn, Poaceae, *Verbena*, and one seed of *Galium* and *Scirpus*. Animal bones included unidentified mammal, field mouse, llama, one duck bone, one unidentified bird bone, and one deer bone. This soil was probably also domestic trash from the secondary use as a storage pit. The common occurrence of field mice in these pits is probably the result of those rodents eating stored foods or domestic trash.

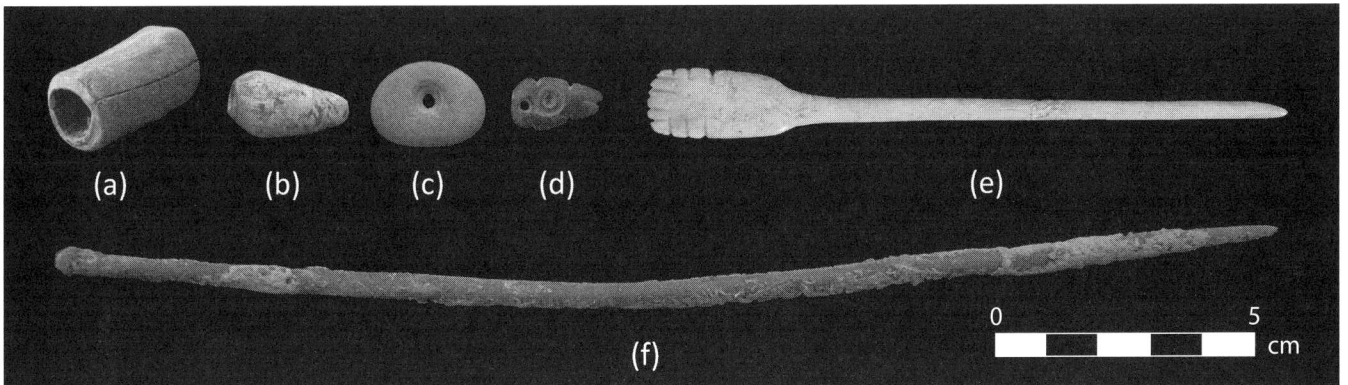

Figure 2.9. Objects used for personal adornment included: beads made of bone (*a*), shell (*b*), and stone (*c, d*); and clothing pins made of bone (*e*) and metal (*f*).

Personal Ornamentation

Very few objects used for personal ornamentation were found at Yuthu (despite sorting the heavy fractions from 1012 liters of flotation samples). These items included: (1) clothing pins made of metal and bone that probably held together garments and (2) beads made of bone, greenstone, and shell (Fig. 2.9; Plate 1). Villagers probably wore these beads and pins during daily life. It is interesting to note that none of these items were found in burial contexts; personal ornaments for the dead were not recovered.

Cranial Modification

Every individual buried at Yuthu (with the exception of Burial 2) had a modified cranium. Cranial modification is a practice carried out every day by mothers and children, and the shape created by modification may mediate social interactions throughout life. According to Spanish chronicles, the intentional reshaping of the head served to indicate group identity within the Inka Empire, but was also practiced before the Inka rose to power (Cobo 1990; de las Casas 1875; Marroquín 1944).

The notion that *intentional* cranial modification marked ethnic identity has been valuable for understanding cases of cranial modification in earlier Andean states (e.g., Blom 2005; Hoshower et al. 1995). These societies were intensely hierarchical, geographically expansive, and ethnically diverse. In these sociopolitical contexts, marking group identity was important: (1) in conflicts between ethnic groups over territory, resources, and status, and (2) as a mechanism for the state to impose order over myriad subjugated groups. Among the Inka, at least, visible markers of ethnicity such as dress and hairstyle were important imperial strategies for tracking and managing the diverse populations within the empire (Mannheim 1991).

In fact, a comparative study of cranial modification in Eurasia and the Andes has suggested that homogeneity of head shaping emerged with increasing state influence in both regions, citing the potential advantages of emulating the powerful state as well as the imposition of standard shapes by imperial powers in order to distinguish and classify groups within the empire (Torres-Rouff and Yablonsky 2005). Additional studies in the Andes support the proposition that cranial modification was more standardized in state-level societies (Allison et al. 1981; Pérez 2007). The lack of standardization within and between Formative Cusco villages raises the question of whether non-standardized cranial modification in pre-state societies may have resulted from practices with goals other than signaling ethnic affiliation.

Despite the evidence that the use of head shape as an ethnic marker arose in multi-ethnic states, most bioarchaeologists have used ethnohistoric descriptions of the Inka as the principal guide to structure research on cranial deformation for all time periods in the Andes. In most approaches, head shape is treated as if it were just one of many objects recovered from a grave that can be used to investigate identity, though with the special advantage of being an immutable characteristic of the individual during life that endured in death (e.g., Blom 2005; Gerszten 1993; Torres-Rouff 2002). Different shapes are typically classified into broad categories based on form so that "types" can be correlated with other archaeological data (especially ceramic types and strontium signatures) in order to identify ethnic groups according to statistically significant correlations among these variables. Because this approach effectively masks some of the most interesting aspects of cranial modification, I propose an alternative approach—that focuses on *cranial modification as the material marker of an everyday social practice that involved interaction between caregivers and very young children during a particular phase in life*.

Although it receives less attention in the literature, there is evidence as to what this social practice was like in certain Andean contexts because dry desert conditions have preserved some devices used for modification. On the north coast, a Late Intermediate period cradleboard that included a device for bind-

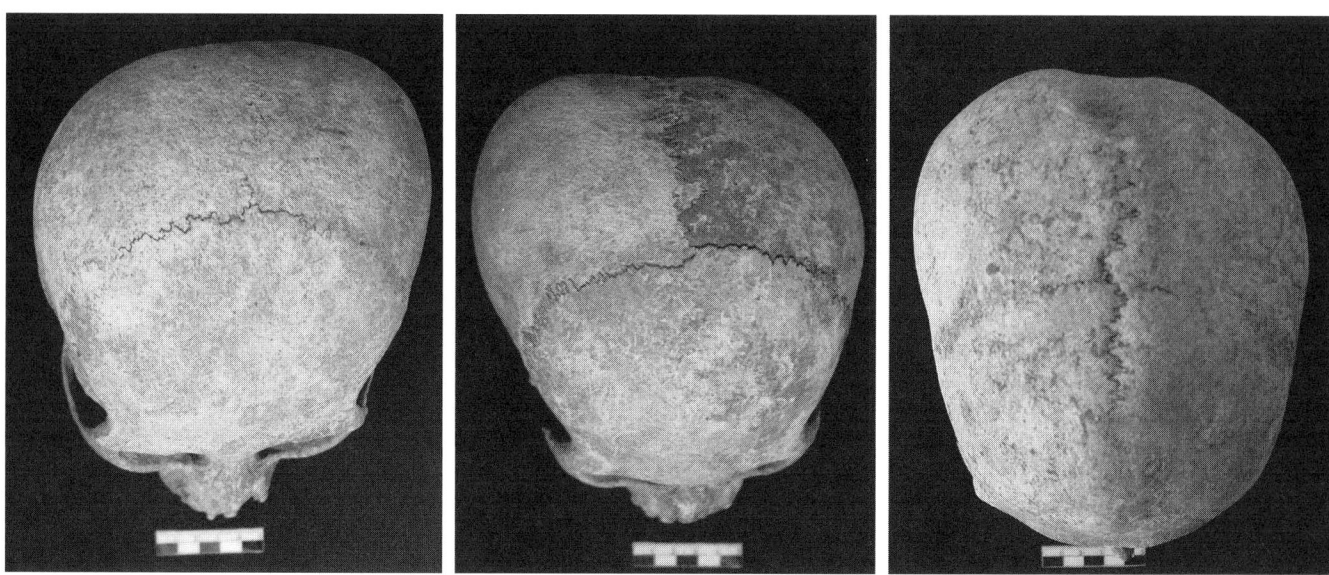

Figure 2.10. Cranial modification at Yuthu: a view from the top. Note the asymmetry and total lack of uniformity in head shape.

ing the infant's head was recovered (Verano 1997). On the south coast, a Middle Horizon period infant was found with a set of three modification devices: one that he was wearing, and two that would have been used as he learned to crawl or walk (Allison et al. 1981). In addition, there have been some attempts to infer modification methods based on the shape of the skulls themselves (Pomeroy et al. 2009). These studies demonstrate that diverse methods were employed for more or less time during childhood. For example, while cradleboarding may have been used only until the child learned to walk, a system of headdresses with flat boards, cords, and ropes could be used for much longer, perhaps until the skull bones had all fused. Therefore, longer processes lasting throughout childhood may have created standardized shapes while short-term practices may have produced more variability.

How can we think about differing kinds of interactions between caregivers and children in terms of whether or not the caregiver was trying to mark the child's ethnic group? Could head shape be entirely unintentional? Although modification from cradleboarding in the Andes has been considered unintentional, ethnography from North America has demonstrated that mothers are conscious that placing an infant on a cradleboard and using particular types of binding will create certain head shapes (Logan et al. 2003). The North American case demonstrates that the term "unintentional" is misleading. It may be more accurate to think of cranial modification in these situations as a secondary effect of the way that an infant is carried.

Instead of trying to infer intentionality, it is more productive to focus on the practice in terms of the goal of uniformity. In the archaeological examples above, the elaborate set of headdresses that would have been worn by the Wari child demonstrates that the main purpose of those objects was to create a specific head shape. It is likely that changing to a new headdress may have accompanied important rites of passage, or steps in becoming a full Wari person. In contrast, the short period of cradleboarding in a non-state society indicates less concern with creating a specific shape—the primary goal may have been the mother's mobility, allowing her to easily transport the infant with no direct concern about modifying the head shape, or a more general and difficult to recognize goal of "proper child rearing." While this discussion has been limited in scope, I would like to emphasize that ethnic marking was not the only possible function of cranial modification in the ancient Andes.

Was cranial modification used to mark group membership in Formative period Cusco? The villagers of Yuthu practiced a single "type" of cranial modification. The frontal and occipital bones were compressed in an anterior-posterior manner that resulted in the non-uniform expansion of the parietal bones, often forming two distinct lobes on either side of the sagittal suture; the lobes were frequently asymmetrical in size and angle (Fig. 2.10). This particular type of asymmetrical "bilobed" modification is often subsumed into a general category of fronto-occipital or tabular oblique modification that is contrasted with the general category of circumferential or annular style in order to make broad comparisons (e.g., Blom 2005; Pomeroy et al. 2009). This lumping makes it seem as though this method produced uniform results, though it rarely did. Conventional scholarly practice has masked the important variation that might be linked to the particular tradition that created this form (see Hoshower et al. 1995; Pomeroy et al. 2009).

At Yuthu, the lack of uniformity of asymmetry and degree of modification suggests that the cultural practice that created this "type" may have involved less standardized methods or may have lasted for a shorter period of the child's life when compared with the more complicated series of headdresses known from later periods. It is possible that cranial deformation during the Formative period was a secondary, though not necessarily unintentional, consequence of a certain child-rearing practice that lasted only as long as the infant was carried by his or her mother. The type of deformation at Yuthu was not the flattened posterior typically produced by cradleboarding, though it is possible that a stronger binding of the infant to the board could have resulted in this more extreme shape. It is more likely that swaddling produced this shape. In fact, certain swaddling devices employed by the Wari were the first of several steps in creating a similar, but more standardized, shape (Allison et al. 1981).

Valerie Andushko (pers. comm.) reports that this modification type and the high degree of variability within it were common throughout the Cusco area during the Formative period. Given that, it is unlikely that head shape was an important marker of group identity in day-to-day interactions. If, however, villagers from Yuthu encountered people with unmodified or markedly different shaped heads while traveling, or when visitors came from distant places, they would take note of it. In those scenarios, the shape of their own heads would become a visible marker of group membership (sensu Wobst 1977, 1999). Outside a multi-ethnic state, however, these kinds of encounters may have been less frequent, and may have involved fewer conflicts that required expression of group membership.

Discussion of Daily Activities at Yuthu

Everyday activities at Yuthu included not only those related to meeting the biological needs of the human body, but also practices that were part of the creation, expression, and negotiation of social identity within the community. We still lack information that would allow us to understand how these tasks were divided among family members or community workgroups. Moving forward, research focused on understanding the social structure of daily life will be particularly important.

Periodic Activities in and around the Village

Some activities were neither elements of production strategies that shaped the annual cycle nor quotidian tasks that filled life every day. Rather, these activities might have been performed as need arose, or as time allowed. The frequency of these practices probably varied—based on season, access to resources, and skill. Some subsistence related activities like hunting, plant collecting, and butchering were probably fairly common, and a subset of craft production activities (like spinning wool or making bone tools) likely filled spare moments during most days. Other activities were probably shorter-duration events of concentrated efforts (like pottery production or chopping wood). In contrast, a few activities were rare and created (or were required for) significant moments in public and/or family life in the village. Such activities included construction of houses and community structures, interpersonal violence, certain rituals, and long-distance trade.

Hunting and Trapping

Hunting and trapping wild animals was not an economically important activity at Yuthu, though it may have been important for social or ritual reasons (see bird related ritual section below). Hunting was also a minor activity at Marcavalle, the only other Formative site for which we have comparable data (Miller 1979). At Yuthu, wild species made up 15.18% of the fauna (NISP). Excluding frogs and mice (12.85%), only 2.33% were animals with economic or social value (Fig. 2.11).

The majority of animals were probably hunted relatively close to the village. The most common were birds (1.63%). Most bird remains were not identified to species, but of those that were, duck was most common, followed by eagle hawk, coot, owl, hawk, heron, and macaw. Water birds like duck, coot, and heron were probably hunted in or around Lake Huaypo, while hawks and owls are common predators on the surrounding plain. All of these species are year-round residents in Cusco (Schulenberg 2007), so it is not possible to specify in which season they were hunted. Deer comprised 0.54% of the total faunal remains. Compared to the total camelids (36.88%), it is clear that deer were a very small part of the diet. Other locally available small mammals such as fox, chinchilla, and viscacha were recovered in small numbers. Predatory cats were present at Yuthu only as single skeletal elements: the upper M3 tooth of a puma and the humerus of a pampas cat.

Species from the lowland forests were probably obtained by trade rather than direct exploitation (see below). The macaw is a bird from the jungle of the departments of Cusco or Puno. A large fish jaw fragment (the only fish bone recovered) was not identified to species, but Vásquez Sánchez and Rosales Tham suggest it may be from a jungle river.

The total absence of local fish at Yuthu may seem surprising given the site's proximity to Lake Huaypo. Though it is possible that very small fish were ground and made into stew, leaving no archaeological trace, it is also possible that villagers did not eat fish. In fact, the Inka did not exploit fish resources from the surrounding lakes and rivers (Kendall 1973).

There is little evidence as to how people might have hunted. Obsidian projectile points may have been used as darts. It is also possible that birds and small mammals were caught with nets or other kinds of traps made of perishable materials, but none have been recovered at Yuthu.

As a final note, it is curious that although the name of the archaeological site is the Quechua word for a tinamou, or Andean partridge, not a single *yuthu* bone was found at Yuthu.

Wild Plant Collecting

Although the villagers of Yuthu relied primarily on domesticated plants for food, some wild plants were also important (17.12% of all identified carbonized plant remains were probably wild species; Fig. 2.12). These plants were probably used for food, as spices, as medicine, to thatch houses, to make baskets, and to make dyes. In many cases, Vásquez Sánchez and Rosales Tham (2009) were not able to identify plants at the species level. Therefore, it is not possible to determine with certainty which plants were used or whether they were domesticated or wild.

Some wild plants were most likely weeds that either were used for fuel or animal fodder or were not exploited economically. Amaranths include many wild species that are considered weeds as well as the domesticated grain *kiwicha*. They are part of the sunflower family (Asteraceae), which is the largest family of flowering plants and includes *wakatay*, a popular savory herb for cooking. Fabaceae, or the pea family, includes *Phaseolus* beans as well as *Trifolium*, which includes some forage (Ugent and Ochoa 2006). The most common wild plant identified at Yuthu was *Ambrosia* (the ragweed genus of flowering plants and weeds). The only species of *Ambrosia* that is widespread in Cusco is *Ambrosia arborescens*, which is a woody shrub, not a weedy plant (Chepstow-Lusty et al. 1998). Its wood was probably used for fuel (discussed above).

Other wild plants were probably used as food or condiments. *Brassica*, part of the mustard family, includes many wild plants used for condiments, to make salads, and to cook as greens. In Peru, there is also a species that produces a tuber that is eaten as food (Ugent and Ochoa 2006). *Oxalis* is a large genus comprised of several species, including domesticated oca (*Oxalis tuberosa*) and a wild species eaten by modern herders in Chinchero (Franquemont et al. 1990; Ugent and Ochoa 2006). *Verbena* is a large genus of fragrant and medicinal plants; in Cusco, some species are used to treat headache and hangovers (Franquemont et al. 1990).

Grasses were probably used as industrial plants. The family Poaceae includes domesticated corn, many wild forage plants, and grasses used today to thatch roofs (Franquemont et al. 1990). Similarly, *Scirpus* is an aquatic grasslike plant that can be used to make baskets, mats, and ropes, and to thatch roofs. It is also the material used to make the famous totora boats of Lake Titicaca (Ugent and Ochoa 2006). We recovered no evidence of watercraft at Yuthu, and with the lack of fish remains, it seems unlikely that boats were used on the small lake.

Vegetable dyes were probably made from wild plants. *Bidens* includes many weeds, but it also includes a genus used for dye. *Galium* also includes plants for making dyes (see below for further discussion).

Practicing Medicine

The frequency with which medicine was practiced probably depended on the community's health, perceived supernatural ailments, social conflict, and even the frequency of celebrations. A few of the genera present at Yuthu include medicinal plants used today in Chinchero. Unfortunately, no medicinal plants were identified to the species level, and many of the genera contain plants that are used not only for medicine, but also for food, dye, or fuel.

Plants that may have been used as medicine at Yuthu (from Franquemont et al. 1990) include:

Galium sp.: *Galium weberbaueri* (*rata rata* or *pisqu sisaq*) is used to make tea and cold drinks. It may be ground and rubbed on a child's tongue when it turns white or rubbed on the eyes for ocular problems.

Verbena sp.: *Verbena hispida* (Quechua name not reported) is boiled to treat a headache (usually from drinking too much alcohol). Alternatively, the entire plant can be rubbed on the body to cleanse and give strength for running.

Bidens sp.: *Bidens andicola* var. *andicola* (*p'irka*) is made into tea to treat pneumonia.

Ambrosia: *Ambrosia arborescens* (*markhu*) leaves are heated in a pot and rubbed on the stomach for pain.

Butchering Animals

Llamas and alpacas may have been slaughtered during annual festivals, when animals were no longer useful, or as needed for food. Cut marks were recorded on camelid bones by Vásquez Sánchez and Rosales Tham (2009). These marks were very rare (only 0.75% of camelid bones) and were generally found on the plantar side of the astragalus and on the first phalange. These kinds of cuts are associated with secondary dismemberment and hide removal (Miller 1979). The overall dearth of cut marks suggests that dismemberment may have been carried out primarily with hatchets or hammer stones, resulting in crushing of the bones rather than cutting. Along with other cooking practices such as boiling and pounding, this type of processing may account for the high proportion of unidentified mammal remains, which are mostly splintered long bone fragments of large mammals.

Textile Production

Tools, dyes, and fibers from Yuthu show that weaving was an important activity during the Formative period. Weaving tools were found in both the Northern and Southern Sectors. The most characteristic tool was the beater (*ruk'i* or *wich'uña* in Quechua; Fig. 2.13c; Plate 1), which is used to pound down the weft when using either a backstrap or horizontal loom. These tools were made from camelid metacarpals or metatarsals. Although this tool is commonly used for weaving, some archaeologists have referred to it more generically as a "bone awl," which could have been used for other activities such as basket making.

Two more bone tool types may have been used for weaving. Long tools with rounded and pointed ends might have been pick-up sticks (*pallana* in Quechua; Fig. 2.13g, i; Plate 1). It is possible

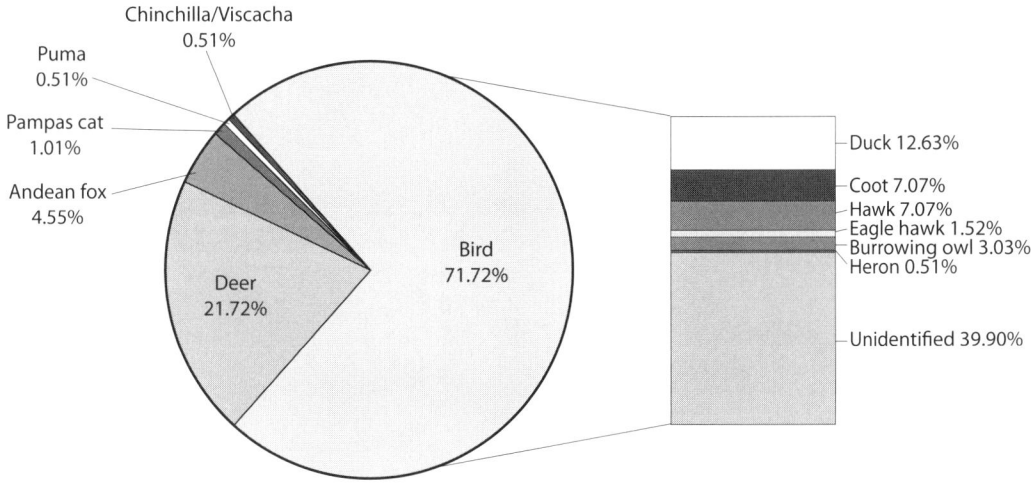

Figure 2.11. Wild species that were hunted or trapped. These species account for only 2.22% of faunal remains at Yuthu.

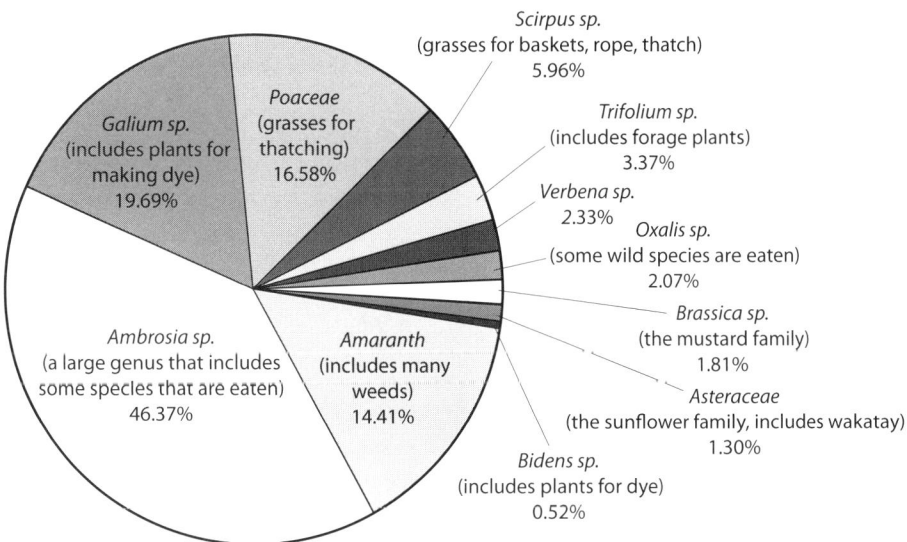

Figure 2.12. Wild plants collected at Yuthu may have been used for food, as spices, as medicine, to thatch houses, to make baskets, and to make dyes. Only 17.12% of all carbonized plant remains were probably wild species. Note that some plant identifications were not specific enough to determine with certainty whether the specimen was wild or domesticated.

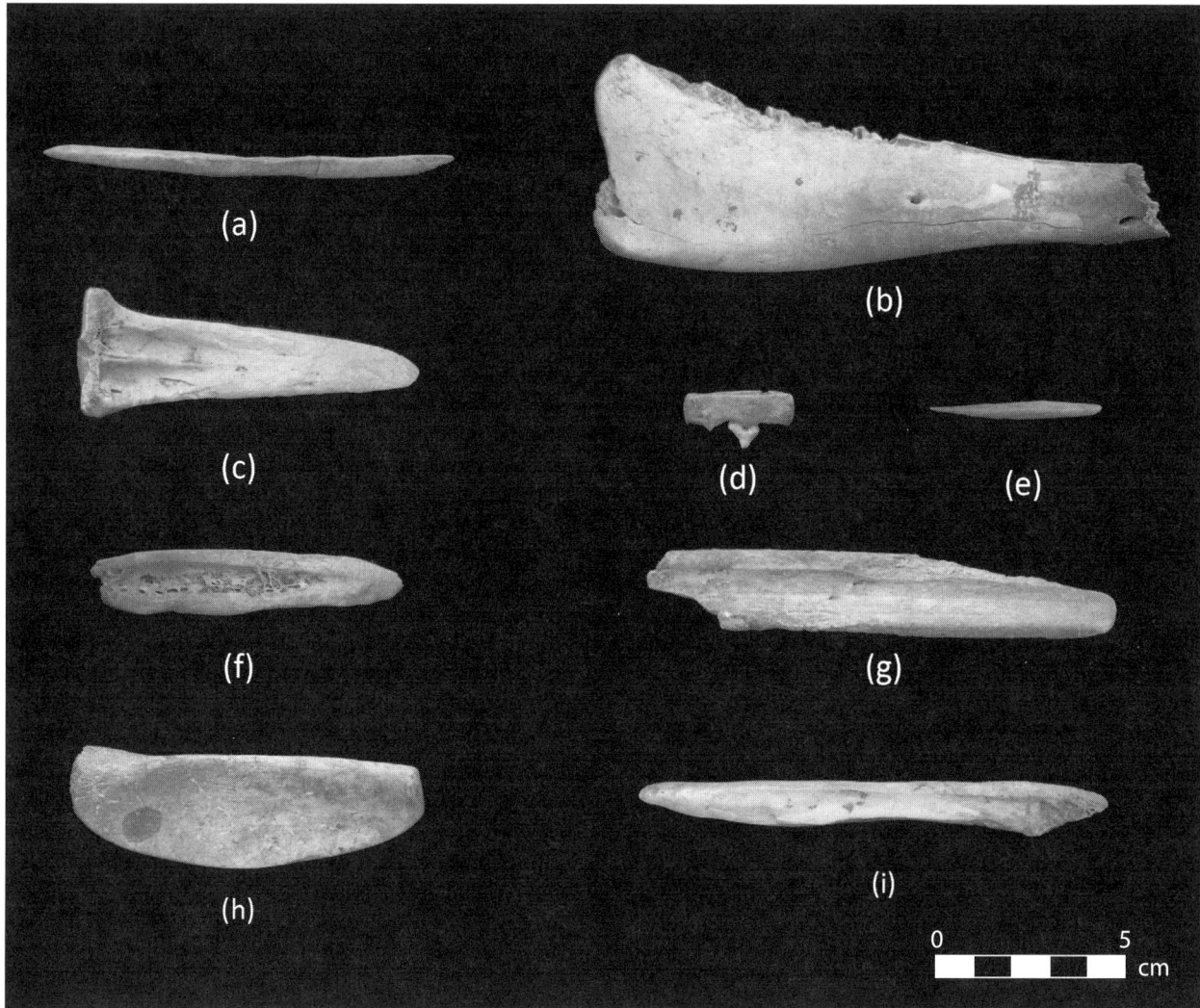

Figure 2.13. Examples of bone tools from Yuthu: *a*, a thin pointed object; *b*, a camelid mandible spatula; *c*, a *ruk'i* or bone awl (see weaving section); *d*, a polished jaw fragment with tooth; *e*, a small needle; *f*, a long bone shaft fragment with smooth rounded tip; *g*, a long bone shaft fragment with square tip; *h*, a camelid scapula scraper; *i*, a long bone shaft fragment with pointed tips.

that some long smoothed bones were used as bobbins (*minikuna*) or weaving swords (*k'allawa*) for making small belts (Fig. 2.13*a*; Plate 1). Unfortunately, the tools could have been used for other activities (like husking corn or punching holes). Many other tools necessary for spinning and weaving were not found at Yuthu, most likely because looms, spindles, whorls, weaving swords, and bobbins were made of wood or other perishable material, just as they are today in Cusco (Callañaupa Alvarez 2007).

The only textile fragments found at Yuthu were made from unidentified plant fiber. They were associated with human burials and may have been special textiles for wrapping bodies during burial preparation. Given the large proportion of llama and alpaca bones found at Yuthu, most spinning and weaving probably used wool fibers.

Yarn is often dyed bright colors before being woven into intricate patterns. Dyes may be made from minerals, insects, or plants. We found carbonized seeds from three plant genera that may have been used to dye wool: *Galium*, *Bidens*, and *Ambrosia*. Two species of *Galium* are used to make red dye—the branch of *Galium aparine* L. is used today in Cusco (Callañaupa Alvarez 2007:52), and *Galium hypocarpium* is used throughout the Andes (Ugent and Ochoa 2006) and was found in Early Horizon contexts at Paracas (1400–400 BC) (Fester 1953). *Bidens andicola* produces orangish-yellow dye, and although *Ambrosia peruviana* is a common weed (ragweed), the leaves can be used to make green dye. Unfortunately, none of these plants were identified to species level, and plants in each genus may have had other uses as medicine or fuel.

The context of the plants, however, does support the proposition that *Galium* and *Ambrosia* were used to dye yarn. Because *Ambrosia* was common (found in 29.7% of flotation samples), and *Bidens* was very rare (one seed was found in a hearth inside the structure in the southeast corner of Unit D), I focused on the contexts where *Galium* was recovered. Except for one seed, which was included with the offering of Burial 11, all *Galium* seeds were found in the domestic Northern Sector. Single seeds were found in many kinds of features including hearths, pits, floors, burials, ash deposits, and compact soil. When more than one *Galium* seed was found, the seeds were found most often in hearths *outside* the structures. Dyeing wool is a messy operation. Therefore, when plants are used to make dyes, they are boiled in large pots over open fires outside. It seems likely, therefore, that *Galium* was used to dye yarn at Yuthu.

Today in Cusco, women are the most visible weavers, and it would be tempting to attribute weaving to women in the Formative period as well. While dyeing wool may be a rare activity involving many people, women spin yarn every day while watching flocks, children, or soccer games. Women and men weave in cooperatives, and men are taught to weave in prison. Cross-culturally, it is true that both men and women weave (Díaz-Andreu 2005:33). Unfortunately, there was no evidence at Yuthu to confirm whether men, women, or both were spinners and weavers.

Bone Tool Manufacture

Many bone tools were found at Yuthu, most made from camelid bone fragments by cutting, smoothing, and polishing. At least in one case, bone tools were made in an outdoor work area next to a large open hearth where a wide variety of domestic activities took place (see Chap. 3). Worked bone recovered from important contexts is described in detail in Chapters 3 and 4.

Pottery Making

Although no unequivocal evidence of pottery manufacturing tools or infrastructure was found at Yuthu (such as piles of clay or special kilns), one sherd that was damaged in the firing process (a "waster") was found on the site's surface. Therefore, it is likely that villagers built and fired pottery at Yuthu on a small scale, using open fires that leave little archaeological trace. Broken ceramic sherds were also reworked to make discs and other shapes whose function is not clear. It is most likely that this activity was carried out according to need or demand.

The pottery was built using coils. The characteristic thick rims of Chanapata neckless *ollas* and open plates were created by folding the clay over and smoothing the seam. The most common finishing technique was burnishing, which would have been done when the clay was leather hard, after drying but before firing. Chanapata redwares and blackwares were decorated with paint. This paint was usually limited to the interior rim of open vessels and the exterior rim of restricted vessels, but red slip was found on the body of a few vessels. Most pots were fired in an oxidizing environment, though some were reduced to create a dark background for the paint.

No whole pots were found at Yuthu, so it was not possible to identify or describe vessel forms in detail. Instead, vessels were categorized as either open or restricted according to rim form (Fig. 2.14). *Open forms* probably included plates and bowls. There were no necks with sharp angles to indicate the presence of flaring-rimmed bowls like *escudillas*. Therefore, open vessels were probably used primarily for serving food. *Restricted forms* were divided into two subgroups: those with a neck and those without a neck. These pots may have included cooking *ollas*, toasters, and storage vessels. They were probably used primarily for storing and preparing food.

The pottery at Yuthu was nearly all Chanapata style or Paqallamocco style (a regional variant of Chanapata-style pottery found on the pampa of Anta). Because these styles cannot be easily distinguished, all were considered Chanapata in this study. Within this style, pottery at Yuthu was divided into subtypes following those originally outlined by Rowe (1944; see Fig. 2.15; Plate 2).

Chanapata plainware is reddish to brown in color. It has no interior or exterior decoration though it may be unevenly burnished or brushed.

Chanapata pattern burnished is similar to Chanapata plainware except that some burnished lines form patterns on the interior of open vessels and the exterior of restricted vessels. The designs are usually a thick, shiny band around the rim and vertical lines descending down the body.

Chanapata incised may be highly burnished and is decorated with lines cut into the clay when it was still somewhat wet.

Chanapata redware is pottery painted with red, cream, or sparkling gray (probably made from hematite). Most commonly, the red was used as a background for the other colors. Paint is found on the exterior of restricted vessels and around the interior rim of open vessels. The area under the paint was often burnished to create a shiny surface. Painting and burnishing rarely extended all the way down the body of the pot. The most common designs were zigzags and circles, though zoomorphic designs sometimes occurred.

Chanapata blackware is the same as Chanapata redware except the pottery is fired in a reducing atmosphere so that the paint appears over a dark brown or black background.

Chanapata painted and incised is similar to Chanapata redware except that deep incisions delimit the painted areas.

Indeterminate style includes several rare styles that might represent trade wares from other parts of the Andes, though no attempt has been made to identify their sources.

Procurement and Working of Chipped Stone

Chipped stone was rarely made into formal tool types. The most common tools were made from relatively low quality materials available in the local ancient marine sedimentary geology

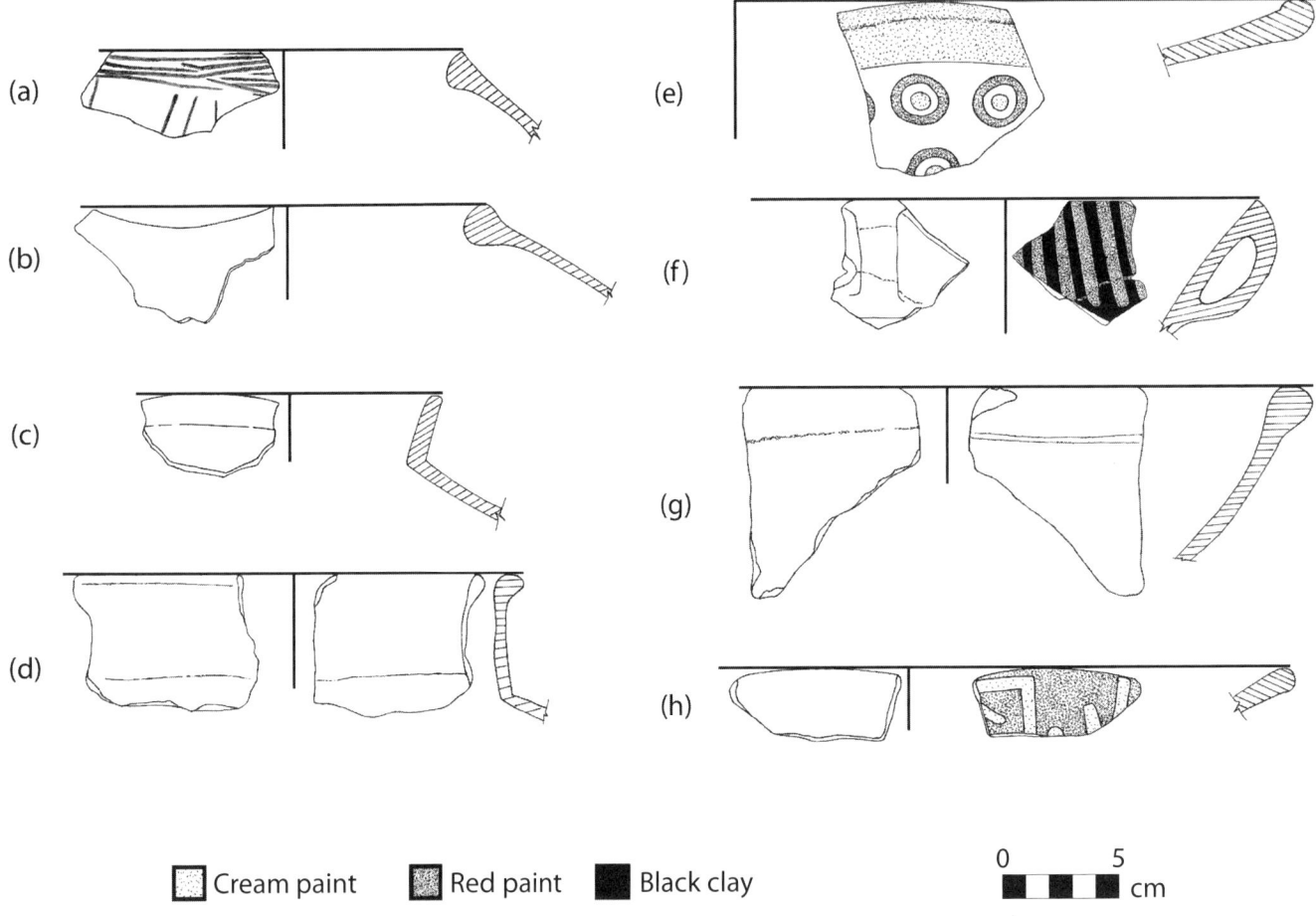

Figure 2.14. Pottery forms at Yuthu were divided into open vessels (*e–h*) and restricted vessels (*a–d*). Restricted vessels were divided into two groups: those without a neck (*a, b*) and those with a neck (*c, d*).

(Fig. 2.16). In fact, several outcrops of red quartzitic sandstone and quartzite surrounded by lithic debitage are located just behind Cerro Huanacaure (about 2 km from Yuthu). Most tools made from this material were simply utilized flakes, and no two tools resembled each other closely. For the most part, chipped stone tools were probably made as need arose, and flakes were discarded when they were no longer sharp.[2] Although no sourcing analysis has been done yet, for now sedimentary and metamorphic rocks are considered together as locally available resources.

Some raw materials were not available in the immediate vicinity of Huaypo, but are present in other parts of Cusco. Slate, a metamorphic rock, is found near Urcos (about 70 km away). It was uncommon at Yuthu, though it was used frequently to make stone tools in later periods. Several igneous rocks available in the region were also present at Yuthu in low quantities.

The only formal tool type at Yuthu was the obsidian projectile point (Fig. 2.17). Although the shape of these points may seem superficially diverse, they are all made with the same technique. The edges of a flake that is short and wide were chipped to create a sharp point and more rounded base (Fig. 2.17). The points were classified as unimarginal flake tools, bimarginal flake tools, or hafted bifaces depending on the location and degree of chipping to achieve the final form. Obsidian tools were reworked fairly frequently to maintain sharp edges. Broken projectile points were also reshaped to make different tools.

Obsidian has no known local source and had to be imported from other parts of the sierra, such as the Alca source in central Arequipa, the Chivay source in southern Arequipa, or the Quispisisa source in Ayacucho (Glascock et al. 2007). At Marcavalle, obsidian came from both Alca and Chivay (Burger et al. 2000). No analyses have been conducted yet to determine the source of obsidian at Yuthu, but obsidian procurement probably occurred periodically as traders with llama caravans passed through Cusco.

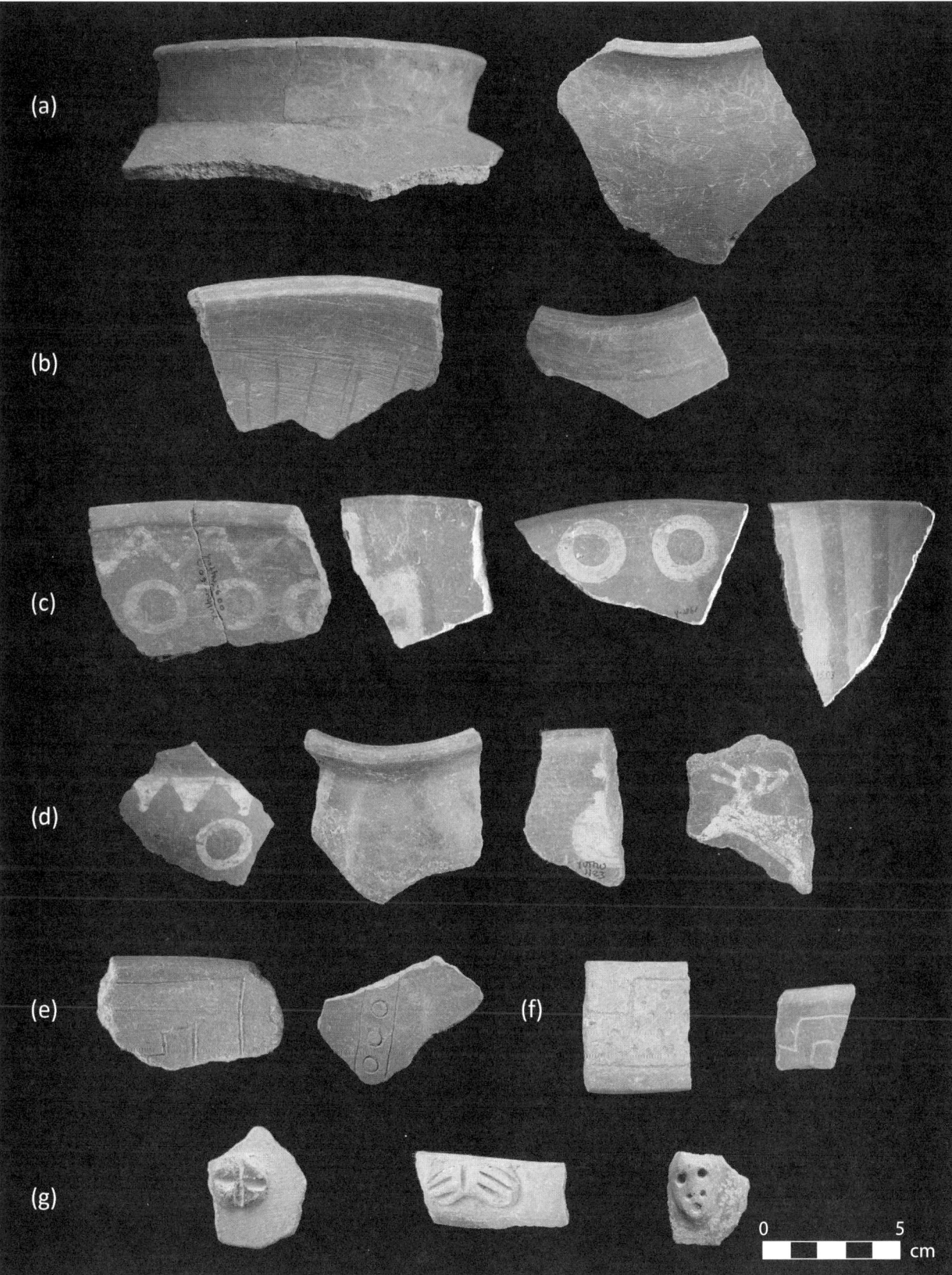

Figure 2.15. Chanapata sub-styles identified at Yuthu: *a*, Chanapata plainware; *b*, Chanapata pattern burnished; *c*, Chanapata redware; *d*, Chanapata blackware; *e*, Chanapata painted and incised; *f*, Chanapata incised. Molded decorations (*g*) were applied to the body or rim of pottery of many different styles.

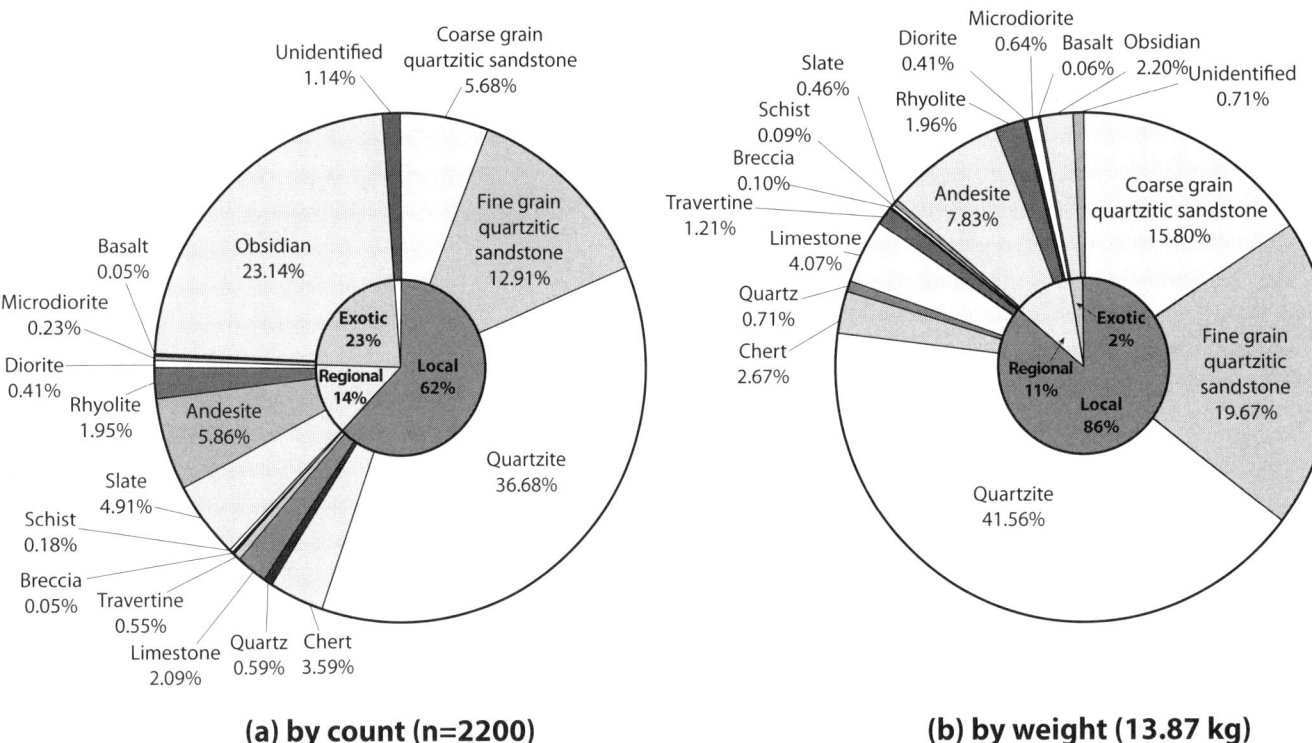

Figure 2.16. Raw materials for chipped stone by count and weight. Locally available sedimentary and metamorphic rocks were the most common materials used to make tools at Yuthu.

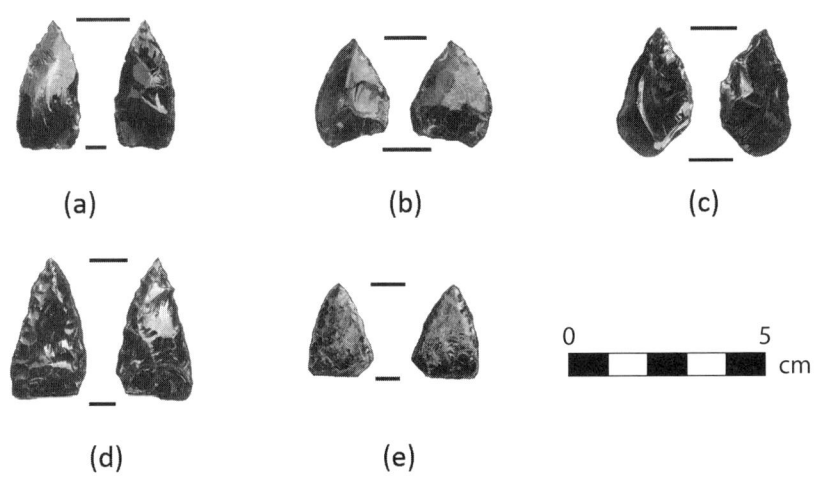

Figure 2.17. Examples of Formative period projectile points found at Yuthu. Although these flakes seem superficially diverse, they are made using the same technique. The edges of a flake that is short and wide are chipped to create a sharp point and more rounded base. The striking platform is located on the center of the dorsal and ventral views.

Chopping and Woodworking

Very few objects for chopping or woodworking were recovered at Yuthu, though there were some fragments of small groundstone axes. The lack of woodworking tools is not surprising given that the area was deforested before 2000 BC (Chepstow-Lusty et al. 2004; Chepstow-Lusty et al. 1998).

Water Manipulation

The villagers of Yuthu understood how to create and take advantage of slope to control water flow. They built both simple drains and elaborate stone canals associated with the ceremonial structure in the Southern Sector. The drains were linear channels cut into bedrock. In contrast, the formal canals at Yuthu were lined on both sides and covered with large flat stones. Rather than bringing water *toward* something like a field, these canals took water *away* from a structure with a sunken floor (see Chap. 4 for further discussion). Constructing and cleaning canals would have been periodic work that may have involved several villagers. It is possible that there were more extensive canal systems located "offsite," used to irrigate agricultural fields.

Construction

At Yuthu, villagers used a wide variety of construction techniques to build domestic and ceremonial structures. While some construction techniques were significant undertakings that would have required labor from a large part of the community, most required little time, labor, or special materials. It is likely that the larger projects were rarer and incorporated many villagers while smaller projects were more frequent and may have required only a few family members. When possible, I include references to other Cusco sites with similar features, though most excavations prior to this study have been very small trenches, which prevent a full understanding of structure shape and type.

Land Leveling and Terracing

The most striking construction was the leveling of a natural hill to create a large platform (about 60 × 30 m). Villagers cut through the topsoil and excavated the relatively soft gypsum bedrock. More modest terracing may exist on the northern slope descending from the larger platform, and along the eastern edge of the site where dense clay is the underlying sterile geologic soil. This kind of leveling is also known from the sites of Batan Urqo and Muyu Orqo (Zapata 1998). It seems that leveling in order to create platforms was a common and important feature of monumental ceremonial architecture in Formative period Cusco.

Clay Floors

There were prepared clay floors in both the ceremonial and domestic sectors. These floors were in open patios or plazas, never inside houses. Paved floors were also found at Chanapata (Bauer 2004).

Masonry

Some structures in the ceremonial sector were built using unmodified field stones set in clean clay mortar. At Yuthu, the bench of the sunken structure (see Chap. 4) and a circular cist were built using this technique. Similar practices have been identified in tomb constructions at Chanapata (Yábar Moreno 1972) and Batan Urqo (Arroyo and Choque 1992). This raises the possibility that the circular stone cist at Yuthu may have also served a mortuary function. Yet no human remains were found in the cist. Although it is impossible to determine, funerary bundles may have been stored in this pit temporarily as part of multiphase burial practices (see below). In addition, the retaining wall of Structure 1 at Yuthu was made of stone *without* mortar. This technique was also found at Chanapata (Bauer 2004) and at Choquepukio (McEwan et al. 1995).

Adobe

Adobes were recovered from Yuthu, though they were not found in situ as part of structures. One adobe was found broken in half. The original brick measured 45 × 20 × 13 cm and was made of clay mixed with grasses. Although no adobe bricks have been found at other Formative period sites, it is possible that adobes were used in construction elsewhere. Zapata (1998) suggests that, at Batan Urqo, the red soil around circular structures was probably adobe melt. In addition, Chávez reported that Marcavalle seemed to have had adobe architecture (Chávez 1980).

Stone Foundations with Walls Made of Perishable Materials

Some small domestic structures at Yuthu had foundations comprised of a single course of stones. These stones were covered with compact red earth (similar to what Zapata found at Batan Urqo). This red earth was probably the remains of a perishable superstructure of adobes, packed mud, or wattle and daub.

Excavated Structures or "Pit Houses"

Some small domestic structures at Yuthu were dug into the earth so that the floor was one meter or more below the ground surface. The "walls" were the sides of the pit, and these houses did not have a superstructure of rock or adobe. Rather, a thatched roof was built directly on the ground. These houses were small and construction would have been quick, requiring little labor, few tools, and only material available locally from the lakeshore. In the *puna*, people still build houses with sunken floors for insulation against the cold and wind (Flannery et al. 1989; Flores Ochoa 1979).

Thatched Roofs

The presence of carbonized *Scirpus* sp. seeds in and around the pit houses suggests that the roofs were thatched with grasses available along the lakeshore.

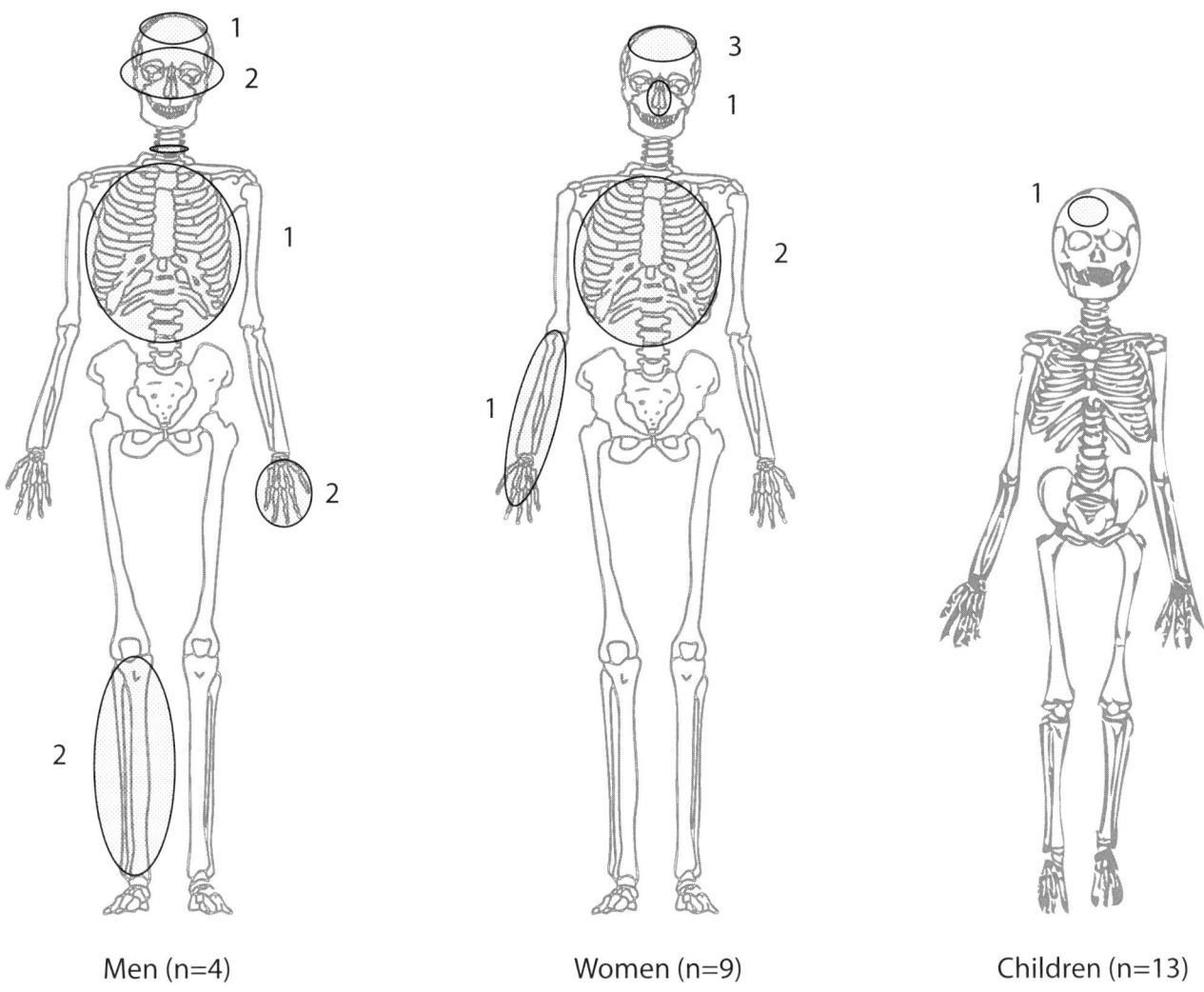

Figure 2.18. Shaded areas highlight the parts of the body where skeletal trauma was observed in men, women, and children. The number that appears beside the shaded area indicates how many individuals had injuries in that area. Human skeletal analysis was conducted by Valerie A. Andrushko.

Interpersonal Violence

While large-scale construction projects and ritual may have brought the community together at times, there is also ample evidence of periodic conflict. Skeletal trauma demonstrates that men, women, and children were the victims of violence at Yuthu (Fig. 2.18). Unfortunately, it is difficult to identify the assailants or understand the motivation for this hostility. Markers of violent trauma on human skeletal remains are often used to demonstrate that raiding or warfare was prevalent in a society. More specifically, when archaeologists study societies undergoing the transition from autonomous villages to multi-village polities, violence is often attributed to escalating inter-village raiding that played a central role in a regional polity's consolidation (sensu Kelly 2000). The level of violence at Yuthu was certainly high enough for us to infer that the Formative period was not peaceful, but there is insufficient evidence to fully understand the social context of this violent behavior.

By considering the social identity of victims, I hope to begin to build a more meaningful picture of interpersonal violence at Yuthu. Because the sample of burials is too small to conduct significant statistical analyses, this section is purely descriptive. Facial trauma is the most reliable evidence for interpersonal violence because it is the injury least likely to have resulted from accidents (Lessa and Mendonça de Souza 2004; Walker 2001). Because facial trauma was not found on individuals without other injuries, I have included all skeletal traumas identified by Valerie A. Andrushko (2008) in this section to help understand possible patterns in violence. It is important to note, however, that not all breaks necessarily co-occurred, and some could have resulted from accidents.

Trauma varied based on age and sex. Adults were more likely to experience violence than children. Eight out of ten adults with greater than 20% skeletal completeness had evidence of healed trauma. Cross-culturally, men are much more likely to experience traumatic injuries, whether from accident or interpersonal violence (Walker 2001). Indeed, all of the men at Yuthu with an intact cranium had facial trauma, often including more than one broken bone. In contrast, only one woman had facial trauma, a broken nose. When cranial injuries are considered, however, three out of four women with crania present had healed depressed skull fractures compared to one out of three men. Clearly men and women experienced different kinds of violence, though the context is not clear.

Among children, only one out of thirteen individuals displayed evidence of violent trauma. An 11- to 12-year old had an unhealed perimortem depressed cranial fracture that almost certainly caused his or her death. That child was buried with two other children (a 7- to 8-year old and a 1- to 2-year old) who did not have unhealed skeletal trauma. The inclusion of three children in the same burial suggests that all of them may have suffered violent deaths. In fact, the neck and head of the 7- to 8-year-old child were absent. It is possible that the child was decapitated, though no cut marks were found on the remaining vertebrae.

Overall, children were unlikely to experience non-lethal violence compared with adults. Male and female villagers began to be involved in certain kinds of socially sanctioned aggression (such as warfare or domestic violence) only after they reached adulthood. Additional research will be necessary to understand this violence among adults.

Mortuary Practice

Men, women, and children were buried in the Northern and Southern Sectors in diverse contexts—from shallow graves near simple pit houses to burials incorporated into the bench of the ceremonial sunken court. With the exception of one red quartzite core and one bird bone, the burials at Yuthu did not include preserved grave goods. All but one of the individuals were buried in a flexed position. Beyond these two commonalities, burial treatment was varied. Therefore, mortuary analyses that focus on identifying correlations between body orientation or grave goods and age, sex, or burial sector were not useful at Yuthu.

Multiphase burial treatments have been most informative about social structure and mortuary practice. The preservation at Yuthu is exceptionally good; many burials included the smallest finger bones, kneecaps, and sternum. Because of this excellent preservation, I have been able to use human skeletal taphonomy to determine that while some burials at Yuthu were primary interments made immediately or relatively soon after the death of the individual, others were the last step in a multiphase burial treatment.

Using a taphonomic approach related to *anthropologie de terrain* (see Duday 2006, 2009; Duday and Guillon 2006; Nilsson Stutz 2003), I have identified four types of burial treatment at Yuthu (described below and diagrammed in Fig. 2.19). The ubiquity of multiphase burials suggests that ongoing interaction with the dead was an important part of life during the Formative period.

(1) Primary Burial

Primary burials had three characteristics: (1) they were found in articulated, or nearly articulated, position; (2) the bones were in good or excellent state of preservation; and (3) all, or nearly all, of the bones were present; missing bones were limited to small or porous elements that decay quickly. In truth, it is not possible to determine whether the body received other mortuary treatments before burial. This definition only excludes additional steps that could be detected through taphonomy.

(2) Secondary Burial of Skeletal Elements of Multiple Individuals

Some burials contained the poorly preserved bones of more than one individual. In this type of burial, the bones were placed together in a small cavity and the deposit was burned. These burials included elements of women, children, and individuals of indeterminate sex. They (Burials 20 and 21) were found in the Northern Sector associated with the early pit houses.

Based on the very small percentage of the skeleton of each individual, it is clear that the remains had been moved to the final resting place at Yuthu after they had been buried or stored in at least one previous location. It is not possible to determine with certainty whether they had been buried in soil or placed in an empty space. But given that buried bone recovered at the site was in excellent condition (even after 2000 years), I would suggest that the poor preservation in these burials indicates storage in above-ground ossuaries or other open places where skeletal elements were exposed to weathering.

(3) Secondary Burial of Individuals Whose Bodies Were Not Preserved by Mummification

Some burials included the bones of a single individual in a fairly poor state of preservation arranged to approximate a flexed body position. Many of the bones that have unstable articulations (such as fingers, toes, and some vertebrae) were absent from these burials. It is likely that the skeletal elements were transported from a previous location. It is clear that the bodies were not bundled or preserved in a way that restricted displacement and loss of small bones after soft tissue decay, but in most cases it is not possible to determine whether the bodies were kept in empty spaces or buried in soil before being brought to Yuthu for final burial. In the case of Burial 14, which was composed of only the long bones and part of the cranium of a 26- to 45-year-old woman, the bones were very weathered and displayed evidence of carnivore gnawing, indicating that the body had been stored

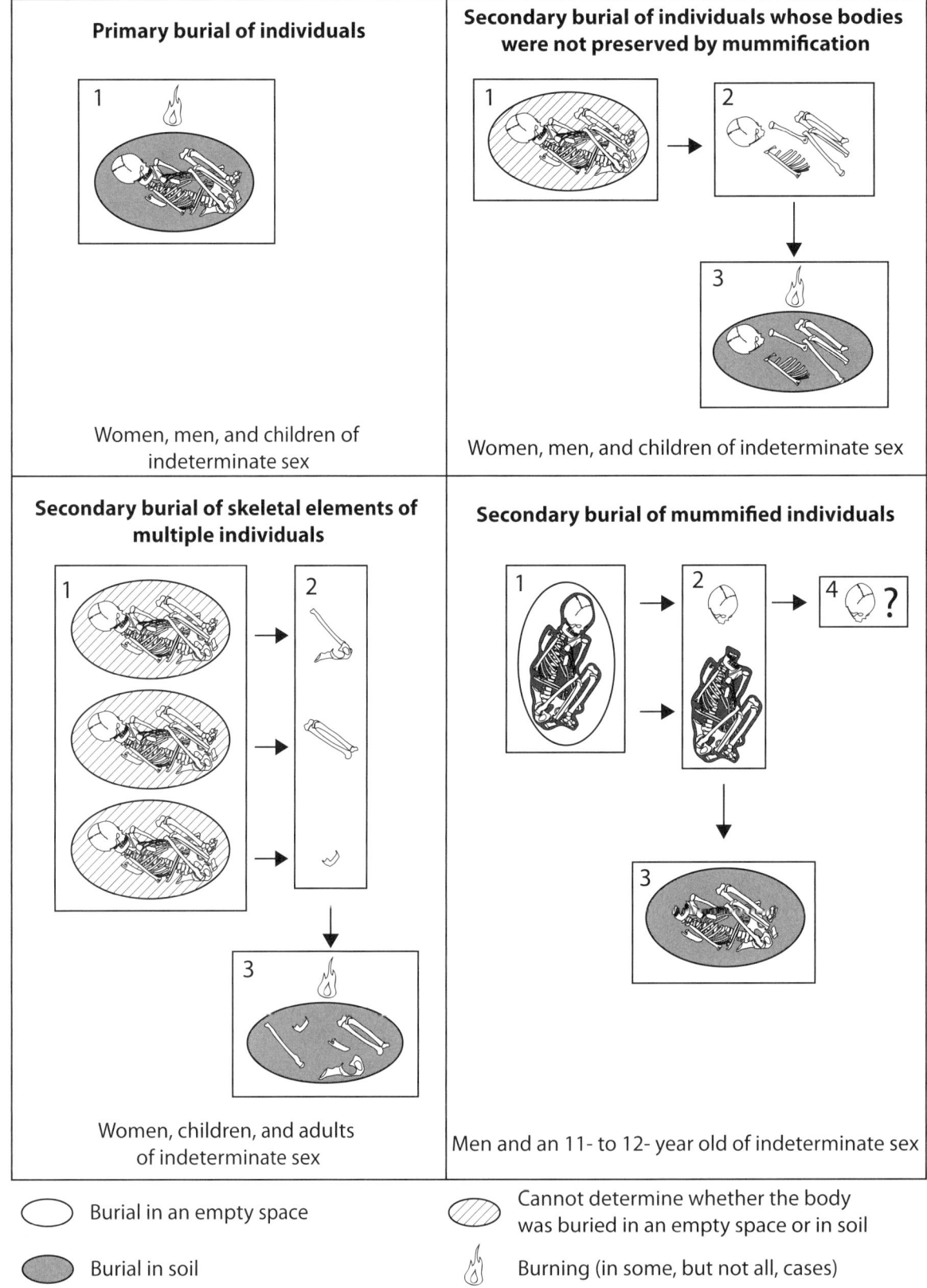

Figure 2.19. There were four types of burial practiced at Yuthu. Each type involved a minimum of 1 to 4 steps (depicted in boxes numbered in the upper left corner) that were detectable based on the position of the body when we excavated it.

in an empty space accessible to scavenging animals. These burials included men, women, and children and were located in the Southern Sector.

(4) Secondary Burials of Mummies

While excavating at Yuthu, I found one burial (a 26- to 35-year-old man) missing the right half of the pelvis with the entire sacrum flipped upside down (see Burial 16, Chap. 3). Despite this significant disturbance, all other bones in the body were in positions very much like that of a living person. Even the fingers from the hand resting in the man's lap were present and in correct anatomical position. Two other individuals at Yuthu were missing the cranium, but were otherwise complete and in articulated positions.

What processes (human or natural) created this pattern? Natural decay can account for the absence of some bones, but taphonomic studies have shown that the cranium is one of the last bones to decay (Bello and Andrews 2006). Although the pelvis is somewhat more fragile, it is not possible that these bones decayed before the small bones of the hands and feet, or the sternum (Bello and Andrews 2006; Waldron 1987). If the bones had not decayed naturally, they must have been removed by someone or something. In both cases, the missing bones were articulated to their neighbors by some of the strongest ligament articulations in the body: the sacroiliac and atlo-occipital joints (Duday 2006; Duday and Guillon 2006). If the elements had been removed before the soft tissue had decayed, these strong ligaments would have to have been cut. However, there were no cut marks on the bones that articulated with the missing elements (mandible, atlas, sacrum, femur, or pelvis) (Andrushko 2008). Therefore, the bones could not have been removed shortly after death while the soft tissue was still strong.

There are no burrowing animals around Lake Huaypo that could have removed these bones. But, there are many people living and working in the area, which raises the possibility that they removed the bones by one of two mechanisms. First, since Yuthu is located in a farm field, plowing with oxen and with tractors could have disturbed burials. Second, the workmen had shared stories that raised suspicions. With a combination of amusement and embarrassment, they described nights when the party in town was particularly good and people came out to the site to find skulls to drink from. Targeted removal of skulls by modern people was a distinct possibility.

I was fairly certain that a tractor was not responsible since no surrounding bones were broken or displaced (in contrast with Burials 17 and 18), but I was more worried about the second possibility. Could modern people have targeted and removed certain bones? Because the bodies are completely skeletonized today, it would no longer be necessary to cut the ligaments. Given that the graves were unmarked, however, it is not likely that a (probably highly inebriated) person could slip away from a party to dig up a single bone without disturbing the rest of the skeleton—not even if that person was an archaeologist.

Having ruled out other possibilities, it became clear that the bone was removed before the body was buried in soil, but after it was in an advanced state of decay. This conclusion highlights what seems to be a contradiction. If the body had reached such an advanced state of decay while stored in an empty space, how could the bones with the weakest articulations still be in correct anatomical position? The body must have been constrained in some way. Indeed, a cloth fragment found in one burial at Yuthu suggests that some individuals were buried in clothing or wrapped in textiles. However, simple wrapping in a textile bundle would not have been sufficient to prevent disarticulation. Rather, it would be necessary for the soft tissue to remain intact to prevent movement of the bones. Such excellent preservation is common on the coast of Peru where the dry desert creates natural mummies by evaporation. But, how could mummification happen in the rainy highlands?

A weekly shopping trip to San Pedro Market in Cusco helped resolve this question. Perfectly preserved naturally freeze-dried llama fetuses hang above every witchcraft vendor's stall. These fetuses are naturally aborted in the high *puna* where the low air pressure and cold temperatures result in flesh desiccated by sublimation (the transition of water from solid ice to gas, skipping the liquid phase). Vendors also sell freeze-dried potatoes (*ch'uñu*) and freeze-dried llama and sheep meat (*ch'arki*). Intentional freeze-drying of food is common today, and was practiced extensively in highland prehispanic Peru at least by the Formative period (Miller and Burger 2000; Shimada 1982, 1985; but see Valdez Cárdenas 2000). A similar process could have easily produced preserved "mummies" whose bodies began to decay only after they were buried in the moist soil at Yuthu. In fact, among Inka and modern populations, mummification was frequently understood in the same terms as the process of making *ch'uñu* (Allen 1982; Sillar 1996).

Unfortunately, it is not possible to determine whether the mummification at Yuthu was intentional or a natural process. Regardless, the best explanation for the unusual completeness, articulation, and preservation of these burials is that they were stored as desiccated mummies in accessible, empty spaces (possibly above ground) for some time before a bone was removed and the rest of the body buried. There is very little evidence as to what happened to the bone after it was removed, though the right half of an adult pelvis was found above the feet of a 1- to 2-year-old child in a multiple burial of children in the Southern Sector (see Chap. 4).

Three individuals received this type of burial: two adult men and one 11- to 12-year-old child of indeterminate sex. These burials were found in the later phases of both the Northern and Southern Sectors of the site. The role of these mummies in the sacred system at Yuthu is discussed further in Chapter 5.

Bird Ritual

We recovered 143 bird bones at the site (10.3% from the heavy fraction of 1012 liters of flotation samples). Excluding unidentified bird bone ($n = 79$), the birds represented in the faunal sample included: (1) birds from the lake that are commonly used for food, like duck, coot, and heron (62.5%); (2) birds of prey including eagle hawk and hawk (26.6%) and the burrowing owl (a single bone); and (3) the beak of a macaw, a bird from the jungle.

Despite the fact that water birds from the lake were more common at Yuthu, ritual focused on birds of prey like hawks and eagles. The most striking example was the burial of an entire eagle hawk in the Northern Sector (see Chap. 3). In addition, we found a bird figurine in the fill of the earliest pit house (Intrusion M, see Chap. 3). Because the ceramic figurine was crudely made, it is not possible to determine what species it might represent. However, the figurine is shaped more like a bird of prey than a water bird (the two common types of birds found at Yuthu). Finally, a man buried during the final use of the site had a bird bone (unidentified species) between his teeth, as if he were chewing it like a toothpick or smoking it like a cigarette (Burial 2, see Chap. 4). The evidence of bird ritual was somewhat rare, so it is likely that these activities were carried out periodically at Yuthu. The ideological significance or meaning of these birds is difficult to determine.

Long-Distance Trade

Although most materials recovered from Yuthu were available locally, long-distance trade was also an important activity. The most common marker of this trade was obsidian, which is available from distant locations in the sierra (see above). The high proportion of obsidian at Yuthu is similar to patterns reported for many Formative sites (Burger et al. 2000; Chávez 1980; McEwan et al. 1995; Rowe 1943; Yábar Moreno 1972). In addition, a macaw beak and a fish jaw that were probably from the jungle were found at Yuthu. Similarly, a peccary tooth associated with Chanapata-style pottery was recovered from the site of Marcavalle (Chávez 1980). These objects were the preserved footprint of what was probably a larger set of traded objects that included textiles, feathers, and other perishable goods. The high proportion of camelids at Yuthu indicates that this trade was probably conducted by long-distance llama caravans, which may have used formalized roads. Arrival and departure of traders was probably a periodic or seasonal occurrence.

Roads and Travel

When the locations of the largest sites are considered against the local topography, it becomes clear that the medium and large sites with Chanapata-style ceramics were located along a natural route from the wetter part of the plain to the Sacred Valley (see Fig. 2.6). Starting at Ak'awillay, the largest site located on the high plain overlooking the pampa of Anta, the route passed by Lake Huaypo, where Yuthu is located. After that, the route continued through the Salineras of Maras, a natural salt spring that has been used at least since Inka times to produce salt (and continues to be used today). Sites gradually became smaller moving north along the route, *away* from the largest site. This linear arrangement resembles the dendritic pattern for down-the-line trade proposed by Renfrew (Banning 2002; Renfrew 1975). This type of pattern is common when sites are located along rivers, roads, or other fixed routes through which exchange takes place.

In fact, this route closely follows footpaths referred to as the "old road" to Maras and Urubamba. The "old road" from Lake Huaypo to Maras and Urubamba passes just above the site of Yuthu. It does not cut through the middle of the site. Rather, it provides a northwestern limit to both the Northern and Southern Sectors (Fig. 2.20). Therefore, it is possible that at least part of this important route to the Sacred Valley was a formal road by 400 BC when Yuthu was settled. Future excavation at Yuthu should clarify whether the road might have been formalized with built features like pavement, stairs, or drains.

Routes like this were probably precursors to the larger and more famous Inka road system (for a description see Hyslop 1984). Many scholars have already argued that a system of roads in the Andes existed during the time of the Wari Empire—both in Cusco (Isbell 1978; Isbell and Schreiber 1978; McEwan 2005) and elsewhere (Lumbreras 1974). On the north coast, formal Early Horizon roads connected valleys to each other (Beck 1979). In Cusco, Ann Kendall (2000) has suggested that the section of the Inka road from Maras to Urubamba was used by about 800 BC based on the abundance of Chanapata pottery along the route. It seems likely that in many cases the Inka may have simply elaborated existing routes with formal paving and road markers. It is interesting to note, however, that the major Inka road that was the primary caravan route to the Chinchaysuyu (which passed along the southern part of the survey area) does not have Formative sites clustered alongside it.

For the Inka, these roads were important for political administration of the vast empire. Although communication might have been important in the Formative period, administration was probably not a major concern in a time when the first multi-village polities were only beginning to form. Within the survey area, the route links two key ecological zones, but beyond the survey area, it may connect even more distant areas. The Inka road that follows the proposed Formative route from Maras to Urubamba continues across the Sacred Valley, to the coca lands of Occobamba (Kendall 2000). It seems likely that these early roads facilitated long-distance trade carried out by llama caravans.

In other parts of the highlands, many scholars have suggested that power and wealth during the Formative period resulted from the control of long-distance exchange. In this scenario, the fortunes of a particular village depended on the importance of the llama caravan routes along which it was located. Exceptional wealth resulted from transit taxes in places through which caravans had to pass. This was true for the well-known centers of Chavín de Huántar (Browman 1975; Burger 1992) and Chiripa (Bandy 2005). It may be that llama caravan trade along this ancient route across the Xaquixaguana Plain played an important role in the emergence of the first complex societies in Cusco as well.

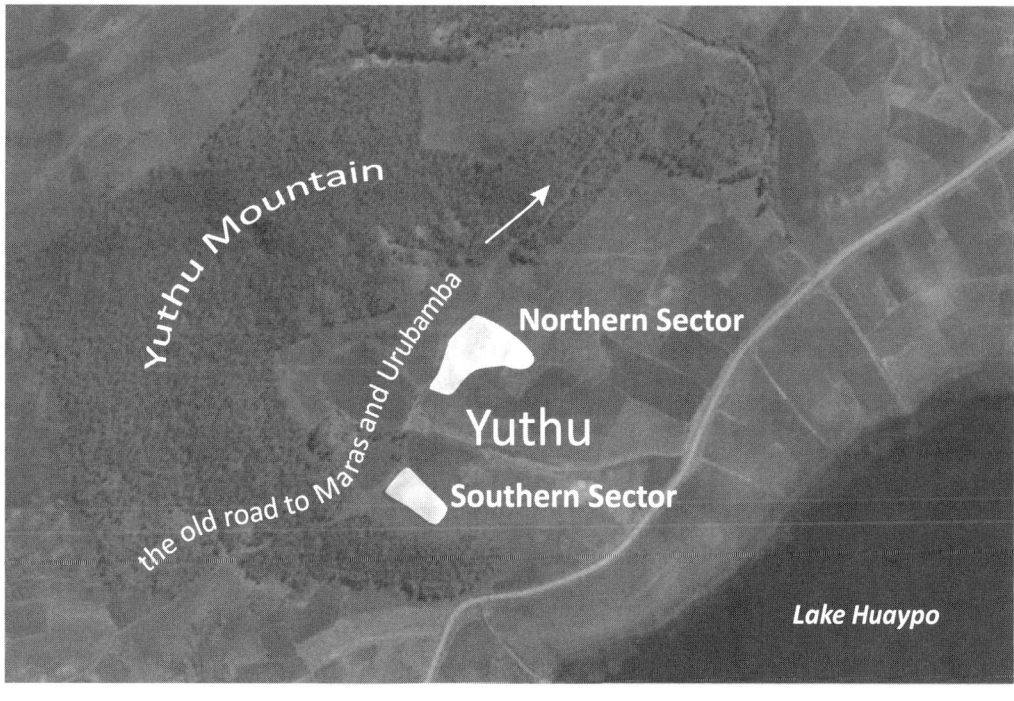

Figure 2.20. The old road (*above*) to Maras and Urubamba is the limit of both the Northern and Southern Sectors at Yuthu. No Formative pottery was found in the fields northwest of the road. Therefore, it is likely that this section of the road existed in the Formative period (by around 400 BC). *below*, close-up of IKONOS satellite imagery of the Lake Huaypo area (courtesy of R. Alan Covey).

Discussion of Periodic Activities

Periodic activities were performed as needed, or as time allowed. Several of these were significant moments in community and family life—providing opportunities to maintain social cohesion as well as venues for conflict, which sometimes involved violent interactions. Other activities, including certain rituals, trade, and travel, provided opportunities for articulation with individuals living outside the village.

Discussion

I have described the activities at Yuthu that left material traces visible to archaeologists. Farming, herding, and storage created an annual frame for all activities, a frame closely tied to the village's particular mountain ecology. Activities such as food preparation and maintenance of social relationships filled each day, regardless of the particular moment in the annual cycle. In contrast, other activities (such as craft production and trade) were periodic and had to be incorporated into the annual cycle according to need. This was also true for ceremonial and political practices, such as large-scale construction and mortuary rituals, that encouraged community cohesion even as they created opportunities for conflict.

Notes

1. See Davis 2010 for a full typology of groundstone objects at Yuthu.

2. Given the variety in the assemblage, I have used methods elaborated by Andrefsky 2005 to classify the chipped stone based on morphology of the piece. Tools are defined as any object that has been modified by use or through purposeful shaping. In contrast, the category of debitage includes objects that are removed from tools and show no other evidence of modification.

—3—

The Spaces of Daily Life

Many everyday activities took place in the Northern Sector of the village, located on the moderate southern slope of Cerro Yuthu. Villagers used a small gully to separate their houses and domestic activity areas from the ceremonial Southern Sector. Until recently, that gully carried water from a spring just above the village to Lake Huaypo.

When I first visited Yuthu, I noticed that compared with the Southern Sector, the density of stone tools, pottery fragments, and human bone on the ground surface was much lower in this area. In addition, the pottery on the surface was mostly undecorated plainware. I was curious to know if the distinctive character of the surface remains was the result of modern plows disturbing different kinds of structures and activity areas below the surface.

I decided that a flat area at the lowest edge of the site, close to Lake Huaypo, would be the best place to address this question and to determine the site's northern limit. In that area, the stepped shape of the land might be the remains of ancient terraces. Unfortunately, I was unable to get authorization from the landowner to dig there. Thus, I opted to excavate in a location about 100 m uphill, in a *chakra* that belonged to the cooperative family that had already given me permission to work in their fields.

In 2006, while most of the excavation team continued to work in the Southern Sector, I sent Jorge Flores to excavate a 2 × 2 m test pit in the Northern Sector. Within that small unit, he found several superimposed layers of ash and trampled surfaces associated with large quantities of burned bones and plants. I was excited that this area seemed promising for finding houses and other domestic activity areas that would allow me to study the daily lives of Yuthu's villagers. When the team returned for a second excavation season in 2007, I extended Unit D to the north and west, creating a single 8 × 8 m excavation unit. During 8 weeks of fieldwork, we found Formative period deposits up to 1.9 m deep that included domestic structures, hearths, storage features, and burials.

Occupation in this area was fairly continuous, creating many thin strata of soil and domestic debris. After the first construction, it is not possible to identify discrete occupations. Therefore, this chapter describes the key contexts in stratigraphic order, beginning with the earliest features. Figure 3.1 is a profile drawing of the stratigraphy of Unit D with each layer of soil labeled with the corresponding number. Although the types of constructions and features changed over time, there was a general pattern of small simple structures associated with outdoor hearths and activity areas in this part of the village.

Archaeological Deposits in the Northern Sector

The Initial Occupation

The first people at Yuthu created structures by digging into very hard red clay, the natural geologic soil in this area. The earliest occupation included a pit house and associated storage pits, a cooking hearth, and human burials (Fig. 3.2).

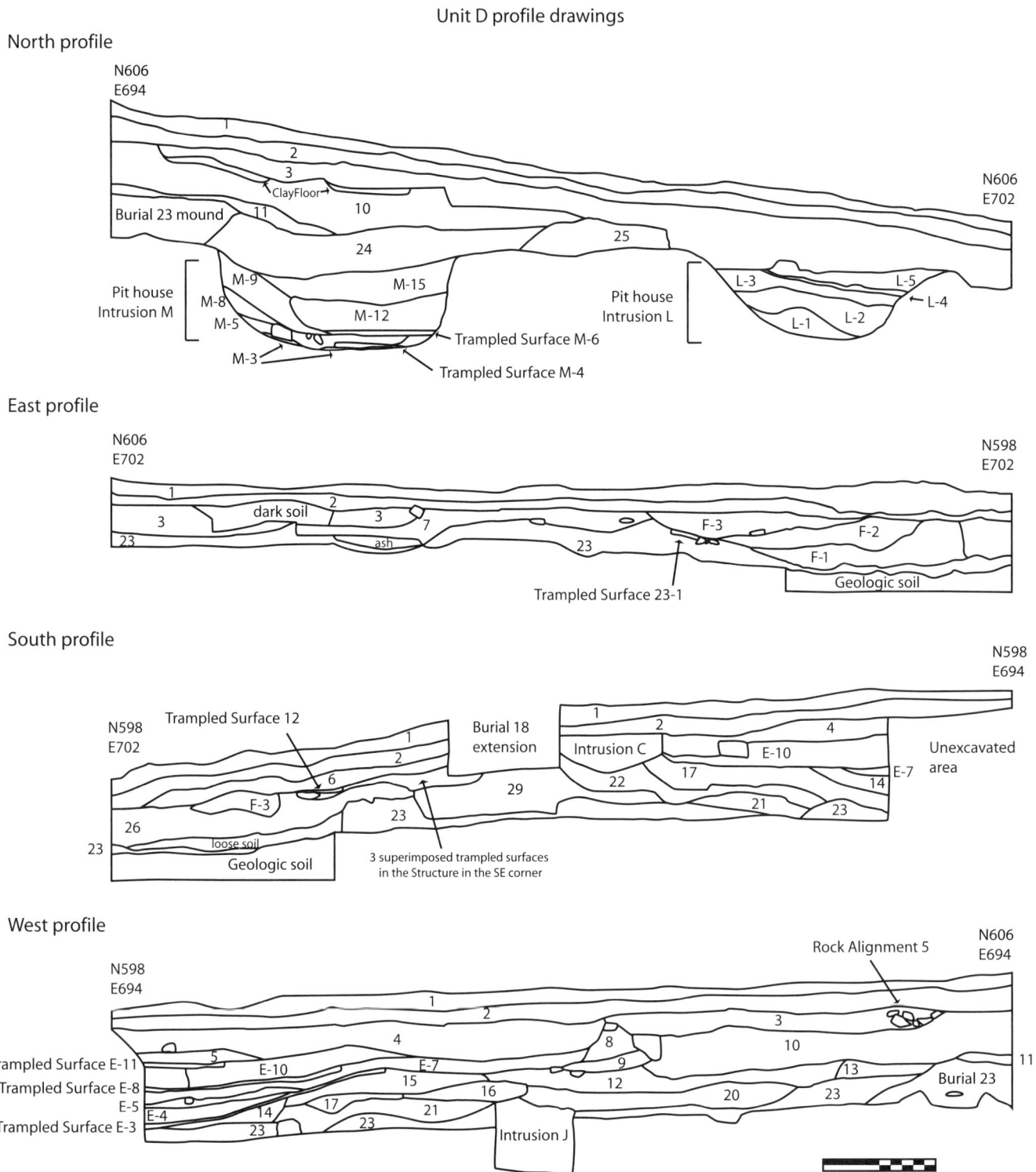

Figure 3.1. The stratigraphy of Unit D. Because the excavation unit was large and many strata did not extend throughout the entire area, it was sometimes impossible to determine if a particular feature or layer of soil was relatively older or younger than another. Therefore, in these cases, the number assigned to a stratum may be misleading in terms of its relative stratigraphic position.

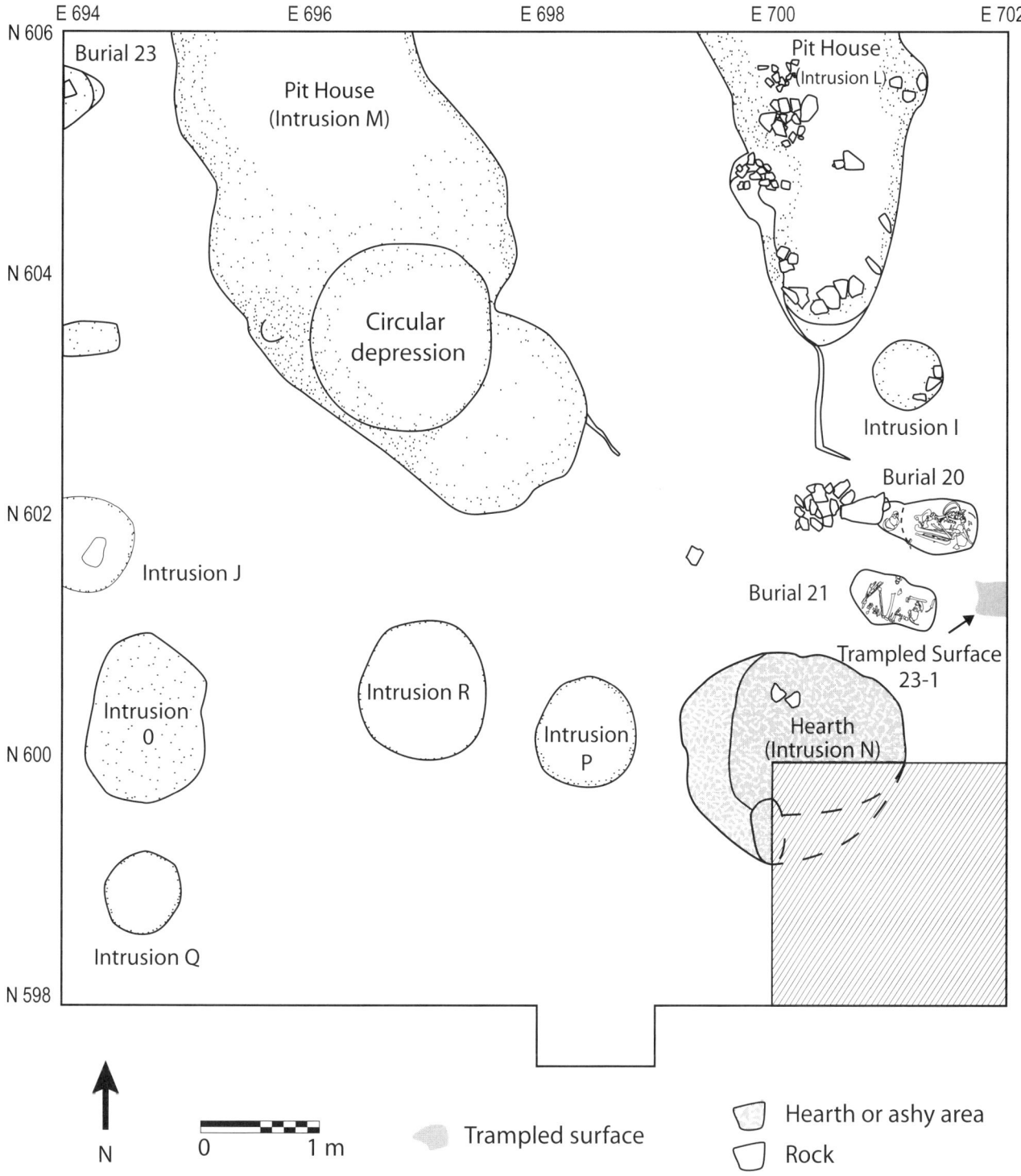

Figure 3.2. The earliest occupation of Yuthu included: storage pits (Intrusions P, Q, R, I); an area for burning and cooking (Intrusion N); two semi-subterranean domestic structures excavated into natural soil (Intrusions M and L); two secondary burials including multiple individuals (Burials 20 and 21); a small trampled surface (23-1); and one infant burial under a mound of soil (Burial 23).

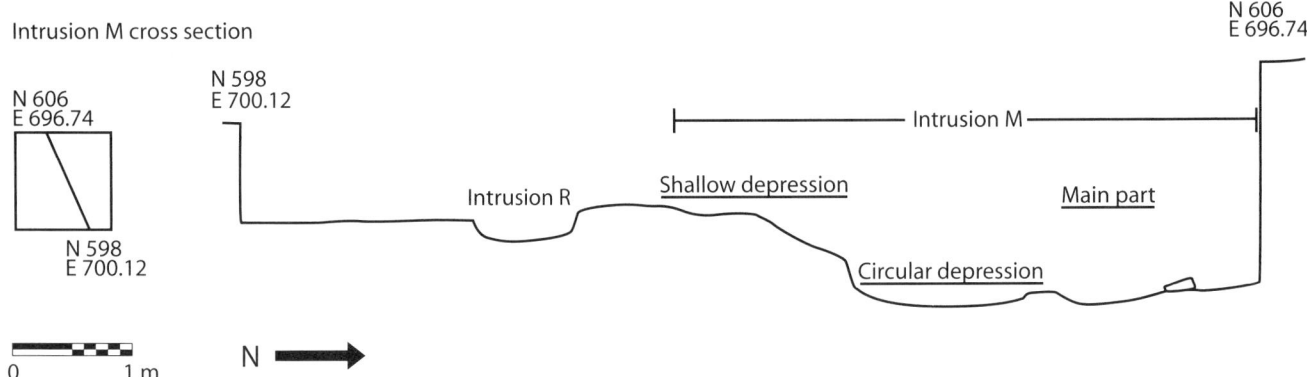

Figure 3.3. A cross section of the final excavation of Intrusion M showing three parts: (1) the main part, (2) the circular depression, and (3) the shallow, sloping depression.

A Semi-Subterranean Domestic Structure (Intrusion M)

On what was supposed to be the last day of fieldwork, all of Unit D had been excavated to geologic soil except the northwest quarter. Although the ground surface was uneven in that area, I felt sure that we would expose geologic soil after quickly scraping off a few centimeters of soil. Then, we would make a final drawing of the unit's plan and head back to the village where the women who usually washed artifacts were preparing a feast of *cuy, cuy* sausage, tortilla española, baked noodles, and at least three kinds of potatoes. I was so confident that we would finish the excavation that I dropped off my contribution for the meal—several cases of Cusqueña beer—*before* going to the field site.

I did not anticipate finding a subterranean feature as large and as deep as Intrusion M. At 6 p.m., the Andean sun disappeared over the hills to the west, and we ran out of excavation forms before reaching the base of the intrusion. We headed back to town without finishing. It was too late for soccer, but we couldn't let the party preparations go to waste. We stuffed ourselves and danced the night away to "No me caso" by Fresia Linda and "Pisao pisao" by Muñequita Sally, the year's hottest *waynus* blaring from the static-making speakers of the taxi that would take us back to Cusco.

Three days later, after a period of recovery, we returned to finish Intrusion M. It took the team a full day to excavate 80 cm of deposits that filled the intrusion, including trampled surfaces, hearths, and accumulations of domestic trash. Although I did not expect to encounter such a significant semi-subterranean feature, Intrusion M turned out to be the most important domestic structure that we found at the site of Yuthu.

This pit house had three components (Fig. 3.3):

(1) The main living area was excavated about 90 cm below the surface of the geologic soil. It had vertical walls, a flat base, and an irregular shape. The maximum width from east to west was 2.6 m. The house extended beyond the northern limit of the excavation unit, so it is unclear what the maximum length might have been, but the excavated portion was 3.3 m long.

(2) A circular storage pit about 1.5 m in diameter and 7 cm deeper than the rest of the house was added at the southern end of the main part after the original construction (see below).

(3) The southern extreme of the house was a shallow depression that sloped gently from 0 to 25 cm below the surface of the natural soil and extended about 1 m southeast of the storage pit.

The deposits that filled this intrusion can be divided into 5 phases of roughly coeval stratigraphic deposits and features (Fig. 3.4).

Phases 1, 2, and 3: Construction and Use of a Domestic Structure (383–118 BC)

During Phase 1, the main part of the intrusion was excavated into the natural soil. Then, soil mixed with artifacts and ash accumulated on the bottom. During Phase 2, a circular storage pit was added to the southern end of the main part of Intrusion M. In addition, a wall or some other type of divider was constructed to separate the storage area from the northern part of the intrusion. Once the divider was built, deposits were distinct on either side. On the northern side, fairly intense foot traffic resulted in a series of trampled surfaces during Phases 2 and 3. In contrast, the circular depression in the southern part was kept clean and only a small trampled surface formed alongside it.

The best explanation for the high degree of foot traffic, the domestic debris, and the form of the circular depression is that Intrusion M was a semi-subterranean domestic structure with a storage feature. There is no evidence of a superstructure of adobes or stone. However, the intrusion was deep enough that a thatch roof would have made a simple, but adequate, house. The presence of *Scirpus* seeds, a species used to thatch the roofs of

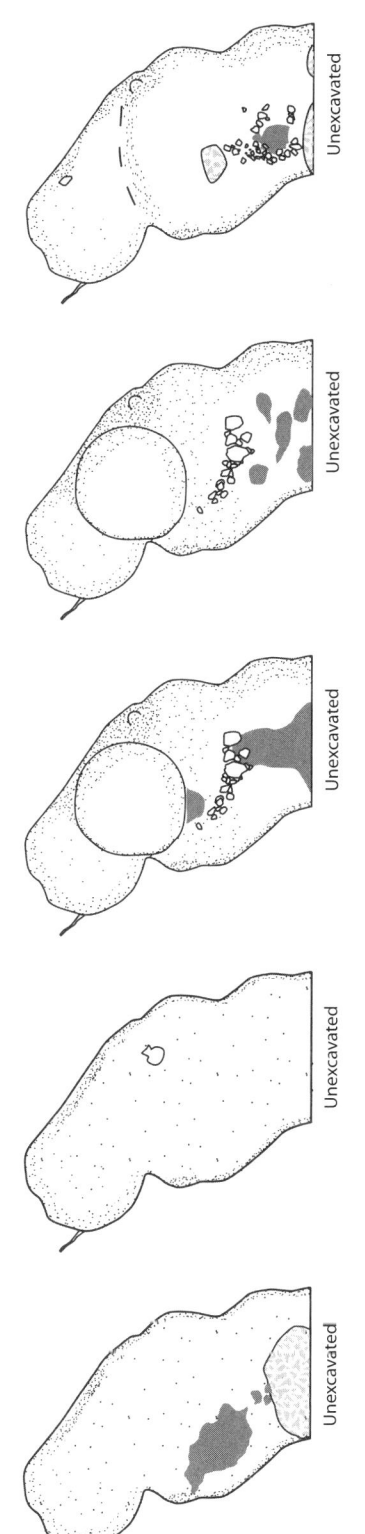

Phase 1

The main part of Intrusion M (north of the dotted line) was excavated 90 cm into geologic soil. The area to the south of the dotted line was a much shallower depression about 25 cm below the level of geologic soil. Dirt mixed with archaeological debris and areas of ash were deposited on the base of the main part of the intrusion. A radiocarbon sample from this phase dated to 383–118 BC (calibrated).

Phase 2

A circular depression, probably used as a storage feature, was added at the southern end of the main part of the intrusion. It was about 7 cm deep. This depression was kept clean of debris during Phases 2 and 3. In addition, an arc-shaped dividing wall was built to separate the storage area from the main part of the intrusion. Trampled surfaces formed to the north of the dividing wall.

Phase 3

The circular depression was kept clean while a small trampled surface formed beside it and a larger trampled surface formed north of the dividing wall. Note that the northern trampled surface meets with two large, flat stones that probably formed a doorway in the dividing wall.

Phase 4

Intrusion H was filled by erosion with three strata of soil. There were no floors or hearths associated with this phase.

Phase 5

The depression left by the partially filled intrusion was used as a cooking area with a hearth along the northern limit of the excavation unit and a trampled surface that led from outside the intrusion to the hearth.

- Depression or pit
- Trampled surface
- Hearth or ashy area
- Rock

Figure 3.4. Intrusion M was filled with five phases of deposits. During Phases 1–3, the intrusion was a simple semi-subterranean domestic structure. During Phases 4 and 5, the intrusion was partly filled in by erosion and then used as a cooking area.

Figure 3.5. Exterior (a) and interior (b) views of a modern semi-subterranean thatched structure excavated into a hillside. Note that the simple roof was built directly on the ground surface.

modern houses (Ugent and Ochoa 2006) in the early levels of the intrusion supports this idea, though interpretation must be cautious because *Scirpus* can also be used to make mats, baskets, and other domestic items.

A similar type of construction, in which a cavity is excavated into a hillside or mountain slope and covered by a simple thatch roof, is used to build temporary-use structures in rural areas of Cusco today (Fig. 3.5; Plate 3). This type of house would have had several advantages for Formative period villagers: this expedient construction would have required only a digging tool and thatching material (which was available from the nearby lake), and would have required little advance preparation (such as making adobes or felling lumber). In fact, Intrusion M was almost certainly built much faster than archaeologists were able to excavate it.

In addition, a subterranean structure would have both blocked the strong cold winds that blow across Cerro Yuthu and insulated the occupants against the chilly air of highland nights. Although similar structures are used only as temporary posts today—when watching herds or working outlying agricultural fields—there is not yet enough evidence to determine whether Intrusion M was used as a permanent or as a short-term dwelling. The presence of a storage feature and an area for raising guinea pigs within the structure, however, does indicate ongoing use as a house at least starting in Phase 2.

Phase 1. The earliest deposits in the house (Levels M-1, M-2, and M-3) rested on top of the geologic soil at the base of the intrusion. During Phase 1, villagers cooked and ate llama, quinoa, maize, and possibly kiwicha (Amaranthus sp.). They used both open and restricted pottery vessels made in plainware, Chanapata redware, and pattern burnished ware. Small flakes of stone indicate that some retouching occurred inside the house. The presence of obsidian shows that the inhabitants were involved in trade networks, and the bone of a pampas cat (a wild cat that preys on small game like guinea pigs and viscacha) may have been procured through hunting or exchange. Burned Scirpus seeds suggest that the structure had a thatched roof and may have held baskets or woven mats.

Level M-1. This level comprised an accumulation of archaeological trash and small rocks (probably occupational debris) in the main part.

Munsell color
  5 YR 5/6 yellowish red

Radiocarbon date
  AA84437\Yuthu RC-255, 2243 ± 36 uncalibrated radiocarbon years BP, 383–118 BC calibrated without modeling (95.4% confidence)

Ceramic vessels
  Total sherds: 130
  Restricted vessels with a neck: 3 plainware
  Restricted vessel without a neck: 1 plainware
  Open vessels: 2 Chanapata redware
  Open vessel with a diameter greater than 30 cm:
    1 Chanapata redware
  Body sherds with diagnostic style: 1 Chanapata redware, 3 pattern burnished

Reworked ceramic sherd
  Non-disc: 1 plainware

Chipped stone
  Locally available stone (66.67% by count, 100% by weight)
    coarse grain quartzitic sandstone
      debitage: 2 proximal flakes (0.2 g)
    fine grain quartzitic sandstone
      tool: 1 unimarginal flake tool (6.7 g)
    quartzite
      debitage: 1 proximal flake (< 0.1 g)
  Exotic stone (33.33% by count, < 1% by weight)
    obsidian
      debitage: 2 proximal flakes (< 0.1 g)

Botanical remains from flotation of 6.2 liters of soil (S-230)
  2 *Chenopodium quinoa* carbonized seeds
  1 *Scirpus* sp. carbonized seed

Animal bone (NISP)
  Mammals
    llama or alpaca (*Lama* sp.): 7 (3 from flotation)
    unidentified: 4 (all from flotation)

Level M-2. Stratigraphically contemporary with Levels M-1 and M-3, Level M-2 was a small very ashy area where burning took place.

Munsell color
  7.5 YR 4/3 brown

Ceramic vessels
  Total sherds: 7
  Restricted vessel without a neck: 1 plainware

Chipped stone
  Locally available stone (100% by count and weight)
    quartzite
      debitage: 1 proximal flake (0.2 g)

Botanical remains from flotation of 6.3 liters of soil (S-228)
  2 *Amaranthus* sp. carbonized seeds
  12 *Chenopodium quinoa* carbonized seeds
  2 *Zea mays* carbonized seeds
  1 *Scirpus* sp. carbonized seed

Botanical remains from flotation of 4.0 liters of soil (S-229)
  1 *Amaranthus* sp. carbonized seed
  10 *Chenopodium quinoa* carbonized seeds
  3 *Scirpus* sp. carbonized seeds

Botanical remains from flotation of 2.1 liters of soil (S-231)
  1 *Amaranthus* sp. carbonized seed
  5 *Chenopodium quinoa* carbonized seeds

Animal bone (NISP)
  Mammals
    llama or alpaca (*Lama* sp.): 1 (from flotation)
    pampas cat (*Felis* cf. *colocolo*): 1
    field mouse (Muridae): 3 (all from flotation)

Level M-3. This was another concentration of ash located along the northern profile that was stratigraphically contemporary with Levels M-1 and M-2.

Munsell color
  5 YR 5/6 yellowish red

Ceramic vessels
  Total sherds: 4
  No diagnostic sherds were found

Botanical remains from flotation of 6.5 liters of soil (S-227)
  1 *Ambrosia* sp. carbonized seed

Phase 2. During Phase 2, a circular depression with a 1.5-m diameter cut through Level M-1 into geologic soil. The base of this intrusion was 7 cm deeper than the surface of Level M-1. Throughout Phase 2, the interior of the circular intrusion was kept clean and no archaeological deposits accumulated within it. The form of this feature was very similar to that of the outdoor storage pits (Intrusions P, Q and R). Because the pit was kept clean, it is unclear what might have been stored in it.

About 60 cm north of the circular intrusion, unworked field stones were arranged in an arc that ran roughly east to west on top of the deposits of Phase 1 (see Fig. 3.4). Although there was no evidence of an adobe, stone, or cane wall above this foundation, it is clear that these rocks divided the space into northern and southern areas and controlled movement between them. By Phase 3 (see below), a trampled surface formed that extended north from two large flat stones in the wall. This indicates that these stones were probably a doorway between the main part of Intrusion M and the new, private storage feature. People used the space north of the arc frequently enough to create trampled surfaces. They continued to prepare llama, quinoa, maize, and possibly *kiwicha* and to use the same kind of pottery. But, there was no evidence of working chipped stone at this time. *Cuy* were kept in the main part of the house, probably close to the hearth where they could stay warm and enjoy cooking scraps.

Trampled Surface M-4. To the north of the dividing arc, a large proportion of the soil surface was compacted by trampling, indicating that there was a passageway from the main part of the house to the storage area.

Munsell color
  5 YR 5/3 reddish brown

Ceramic vessels
  Total sherds: 8
  Restricted vessels with a neck: 2 plainware
  Body sherd with diagnostic style: 1 pattern burnished

Botanical remains from flotation of 6.7 liters of soil (S-226)
  1 *Amaranthus* sp. carbonized seed
  6 *Chenopodium quinoa* carbonized seeds
  2 *Zea mays* carbonized cupule fragments

Level M-5. A thin layer of light brown soil accumulated on top of this floor. This soil included the coprolite of a *cuy*. In many modern Andean homes, guinea pigs are kept in kitchens near hearths. It seems that this practice extends back to this early subterranean house as well.

Munsell color
  7.5 YR 4/4 brown

Ceramic vessels
  Total sherds: 68
  Restricted vessels with a neck: 4 plainware
  Open vessel: 1 plainware
  Body sherds with diagnostic style: 1 Chanapata redware,
    1 pattern burnished

Reworked ceramic sherd
  Non-disc: 1 plainware

Botanical remains from flotation of 7.1 liters of soil (S-222)
  1 *Amaranthus* sp. carbonized seed
  2 *Chenopodium quinoa* carbonized seeds

Botanical remains from flotation of 6.8 liters of soil (S-225)
  1 *Poaceae* carbonized seed

Animal bone (NISP)
  Mammals
    llama or alpaca (*Lama* sp.): 1
  Human bone: 3

Other items
  Cuy coprolite

Phase 3. Phase 3 was a stratigraphically higher set of trampled surfaces in the northern and southern areas of the main part of Intrusion M. When comparing the trampled surfaces north and south of the dividing wall, the botanical remains to the south were much denser (6.43 seeds/liter in the south and 0.33 seed/liter in the north). While there were only 2 quinoa seeds in the main part of the house, the diversity of plants near the storage pit was much higher, including food plants such as quinoa, corn, possibly *kiwicha*, as well as fuel and forage plants like *Ambrosia* and *Trifolium*. It seems likely that plants remains were trampled into the surface as people moved them in and out of the pit. The presence of field mice also suggests storage of food in this pit.

Trampled Surface M-6. Trampled Surface M-6 was large and extended north from the doorway. It was stratigraphically contemporary with Trampled Surface M-7.

Munsell color
7.5 YR 4/4 brown

Ceramic vessels
Total sherds: 4
Restricted vessel with a neck: 1 plainware
Body sherd with diagnostic style: 1 pattern burnished

Botanical remains from flotation of 6.0 liters of soil (S-221)
2 *Chenopodium quinoa* carbonized seeds

Trampled Surface M-7. South of the arc of stones, there was a small trampled area along the northeastern edge of the storage pit.

Munsell color
7.5 YR 4/4 brown

Ceramic vessels
Total sherds: 3
No diagnostic sherds were found

Chipped stone
Locally available stone (33.33% by count, unknown percent by weight)
quartzite
debitage: 1 proximal flake (< 0.1 g)
Exotic stone (66.67% by count, unknown percent by wt)
obsidian
debitage: 2 proximal flakes (< 0.1 g)

Botanical remains from flotation of 5.8 liters of soil (S-224)
6 *Amaranthus* sp. carbonized seeds
12 *Chenopodium quinoa* carbonized seeds
1 *Trifolium* sp. carbonized seed
10 *Ambrosia* sp. carbonized seeds
8 *Zea mays* carbonized rachis fragments, 4 carbonized seeds

Animal bone (NISP)
Mammals
field mouse (*Muridae*): 13 (all from flotation)
unidentified: 4 (all from flotation)

Phases 4 and 5: Fill and Reuse of the Depression Left after the Structure was Abandoned

During Phase 4, Intrusion M was filled in by several strata of soil that probably washed into the depression after it was no longer used as a house. These strata contained no evidence of human use such as floors or hearths. During Phase 5, however, after the intrusion was partly filled, the shallow depression that remained was used for a new purpose. Villagers took advantage of the cavity as a windbreak for cooking fires. They made a hearth at the excavation unit's northern limit, and a trampled surface formed that led from outside the intrusion to that hearth. They probably used *markhu* as fuel for cooking camelid, quinoa, corn, and possibly *kiwicha*. The foods were prepared here partly by grinding and were cooked only in *ollas* with a neck. In contrast with most hearths, no serving vessels were found in this area. Villagers also used and possibly sharpened a variety of stone tools in this area.

Phase 5. Villagers built a hearth in the depression left after the pit house was partially filled.

Hearth M-12. The hearth was a deep intrusion of very ashy loose soil.

Munsell color
10 YR 5/2 grayish brown

Ceramic vessels
Total sherds: 277
Restricted vessels with a neck: 14 plainware
Body sherds with diagnostic style: 2 Chanapata blackware

Chipped stone
Locally available stone (80% by count, 100% by wt)
coarse grain quartzitic sandstone
debitage: 2 proximal flakes (0.3 g)
fine grain quartzitic sandstone
debitage: 2 proximal flakes (< 0.1 g)
quartzite
debitage: 4 proximal flakes (0.2 g)
organic limestone
tool: 1 unimarginal flake tool (5.1 g)
debitage: 3 fragments of angular shatter (0.3 g)
Regionally available stone (6.67% by count, < 1% by wt)
andesite
debitage: 1 proximal flake (0.1 g)
Exotic stone (13.33% by count, < 1% by weight)
obsidian
debitage: 2 proximal flakes (< 0.1 g)

Groundstone
Grinding stone that fit in one hand with plano-convex cross section and flattened surfaces created by grinding with back and forth and rocking motions (Group 1, Type B). The stone measured 11.23 × 8.80 × 4.21 cm; it weighed 640 g.

Botanical remains from flotation of 4.5 liters of soil (S-213)
    3 *Amaranthus* sp. carbonized seeds
    10 *Chenopodium quinoa* carbonized seeds
    3 *Ambrosia* sp. carbonized seeds
    5 *Zea mays* carbonized cupule fragments

Animal bone (NISP)
    Mammals
        llama or alpaca (*Lama* sp.): 19 (10 from flotation)

Trampled Surface M-13. This was a long and narrow area of compacted soil that formed along the intrusion's eastern edge, probably as a result of people entering and exiting the depression on the way to and from the hearth.

Munsell color
    7.5 YR 4/4 brown

Ceramic vessels
    Total sherds: 2
    No diagnostic sherds were found

Chipped stone
    Locally available stone (100% by count and weight)
        quartzite
            debitage: 3 proximal flakes (< 0.1 g)

Botanical remains from flotation of 5.6 liters of soil (S-215)
    2 *Chenopodium quinoa* carbonized seeds

Animal bone (NISP)
    Mammals
        unidentified: 4 (all from flotation)

Burial 23

In the northwest corner of Unit D next to the pit house, a small depression that cut into geologic soil contained Burial 23, an infant (newborn to 6 months of age). The burial was covered by loose brown dirt. Although the limits of the unit prevented us from excavating this soil completely, it is possible that it was a small mound, about 44 cm high and 80 cm in diameter, constructed to cover and mark the burial. The mound was almost entirely on top of geologic soil except for a small part that overlapped Stratum 24, the last layer that filled the pit house (Intrusion M, see Fig. 3.1, northern profile). If the mound were constructed on top of Stratum 24, it would have been built long after the semi-subterranean house was abandoned. However, if the superposition of the mound on top of Stratum 24 resulted from slumping or erosion, it is possible that this burial mound was coeval with construction of the house and that the child was a member of the family that lived there.

Unfortunately, the orientation and position of the body were not recorded because my assistant did not recognize that he was excavating a human burial. Despite this, 57% of the bones of the individual were salvaged from the fauna bag. Since the skeleton was nearly complete and the delicate infant bones were in excellent condition, it is likely that Burial 23 was a primary interment made very soon after death (Burial Type 1).

The infant had a double-headed first rib, a congenital condition that he or she shared with a woman buried during the final use of the Northern Sector (Andrushko 2008; see Burial 18 below). Although these two individuals shared a heritable trait, the burials were from the stratigraphically lowest and highest cultural deposits, making it impossible that they were mother and child. Rather, this shared condition demonstrates the continued occupation of the site by related people from the earliest to latest phases.

Shallow Circular Storage Pits with Vertical Walls

The pit house was associated with three circular intrusions (Intrusions R, Q, and P) with vertical walls and slightly rounded bottoms that were dug into the dense red clay. The form and contents of these features indicate they were probably storage pits that contained food and/or other implements.

Intrusion R

Intrusion R was 110 cm in diameter and 15 cm deep. Two distinct levels of soil filled this pit.

Level R-1. This stratigraphically deepest level was stuck to the pit's corners and base. It was composed of semi-compact soil containing a high proportion of blocks of ash and charcoal. It is possible that this layer was the remains of items that accumulated in the pit while it was used for storage, but were burned when pests made the pit unusable. If that was the case, it seems that quinoa and medicinal or dye plants (*Galium* sp. and *Verbena* sp.) were stored in the pit and that *markhu* was used as fuel to burn the contents.

Munsell color
    7.5 YR 4/3 brown

Ceramic vessels
    Total sherds: 21
    Restricted vessels with a neck: 3 plainware

Chipped stone
    Regionally available stone (100% by count and weight)
        andesite
            debitage: 1 proximal flake (0.2 g)

Botanical remains from flotation of 5.8 liters of soil (S-196)
    8 *Chenopodium quinoa* carbonized seeds
    4 *Galium* sp. carbonized seeds
    1 *Verbena* sp. carbonized seed
    2 *Ambrosia* sp. carbonized seeds

Animal bone (NISP)
    Mammals
        field mouse (Muridae): 1 (from flotation)
        unidentified: 16 (all from flotation)

Level R-2. This comprised looser soil mixed with some ash and charcoal that filled the rest of the intrusion. The items in the pit were typical of what might be found in domestic trash. They included fragments of restricted vessels with a neck made of redware, plainware, and pattern burnished pottery. The pit held food scraps such as quinoa, corn, camelid, and guinea pig as well as plants used for medicine and fuel. Bones of field mice suggest that those rodents ate the discarded food. The organic rubbish was mixed with discarded tools such as a ceramic disc and primary debris from chipped stone tool manufacture.

Munsell color
    7.5 YR 4/3 brown

Ceramic vessels
    Total sherds: 161
    Restricted vessels with a neck: 2 Chanapata redware,
        7 plainware
    Body sherds with diagnostic style: 1 Chanapata redware,
        1 Chanapata incised, 2 pattern burnished

Reworked ceramic sherd
    Disc: 1 plainware

Chipped stone
    Locally available stone (100% by count and weight)
        fine grain quartzitic sandstone
            tool: 1 unidirectional core (33.1 g)
            debitage: 1 fragment angular shatter (51.4 g)
        organic limestone
            tool: 1 multidirectional core (23.8 g)

Botanical remains from flotation of 5.7 liters of soil (S-195)
    1 *Amaranthus* sp. carbonized seed
    25 *Chenopodium quinoa* carbonized seeds
    1 *Galium* sp. carbonized seed
    2 *Ambrosia* sp. carbonized seeds
    4 *Zea mays* carbonized cupule fragments

Animal bone (NISP)
    Mammals
        llama or alpaca (*Lama* sp.): 1
        guinea pig (*Cavia porcellus*): 3 (all from flotation)
        field mouse (Muridae): 5 (all from flotation)
        unidentified: 17 (all from flotation)

Intrusion Q

Intrusion Q was a shallow circular pit similar to Intrusion R. It was 80 cm in diameter and 20 cm deep. Loose soil with flecks of charcoal filled this feature. Like Intrusion R, this pit included domestic trash such as food scraps and fragments of restricted vessels with a neck. Mice were attracted to this rubbish, which also contained several utilized flakes from local and exotic stone.

Munsell color
    7.5 YR 4/4 brown

Ceramic vessels
    Total sherds: 49
    Restricted vessels with a neck: 3 plainware
    Body sherd with diagnostic style: 1 pattern burnished

Chipped stone
    Locally available stone (33.3% by count, 81.5% by wt)
        quartzite
            tool: 1 unimarginal utilized flake (10.3 g)
            debitage: 1 proximal flake (0.3 g)
    Regionally available stone (33.3% by count, 15.4% by wt)
        slate
            tool: 1 unimarginal retouched or shaped flake tool
                (2.0 g)
            debitage: 1 proximal flake (< 0.1 g, from flotation)
    Exotic stone (33.3% by count, 3.1% by weight)
        obsidian
            tool: 1 unimarginal utilized flake (0.4 g)
            debitage: 1 proximal flake (< 0.1 g)

Botanical remains from flotation of 4.8 liters of soil (S-192)
    18 *Chenopodium quinoa* carbonized seeds
    1 *Trifolium* sp. carbonized seed
    4 *Zea mays* carbonized cupule fragments

Animal bone (NISP)
    Mammals
        llama or alpaca (*Lama* sp.): 1
        field mouse (Muridae): 7 (all from flotation)
        unidentified: 8 (all from flotation)

Intrusion P

Intrusion P was a shallow circular storage pit similar to Intrusions Q and R. It was 100 cm in diameter and 19 cm deep. The soil that filled the pit was full of ash and bits of charcoal. The contents were most likely refuse. There were flakes of local stone and obsidian, fragments of restricted vessels with and without a neck, and a one-handed grinding stone. Compared with the other two pits, food scraps were less dense and there were no field mice.

Munsell color
7.5 YR 5/2 brown

Ceramic vessels
Total sherds: 53
Restricted vessels with a neck: 3 plainware
Restricted vessels without a neck: 1 Chanapata redware, 1 plainware

Groundstone
Grinding stone that fit in one hand with plano-convex cross section and flattened surfaces created by grinding with back and forth and rocking motions (Group 1, Type B). The stone measured 7.41 × 6.89 × 4.53 cm; it weighed 340 g.

Chipped stone
Locally available stone (33.33% by count, 26.67% by wt)
fine grain quartzitic sandstone
debitage: 1 proximal flake (0.4 g)
Exotic stone (66.67% by count, 73.33% by weight)
obsidian
debitage: 1 proximal flake (< 0.1 g), 1 fragment of flake shatter (1.1 g)

Botanical remains from flotation of 7.8 liters of soil (S-210)
10 *Chenopodium quinoa* carbonized seeds
1 *Galium* sp. carbonized seed
1 *Zea mays* carbonized cupule fragment, 2 carbonized seeds

Animal bone (NISP)
Mammals
unidentified: 27 (all from flotation)

Circular Hearth Filled with Multiple Layers of Soil and Ash (Intrusion N)

In the southeast corner of Unit D, several superimposed hearths were excavated into natural soil. The area that held these intrusions had a diameter between 1.6 and 1.9 m and a maximum depth of 40 cm. This hearth contained fragments of open and restricted vessels from every subtype of Chanapata pottery (redware, blackware, painted and incised, incised, pattern burnished, and plainware). There were flakes of local and regional stone, but no obsidian. There were also diverse animal remains like camelids, *cuy*, and bird. Plant remains included not only foods (like quinoa and corn), but also plants for dyes. Field mice recovered from upper levels of the hearth indicate that the feature was full of organic matter. The activities performed around this hearth were very diverse, including not only the cooking and serving of a variety of foods, but also craft production such as dyeing textiles.

Intrusion N-1

The earliest of these hearths was a pit about 30 cm in diameter, between 10 and 20 cm deep. The semi-compact soil that filled this depression was slightly orange in color and contained burned plant remains. Most of this pit was destroyed by the later Intrusions N-2 and N-3.

Munsell color
10 YR 5/1 gray

Ceramic vessels
Total sherds: 7
Open vessel: 1 plainware
Body sherds with diagnostic style: 5 pattern burnished

Botanical remains from flotation of 5.1 liters of soil, the entire contents of the intrusion (S-199)
6 *Chenopodium quinoa* carbonized seeds

Animal bone (NISP)
Mammals
unidentified: 17 (all from flotation)

Intrusion N-2

Intrusion N-2 cut through part of Intrusion N-1 into natural soil. It had a diameter of about 140 cm and a maximum depth of 10 cm and was filled with ashy soil.

Munsell color
7.5 YR 5/3 brown

Ceramic vessels
Total sherds: 34
Restricted vessels with a neck: 4 plainware, 1 Chanapata incised and painted
Body sherds with diagnostic style: 3 pattern burnished

Chipped stone
Locally available stone (66.67% by count, < 1% by wt)
quartzite
debitage: 2 proximal flakes (< 0.1 g)

Regionally available stone (33.33% by count, 100% by wt)
   andesite
      debitage: 1 proximal flake (0.3 g)

Botanical remains from flotation of 6.5 liters of soil (S-207)
   2 *Amaranthus* sp. carbonized seeds
   6 *Chenopodium quinoa* carbonized seeds
   2 *Galium* sp. carbonized seeds
   2 *Zea mays* carbonized cupule fragments
   2 *Scirpus* sp. carbonized seeds

Animal bone (NISP)
   Mammals
      llama or alpaca (*Lama* sp.): 3
      unidentified: 10 (all from flotation)

Intrusion N-3

Intrusion N-3 held very ashy soil and cut through the eastern edge of Intrusion N-2 into geological soil. This area was 35 × 60 cm and between 5 and 10 cm deep.

Munsell color
   7.5 YR 5/3 brown

Ceramic vessels
   Total sherds: 12
   Restricted vessel without a neck: 1 plainware
   Body sherd with diagnostic style: 1 pattern burnished

Chipped stone
   Locally available stone (100% by count and weight)
      quartzite
         debitage: 2 proximal flakes (0.3 g)

Botanical remains from flotation of 6.9 liters of soil (S-205)
   8 *Chenopodium quinoa* carbonized seeds
   2 *Zea mays* carbonized cupule fragments

Animal bone (NISP)
   Mammals
      unidentified: 9 (all from flotation)

Intrusion N-4

Intrusion N-4 was an ashy stratum 10 cm thick that covered both Intrusions N-2 and N-3. This stratum extended over the entire area of Intrusion N.

Munsell color
   10 YR 5/1 gray

Ceramic vessels
   Total sherds: 154
   Restricted vessels with a neck: 1 Chanapata redware,
     2 Chanapata blackware, 9 plainware
   Body sherds with diagnostic style: 3 Chanapata redware,
     2 Chanapata incised, 7 pattern burnished

Animal bone (NISP)
   Mammals
      llama or alpaca (*Lama* sp.): 14
      guinea pig (*Cavia porcellus*): 2
      field mouse (Muridae): 4
      unidentified: 4
   Birds
      unidentified: 1

Intrusion N-5

Intrusion N-5 was a shallow circular intrusion with a diameter of about 120 cm and a depth of only 5 cm, filled with reddish brown soil that had less ash than the previous intrusions. It cut through most of Level N-4, but the center was located slightly to the west of that of Intrusion N-4.

Munsell color
   5 YR 4/6 yellowish red

Ceramic vessels
   Total sherds: 89
   Body sherds with diagnostic style: 2 Chanapata redware

Chipped stone
   Locally available stone (60% by count, 100% by wt)
      fine grain quartzitic sandstone
         debitage: 1 fragment of angular shatter (0.6 g)
      quartzite
         debitage: 2 proximal flakes (0.1 g)
   Regionally available stone (40% by count, < 1% by wt)
      slate
         debitage: 2 proximal flakes (< 0.1 g)

Groundstone
   Nondescript fragment of grinding stone that weighed 100 g

Botanical remains from flotation of 6.7 liters of soil (S-200)
   8 *Chenopodium quinoa* carbonized seeds

Animal bone (NISP)
   Mammals
      llama or alpaca (*Lama* sp.): 6
      field mouse (Muridae): 3 (all from flotation)

Shallow Depression Filled with Ash (Intrusion O)

Intrusion O was a shallow, irregularly-shaped depression between 5 and 10 cm deep excavated into the natural soil. From north to south, the diameter was 138 cm, and from east to west the diameter was 96 cm. The soil that filled the depression was ashy and full of flecks of carbon, indicating that burning took place in this area.

Munsell color
   7.5 YR 4/3 brown

Ceramic vessels
   Total sherds: 12
   Restricted vessel with a neck: 1 plainware

Botanical remains from flotation of 5.7 liters of soil (S-194)
   6 *Chenopodium quinoa* carbonized seeds
   2 *Ambrosia* sp. carbonized seeds
   4 Poaceae carbonized seeds

Animal bone (NISP)
   Mammals
      unidentified: 8 (all from flotation)
   Birds
      unidentified: 2

A Semi-Subterranean Domestic Structure (Intrusion L)

After the first pit house had been filled and covered with a thick stratum of soil, another similar intrusion was excavated through Stratum 25 into geologic soil. Like the earlier house, it had an irregular shape, vertical walls, and a flat base. Both pit houses were excavated about 90 cm below the western ground surface that existed at the time of their construction. The second pit house had a maximum width that was 2 m from east to west. The excavated portion of the intrusion measured 2.6 m north to south, but the true length of the feature is not known because it extended beyond the northern limit of Unit D. A radiocarbon sample from the base of the feature dated it to 366–96 BC (calibrated), very close in time to the earlier house (383–118 BC).

The house was kept relatively clean during initial use. Several accumulations of rocks were left on the intrusion's base (Fig. 3.6). In addition, two unique artifacts were found resting on the floor, leaning against the eastern wall (Fig. 3.6). The first was a long, narrow bifacial stone tool made of andesite (22 × 5 cm); this tool was probably the blade of a hoe or axe that had been hafted to a perishable handle. The second was a white cone-shaped object, carved out of gypsum, that measured roughly 22 cm long and 12 cm in diameter. Narrow linear grooves were incised into the flat base of the cone, as if the bottom had been scraped against a harder object or surface, but it is unclear what its function might have been. No comparable objects were found at Yuthu, but very similar artifacts were recovered from domestic contexts at Lukurmata and other Lake Titicaca Formative period sites (Bermann 1994).

There were important differences between the two semi-subterranean structures. Unlike Intrusion M, Intrusion L did not have a dividing wall or carbonized *Scirpus* seeds that may have come from a thatch roof. Therefore, it is possible that the intrusions did not have the same type of superstructure. In addition, Intrusion L did not contain trampled surfaces and it lacked an interior storage feature. It was closely associated with Intrusion I (described below), a small storage pit 30 cm southeast. While Intrusion L had in situ artifacts on its floor, no artifacts were found resting on the bottom of Intrusion M.

Despite some differences, I propose that Intrusion L was also a semi-subterranean domestic structure, based on the similarity in form and size to Intrusion M and the artifacts found on the feature's base. The contrasts (described above) may have resulted from a shorter period of use that did not produce trampled surfaces and did not include a restructuring of space like that of Intrusion M. Alternatively, the differences between the two structures may reflect functionally distinct uses of the spaces—such as cooking and food storage in Intrusion M versus sleeping and tool storage in Intrusion L. In fact, the small size of these structures may preclude these kinds of divisions into distinct activity areas within a single semi-subterranean structure.

To understand daily life in a Formative village, it is necessary to determine whether households included more than one domestic structure, each with a different use. Unfortunately, entire household complexes were not found in the relatively small unit and more extensive excavations will be necessary to identify the full range of structures and activities within Formative households.

Radiocarbon date
   AA84436\Yuthu RC-251, 2223 ± 36 uncalibrated radiocarbon years BP, 366–96 BC calibrated without modeling (95.4% confidence)

Storage Pit (Intrusion I)

Intrusion I was a storage pit with vertical walls and a flat base, located only 30 cm southeast of the second semi-subterranean house (Intrusion L; see Fig. 3.2). The diameter was 25 cm and it was 7–10 cm deep. The depression was filled with semi-compact orange soil that contained very little cultural material, suggesting that the pit was kept empty for storage until it was no longer used.

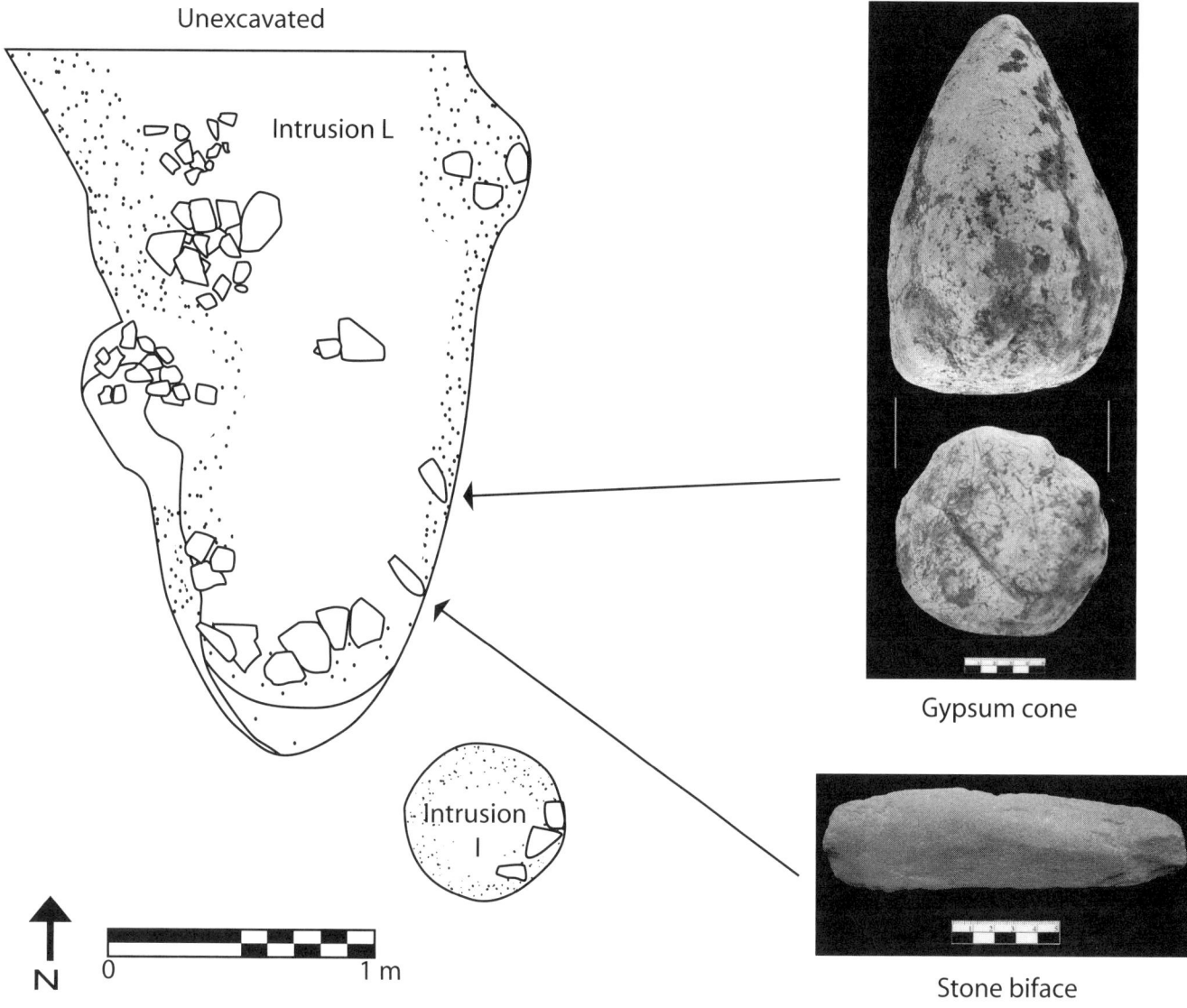

Figure 3.6. Two unique artifacts were found on the floor of Intrusion L, a semi-subterranean domestic structure that dated to 366–96 BC: a white gypsum cone with flat bottom with linear scrape marks whose function is unknown, and an andesite biface whose form suggests that it was hafted to the handle of a foot plow.

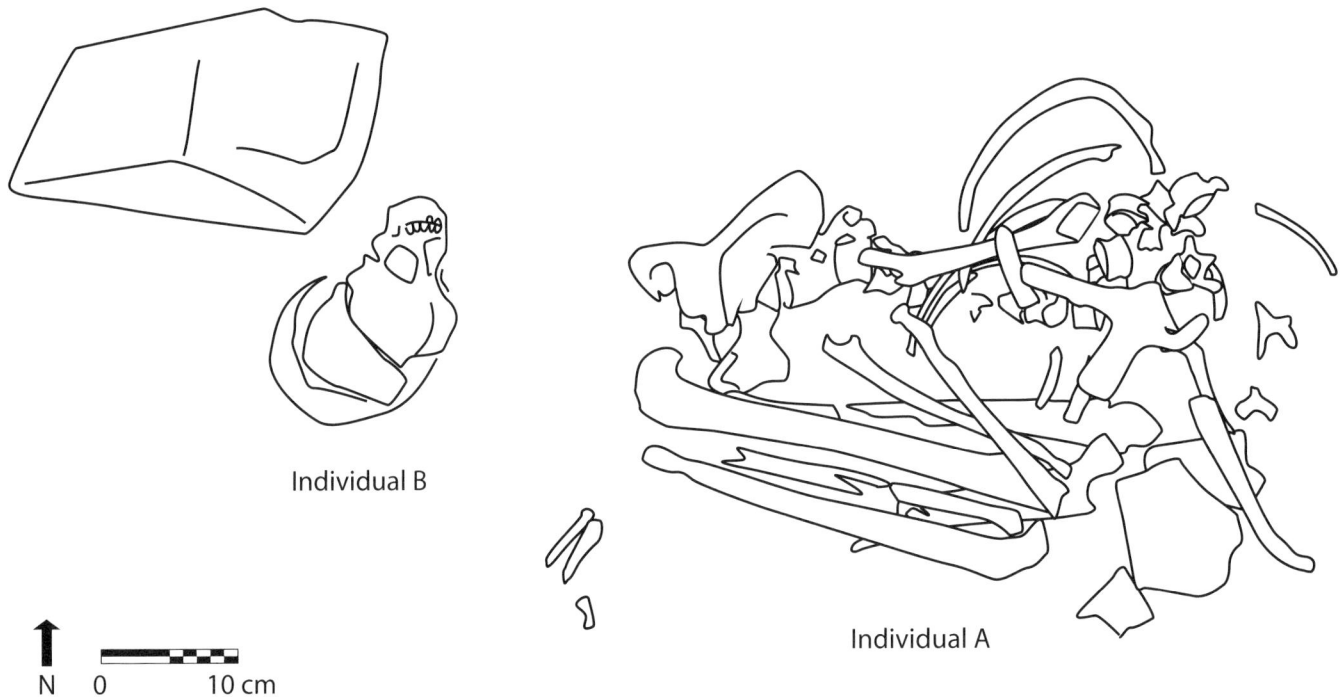

Figure 3.7. Burial 20 was a secondary burial that included the incomplete skeletons of two individuals. Individual A was a woman between 26 and 35 years of age. Individual B was the head of a 1- to 2-year-old child of indeterminate sex that exhibited signs of possible burning.

Area with Burials, a Trampled Surface, and Small Distinct Soil Deposits

Just south of the second semi-subterranean house, several closely associated features cut through Stratum 23. These included: two burials, an area of orange compact soil, a small trampled surface, an ash layer, and an area of dark soil that contained a concentration of pottery. The ashy soil contained plants that could be used as fuel, food, or medicine, as well as human and camelid bone. There were both restricted and open vessels in this area. This set of features seems to be the remains of funerary rituals associated with the second pit house. At this time, the partial remains of several women and children were brought to the new village and interred during rituals that included burning offerings.

Burial 20

Burial 20 included two individuals buried in a shallow cavity that cut through Stratum 23 into geologic soil (Fig. 3.7). Individual A was an adult woman between 26 and 35 years old buried in flexed position on her right side. The skeleton was incomplete (29% complete) and included elements primarily from the right side of the trunk, arms, and upper portion of the legs. The head, hands, and feet were missing, and the bones were poorly preserved. Individual B consisted of a cranium and part of a mandible (0% complete) of a 1- to 2-year-old child of indeterminate sex. The child's head had been placed at the woman's feet. The bones were in poor condition and their dark gray color may have been the result of burning, though other characteristics of burning were not present (Andrushko 2008). Although there is not yet genetic or skeletal morphological evidence of relatedness between these two individuals, it is an intriguing possibility that the burial represents a mother and child who were reunited through reburial in a secondary interment.

Considering the incompleteness and preservation of the skeletal remains of both individuals, it is clear that Burial 20 was not a primary interment (Burial Type 2). While discoloration of the child's cranium may be the result of burning or another special treatment, there is no such discoloration of the woman's bones. Therefore, the treatment of the cranium probably occurred before it was placed in the grave. It is not possible to determine if it was prior to or during the inhumation ritual. Hard purplish soil under the woman's body may represent the remains of another aspect of mortuary ritual. This burial was not associated with any grave goods, but there was a large rock to the west of the child's cranium that may have marked the grave.

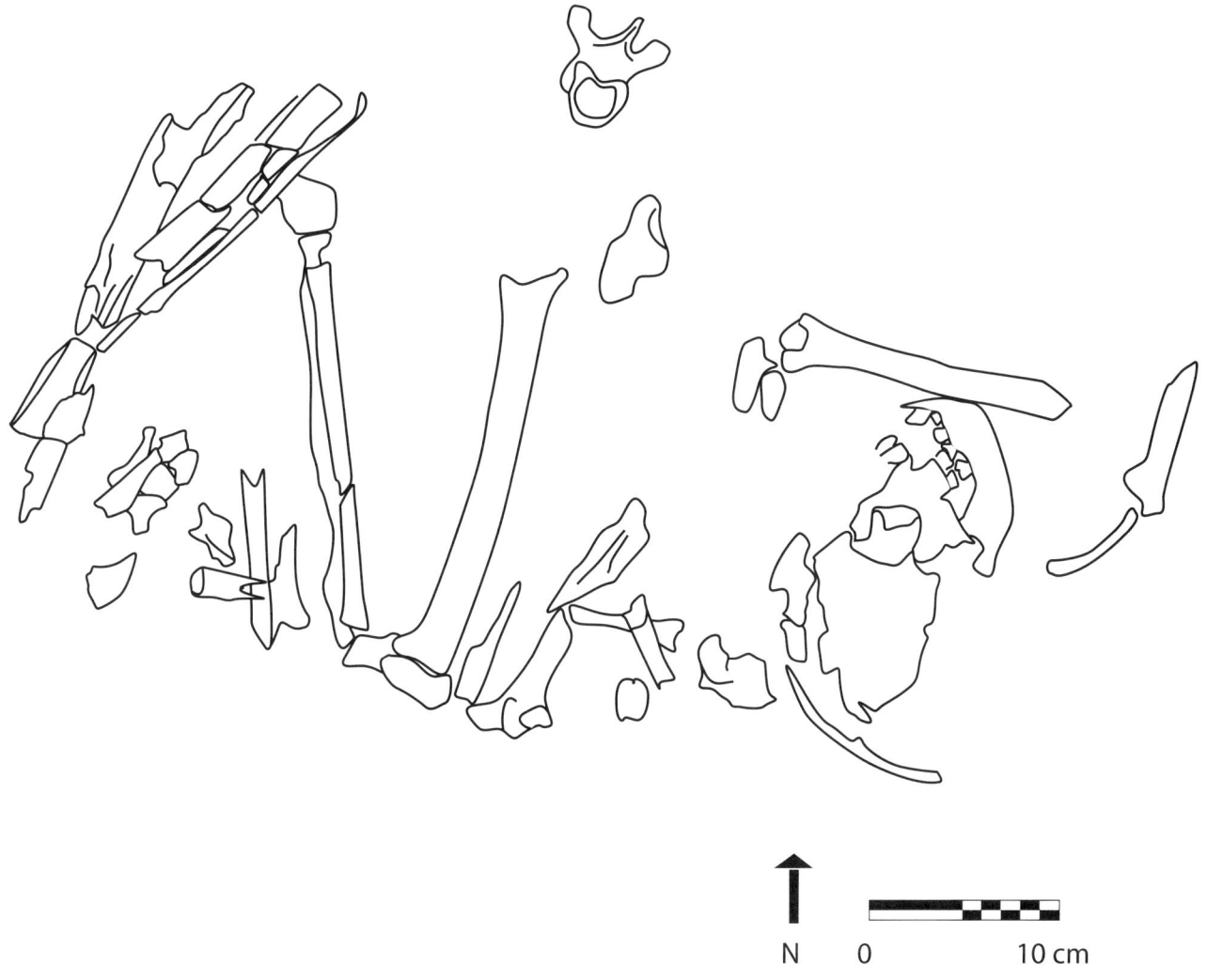

Figure 3.8. Burial 21 was a burned secondary interment of two individuals who were probably about 3 months of age, a 5- to 6-year-old child, and an adult (of indeterminate sex) more than 25 years old.

Burial 21

Burial 21 included the burned partial remains of four individuals buried in a cavity that cut through Stratum 23 into geologic soil (Fig. 3.8). Individuals A (29% complete) and B (29% complete) were cranial and post cranial bone fragments of two infants about 3 months old. The bones were in poor condition and showed signs of weathering. Individual C consisted of elements primarily from the right side of the head, trunk, and legs of a 5- to 6-year-old child (7% complete) in a poor state of preservation. The child had tabular erect cranial modification. Individual D was represented by very fragmentary bits of bone from the head, trunk, legs, and arms of an adult of indeterminate sex who was at least 25 years old (Andrushko 2008).

The very fragmentary nature of the bones of all individuals in the grave demonstrates that this was a secondary burial (Burial Type 2). The small fraction of bones from any one person suggests that before being moved and reburied, the individuals were interred either in different graves or in an open ossuary. In addition, the clear evidence for burning of all skeletal elements implies that the bones and other combustible materials were burned at the time of the inhumation. There were no grave goods associated with this burial.

Small Area of Orange Soil

A small area of orange, possibly burned soil was located just south of Burial 20. It was about 80 cm from east to west, 60 cm from north to south, and 9 cm deep.

Munsell color
   7.5 YR 3/3 dark brown

Ceramic vessels
   Total sherds: 34
   Restricted vessel with a neck: 1 plainware
   Restricted vessel without a neck: 1 plainware

Chipped stone
   Locally available stone (100% by count and weight)
     quartzite
       debitage: 1 proximal flake (0.6 g)

Animal bone (NISP)
   Mammals
     unidentified: 10

Area of Soil Mixed with Ash

A small ash concentration 9 cm thick that measured 1.2 m from north to south and 80 cm from east to west was adjacent to the southern edge of the area with orange soil.

Munsell color
   7.5 YR 4/3 brown

Ceramic vessels
   Total sherds: 142
   Restricted vessels with a neck: 4 plainware
   Open vessels: 2 plainware
   Lid: 1 plainware
   Body sherds with diagnostic style: 2 pattern burnished

Chipped stone
   Locally available stone (75% by count, 99.41% by wt)
     fine grain quartzitic sandstone
       debitage: 1 proximal flake (5.5 g)
     quartzite
       debitage: 2 proximal flakes (1.1 g), 3 fragments of angular shatter (10.3 g)
   Regionally available stone (25% by count, 0.59% by wt)
     slate
       debitage: 2 proximal flakes (0.1 g)

Botanical remains from flotation of 5.2 liters of soil (S-176)
   2 *Chenopodium quinoa* carbonized seeds
   1 *Brassica* sp. carbonized seed
   1 *Ambrosia* sp. carbonized seed

Animal bone (NISP)
   Mammals
     llama or alpaca (*Lama* sp.): 3
     field mouse (Muridae): 5 (all from flotation)
     unidentified: 28 (all from flotation)
   Human bone: 2 (all from flotation)

Trampled Surface 23-1

Trampled Surface 23-1 formed on top of the soil mixed with ash described above. It was a small area about 30 cm from north to south that extended beyond the western limit of Unit D. The entire floor was taken as a flotation sample.

Munsell color
   7.5 YR 4/4 brown

Ceramic vessels
   Total sherds: 4
   Restricted vessel with a neck: 1 plainware

Chipped stone
   Locally available stone (100% by count and weight)
     fine grain quartzitic sandstone
       tool: 1 unimarginal flake tool (11.7 g)

Botanical remains from flotation of 1.2 liters of soil (S-175)
   6 *Chenopodium quinoa* carbonized seeds

Animal bone (NISP)
   Mammals
     llama or alpaca (*Lama* sp.): 2 (all from flotation)
     field mouse (Muridae): 3 (all from flotation)

Dark Soil Containing a Concentration of Pottery

A small area of very dark soil 9 cm thick that measured 60 cm from east to west and 85 cm north to south contained a high quantity of pottery and some loose stones.

Munsell color
   7.5 YR 3/4 dark brown

Ceramic vessels
   Total sherds: 61
   Open vessel: 1 pattern burnished
   Body sherd with diagnostic style: 1 Chanapata incised and painted

Chipped stone
   Locally available stone (100% by count and weight)
     fine grain quartzitic sandstone
       debitage: 1 proximal flake (2.8 g)

quartzite
tool: 1 bimarginal flake tool (23.9 g)
debitage: 1 fragment of angular shatter (8.1 g)

Animal bone (NISP)
Mammals
llama or alpaca (*Lama* sp.): 1

Ashy Intrusion 3 in the Northwest Corner (Intrusion K)

Thirty-eight cm of soil accumulated over the pit house in the northwest corner before a series of superimposed ashy deposits (partly or fully separated by intervening strata of non-ashy soil) filled in the slight depression left by the semi-subterranean structure. Ashy Intrusion 3 was the deepest of these deposits. It held food remains, grinding stones, and a large variety of pottery for both serving and preparing food. In addition, there were utilized flakes and debitage from working local and exotic stone. The presence of *Galium* suggests that people prepared medicine or dyed textiles in this hearth. Like other hearths in the Northern Sector, it seems that a wide variety of activities took place in and around this one.

Munsell color
10 YR 5/2 grayish brown

Ceramic vessels
Total sherds: 757
Restricted vessels with a neck: 13 plainware
Restricted vessel without a neck: 1 plainware
Open vessels: 5 plainware
Open vessel with a diameter greater than 30 cm:
 1 plainware
Lid: 1 plainware
Body sherds with diagnostic style: 2 Chanapata redware,
 3 pattern burnished

Reworked ceramic sherd
Non-disc: 1 plainware

Chipped stone
Locally available stone (55.56% by count, 100% by wt)
quartz
debitage: 1 proximal flake (0.7 g)
breccia
tool: 1 unimarginal flake tool (13.8 g)
Regionally available stone (22.22% by count, < 1% by wt)
slate
debitage: 2 proximal flakes (< 0.1g)
Exotic stone (22.2% by count, < 1% by weight)
obsidian
debitage: 1 proximal flake (< 0.1 g), 1 fragment of
 angular shatter (< 0.1 g)

Groundstone
Grinding stone that fit in one hand with plano-convex cross section and flattened surfaces created by grinding with back and forth and rocking motions (Group 1, Type B). The object had evidence of pecking. The stone measured 10.60 × 9.60 × 4.41 cm; it weighed 620 g.

Stone that could be pinched between the fingers with a flattened surface created by back and forth or circular strokes (Small Group 3, Type P). The stone measured 5.92 × 3.47 × 3.42 cm; it weighed 90 g.

Nondescript fragment of grinding stone that weighed 260 g.

Botanical remains from flotation of 5.2 liters of soil (S-158)
18 *Chenopodium quinoa* carbonized seeds
1 Asteraceae carbonized seed

Botanical remains from flotation of 6.0 liters of soil (S-165)
12 *Chenopodium quinoa* carbonized seeds
2 *Galium* sp. carbonized seeds
2 *Ambrosia* sp. carbonized seeds
2 *Zea mays* carbonized seeds

Botanical remains from flotation of 6.1 liters of soil (S-168)
6 *Chenopodium quinoa* carbonized seeds
2 Poaceae carbonized seeds

Animal bone (NISP)
Mammals
llama or alpaca (*Lama* sp.): 16 (4 from flotation)
field mouse (Muridae): 16 (all from flotation)
unidentified: 44 (all from flotation)
Birds
unidentified: 2

Intrusion J

Intrusion J was a cylindrical pit about 60 cm in diameter and 60 cm deep that cut through Stratum 23 into geologic soil. The soil that filled this feature was reddish brown with chunks of burned earth and flecks of charcoal. It contained a mixture of food remains and tools that is typical of domestic trash.

Munsell color
5 YR 4/4 reddish brown

Ceramic vessels
Total sherds: 71
Body sherds with diagnostic style: 1 Chanapata redware,
 4 pattern burnished

Chipped stone
    Locally available stone (66.67% by count, < 1% by wt)
        coarse grain quartzitic sandstone
            debitage: 1 proximal flake (< 0.1 g)
        quartzite
            debitage: 1 fragment of angular shatter (< 0.1 g)
    Exotic stone (33.33% by count, 100% by weight)
        obsidian
            debitage: 1 fragment of angular shatter (0.5 g)

Botanical remains from flotation of 6.2 liters of soil from a lower part of the intrusion fill (S-186)
    18 *Chenopodium quinoa* carbonized seeds
    2 *Verbena* sp. carbonized seeds
    4 *Ambrosia* sp. carbonized seeds

Botanical remains from flotation of 6.9 liters of soil from a higher part of the intrusion fill (S-185)
    20 *Chenopodium quinoa* carbonized seeds
    4 *Ambrosia* sp. carbonized seeds
    3 *Zea mays* carbonized seeds
    6 Poaceae carbonized seeds

Animal bone (NISP)
    Mammals
        llama or alpaca (*Lama* sp.): 2 (all from flotation)
        field mouse (Muridae): 12 (all from flotation)
        unidentified: 8 (7 from flotation)

Eagle Hawk Burial

Close to the excavation unit's western limit, the intentional burial of a bird intruded into Stratum 20. The bird was an eagle hawk (*Geranoetus* sp.), also known as the buzzard eagle or *aguilucho*, a species that inhabits forests, open areas, and mountainsides and eats rodents, reptiles, and carrion (Koepcke 1970). There were no other objects buried with the bird.

The bird burial was closely associated with two areas of burned earth 9 cm thick that rested on Stratum 20 (Fig. 3.9). The low density of carbonized botanical remains from these features suggests that the burning that created them was probably not a cooking fire. Rather, it might have been part of a ritual performed when the eagle hawk was buried. The materials below were recovered from the compact soil.

Munsell color
    2.5 YR 4/4 reddish brown

Ceramic vessels
    Total sherds: 79
    Body sherd with diagnostic style: 1 Chanapata redware

Reworked ceramic sherd
    Non-disc: 1 plainware

Botanical remains from flotation of 6.4 liters of soil (S-183)
    1 Fabaceae carbonized seed
    1 *Ambrosia* sp. carbonized seed

Animal bone (NISP)
    Mammals
        field mouse (Muridae): 6 (all from flotation)
        unidentified: 7 (5 from flotation)

A Prepared Clay Floor Associated with a Large Open Hearth

Semicircular Clay Floor

Floor 2 was the only formally prepared floor in Unit D. It was made of hard, brown clay. The floor extended beyond the northern limit of Unit D, so the entire size and shape are not known. However, the excavated portion was shaped like the head of a wrench with the "mouth" facing south toward Ashy Intrusion 2 in the northwest corner (Fig. 3.9). It was 10 cm thick and measured 1.63 m east to west and 84 cm north to south. It is unclear whether this floor was covered by a superstructure.

Munsell color
    7.5 YR 5/3 brown

Ceramic vessels
    Total sherds: 63
    Body sherd with diagnostic style: 1 Chanapata redware

Chipped stone
    Regionally available stone (50% by count, percent by weight unknown)
        slate
            debitage: 1 proximal flake (< 0.1 g)
    Exotic stone (50% by count, percent by weight unknown)
        obsidian
            debitage: 1 proximal flake (< 0.1 g)

Botanical remains from flotation of 5.8 liters of soil (S-163)
    6 *Chenopodium quinoa* carbonized seeds

Animal bone (NISP)
    Mammals
        llama or alpaca (*Lama* sp.): 3 (all from flotation)
        guinea pig (*Cavia porcellus*): 1 (from flotation)
        unidentified: 27 (all from flotation)

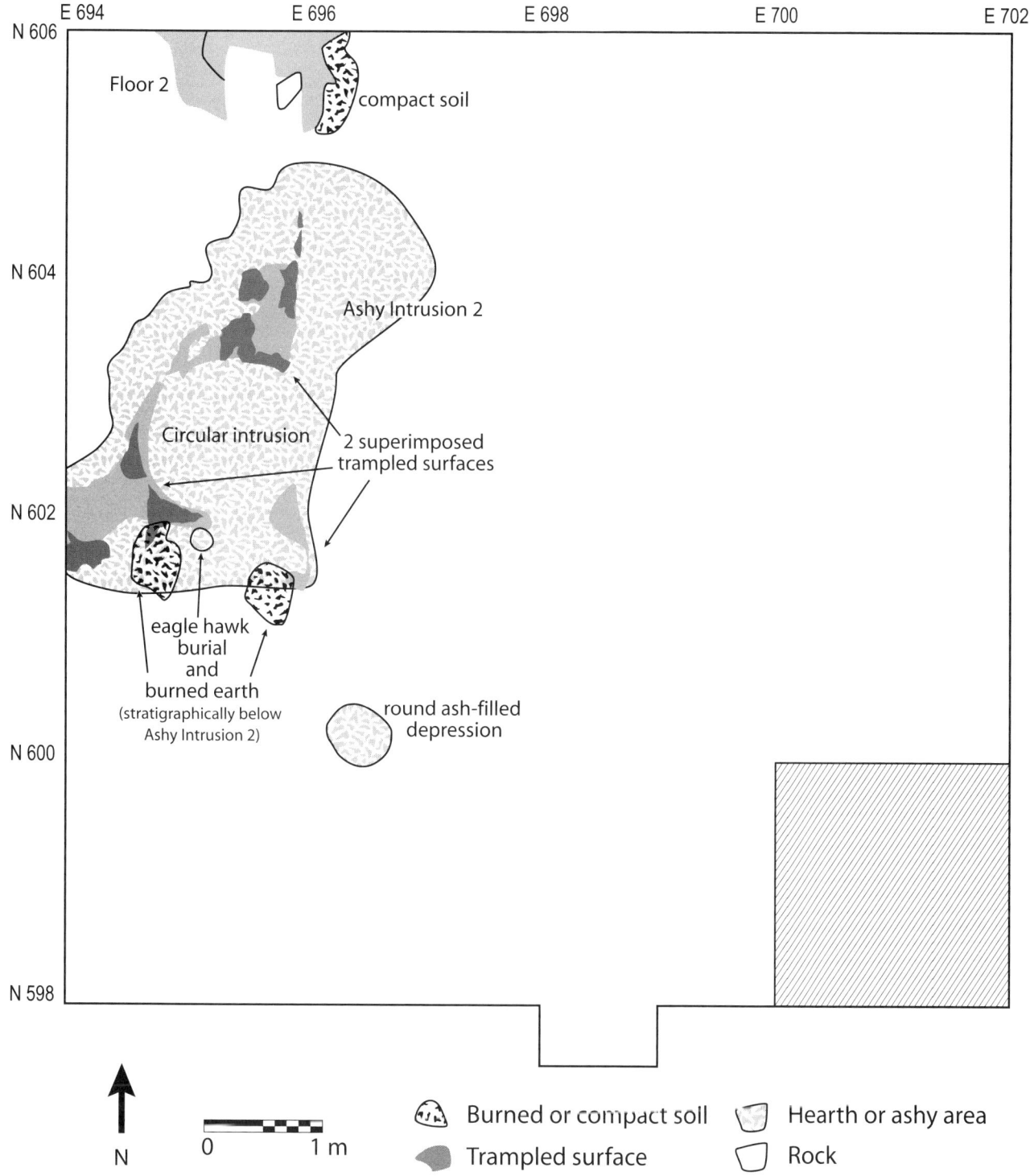

Figure 3.9. The semicircular floor in the northwest corner was the only prepared floor made of very hard clay in Unit D. It was associated with Ashy Intrusion 2 (Intrusion G) in the northwest corner that was a large irregular-shaped cavity filled with alternating layers of ash and trampled surfaces. This plan drawing also includes the eagle hawk burial, the round ash-filled depression, and a cluster of adobe and stones.

Ashy Intrusion 2 in the Northwest Corner (Intrusion G)

This ash-filled intrusion was located directly above Ashy Intrusion 3 in the northwest corner. Although both features were ash-filled depressions, they were not the same size or shape, and they were separated by Stratum 10, a non-ashy layer that covered Ashy Intrusion 3. Ashy Intrusion 2 was between 10 and 25 cm deep with a rounded bottom. It was filled with alternating ash deposits and trampled surfaces (described below), which indicate frequent use of this area. As might be expected, this large hearth contained dense and varied food remains. Food was prepared and served primarily in restricted vessels with a neck and open vessels. Restricted vessels without a neck were uncommon. In addition to food preparation and serving items, evidence for other tasks was recovered from this area. Carbonized plant remains included those for making dye and medicine. There were several bone tools and grinding stones, but the large number of obsidian projectile points and other formal tools is particularly striking (Fig. 3.10; Plate 3). This suggests that these tools were used for one or more craft activities that took place alongside day-to-day cooking and eating.

Figure 3.10. Several obsidian tools were found in Ashy Intrusion 2 in the northwest corner. It is likely that they were used for craft production of some kind.

Level G-1

The stratigraphically lowest level in this intrusion was semi-compact, gray soil mixed with ash that was 40 cm deep.

Munsell color
    2.5 YR 5/2 grayish brown

Ceramic vessels
    Total sherds: 437
    Restricted vessels with a neck: 2 Chanapata redware, 19 plainware
    Open vessels: 12 plainware
    Lid: 1 plainware
    Body sherds with diagnostic style: 6 Chanapata redware, 6 pattern burnished, 1 indeterminate

Reworked ceramic sherd
    Non-disc: 1 plainware

Chipped stone
    Locally available stone (30.77% by count, 73.89% by wt)
        fine grain quartzitic sandstone
            debitage: 1 fragment of angular shatter (0.8 g)
        quartzite
            tool: 1 bimarginal flake tool (14.5 g)
            debitage: 4 proximal flakes (5.6 g), 1 fragment of flake shatter (2.8 g), 1 fragment of angular shatter (8.0 g)
    Regionally available stone (19.23% by count, 1.17% by wt)
        slate
            debitage: 2 proximal flakes (< 0.1 g)
        andesite
            debitage: 1 proximal flake (0.1 g)
        diorite
            debitage: 2 proximal flakes (0.4 g)
    Exotic stone (50% by count, 24.94% by weight)
        obsidian
            tools: 2 hafted biface reutilized projectile points (8.1 g), 1 unimarginal flake tool reutilized projectile point (0.5 g), 1 bimarginal flake tool (2.1 g)
            debitage: 9 proximal flakes (< 0.1 g)

Groundstone

A roughly spherical stone that fit into one hand with flattened surfaces created by grinding with back and forth or circular strokes (Group 1, Type A). The stone had pecking marks. It measured 7.29 × 6.91 × 4.95 cm; it weighed 350 g.

Stone that could be pinched between the fingers with a flattened surface created by back and forth or circular strokes (Small Group 3, Type P). The stone measured 2.11 × 1.99 × 1.88 cm; it weighed 10 g.

Fragment of a palm-sized mortar (Type R). The length was unknown; it was 9.17 cm long and 4.10 cm tall. The fragment weighed 500 g.

Three nondescript fragments of grinding stones that weighed 170, 120, and 20 g.

Botanical remains from flotation of 5.8 liters of soil (S-143)
    10 *Chenopodium quinoa* carbonized seeds
    2 *Galium* sp. carbonized seeds

Botanical remains from flotation of 4.8 liters of soil (S-145)
    50 *Chenopodium quinoa* carbonized seeds
    1 *Galium* sp. carbonized seed
    8 *Zea mays* carbonized cupule fragments
    1 Poaceae carbonized seed

Botanical remains from flotation of 5.4 liters of soil (S-182)
18 *Chenopodium quinoa* carbonized seeds
1 Fabaceae carbonized seed
1 *Ambrosia* sp. carbonized seed
1 *Zea mays* carbonized seed

Animal bone (NISP)
Mammals
llama or alpaca (*Lama* sp.): 17 (7 from flotation)
white-tailed deer (*Odocoileus virginianus*): 3
guinea pig (*Cavia porcellus*): 7 (3 from flotation)
field mouse (Muridae): 25 (all from flotation)
unidentified: 51 (all from flotation)
Birds
coot (*Fulica* sp.): 1
eagle hawk (*Geranoetus* sp.): 1

Trampled Surface G-2

This trampled surface formed on part of the surface of Level G-1. It was dark gray, with an irregular shape, and measured 2.5 m north to south and 60 cm east to west.

Munsell color
2.5 YR 5/2 grayish brown

Ceramic vessels
Total sherds: 7
Body sherd with diagnostic style: 1 pattern burnished

Chipped stone
Regionally available stone (50% by count, percent by weight unknown)
andesite
debitage: 1 proximal flake (< 0.1 g)
Exotic stone (50% by count, percent by weight unknown)
obsidian
debitage: 1 proximal flake (< 0.1 g)

Botanical remains from flotation of 3.7 liters of soil (S-151)
18 *Chenopodium quinoa* carbonized seeds
4 *Galium* sp. carbonized seeds
2 *Zea mays* carbonized cupule fragments
10 Poaceae carbonized seeds

Animal bone (NISP)
Mammals
field mouse (Muridae): 8 (all from flotation)
unidentified: 10 (all from flotation)

Level G-3

Levels G-1 and G-2 were covered with semi-compact ashy soil 42 cm deep that was grayish brown. Compared with the first ash level, the density of carbonized plant remains was lower.

Munsell color
2.5 YR 5/2 grayish brown

Ceramic vessels
Total sherds: 635
Restricted vessels with a neck: 1 Chanapata redware, 19 plainware
Restricted vessels without a neck: 3 plainware
Open vessel: 1 plainware
Open vessel with a diameter greater than 30 cm: 1 plainware
Lid: 1 plainware
Body sherds with diagnostic style: 5 pattern burnished

Chipped stone
Locally available stone (30% by count, 65.19% by wt)
fine grain quartzitic sandstone
debitage: 2 proximal flakes (2.6 g)
quartzite
debitage: 4 proximal flakes (13.8 g), 2 fragments of angular shatter (5.3 g)
chert
debitage: 1 fragment of angular shatter (0.4 g)
Regionally available stone (10% by count, 4.42% by wt)
andesite
debitage: 3 proximal flakes (1.5 g)
Exotic stone (60% by count, 30.38% by weight)
obsidian
tools: 1 unhafted biface projectile point (1.0 g), 4 unimarginal flake tools (0.9 g), 2 bimarginal flake tools (1.7 g), 1 bimarginal flake tool projectile point (2.1 g), 1 combination flake tool (1.4 g), 1 unidirectional core (1.1 g), 1 multidirectional core (0.8 g)
debitage: 7 proximal flakes (1.3 g)

Reworked ceramic sherd
Disc: 1 plainware

Worked bone
1 tool made from a single carnivore tooth set in a cut and polished jaw fragment
1 broad, flat long bone shaft fragment with pointed tip

Botanical remains from flotation of 5.0 liters of soil (S-134)
10 *Chenopodium quinoa* carbonized seeds
2 *Galium* sp. carbonized seeds
3 *Ambrosia* sp. carbonized seeds

Botanical remains from flotation of 5.0 liters of soil (S-137)
16 *Chenopodium quinoa* carbonized seeds
3 *Galium* sp. carbonized seeds
4 *Ambrosia* sp. carbonized seeds
4 *Zea mays* carbonized cupule fragments

Animal bone (NISP)
Mammals
llama or alpaca (*Lama* sp.): 29 (7 from flotation)
guinea pig (*Cavia porcellus*): 8
unidentified: 36 (23 from flotation)
Birds
duck (*Anas* sp.): 2

Trampled Surface G-4

Part of the top of Level G-3 was trampled, forming a hard, dark grayish brown surface. It was located directly above Trampled Surface G-2 and had nearly the same spatial extent, measuring 2.6 m north to south by 80 cm east to west. The traffic patterns within this hearth (and therefore the way the space was used) remained the same over time.

Munsell color
10 YR 4/2 dark grayish brown

Ceramic vessels
Total sherds: 101
Open vessel: 1 plainware
Lids: 2 plainware
Body sherds with diagnostic style: 3 pattern burnished

Reworked ceramic sherd
Disc: 1 plainware

Botanical remains from flotation of 3.9 liters of soil (S-148)
2 *Chenopodium quinoa* carbonized seeds
2 *Zea mays* carbonized cupule fragments

Animal bone (NISP)
Mammals
llama or alpaca (*Lama* sp.): 5
unidentified: 5 (3 from flotation)

Level G-5

The stratigraphically highest level in the intrusion was loose, gray ash 16 cm deep. No trampled surfaces formed on top of this level. Compared to earlier levels, the density of carbonized plant remains was lower.

Munsell color
10 YR 5/1 gray

Ceramic vessels
Total sherds: 96
Restricted vessels with a neck: 4 plainware
Restricted vessels without a neck: 5 plainware
Lids: 2 plainware
Body sherds with diagnostic style: 1 Chanapata redware, 6 pattern burnished

Chipped stone
Locally available stone (33.33% by count, 20.78% by wt)
fine grain quartzitic sandstone
debitage: 1 proximal flake (0.2 g)
quartzite
debitage: 1 proximal flake (1.1 g), 1 fragment of angular shatter (0.3 g)
Exotic stone (66.67% by count, 79.22% by weight)
obsidian
tools: 2 unimarginal flake tools (2.6 g), 2 bimarginal flake tools (3.5 g)
debitage: 2 proximal flakes (< 0.1 g)

Botanical remains from flotation of 4.7 liters of soil (S-131)
8 *Chenopodium quinoa* carbonized seeds
1 *Galium* sp. carbonized seed

Animal bone (NISP)
Mammals
llama or alpaca (*Lama* sp.): 1
unidentified: 7

The House of the Earliest Mummy Found at Yuthu

When I first began to excavate in the Northern Sector, I hoped to find the material remains of daily domestic life. I never expected to be able to study the origins of mummy veneration in Cusco. Yet, the earliest known mummy from Cusco was found alongside the latest domestic structure that we discovered, an above-ground house with a large outdoor activity area in the southern half of Unit D (Fig. 3.11).

This house was stratigraphically later than the pit houses. In some ways, spaces for day-to-day activity at Yuthu did not change much over time. Throughout the occupation, houses in this area were small and most quotidian activities took place outside around large hearths. The most striking difference, however, was that the later structure was built above ground. In addition, whereas the earlier houses were associated with the primary burial of an infant and two secondary burials of women and children, the later house was next to the burial of the earliest mummy found at Yuthu (Burial 19, Burial Type 4). This mummy was a child who died at 11 or 12 years and was eventually buried in the same space where people worked, relaxed, ate, and slept every day. In contrast, the two later mummies found at the site had been taken away from other villages (where their

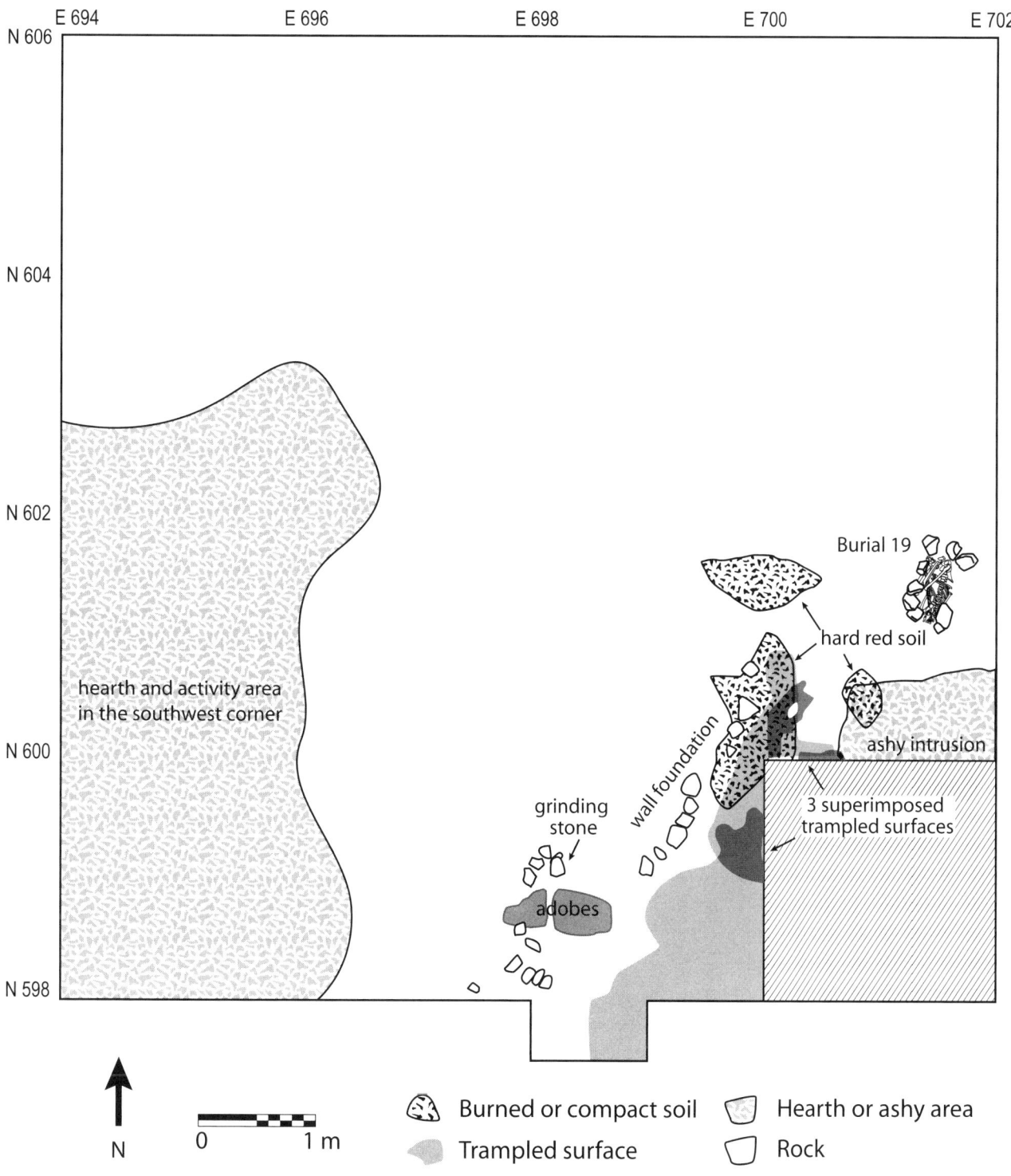

Figure 3.11. The structure in the southeast corner included three superimposed trampled surfaces bordered on the northwest by a simple wall foundation and to the east by an ashy intrusion. This structure was closely associated with the mummy burial of an 11- to 12-year-old child (Burial 19). The large hearth in the southwest corner was filled with four phases of alternating ash and trampled surfaces, suggesting that it was used for some time as an open-air cooking pit (Intrusion E). It seems likely that this hearth and activity area was used at the same time as the structure in the southeast corner.

Figure 3.12. An above-ground domestic structure in the southeast corner of Unit D had three parts: (1) a series of superimposed trampled surfaces (the latest appears in this photo and dates to 391–203 BC), (2) a possible wall foundation along the northwest corner of the trampled surfaces, and (3) an interior hearth filled with multiple layers of ash.

descendants presumably lived) to be buried at Yuthu after it had been converted to a cemetery (see Burial 16 in this chapter and Burial 4 in Chap. 4).

The Above-Ground Domestic Structure

Several closely associated features in the southeast corner rested on or intruded into Stratum 7 (Fig. 3.12). Although the features were disturbed, several characteristics suggest they were the remains of an above-ground domestic structure with a stone foundation and perishable walls that included mud or mud brick. On what was most likely the interior of the structure, heavy foot traffic created trampled surfaces that extended to the wall. In addition, there was an ashy intrusion inside the structure that was likely a cooking feature. Unlike the earlier pit houses, there were no carbonized *Scirpus* seeds that would suggest that the house had a thatched roof, but it is possible that the roof was made of another type of grass or brush, or that the roofing material was not burned.

Although the poorly preserved structure may not have been very sturdy or substantial, the series of 3 superimposed living floors and 4 strata filling the hearth indicate that it was probably used as a house for some time. The latest floor dated to 391–203 BC (contemporary with the hearth, which dated to 403–206 BC).

The structure is described below in three sections: (1) the series of trampled surfaces alternating with ashy deposits inside the structure, (2) the wall located along the northwest edge of the floors, and (3) the interior hearth east of the floors.

Figure 3.13. A carved antler found on the first trampled surface of the structure in the southeast corner.

Alternating Trampled Surfaces and Layers of Ash

Three superimposed trampled surfaces separated by thin layers of ashy soil formed part of the interior of the above-ground domestic structure. These alternating layers appear in the southern profile (see Fig. 3.1). The floors were kept relatively clean, but the soil between them contained typical domestic trash as well as a bone bead and a carved deer antler (Fig. 3.13; Plate 3). A radiocarbon sample from the latest floor dates the structure to 391–203 BC (calibrated).

The First Trampled Surface. This was the stratigraphically lowest living surface. It measured 140 by 40 cm.

Munsell color
    7.5 YR 5/3 brown

Ceramic vessels
    Total sherds: 7
    Restricted vessels without a neck: 2 plainware

Worked bone
    1 carved antler (Fig. 3.13)
    1 broad, flat long bone shaft fragment with pointed tip

Bead
    1 bone bead

Botanical remains from flotation of 5.6 liters of soil (S-162)
  8 *Chenopodium quinoa* carbonized seeds
  1 *Verbena* sp. carbonized seed
  3 *Ambrosia* sp. carbonized seeds
  3 *Zea mays* carbonized seeds

Animal bone (NISP)
  Mammals
    unidentified: 36 (all from flotation)

The Second Trampled Surface. This surface formed on top of a very thin layer of ash that rested on top of the first trampled surface. It measured 110 cm by 80 cm. The ash could not be separated during excavation, so it was excavated along with this trampled surface.

Munsell color
  7.5 YR 5/3 brown

Ceramic vessels
  Total sherds: 175
  Restricted vessels with a neck: 8 plainware
  Restricted vessels without a neck: 3 plainware
  Open vessels: 4 plainware
  Open vessels with a diameter greater than 30 cm:
    4 plainware
  Lid: 1 plainware
  Body sherds with diagnostic style: 2 Chanapata redware,
    1 Chanapata blackware

Botanical remains from flotation of 5.6 liters of soil (S-152)
  14 *Chenopodium quinoa* carbonized seeds
  2 *Ambrosia* sp. carbonized seeds
  2 *Zea mays* carbonized cupule fragments

Ashy Soil between the Second and Third Trampled Surfaces. The second trampled surface was covered by a stratum of ashy soil about 4 cm thick.

Munsell color
  7.5 YR 4/3 brown

Ceramic vessels
  Total sherds: 161
  Restricted vessel with a neck: 1 plainware
  Restricted vessels without a neck: 8 plainware
  Open vessels: 2 plainware
  Open vessel with a diameter greater than 30 cm: 1 plainware
  Body sherd with diagnostic style: 1 pattern burnished

Chipped stone
  Locally available stone (66.67% by count, 98.78% by wt)
    fine grain quartzitic sandstone
      debitage: 1 fragment of angular shatter (12.7 g)
    quartzite
      tool: 1 unhafted biface (43.70 g)
      debitage: 2 proximal flakes (0.2 g)
  Regionally available stone (16.67% by count, 0.87% by wt)
    slate
      debitage: 1 proximal flake (0.5 g)
  Exotic stone (16.67% by count, 0.35% by weight)
    obsidian
      tool: 1 bimarginal flake tool (0.2 g)

Metal
  One broken point of a metal pin was found within the matrix of this trampled surface (in the heavy fraction of S-135). It had a round cross section and weighed less than 0.1 g.

Botanical remains from flotation of 5.9 liters of soil (S-135)
  12 *Chenopodium quinoa* carbonized seeds

Animal bone (NISP)
  Mammals
    llama or alpaca (*Lama* sp.): 4 (2 from flotation)
    unidentified: 8 (7 from flotation)
  Birds
    unidentified: 1

The Third Trampled Surface. The latest trampled surface formed on top of ashy soil (Fig. 3.12). It was the largest of the three superimposed floors, though its full size and shape are unknown because it extended beyond the excavation unit's southern limit. The excavated portion measured 2.2 m north to south and 1.3 m east to west. There was a concentration of pottery located on the surface. A seed that was trampled into this floor was processed as a radiocarbon date.

Munsell color
  7.5 YR 4/1 dark gray

Radiocarbon date
  AA84435\Yuthu RC-216, 2295 ± 38 uncalibrated radiocarbon years BP, 391–203 BC calibrated without modeling (95.4% confidence)

Ceramic vessels from the concentration of pottery on the floor surface
  Total sherds: 56
  Restricted vessels with a neck: 2 plainware
  Restricted vessels without a neck: 3 plainware
  Lid: 1 plainware

Ceramic vessels in the matrix of the trampled surface
    Total sherds: 34
    Restricted vessel with a neck: 1 plainware
    Restricted vessels without a neck: 2 plainware
    Body sherds with diagnostic style: 2 Chanapata incised,
        4 pattern burnished

Chipped stone
    Exotic stone (100% by count and weight)
        obsidian
            debitage: 2 proximal flakes (< 0.1 g), 2 fragments
                of angular shatter (< 0.1 g)

Botanical remains from flotation of 6.7 liters of soil (S-133)
    10 *Chenopodium quinoa* carbonized seeds
    1 *Trifolium* sp. carbonized seed
    1 *Ambrosia* sp. carbonized seed

Animal bone (NISP)
    Mammals
        llama or alpaca (*Lama* sp.): 1
        guinea pig (*Cavia porcellus*): 2 (1 from flotation)
        unidentified: 10 (all from flotation)

Ashy Soil on Top of the Third Trampled Surface. Ashy soil about 2 cm thick accumulated on top of the third trampled surface.

Munsell color
    7.5 YR 5/3 brown

Ceramic vessels
    Total sherds: 144
    Restricted vessel with a neck: 1 plainware
    Restricted vessels without a neck: 3 plainware
    Open vessels: 3 plainware
    Body sherds with diagnostic style: 2 Chanapata redware,
        1 pattern burnished

Chipped stone
    Locally available stone (100% by count and weight)
        quartzite
            debitage: 1 proximal flake (9.6 g), 1 fragment of
                angular shatter (11.2 g)

Groundstone
    Fragment of a grinding stone that fit in one hand with plano-convex cross section and flattened surfaces created by grinding with back and forth and rocking motions (Group 1, Type B). The stone had pecking marks. About 50% of the object was present. Length was unknown; it was 10.36 cm wide and 4.96 cm long. The fragment weighed 480 g.
    An unmodified flat stone that may have been used as a base for small-scale grinding or pulverizing (Type R). The stone measured 3.96 × 3.96 × 0.85 cm; it weighed 20 g.

Botanical remains from flotation of 2.5 liters of soil (S-141)
    2 *Chenopodium quinoa* carbonized seeds

Animal bone (NISP)
    Mammals
        llama or alpaca (*Lama* sp.): 3 (all from flotation)
        field mouse (Muridae): 4 (all from flotation)
        unidentified: 13 (10 from flotation)

A Wall along the Northwest Edge of the Trampled Surfaces

There was a one-course alignment of unworked field stones along the northwest edge of the trampled surfaces. These stones probably formed a simple wall foundation and were covered by two layers of soil, described below.

Loose Dark Red Soil. Loose, dark red or orange soil about 4 cm thick surrounded the stones.

Munsell color
    7.5 YR 3/3 dark reddish brown

Ceramic vessels
    Total sherds: 305
    Restricted vessels with a neck: 1 Chanapata redware,
        13 plainware
    Restricted vessels without a neck: 4 plainware
    Open vessels: 2 plainware
    Open vessels with a diameter greater than 30 cm:
        2 plainware
    Lid: 1 Chanapata redware
    Body sherds with diagnostic style: 1 Chanapata redware,
        1 pattern burnished

Worked bone
    2 thin objects with square cross section and pointed ends

Groundstone
    Fragment of a grinding stone that fit in two hands with plano-convex cross section and flattened surfaces created by grinding with back and forth and rocking motions (Group 1, Type C). The stone had pecking marks. The length was unknown; it was 9.21 cm wide and 5.51 cm tall. The fragment weighed 460 g.
    Nondescript fragment of grinding stone that weighed 20 g.

Animal bone (NISP)
    Mammals
        llama or alpaca (*Lama* sp.): 11
        guinea pig (*Cavia porcellus*): 5
        unidentified: 13

Compact Red Soil. Compact red soil covered the stones and loose reddish soil. This stratum was 6 cm thick, mixed with and surrounded by bits of ash. It is likely that this soil was the remains of mortar, a superstructure made partially of mud or clay (like wattle and daub), or adobe blocks (like those located just west of the structure). The very compact texture and deep red color of the soil as well as the nearby bits of ash suggest that this structure might have been burned.

Munsell color
   7.5 YR 4/4 brown

Ceramic vessels
   Total sherds: 45
   Restricted vessels with a neck: 2 plainware
   Restricted vessel without a neck: 1 plainware

Groundstone
   Fragment of a doughnut-shaped clod-breaker. About 50% of the stone was present. It was 7.14 cm in diameter and 3.26 cm in height; the fragment weighed 110 g.

Animal bone (NISP)
   Mammals
      llama or alpaca (*Lama* sp.): 1
      unidentified: 4
   Human bone: 3

The Interior Hearth (Intrusion F)

The hearth was 1.35 m from east to west, 75 cm from north to south, and 44 cm deep. Although the edges of the trampled surfaces and the edge of this hearth do not meet, this intrusion cut into the same stratum that the earliest trampled surfaces were seated on, suggesting that the floors and hearth were roughly contemporary. The hearth was filled with 3 strata (described below).

Compared with most cooking features, this hearth had low densities of carbonized plant remains. Meals prepared in this area included at least quinoa, corn, greens, and possibly oca. There was very little variety in meat prepared. Faunal remains of economically useful animals were almost exclusively domesticated camelid and *cuy*. Many field mice were attracted to the organic material left behind in this hearth. The feature also contained a wide variety of bone tools and chipped stone tools and debitage made of both local material and obsidian (Fig. 3.14; Plate 3).

Figure 3.14. Chipped stone tools found in the ashy intrusion: *a*, obsidian hafted biface projectile point (Level F-1); *b*, quartzite unidirectional core tool (Level F-2); *c*, quartzite multidirectional core tool (Level F-3); *d*, coarse grain quartzitic sandstone bimarginal flake tool (Level F-3).

Level F-1. The lowest stratum that filled this intrusion was loose soil mixed with ash, 25 cm thick, that sloped upward along the southern edge.

Munsell color
   7.5 YR 4/4 brown

Ceramic vessels
   Total sherds: 87
   Restricted vessels with a neck: 8 plainware
   Open vessels: 4 plainware
   Body sherds with diagnostic style: 2 pattern burnished

Chipped stone
   Locally available stone (68.75% by count, 89.47% by wt)
      fine grain quartzitic sandstone
         debitage: 1 proximal flake (0.2 g)
      quartzite
         debitage: 8 proximal flakes (0.5 g)
      chert
         debitage: 1 proximal flake (4.4 g)
      organic limestone
         debitage: 1 fragment of flake shatter (< 0.1 g)
   Regionally available stone (25% by count, < 1% by wt)
      slate
         debitage: 3 proximal flakes (< 0.1 g)
      andesite
         debitage: 1 proximal flake (< 0.1 g)
   Exotic stone (6.25% by count, 10.53% by weight)
      obsidian
         tool: 1 hafted biface projectile point (0.6 g)

Botanical remains from flotation of 6.9 liters of soil (S-187)
   2 *Chenopodium quinoa* carbonized seeds
   4 *Brassica* sp. carbonized seeds

Botanical remains from flotation of 6.2 liters of soil (S-188)
   2 *Chenopodium quinoa* carbonized seeds
   2 *Ambrosia* sp. carbonized seeds
   2 *Zea mays* carbonized cupule fragments

Animal bone (NISP)
   Mammals
      llama or alpaca (*Lama* sp.): 3
      guinea pig (*Cavia porcellus*): 1
      field mouse (Muridae): 15 (all from flotation)
      unidentified: 16 (all from flotation)

Level F-2. The second stratum of soil in the hearth was compact ashy soil about 20 cm deep.

Munsell color
   7.5 YR 4/4 brown

Ceramic vessels
   Total sherds: 245
   Restricted vessels with a neck: 3 plainware
   Restricted vessels without a neck: 2 plainware, 3 pattern burnished
   Lid: 1 plainware
   Body sherd with diagnostic style: 1 Chanapata incised

Chipped stone
   Locally available stone (64.29% by count, 92.80% by wt)
      coarse grain quartzitic sandstone
         debitage: 1 proximal flake (1.3 g)
      quartzite
         tool: 1 unidirectional core (10.3 g)
         debitage: 5 proximal flakes (19.8 g), 2 fragments of angular shatter (15.0 g)
   Regionally available stone (28.57% by count, 6% by wt)
      slate
         debitage: 3 proximal flakes (< 0.1 g)
      rhyolite
         debitage: 1 proximal flake (3.0 g)
   Exotic stone (7.14% by count, 1.20% by weight)
      obsidian
         debitage: 1 fragment of angular shatter (0.6 g)

Botanical remains from flotation of 6.6 liters of ashy soil (S-114)
   8 *Chenopodium quinoa* carbonized seeds
   2 *Ambrosia* sp. carbonized seeds

Botanical remains from flotation of 4.7 liters of soil (S-128)
   1 *Chenopodium quinoa* carbonized seed

Animal bone (NISP)
   Mammals
      llama or alpaca (*Lama* sp.): 6
      guinea pig (*Cavia porcellus*): 3
      field mouse (Muridae): 13 (all from flotation)
      unidentified: 32 (all from flotation)

Level F-3. A layer of ashy soil about 20 cm deep filled the rest of the intrusion.

Munsell color
    7.5 YR 4/3 brown

Ceramic vessels
    Total sherds: 643
    Restricted vessels with a neck: 1 Chanapata redware,
      25 plainware
    Restricted vessels without a neck: 14 plainware
    Open vessels: 1 Chanapata redware, 1 Chanapata painted
      and incised, 7 plainware
    Lid: 1 plainware
    Body sherds with diagnostic style: 1 Chanapata blackware,
      3 pattern burnished

Chipped stone
    Locally available stone (77.78% by count, 99.77% by wt)
      coarse grain quartzitic sandstone
        tool: 1 bimarginal flake tool (177.9 g)
        debitage: 2 proximal flakes (114.4 g)
      fine grain quartzitic sandstone
        debitage: 2 proximal flakes (5.0 g)
      quartzite
        tools: 2 unimarginal flake tools (11.4 g), 1 bimarginal
          flake tool (4.6 g), 1 multidirectional core (20.8 g)
        debitage: 4 proximal flakes (4.7 g), 1 fragment of
          angular shatter (7.7 g)
    Regionally available stone (16.67% by count, < 1% by wt)
      slate
        debitage: 3 proximal flakes (< 0.1 g)
    Exotic stone (5.56% by count, 0.23% by weight)
      obsidian
        tool: 1 unimarginal flake tool (0.8 g)

Reworked ceramic sherd
    Non-disc: 1 plainware

Worked bone
    1 thin object with square cross section and pointed end

Groundstone
    Stone that could be pinched between the fingers with a flattened surface created by back and forth or circular strokes (Small Group 3, Type P). The stone measured 1.76 × 1.64 × 1.18 cm; it weighed 10 g.
    Nondescript fragment of a grinding stone that weighed 10 g.

Botanical remains from flotation of 6.7 liters of soil (S-111)
    1 *Oxalis* sp. carbonized seed

Botanical remains from flotation of 5.0 liters of soil (S-160)
    6 *Chenopodium quinoa* carbonized seeds
    2 *Ambrosia* sp. carbonized seeds

Animal bone (NISP)
    Mammals
      llama or alpaca (*Lama* sp.): 11
      guinea pig (*Cavia porcellus*): 1
      field mouse (Muridae): 16 (15 from flotation)
      unidentified: 32 (20 from flotation)
    Birds
      heron (Ardeidae): 1
    Amphibians
      toad (*Bufo* sp.): 1 (from flotation)

Level F-4. A narrow boot-shaped intrusion of loose ash intruded into Level F-3 and then into Levels F-2 and F-1. It was 40 cm from north to south, 20 cm from east to west and 44 cm deep.

Munsell color
    7.5 YR 3/3 dark brown

Ceramic vessels
    Total sherds: 42
    Restricted vessel without a neck: 1 plainware
    Open vessel: 1 plainware
    Body sherd with diagnostic style: 1 Chanapata incised

Chipped stone
    Locally available stone (44.44% by count, 99.08% by wt)
      quartzite
        debitage: 4 fragments of angular shatter (21.6 g)
    Regionally available stone (55.56% by count, 0.92% by wt)
      slate
        debitage: 4 proximal flakes (< 0.1 g)
      andesite
        debitage: 1 proximal flake (0.2 g)

Botanical remains from flotation of 1.3 liters of soil higher in the intrusion (S-129)
    3 *Chenopodium quinoa* carbonized seeds
    1 *Ambrosia* sp. carbonized seed

Botanical remains from flotation of 5.3 liters of soil lower in the intrusion (S-130)
    20 *Chenopodium quinoa* carbonized seeds
    6 Poaceae carbonized seeds

Animal bone (NISP)
    Mammals
      llama or alpaca (*Lama* sp.): 8 (7 from flotation)
      field mouse (Muridae): 9 (all from flotation)
      unidentified: 26 (2 from flotation)

Burial 19

Burial 19, an 11- to 12-year-old child of indeterminate sex, was buried in a cavity that cut down into Stratum 7. The body was tightly flexed and surrounded by a rectangle of stones (Fig. 3.15). There were no associated grave goods. The skeleton was in excellent condition and complete except for the cranium (100% completeness; Fig. 3.16). All other bones were found in the correct anatomical position, including fingers, toes, and all vertebrae. There were no cut marks to indicate that the cranium had been cut from the mandible or vertebra (Andrushko 2008).

This individual likely underwent at least two phases of mortuary treatment after his or her death. The presence of some upper teeth in the burial clearly demonstrates that the cranium was present in an early phase of funerary ritual. The absence of cut marks on the vertebrae and mandible indicates that the body must have been in an advanced state of decay when the cranium was removed. The soft tissue, including muscles and tendons, must have decayed sufficiently for the cranium to be taken without cutting and without disturbing the attached bones (Fig. 3.16). Yet, the soft tissue must have remained in place to prevent displacement of unstable articulations like those of the fingers and toes. This individual was the first person who was stored as a mummy before final burial at Yuthu (Burial Type 4).

Although scholars sometimes suggest that a tightly flexed position (like that of Burial 19) indicates that a body was wrapped as a bundle, taphonomic studies show that this can result from compression from the sediment covering the body during the decay process (Duday and Guillon 2006). Although the flexed position does not provide convincing evidence that the body was wrapped, keeping the mummy in a bundle would have provided an extra level of security against loss and would have allowed the targeted removal of the cranium without disturbing any other bones since the head would have been easily identifiable. If the bundle had been buried originally, even careful exhumation targeting a single bone would have disturbed other elements. Therefore, the mummy was probably stored in an accessible space before the cranium was removed. No evidence recovered at Yuthu indicates where the head was stored or how it was used after it was detached.

A Large Hearth in the Southwest Corner (Intrusion E)

A large outdoor hearth was located west of the above-ground domestic structure. The hearth was used sometime between 403 and 206 BC (calibrated), contemporary with the above-ground structure, which dated to 391–203 BC. The true length and width of the hearth are not known because it extended beyond the southern and western limits of the excavation unit. However, the dimensions of the excavated portion (2.73 m north to south and 2.68 m east to west) indicate that it was probably very large. The pit was filled with a series of ash layers and trampled surfaces, suggesting frequent and repetitive use. Unworked field stones were arranged to support a cooking pot, or *olla,* at the base of the feature. Therefore, the feature was probably used as an open cooking pit, rather than a buried roasting pit. *Markhu* was likely used as fuel.

Most cooking took place in restricted vessels with a neck. (There were more than 7 sherds of this form for each fragment of restricted vessels without a neck.) Although there were relatively more cooking and storage vessels compared with serving forms (5 sherds of closed vessels for every 1 sherd of an open vessel), it is likely that both preparation and consumption took place in this area. There were several one- and two-handed grinding stones, smaller stones held between the fingers, and flat base stones for food preparation and other grinding activities. Carbonized plant foods included quinoa and corn. The meat remains were varied; they included not only camelid and *cuy*, but also duck, coot, and white-tailed deer.

The discarded or lost remnants of craft production activities indicate that the hearth was the main attraction in a generalized outdoor activity area where people gathered to eat, socialize, and work. At least two steps in textile production likely took place in this area. *Galium*, a plant used to dye fiber, was fairly common, and we found a bone sword, which could have been used to weave. Like the other large outdoor hearth, this area contained many finished obsidian projectile points and formal tools that were probably used to make unknown (probably perishable) items. Large cores and several large flakes of quartzitic sandstone and quartzite were the remains of primary reduction of chipped stone tools made from locally available materials (Figs. 3.17, 3.19; Plate 3). Pre-formed fragments of long bones and finished pointed bone tools indicate bone tool manufacture in this area (Figs. 3.18, 3.20). *Scirpus* and Poaceae may have been used to make basketry or other items.

The strata that filled the hearth are described below, starting with the earliest deposits.

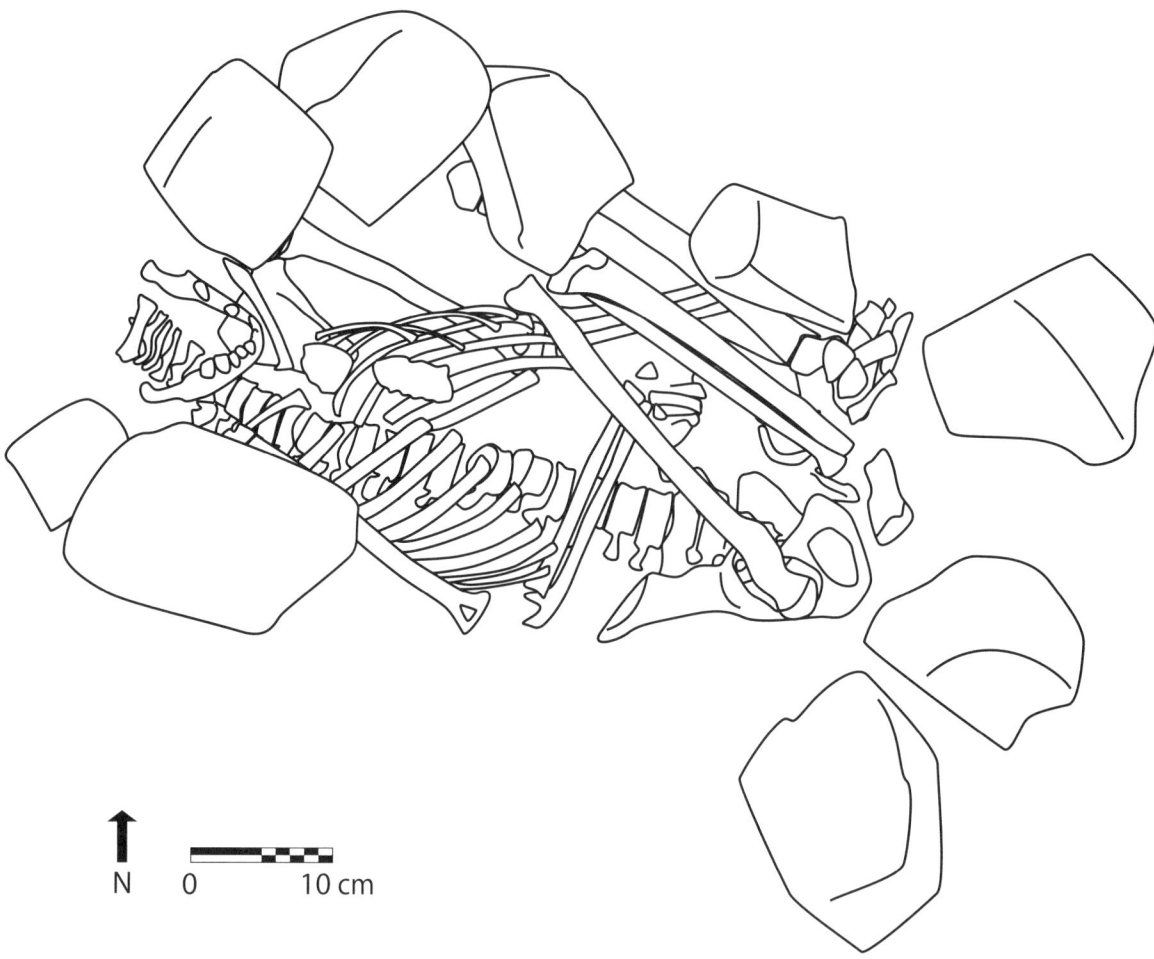

Figure 3.15. Burial 19 was an 11- to 12-year-old child, in a tightly flexed position, that was complete except for the cranium.

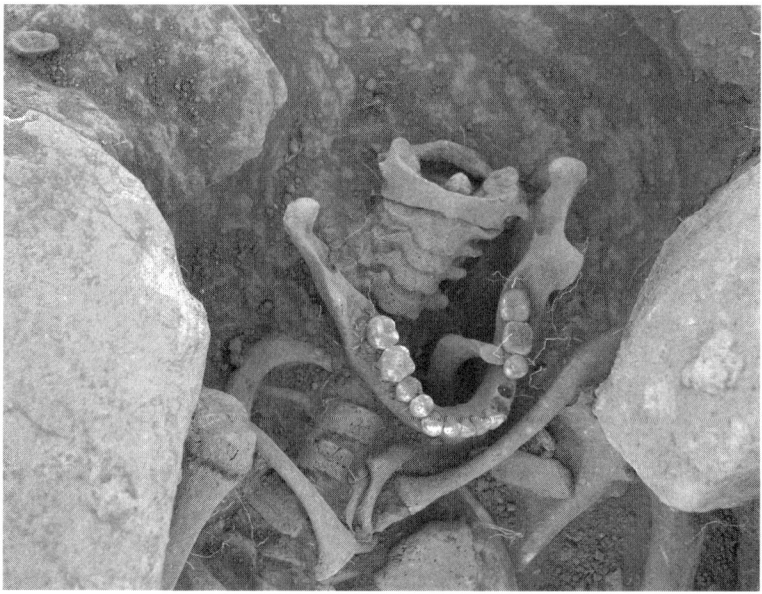

Figure 3.16. The cranium of Burial 19 was removed without disturbing any of the surrounding bones.

Figure 3.17. Several chipped stone tools were in Level E-7 (*left to right starting at the top*): obsidian unimarginal flake tool, obsidian combination flake tool, obsidian bimarginal flake tool projectile point, obsidian multidirectional core tool, obsidian unimarginal flake tool reutilized projectile point, chert combination flake tool, quartzite unidirectional core, quartzite multidirectional core, quartzite bimarginal flake tool, laminar andesite bimarginal flake tool.

Figure 3.18. Worked bone from Level E-7: *a*, one pointed tool made from a long bone shaft (*bottom*) and five unworked shaft fragments that may have been preforms for making similar tools; these bones were all found near Trampled Surface E-1; *b, c*, broad, flat pointed tools made from long bone shaft fragments; *d*, a tool with a pointed tip off to one side made from a long bone shaft.

Figure 3.19. Chipped stone from Level E-10 of the hearth in the southwest corner (*left to right*): obsidian bimarginal flake tool projectile point, unimarginal flake tool projectile point, multidirectional core reutilized projectile point.

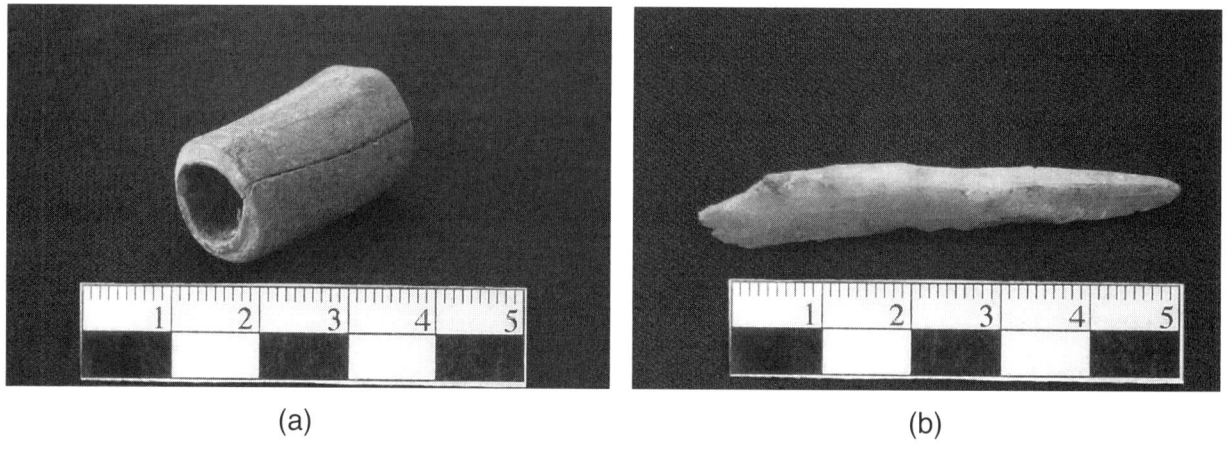

Figure 3.20. Worked bone from Level E-10 of the hearth in the southwest corner: *a*, a tubular bead made from a long bone shaft; *b*, a long bone shaft fragment with pointed tip.

Trampled Surface E-1[1]

Trampled Surface E-1 formed on top of the exposed surface of Stratum 17; it was 45 cm north to south and 50 cm east to west. This feature was excavated along with Level E-7.

Munsell color
10 YR 4/2 dark grayish brown

No artifacts were analyzed from this feature.

Trampled Surface E-2

Trampled Surface E-2 formed on top of the exposed surface of Stratum 17. It comprised two sections of floor that measured 1.57 m from northwest to southeast and 46 cm from southwest to northeast.

Munsell color
7.5 YR 4/3 brown

Ceramic vessels
Total sherds: 17
Restricted vessels with a neck: 1 Chanapata blackware, 1 plainware
Body sherd with diagnostic style: 1 Chanapata blackware

Chipped stone
Exotic stone (100% by count and weight)
obsidian
debitage: 1 proximal flake (< 0.1 g)

Botanical remains from flotation of 5.6 liters of soil (S-184)
8 *Chenopodium quinoa* carbonized seeds

Animal bone (NISP)
Mammals
field mouse (Muridae): 4 (all from flotation)
unidentified: 19 (all from flotation)

Trampled Surface E-3

Trampled Surface E-3 formed on top of the exposed surface of Stratum 20. It extended beyond the unit's southwest corner, but the excavated portion measured 1.4 m north to south by 2 cm east to west.

Ceramic vessels
Total sherds: 282
Restricted vessels with a neck: 2 Chanapata redware, 12 plainware
Restricted vessel without a neck: 1 plainware
Open vessels: 2 Chanapata redware
Body sherds with diagnostic style: 5 Chanapata redware, 2 Chanapata blackware

Reworked ceramic sherds
Discs: 2 plainware

Chipped stone
Locally available stone (83.33% by count, 100% by wt)
fine grain quartzitic sandstone
debitage: 1 proximal flake (< 0.1 g)
quartzite
debitage: 2 proximal flakes (3.7 g), 1 fragment of angular shatter (18.3 g)
Exotic stone (16.67% by count, < 1% by weight)
obsidian
debitage: 1 proximal flake (< 0.1 g)

Groundstone
Small oval stone with plano-convex cross section that could be held between the fingers (Small Group 2, Type O). The stone measured 6.00 × 3.65 × 3.25 cm; it weighed 100 g.

Grinding stone that fit in one hand with plano-convex cross section and flattened surfaces created by grinding with back and forth and rocking motions (Group 1, Type B). The stone had pecking marks. It measured 10.88 × 9.20 × 3.98 cm; it weighed 660 g.

Nondescript fragment of a grinding stone that weighed 30 g.

Botanical remains from flotation of 5.7 liters of soil (S-173)
24 *Chenopodium quinoa* carbonized seeds
3 *Ambrosia* sp. carbonized seeds
2 *Zea mays* carbonized seeds
1 *Scirpus* sp. carbonized seed

Animal bone (NISP)
Mammals
llama or alpaca (*Lama* sp.): 7 (6 from flotation)
field mouse (Muridae): 4 (all from flotation)
unidentified: 25 (17 from flotation)

Level E-4

Level E-4 was very ashy, gray soil 10 cm deep that included rocks arranged to support a cooking pot.

Munsell color
   10 YR 5/2 grayish brown

Ceramic vessels
   Total sherds: 375
   Restricted vessels with a neck: 1 Chanapata redware, 8 plainware
   Open vessels: 3 Chanapata redware, 5 plainware
   Body sherds with diagnostic style: 11 Chanapata redware, 2 Chanapata blackware, 2 pattern burnished

Reworked ceramic sherds
   Discs: 2 plainware
   Non-disc: 1 plainware

Chipped stone
   Locally available stone (20% by count, 17.53% by weight)
      quartzite
         tool: 1 unimarginal flake tool (1.7 g)
         debitage: 1 proximal flake (< 0.1 g)
   Regionally available stone (10% by count, 65.98% by wt)
      microdiorite
         tool: 1 unimarginal flake tool (6.4 g)
   Exotic stone (70% by count, 16.49% by weight)
      obsidian
         tool: 1 unimarginal flake tool (1.5 g)
         debitage: 6 proximal flakes (0.1 g)

Worked bone
   1 broad, flat long bone shaft fragment with square tip (possibly a weaving sword)

Groundstone
   Roughly spherical stone that fit into one hand with flattened surfaces created by grinding with back and forth or circular strokes (Group 1, Type A). The stone had pecking marks. It measured 6.88 × 6.08 × 5.56; it weighed 320 g.
   Roughly spherical stone that fit into one hand with flattened surfaces created by grinding with back and forth or circular strokes (Group 1, Type A). The stone had pecking marks. It measured 7.11 × 6.93 × 5.41; it weighed 340 g.
   Roughly spherical stone that fit into one hand with flattened surfaces created by grinding with back and forth or circular strokes (Group 1, Type A). The stone had pecking marks. It measured 9.98 × 7.21 × 5.42; it weighed 500 g.
   Roughly spherical stone that fit into one hand with flattened surfaces created by grinding with back and forth or circular strokes (Group 1, Type A). It measured 9.69 × 7.81 × 5.27; it weighed 520 g.

   Fragment of a grinding stone that fit in two hands with plano-convex cross section and flattened surfaces created by grinding with back and forth and rocking motions (Group 1, Type C). The length and height were unknown; it was 7.21 cm wide. The fragment weighed 530 g.

Botanical remains from flotation of 4.5 liters of soil (S-174)
   8 *Chenopodium quinoa* carbonized seeds
   2 *Galium* sp. carbonized seeds
   2 *Ambrosia* sp. carbonized cupule fragments

Botanical remains from flotation of 5.2 liters of soil (S-159)
   1 *Amaranthus* sp. carbonized seed
   8 *Chenopodium quinoa* carbonized seeds
   4 *Galium* sp. carbonized seeds

Animal bone (NISP)
   Mammals
      llama or alpaca (*Lama* sp.): 17 (1 from flotation)
      field mouse (Muridae): 38 (all from flotation)
      unidentified: 11 (3 from flotation)

Level E-5

Level E-5 was gray soil about 6 cm thick composed primarily of ash. It was associated with a few unworked stones that were arranged to support a cooking pot.

Munsell color
   7.5 YR 4/2 brown

Ceramic vessels
   Total sherds: 540
   Restricted vessels with a neck: 20 plainware
   Open vessels: 1 Chanapata redware, 2 plainware
   Body sherds with diagnostic style: 5 Chanapata redware, 3 pattern burnished

Chipped stone
   Exotic stone (100% by count and weight)
      obsidian
         debitage: 4 proximal flakes (< 0.1 g)

Groundstone
   Stone that could be pinched between the fingers with a flattened surface created by back and forth or circular strokes (Small Group 3, Type P). The stone measured 5.35 × 3.85 × 3.29 cm; it weighed 90 g.

Botanical remains from flotation of 5.0 liters of soil (S-155)
   18 *Chenopodium quinoa* carbonized seeds
   6 *Galium* sp. carbonized seeds
   8 *Ambrosia* sp. carbonized seeds
   7 *Zea mays* carbonized cupule fragments

Animal bone (NISP)
    Mammals
        llama or alpaca (*Lama* sp.): 50 (47 from flotation)
        unidentified: 6

Trampled Surface E-6

Trampled Surface E-6 formed on the surface of Level E-5. It was 60 cm north to south by 65 cm east to west.

Munsell color
    7.5 YR 5/1 gray

Ceramic vessels
    Total sherds: 6
    Body sherd with diagnostic style: 1 pattern burnished

Botanical remains from flotation of 1.9 liters of soil (S-154)
    4 *Chenopodium quinoa* carbonized seeds
    1 *Galium* sp. carbonized seed
    2 Poaceae carbonized seeds
    1 *Scirpus* sp. carbonized seed

Animal bone (NISP)
    Mammals
        llama or alpaca (*Lama* sp.): 1 (from flotation)
        unidentified: 4 (all from flotation)

Level E-7

Level E-7 was a layer of very ashy loose soil that was 12 cm deep. This stratum contained several finished, pointed long bone shaft tools as well as several bones that might have been preforms for these tools (Fig. 3.18). Therefore, bone tool manufacture probably took place near the hearth, perhaps utilizing bones from the same animals that were being cooked. The stratum also contained several chipped stone tools and debitage that may have been the remains of other craft production activities (Fig. 3.17; Plate 3).

Munsell color
    10 YR 4/2 dark grayish brown

Radiocarbon date
    AA84434\Yuthu RC-214, 2329 ± 37 uncalibrated radiocarbon years BP, 403–206 BC calibrated without modeling (95.4% confidence)

Ceramic vessels
    Total sherds: 2524
    Restricted vessels with a neck: 1 Chanapata redware, 84 plainware
    Restricted vessels without a neck: 17 plainware
    Open vessels: 1 Chanapata redware, 13 plainware
    Open vessels with a diameter greater than 30 cm: 1 Chanapata redware, 3 plainware
    Lids: 2 Chanapata incised
    Body sherds with diagnostic style: 16 Chanapata redware, 3 Chanapata blackware, 2 Chanapata incised, 44 pattern burnished

Reworked ceramic sherds
    Non-discs: 4 plainware

Chipped stone
    Locally available stone (59.26% by count, 95.05% by wt)
        coarse grain quartzitic sandstone
            tools: 1 unimarginal flake tool (22.0 g), 1 unidirectional core (23.3 g)
            debitage: 2 proximal flakes (97.6 g)
        quartzite
            tools: 1 bimarginal flake tool (5.7 g), 1 unidirectional core (46.3 g), 1 multidirectional core (34.4 g)
            debitage: 3 proximal flakes (19.2 g), 1 fragment of flake shatter (3.0 g), 3 fragments of angular shatter (10.2 g)
        chert
            tools: 1 combination flake tool (2.3 g), 1 multidirectional core (12.5 g)
    Regionally available stone (3.70% by count, 2.92% by wt)
        andesite
            tool: 1 bimarginal flake tool (8.5 g)
    Exotic stone (37.04% by count, 2.03% by weight)
        obsidian
            tools: 3 unimarginal flake tools (2.0 g), 1 unimarginal flake tool reutilized projectile point (0.7 g), 1 bimarginal flake tool projectile point (1.8 g), 1 combination flake tool (< 0.1 g), 1 multidirectional core (1.4 g)
            debitage: 3 proximal flakes (< 0.1 g)

Worked bone
    4 broad, flat long bone shaft fragments with pointed tips
    1 broad, flat long bone shaft fragment with pointed end off to one side

Groundstone

Small oval stone with plano-convex cross section that could be held between the fingers (Small Group 2, Type O). The stone had pecking marks. It measured 5.90 × 2.83 × 1.96 cm; it weighed 50 g.

Stone that could be pinched between the fingers with a flattened surface created by back and forth or circular strokes (Small Group 3, Type P). The stone measured 2.55 × 1.83 × 1.33 cm; it weighed 10 g.

Unmodified flat stone that may have been used as a base for small-scale grinding or pulverizing. Length and width were unknown. The stone was 8.7 cm thick and weighed 30 g.

Unmodified flat stone that may have been used as a base for small-scale grinding or pulverizing. Length was unknown; the stone was 4.49 cm wide and 1.23 cm thick. The fragment weighed 20 g.

Nondescript fragment of a grinding stone that weighed 20 g.

Botanical remains from flotation of 5.1 liters of soil (S-132)
    24 *Chenopodium quinoa* carbonized seeds
    1 *Galium* sp. carbonized seed
    3 *Ambrosia* sp. carbonized seeds

Botanical remains from flotation of 5.5 liters of soil (S-146)
    3 *Chenopodium quinoa* carbonized seeds
    1 *Galium* sp. carbonized seed

Animal bone (NISP)
    Mammals
        llama or alpaca (*Lama* sp.): 72
        white-tailed deer (*Odocoileus virginianus*): 2
        guinea pig (*Cavia porcellus*): 8
        unidentified: 86 (54 from flotation)
    Birds
        duck (*Anas* sp.): 2
        coot (*Fulica* sp.): 1
        unidentified: 1

Trampled Surface E-8

Two trampled surfaces formed along the western limit of the hearth feature. Trampled Surface E-8 was the stratigraphically lower of these two floors and formed on the surface of Level E-7. The floor extended beyond the western limit of Unit D, so its width is not known. However, the excavated portion measured 70 cm east to west and 60 cm north to south.

Munsell color
    7.5 YR 4/4 brown

Ceramic vessels
    Total sherds: 10
    Restricted vessel with a neck: 1 plainware
    Restricted vessel without a neck: 1 plainware
    Body sherd with diagnostic style: 1 pattern burnished

Botanical remains from flotation of 6.2 liters of soil (S-157)
    12 *Chenopodium quinoa* carbonized seeds
    4 *Ambrosia* sp. carbonized seeds
    6 *Zea mays* carbonized seeds
    2 *Scirpus* sp. carbonized seeds

Animal bone (NISP)
    Mammals
        guinea pig (*Cavia porcellus*): 2 (all from flotation)
        unidentified: 8 (all from flotation)

Trampled Surface E-9

Trampled Surface E-9 formed on top of Trampled Surface E-8. It was 60 cm long, but only 10 cm extended out from the western profile, so it was not excavated.

Munsell color
    7.5 YR 4/4 brown

No artifacts were recovered from this feature.

Level E-10

Level E-10 was dirt mixed with ash and bits of charcoal 22 cm deep.

Munsell color
    7.5 YR 2/4 brown

Ceramic vessels
    Total sherds: 526
    Restricted vessels with a neck: 20 plainware, 2 pattern burnished
    Restricted vessels without a neck: 1 Chanapata redware, 1 plainware
    Open vessels: 2 Chanapata redware, 1 plainware
    Body sherds with diagnostic style: 2 Chanapata redware, 1 pattern burnished

Reworked ceramic sherds
    Non-discs: 2 plainware

Chipped stone
    Locally available stone (18.75% by count, < 1% by wt)
        quartzite
            debitage: 3 proximal flakes (< 0.1 g)
    Regionally available stone (6.25% by count, 2.56% by wt)
        andesite
            debitage: 1 proximal flake (< 0.1 g)
    Exotic stone (75.00% by count, 97.44% by weight)
        obsidian (Fig. 3.19)
            tools: 1 unimarginal flake tool reutilized projectile point (0.4 g), 1 bimarginal flake tool projectile point (0.3 g), 1 multidirectional core reutilized projectile point (1.1 g)
            debitage: 7 proximal flakes (0.4 g), 2 fragments of flake shatter (1.6 g)

Worked bone (Fig. 3.20)
  1 tubular bead
  1 broad, flat long bone shaft fragment with pointed tip

Metal
  A very small fragment of metal was found in the heavy fraction of S-115 from Level E-10. It was 1.9 mm long and 0.6 mm in diameter. It weighed less than 0.1 g.

Botanical remains from flotation of 5.4 liters of soil (S-115)
  No identifiable plant remains were recovered from this sample

Botanical remains from flotation of 5.43 liters of soil (S-144)
  20 *Chenopodium quinoa* carbonized seeds
  1 *Galium* sp. carbonized seed
  2 *Ambrosia* sp. carbonized seeds
  2 *Zea mays* carbonized seeds

Animal bone (NISP)
  Mammals
    llama or alpaca (*Lama* sp.): 29 (7 from flotation)
    guinea pig (*Cavia porcellus*): 3
    field mouse (Muridae): 8 (all from flotation)
    unidentified: 52 (35 from flotation)
  Birds
    duck (*Anas* sp.): 1
    coot (*Fulica* sp.): 1
    unidentified: 4 (2 from flotation)

Trampled Surface E-11

A trampled surface formed on top of Level E-10. It was 72 cm from north to south, but it was not excavated because only 7 cm extended into Unit D. This was the last deposit that formed while the intrusion was used as a cooking hearth.

Munsell color
  7.5 YR 4/4 brown

No artifacts were recovered from this level.

Later Circular Intrusions and Ashy Deposits

Unit D contained storage pits and ashy deposits that were stratigraphically later than the above-ground house and hearth (Fig. 3.21). While the earliest pit (Intrusion D) was filled with domestic trash, the later pit and ashy deposits lacked high densities of food remains and may have been used for non-cooking activities. It is possible that these features were associated with a house located outside the limits of Unit D. In fact, stones in the southwest corner may have been the foundation of a rectangular above-ground structure just south of the unit. Of course, it is also possible that these activities were not associated with a domestic occupation and that the deposits were made after people no longer lived at the site. Further excavation will be necessary to understand village occupation and abandonment at Yuthu.

Circular Pit (Intrusion D)

A cylindrical intrusion cut through Stratum 4 into Ashy Intrusions 1 and 2 in the northwest corner. It was 110 cm east to west, 95 cm north to south, and 62 cm deep. It seems likely that this intrusion was used as a storage pit. Then after it was abandoned, the intrusion was filled with discarded construction materials and other rubbish. Based on the high density of carbonized seeds and animal bone, the trash probably included ash removed from a hearth during cleaning. Field mice were probably drawn to organic matter in the pit.

The strata that filled the intrusion are described below, starting with the earliest or stratigraphically lowest.

Level D-1

Several rocks and an adobe brick broken into two large pieces rested on the bottom of the intrusion. Those items were surrounded by a stratum of semi-compact brown soil about 15 cm deep. This level had a high density of carbonized quinoa seeds, but there were no other carbonized plant remains.

Munsell color
  5 YR 4/3 reddish brown

Ceramic vessels
  Total sherds: 101
  Restricted vessels with a neck: 1 Chanapata incised,
    5 plainware
  Open vessel with a diameter greater than 30 cm:
    1 Chanapata redware
  Body sherds with diagnostic style: 1 Chanapata blackware,
    4 pattern burnished

Reworked ceramic sherds
  Discs: 2 plainware

Chipped stone
  Locally available stone (87.50% by count, 100% by wt)
    quartzite
      debitage: 3 proximal flakes (3.1 g), 3 fragments of
        angular shatter (28.0 g)
    chert
      tool: 1 multidirectional core (1.7 g)
  Regionally available stone (12.50% by count, < 1% by wt)
    slate
      debitage: 1 proximal flake (< 0.1 g)

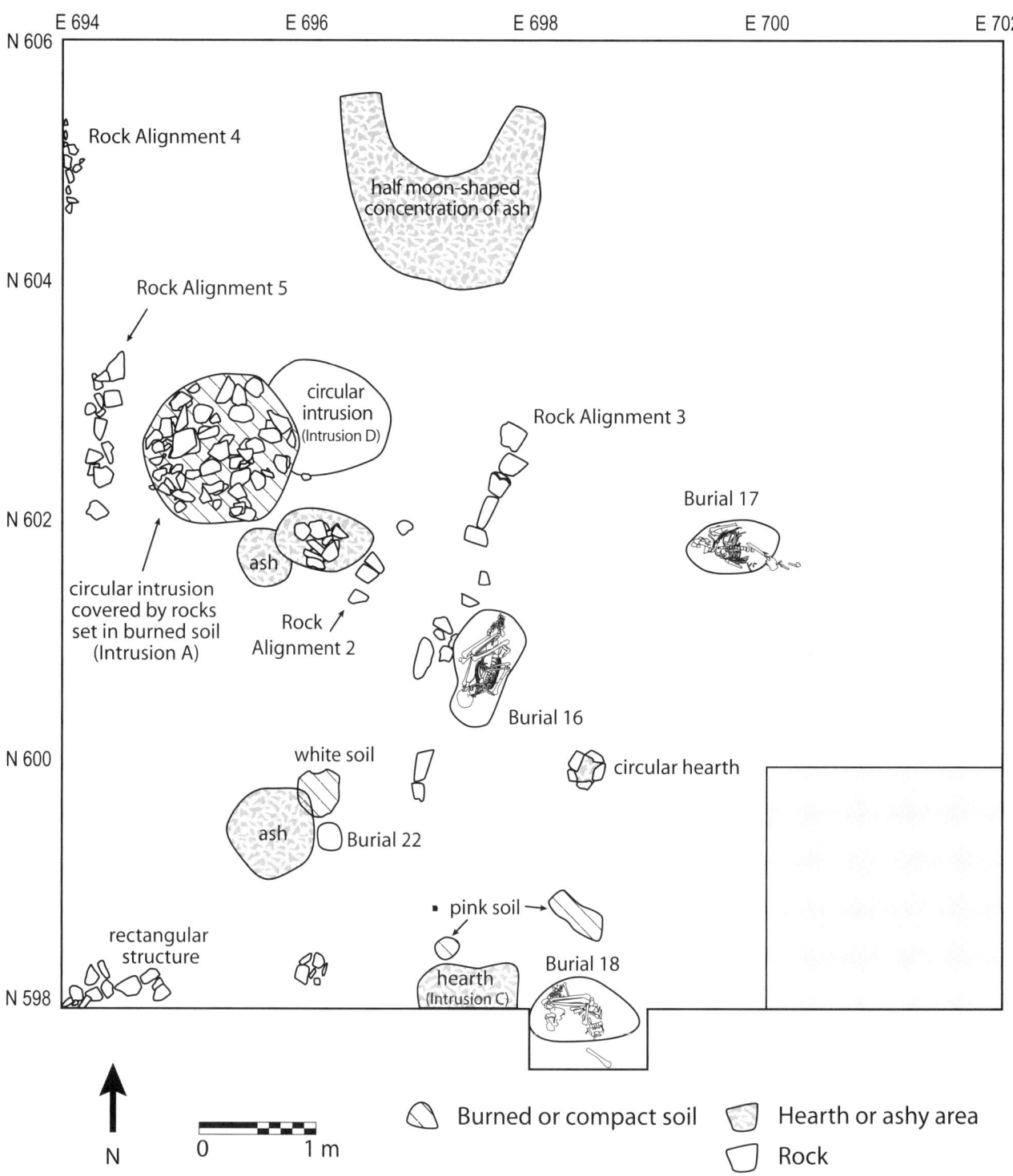

Figure 3.21. The final phase of use in Unit D included a half-moon-shaped ash deposit in the northwest corner, two circular intrusions, four stone alignments, a small hearth along the southern profile, and several small deposits of ash and colored soil. Four human burials were associated with a small circular stone hearth including the mummy burial of a 26- to 35-year-old man (Burial 16), a 16- to 17-year-old young woman (Burial 17), a 26- to 35-year-old woman (Burial 18), and an infant (Burial 22).

Botanical remains from flotation of 7.1 liters of soil (S-124)
  60 *Chenopodium quinoa* carbonized seeds

Animal bone (NISP)
  Mammals
    llama or alpaca (*Lama* sp.): 3
    field mouse (Muridae): 32 (30 from flotation)
    unidentified: 2 (all from flotation)

Level D-2

Level D-2 was a layer of loose brown dirt about 20 cm deep that covered the tops of loose stones.

Munsell color
  7.5 YR 5/2 brown

Ceramic vessels
  Total sherds: 218
  Restricted vessels with a neck: 13 plainware
  Restricted vessels without a neck: 4 plainware
  Lid: 1 plainware
  Body sherds with diagnostic style: 3 Chanapata redware, 3 pattern burnished

Chipped stone
  Locally available stone (33.33% by count, 96.81% by wt)
    fine grain quartzitic sandstone
      debitage: 3 proximal flakes (8.0 g)
    quartzite
      debitage: 1 proximal flake (1.1 g)
  Regionally available stone (50.00% by count, 3.19% by wt)
    slate
      debitage: 6 proximal flakes (0.3 g)
  Exotic stone (16.67% by count, < 1% by weight)
    obsidian
      debitage: 2 proximal flakes (< 0.1 g)

Worked bone
  1 carved bone

Groundstone
  Roughly spherical stone that fit into one hand with flattened surfaces created by grinding with back and forth or circular strokes (Group 1, Type A). The stone had pecking marks. It measured 7.93 × 7.07 × 5.87 cm; it weighed 420 g.
  Roughly spherical stone that fit into one hand with flattened surfaces created by grinding with back and forth or circular strokes (Group 1, Type A). The stone had pecking marks. It measured 8.66 × 7.41 × 5.16 cm; it weighed 480 g.
  Fragment of an oval stone with rectangular cross section created by rocking the stone side to side along its edge (Group 2, Type D). About 20% of the object was present. The length and width were unknown; it was 4.72 cm tall. The fragment weighed 300 g.
  Nondescript fragment of a grinding stone that weighed 10 g.

Botanical remains from flotation of 6.9 liters of soil lower in the level (S-120)
  14 *Chenopodium quinoa* carbonized seeds
  2 *Zea mays* carbonized cupule fragments
  1 *Scirpus* sp. carbonized seed

Botanical remains from flotation of 7.2 liters of soil higher in the level (S-119)
  14 *Chenopodium quinoa* carbonized seeds
  1 *Galium* sp. carbonized seed
  1 *Ambrosia* sp. carbonized seed

Animal bone (NISP)
  Mammals
    llama or alpaca (*Lama* sp.): 12 (3 from flotation)
    white-tailed deer (*Odocoileus virginianus*): 1
    field mouse (Muridae): 5 (all from flotation)
    unidentified: 50 (46 from flotation)
  Birds
    duck (*Anas* sp.): 1
    unidentified: 1

Level D-3

Level D-3 was a round deposit of compact brown soil about the same shape as the intrusion, but smaller with a diameter of 80 cm. It cut into Level D-2 and was 15 cm deep.

Munsell color
  7.5 YR 4/3 brown

Ceramic vessels
  Total sherds: 60
  Restricted vessels with a neck: 2 plainware

Chipped stone
  Locally available stone (100% by count and weight)
    quartzite
      tool: 1 unidirectional core (11.7 g)
      debitage: 1 fragment of angular shatter (12.2 g)

Animal bone (NISP)
  Mammals
    unidentified: 2

A Circular Intrusion Covered by Rocks Set in Burned Soil (Intrusion A)

A second circular intrusion (78 cm deep) cut through Stratum 3 and the earlier circular intrusion (Fig. 3.22). It was covered by rocks set in hard, burned soil that measured 130 cm east to west and 135 cm north to south. The rocks were mostly loose field stones, but also included a mortar for grinding with a deep circular depression. Under the hard cap, we found a variety of non-food plants. Many could have been used for fuel (quinoa and *Ambrosia*) or forage (Poaceae and *Trifolium*). There were also plants for dye and/or medicine (*Galium* and *Verbena*). There were some camelid and field mouse bones. Most pottery vessels were restricted with a neck, and the intrusion held several grinding stones. Nearly all chipped stone items were flakes (rather than formal tools) made of local, regional, and exotic materials. This feature is intriguing because it is unlike any other that we found at Yuthu, but it is very difficult to understand its purpose.

The intrusion was filled with several layers of soil that are described below, starting with the earliest, or stratigraphically lowest, and ending with the cap of burned earth and rocks.

Figure 3.22. The circular intrusion covered by rocks set in burned soil cut into Stratum 3 and the earlier circular intrusion. The hole in the center of the stones was soil removed for a flotation sample.

Level A-1

The deepest level in this intrusion was light brown semi-compact soil with flecks of charcoal 3 cm deep.

Munsell color
    7.5 YR 5/3 brown

Ceramic vessels
    Total sherds: 23
    No diagnostic sherds were recovered from this context

Chipped stone
    Locally available stone (25% by count, 100% by weight)
        quartzite
            debitage: 2 proximal flakes (0.3 g)
    Regionally available stone (25% by count, < 1% by wt)
        slate
            debitage: 1 proximal flake (< 0.1 g)
        rhyolite
            debitage: 1 proximal flake (< 0.1 g)
    Exotic stone (50% by count, < 1% by weight)
        obsidian
            debitage: 4 proximal flakes (< 0.1 g)

Botanical remains from flotation of 6.0 liters of soil (S-179)
    18 *Chenopodium quinoa* carbonized seeds
    2 *Verbena* sp. carbonized seeds

Animal bone (NISP)
    Mammals
        llama or alpaca (*Lama* sp.): 2
        field mouse (Muridae): 2 (all from flotation)
        unidentified: 14 (all from flotation)

Level A-2

A narrow strip of loose, light brown soil cut into Level A-1 along the western side of the intrusion. It was 40 cm east to west, 90 cm north to south, and 3 cm deep.

Munsell color
    7.5 YR 4/4 brown

Ceramic vessels
    Total sherds: 6
    Open vessel: 1 plainware
    Body sherd with diagnostic style: 1 pattern burnished

Chipped stone
    Locally available stone (60% by count, 100% by weight)
        fine grain quartzitic sandstone
            debitage: 1 proximal flake (0.2 g)
        quartzite
            debitage: 2 proximal flakes (< 0.1 g)
    Exotic stone (40% by count, < 1% by weight)
        obsidian
            debitage: 1 proximal flake (< 0.1 g), 1 fragment of angular shatter (< 0.1 g)

Botanical remains from flotation of 6.2 liters of soil (S-178)
    26 *Chenopodium quinoa* carbonized seeds

Level A-3

A layer of reddish brown soil 15 cm deep included some burned earth, which was taken as a flotation sample.

Munsell color
    5 YR 5/3 reddish brown

Ceramic vessels
    Total sherds: 99
    Restricted vessels with a neck: 5 plainware
    Restricted vessel without a neck: 1 plainware
    Open vessel: 1 plainware
    Body sherds with diagnostic style: 4 Chanapata blackware, 1 Chanapata incised

Chipped stone
    Locally available stone (100% by count and weight)
        quartzite
            debitage: 2 proximal flakes (< 0.1 g)
        chert
            debitage: 1 proximal flake (0.1 g)

Groundstone
    Fragment of a grinding stone that fit in one hand with plano-convex cross section and flattened surfaces created by grinding with back and forth and rocking motions (Group 1, Type B). About 50% of the object was present. Length was unknown; it was 8.35 cm wide and 3.45 cm tall. The fragment weighed 280 g.

Botanical remains from flotation of 6.3 liters of soil (S-177)
    6 *Chenopodium quinoa* carbonized seeds
    1 *Trifolium* sp. carbonized seed
    1 *Galium* sp. carbonized seed
    1 *Ambrosia* sp. carbonized seed
    3 Poaceae carbonized seeds

Animal bone (NISP)
    Mammals
        llama or alpaca (*Lama* sp.): 1
        unidentified: 9 (7 from flotation)

Level A-4

Level A-4 was very hard, burned earth 50 cm thick with inset rocks forming an uneven circular surface. The stones included unworked field stones, grinding stones, and mortars.

Munsell color
    5 YR 5/3 reddish brown

Ceramic vessels
    Total sherds: 373
    Restricted vessels with a neck: 12 plainware
    Restricted vessel without a neck: 1 plainware
    Open vessels: 1 Chanapata redware, 4 plainware
    Body sherds with diagnostic style: 4 Chanapata redware, 2 Chanapata blackware, 1 Chanapata incised, 1 pattern burnished

Chipped stone
    Locally available stone (88.89% by count, 100% by wt)
        coarse grain quartzitic sandstone
            debitage: 2 proximal flakes (12.9 g)
        fine grain quartzitic sandstone
            debitage: 3 proximal flakes (25.5 g), 3 fragments of angular shatter (28.1 g)
        quartzite
            tools: 1 unimarginal flake tool (3.6 g), 1 unidirectional core (3.5 g)
            debitage: 3 proximal flakes (5.7 g), 3 fragments of angular shatter (8.4 g)
    Regionally available stone (5.56% by count, < 1% by wt)
        andesite
            debitage: 1 proximal flake (< 0.1 g)
    Exotic stone (5.56% by count, < 1% by weight)
        obsidian
            debitage: 1 fragment of angular shatter (< 0.1 g)

Worked bone
    2 tube-shaped beads

Groundstone

Fragment of a grinding stone that fit in two hands with plano-convex cross section and flattened surfaces created by grinding with back and forth and rocking motions (Group 1, Type C). About 80% of the object was present. The length was unknown; it was 8.74 cm wide and 6.30 cm tall. The fragment weighed 1 kg.

Stone that could be pinched between the fingers with a flattened surface created by back and forth or circular strokes (Small Group 3, Type P). The stone measured 5.21 × 3.97 × 2.94 cm; it weighed 90 g.

A grinding slab with a concave surface and an additional deep cuplike grinding surface that could have been used as a mortar for a pestle. This stone was set into hard mud mortar.

Botanical remains from flotation of 6.1 liters of soil (S-104)
    1 *Chenopodium quinoa* carbonized seed
    1 *Ambrosia* sp. carbonized seed

Animal bone (NISP)
    Mammals
        llama or alpaca (*Lama* sp.): 11
        field mouse (Muridae): 37 (29 from flotation)
        unidentified: 7

Ashy Intrusion 1 in the Northwest Corner (Intrusion B)

Ashy Intrusion 1 cut into Stratum 3. It was 2.9 m north to south by 2.11 m east to west and about 30 cm deep. This ashy feature was the latest of three that were located in roughly the same location. Compared with the earlier ash deposits in this area, the density of food remains was low. In fact, all of the carbonized plants recovered could have been used as fuel, and although field mice were typically found in areas with high organic content at Yuthu, there were none in this feature. We did find grinding stones, bone tools, and a variety of chipped stone objects. Although the burning in this area was probably not for cooking food, it is difficult to determine what the primary activity might have been.

The strata that filled the intrusion are described below, starting with the stratigraphically lowest deposit.

Level B-1

The lowest level that filled in this intrusion was 18 cm of dark gray semi-compact ash.

Munsell color
    10 YR 4/2 dark grayish brown

Ceramic vessels
    Total sherds: 200
    Restricted vessels with a neck: 8 plainware
    Restricted vessel without a neck: 1 plainware
    Open vessels: 4 plainware
    Body sherd with diagnostic style: 1 pattern burnished

Chipped stone
    Locally available stone (30% by count, 10.64% by weight)
        fine grain quartzitic sandstone
            tool: 1 unimarginal flake tool (0.3 g)
        quartzite
            debitage: 2 proximal flakes (0.2 g)
    Regionally available stone (20% by count, < 1% by weight)
        andesite
            debitage: 2 proximal flakes (< 0.1 g)

Exotic stone (50% by count, 89.36% by weight)
  obsidian
    tools: 1 unhafted biface reutilized projectile point (1.8 g), 1 bimarginal flake tool (2.4 g)
    debitage: 3 proximal flakes (< 0.1 g)

Worked bone
1 broad, flat long bone shaft fragment with pointed tip

Groundstone
Fragment of a roughly spherical stone that fit into one hand with flattened surfaces created by grinding with back and forth or circular strokes (Group 1, Type A). The stone had pecking marks. About 45% of the object was present. It was 7.92 cm long and 7.12 cm wide; the height was unknown. The fragment weighed 260 g.

Fragment of a roughly spherical stone that fit into one hand with flattened surfaces created by grinding with back and forth or circular strokes (Group 1, Type A). About 45% of the object was present. It was 7.94 cm long and 7.11 cm wide; the height was unknown. The fragment weighed 280 g.

Botanical remains from flotation of 4.6 liters of soil (S-106)
  3 *Chenopodium quinoa* carbonized seeds
  2 *Ambrosia* sp. carbonized seeds

Animal bone (NISP)
  Mammals
    llama or alpaca (*Lama* sp.): 6
    unidentified: 9 (all from flotation)

Level B-2

Level B-2 was loose brown dirt (without ash) 15 cm deep.

Munsell color
  7.5 YR 5/3 brown

Ceramic vessels
  Total sherds: 87
  Restricted vessels with a neck: 3 plainware
  Restricted vessel without a neck: 1 plainware
  Open vessel: 1 plainware
  Open vessel with a diameter greater than 30 cm: 1 plainware
  Body sherds with diagnostic style: 2 Chanapata redware

Animal bone (NISP)
  Mammals
    llama or alpaca (*Lama* sp.): 3
  Birds
    unidentified: 3

Trampled Surface B-3

Part of the top of Level B-2 became a thin, light brown trampled surface that measured 95 cm from north to south and 30 cm from east to west.

Munsell color
  5 YR 4/3 reddish brown

Ceramic vessels
  Total sherds: 4
  No diagnostic sherds were found

Chipped stone
  Locally available stone (100% by count and weight)
    chert
      debitage: 1 proximal flake (< 0.1 g), 1 fragment of angular shatter (0.4 g)

Botanical remains from flotation of 2.3 liters of soil (S-123)
  1 *Zea mays* carbonized cupule fragment

Animal bone (NISP)
  Mammals
    unidentified: 1 (from flotation)

Half-Moon-shaped Ashy Area

A thin, half-moon-shaped layer of ashy soil 4 cm thick was located near the northern edge of Unit D. It was 1.64 m from north to south and 1.73 m from east to west. It cut into Stratum 4 and Ashy Intrusion 1 in the northwest corner. This ash was probably discarded or blown in from another area.

Munsell color
  7.5 YR 4/3 brown

Ceramic vessels
  Total sherds: 8
  Restricted vessel without a neck: 1 plainware
  Body sherd with diagnostic style: 1 pattern burnished

Chipped stone
  Regionally available stone (40% by count, 100% by weight)
    slate
      debitage: 2 proximal flakes (0.1 g)
  Exotic stone (60% by count, < 1% by weight)
    obsidian
      debitage: 2 proximal flakes (< 0.1 g), 1 fragment of angular shatter (< 0.1 g)

Botanical remains from flotation of 5.1 liters of soil (S-103)
  16 *Chenopodium quinoa* carbonized seeds

Animal bone (NISP)
    Mammals
        llama or alpaca (*Lama* sp.): 5
    Birds
        unidentified: 1

An Area with Burials Surrounding a Small Circular Stone Hearth

Although there were more burials in total in the Southern Sector than the Northern Sector (15 vs. 7), the number of burials in the last phase in each area was nearly the same: there were five in the Southern Sector and four in the Northern Sector. One of the most intriguing areas from the last phase of Formative period use of the Northern Sector held four human burials surrounding a small circular stone hearth (Fig. 3.23). These included one man who had been stored as a mummy before interment, two adult women, and one infant. Although these burials were clearly related, it is not possible to determine whether they were buried at the same moment or separately over time.

The circular hearth was filled with ash and was surrounded by scattered ash mixed with soil. This feature was nearly identical to a hearth found inside the mud structure in Unit A (see Chap. 4). There was another small pit used for burning located next to the burial of a woman. The lack of carbonized food remains in both hearths suggests that they were not used for cooking. It is more likely that they were used to burn materials during mortuary rituals—either when individuals were buried or as part of repetitive periodic rituals that continued after interment.

Inside the Stone Circle

    Munsell color
        7.5 YR 4/3 brown

    Ceramic vessels
        Total sherds: 5
        Restricted vessel with a neck: 1 plainware

    Botanical remains from flotation of 1.3 liters of soil, the entire contents of the hearth (S-127)
        1 *Chenopodium quinoa* carbonized seed

    Animal bone (NISP)
        Mammals
            field mouse (Muridae): 3 (all from flotation)
            unidentified: 3 (all from flotation)

Ashy Soil Surrounding the Stone Circle

    Munsell color
        7.5 YR 4/3 brown

    Ceramic vessels
        Total sherds: 198
        Restricted vessels with a neck: 3 plainware
        Restricted vessel without a neck: 1 plainware
        Open vessels: 1 Chanapata blackware, 1 plainware
        Body sherds with diagnostic style: 2 Chanapata redware, 1 Chanapata blackware, 3 pattern burnished

    Chipped stone
        Locally available stone (69.23% by count, 96.07% by wt)
            coarse grain quartzitic sandstone
                debitage: 2 proximal flakes (9.2 g)
            fine grain quartzitic sandstone
                debitage: 1 fragment of angular shatter (3.2 g)
            quartzite
                tools: 1 unimarginal flake tool (3.0 g), 1 multidirectional core (14.6 g)
                debitage: 3 proximal flakes (5.8 g), 1 fragment of angular shatter (0.9 g)
        Regionally available stone (7.69% by count, 1.83% by wt)
            andesite
                debitage: 1 proximal flake (0.7 g)
        Exotic stone (23.08% by count, 2.09% by weight)
            obsidian
                tool: 1 multidirectional core (0.8 g)
                debitage: 1 proximal flake (< 0.1 g), 1 fragment of angular shatter (< 0.1 g)

    Botanical remains from flotation of 7.2 liters of soil (S-109)
        4 *Chenopodium quinoa* carbonized seeds

    Animal bone (NISP)
        Mammals
            llama or alpaca (*Lama* sp.): 2 (all from flotation)
            guinea pig (*Cavia porcellus*): 5 (3 from flotation)
            unidentified: 55 (35 from flotation)

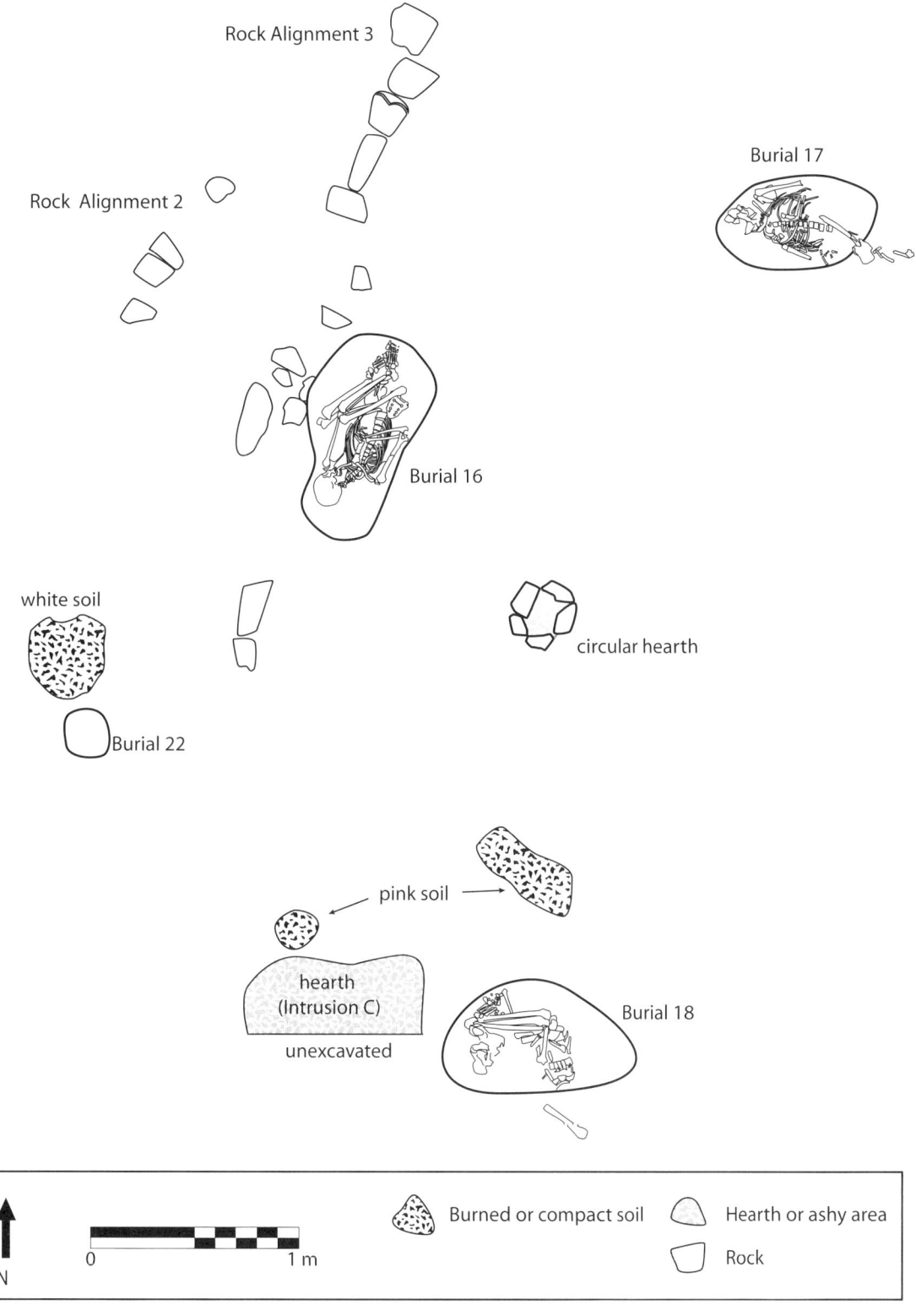

Figure 3.23. Four human burials surrounded a small circular stone hearth including the secondary burial of a 26- to 35-year-old man (Burial 16), a 16- to 17-year-old young woman (Burial 17), a 26- to 35-year-old woman (Burial 18), and an infant (Burial 22). Burial 18 was associated with a small hearth, and there were several deposits of pink and white soil surrounding the burials. Burials 17 and 18 were disturbed by modern plowing.

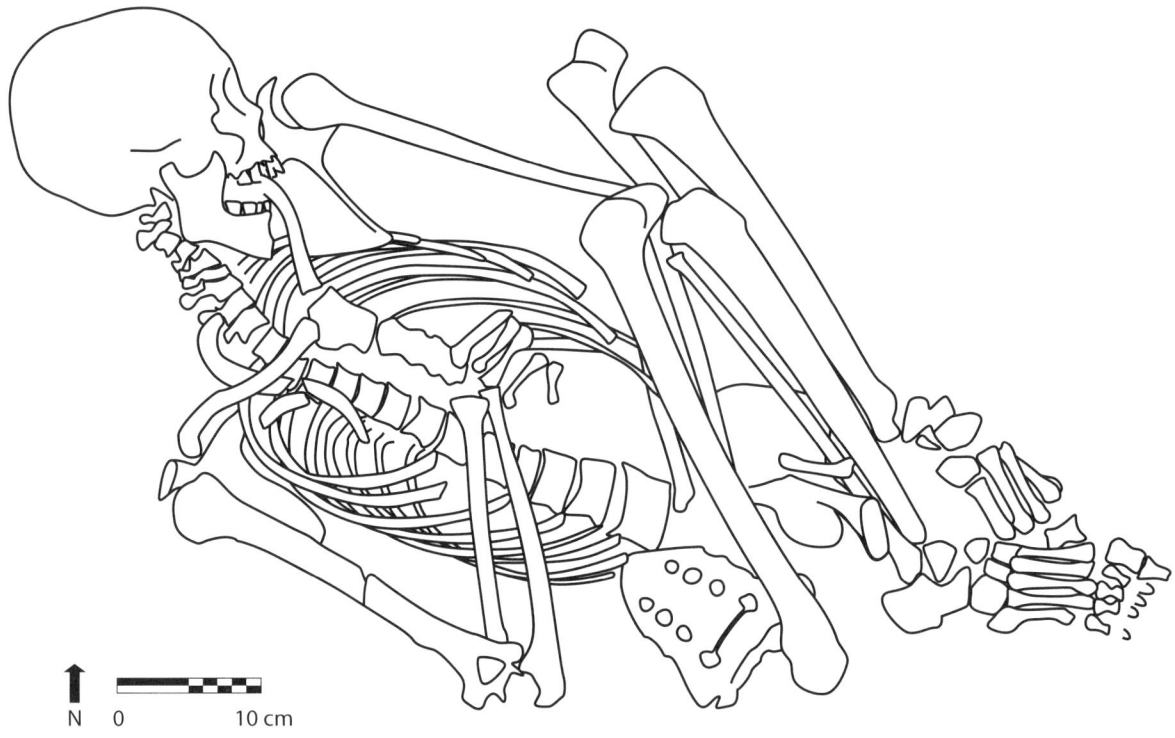

Figure 3.24. Burial 16 was the burial of a 26- to 35-year-old man who had been stored as a mummy before interment. When the right side of the pelvis was removed, the sacrum was rotated approximately 180 degrees from its natural position.

Burial 16

Burial 16 was a man between 26 and 35 years of age with tabular erect cranial modification buried in a cavity that cut into Stratum 4. There were no grave goods associated with this burial, though there was a small rock located at his right elbow. The skeleton was tightly flexed on its back, in good condition, and was complete except for the right half of the pelvis (100% complete; Fig. 3.24) (Andrushko 2008). The skeleton was in correct articulated position except for the sacrum, which was rotated 180 degrees from its original position, and the scattered fingers of the left hand, which were originally located in the man's lap. There were no cut marks on the sacrum, femur, or left side of the pelvis. Yet, the pelvis would have been impossible to remove without cutting if the connective tissue were not already very decayed. Like Burial 19, the tightly flexed position, completeness, and articulation of the skeleton suggest that this man was stored above ground as a mummy for a significant amount of time before being buried at Yuthu (Burial Type 4).

Although I found no evidence of where or how the pelvis of this man was used after removal, a fragment of the right ilium (pelvis) of an adult was found resting on the feet of a 1- to 2-year old in a group burial of three children in the Southern Sector (see Chap. 4). At least in that case, it seems that a curated bone from a mummy was eventually buried after it circulated among the living.

This individual showed many signs of healed trauma including a cranial vault fracture; fractures of the right and left nasals; healed fractures to the left frontal, zygomatic process, and left zygomatic body; and a fracture of the transverse process of the seventh cervical vertebra (Andrushko 2008).

Burial 17

Burial 17 was a 16- to 17-year-old young woman with tabular erect cranial modification buried in a cavity that intruded into Stratum 4 (Andrushko 2008). The skeleton was incomplete (21%) and in poor condition because it had been disturbed by modern plowing. The body may have been buried in a flexed position facing up, though this cannot be determined with certainty. Although it is difficult to say for sure, I would suggest that this was a primary burial (Burial Type 1). There were no grave goods associated with this burial.

Burial 18

Burial 18 was a 26- to 35-year-old woman buried in a cavity that cut into Stratum 4. It was associated with a hearth (Intrusion C) and two areas of pinkish earth with white flecks. The condition of the skeleton was fair even though it had been disturbed by modern plowing and was incomplete (57%). The body was flexed and buried on the right side, facing north. It is impossible to determine with any certainty, but I suspect that this was a primary interment (Burial Type 1).

The skeleton had many healed traumas, including a fracture to a right middle rib, a healed clavicle fracture, a Colles' fracture to the left radius, a fractured distal left ulna, and a fractured fifth metacarpal (Andrushko 2008). This woman shared the congenital trait of a double-headed first right rib with the infant in Burial 23 (see above) (Andrushko 2008). Because this burial was one of the latest in Unit D, this demonstrates that related people (at least related women) used the site from the earliest through latest periods.

Hearth (Intrusion C)

A hearth filled with loose, ashy soil 32 cm deep cut into Stratum 4 just west of Burial 18. It was 40 cm north to south by 90 cm east to west. This intrusion was full of ash, but it did not contain food remains. There were a few ceramic fragments of open and closed vessels and three one-handed grinding stones. It seems that this hearth was not used for cooking meals, but rather for ritual burning that took place when the woman was interred.

Munsell color
    10 YR 5/2 grayish brown

Ceramic vessels
    Total sherds: 68
    Restricted vessels with a neck: 2 plainware
    Restricted vessels without a neck: 2 plainware
    Open vessel: 1 plainware
    Open vessel with a diameter greater than 30 cm: 1 plainware
    Body sherd with diagnostic style: 1 pattern burnished

Groundstone
    Roughly spherical stone that fit into one hand with flattened surfaces created by grinding with back and forth or circular strokes (Group 1, Type A). The stone had pecking marks. It measured 103.5 × 7.56 × 6.26 cm; it weighed 800 g.
    Roughly spherical stone that fit into one hand with flattened surfaces created by grinding with back and forth or circular strokes (Group 1, Type A). The stone measured 9.60 × 7.01 × 5.38; it weighed 500 g.
    Fragment of an oval stone with rectangular cross section created by rocking the stone side to side along its edge (Group 2, Type D). About 25% of the object was present. The length and width were unknown; it was 4.41 cm tall. The fragment weighed 460 g.

Botanical remains from flotation of 7.3 liters of soil (S-108)
    6 *Chenopodium quinoa* carbonized seeds

Animal bone (NISP)
    Mammals
        field mouse (Muridae): 1
        unidentified: 12

Burial 22

Burial 22, an infant who likely did not survive childbirth, was buried in a cavity in Stratum 4. Fifty percent of the delicate skeleton was in good condition, indicating that this was a primary burial in which the individual was probably interred shortly after he or she died (Burial Type 1). A circular area of loose dirt with chunks of white soil, which contained two ceramic discs, was located about 40 cm north of Burial 22. It was 40 cm in diameter and 9 cm deep and may have been the remains of part of the burial ritual.

Discussion of the Deposits and Features in the Northern Sector

In general, the deposits in Unit D had a distinctive quality. Most soil strata were deposited gradually in fine layers and contained compacted surfaces that formed from repeated trampling. These surfaces were the results of habitually performed tasks like walking to and from a hearth or entering and exiting a house through the door.

This area had a sequence of simple domestic structures, storage features, and cooking features. The earliest occupation comprised two semi-subterranean domestic structures with simple thatched roofs, storage pits, a cooking pit, and human burials. A thick soil layer mixed with many artifacts (but without cultural features) covered the remains of that early occupation. It was probably sediment deposited by erosion of soil from uphill. The next significant feature was a large cooking pit in the northwest corner, associated with the only prepared clay floor in Unit D. Then, the first above-ground house with a simple stone foundation (and walls made of mud, adobe, or wattle and daub) was built in the southeast corner. This structure was associated with the earliest mummy burial found at Yuthu. A very large hearth in the southwest corner was roughly contemporaneous with the above-ground house. These features were also covered by soil without cultural features. The final use of Unit D included primary and secondary burials that surrounded a small stone hearth. These burials were contemporary with stone alignments that were not associated with the remains of floors or walls.

Even though the two sets of strata without cultural features indicate that use of this area was not continuous, it is not clear what this means in terms of continuity of occupation. Further excavation will be necessary to determine whether houses were simply located outside the area excavated or whether the site was briefly abandoned and reoccupied.

The final use of the Northern Sector seems to have been exclusively mortuary. This was also true in Unit A in the Southern Sector. Although I excavated only a small portion of the site, the lack of community buildings or houses and the ubiquity of human burials suggest that Yuthu may have been used as a cemetery after people no longer lived there. Although Unit D was only a small fraction of the Northern Sector, excavations in this area provided important data on domestic life in Formative Cusco society.

Domestic Architecture at Yuthu in a Regional Perspective

Before beginning excavations in the Northern Sector, I wanted to know if the distinctive pottery, stone tools, and bones found on the surface were indicative of what lay beneath. Were the kinds of structures and activity areas under the surface different from the Southern Sector? I was excited at the possibility that excavation in this area would allow me to begin to learn about the everyday experiences of the families that lived at Yuthu. Before my excavations, archaeologists knew almost nothing about the daily lives of Formative villagers, a significant shortcoming of Formative period research not only in Cusco, but throughout the region.

Very few Formative period households have been excavated in the Andean highlands. Roughly contemporary structures from Batan Urqo in Cusco include four circular houses 2 to 2.8 m in diameter with post holes, red clay walls, and a stone foundation. These structures are distinct from those found at Yuthu and are slightly later; one dated to 151 BC–AD 68 (Zapata 1998).

Far north of Cusco, at Chavín de Huántar, houses were made of stone during the Janabarriu phase (400–200 BC). They were rectangular with two or more rooms and occasionally had niches in the walls (Burger 1998). In the Jauja-Huancayo Basin of Junín, there were circular and rectangular subterranean pithouses with perishable superstructures dating roughly to 1300–50 BC (Browman 1977). Near Huancavelica, houses consisted of one small and one large circular semi-subterranean structure, each with foundations made of uncoursed stones (Burger and Matos Mendieta 2002).

South of Cusco, in the Titicaca Basin, the earliest structure excavated at Lukurmata (200 BC–AD 50) consisted of a stone foundation and walls of adobe, cane, or brush. The house had no internal features; hearths and refuse pits were outside. Therefore, most activities took place outdoors (Bermann 1994). Further south in highland Bolivia, Wankarani houses varied (1800 BC–AD 300). In the early part of this period (2014–1525 calibrated years BC), domestic units were groups of multiple dwellings with smaller ancillary buildings. Each structure was circular with a sunken floor about 10 cm below a wall foundation made of stone (Rose 2001). Structures abandoned by the twelfth century BC were oval with stone foundations and mud brick or cut sod walls and interior stone hearths (Bermann and Estévez Castillo 1995).

No previously excavated Formative house was exactly like any structure at Yuthu, but there were some common construction techniques such as subterranean floors and simple one- or two-row stone foundations for perishable superstructures. Perhaps the most widespread characteristic is that structures were small and were associated with large outdoor activity areas. In many time periods, outdoor spaces were an important element of highland domestic areas (Nash 2009). Additional excavations may identify regional patterns in domestic architecture, but as of now, it seems that the ways in which families organized their activities in domestic space varied greatly during the Formative period.

Domestic Ritual

Ultimately, a village is not defined by the monumental architecture it contains or the position it holds in a settlement hierarchy. Rather, it is made up of the people who eat, marry, dance, and die as neighbors. I am happy that excavations in the Northern Sector have provided important new information about domestic life in a Formative village. The area was not, however, used exclusively for mundane endeavors. Although the principal features in this sector were houses with cooking and storage features, there was ample evidence of ritual behavior as well. Human burials were found in every phase of occupation. Figurines, carved bone, and the intentional burial of an eagle hawk were rare finds, but all provided evidence that ritual was an important part of daily life for the families of Yuthu. Even so, rituals conducted in this area were unlike those that took place on the platform in the Southern Sector, which was intentionally separated from the space of quotidian life. The archaeological remains of ceremonial life will be described in the next chapter.

Note

1. Three trampled surfaces (E-1, E-2, and E-3) formed along the base of the intrusion, on top of the newly re-exposed strata that had been cut through. Therefore, when considering the contents of the earliest trampled surfaces, it is important to remember their matrix formed from soil that was deposited long before this hearth was built and used. As a result, only a small proportion of cultural materials recovered from the floors were deposited during the use of the hearth.

— 4 —

Ceremonial Life at Yuthu

The Southern Sector is an eye-catching feature on the southern slope of Cerro Yuthu (Fig. 4.1; Plate 4). Today it is a very flat rectangular barley field located on a prominence that extends out from the mountain like a finger pointing toward Lake Huaypo. Because of the unusual form of the land, this part of the site was quickly identified by the Xaquixaguana Plain Archaeological Survey in 2004.

When I visited Yuthu for the first time in 2005, as I walked up the slope to the Southern Sector I was impressed by the density of Formative period artifacts lying on the surface. Compared with many Formative period sites that I had identified nearby, this site was packed with painted pottery, stone tools, and even human remains. When I arrived at the top of the hill, I was struck by even more unique characteristics of the site. The yellowed barley drying in the *chakra* highlighted the remarkably rectangular shape of the field and the straight, steep banks that delimited it. The southern hillside was planted with eucalyptus because it was too steep to farm. To the west, the farm field and the scatter of Formative pottery ended suddenly at the trail to Maras. I had never seen any *chakra* like it, despite having surveyed hundreds of square kilometers of the rolling Andean plains of Anta and Chinchero.

When my archaeologist eyes finally looked up from the ground, I realized that I was in one of the most beautiful places that I had seen on the plain, overlooking Lake Huaypo with its marshy perimeter and the patchwork quilt of fields planted in barley, potatoes, beans, quinoa, and tarwi that covered the rolling hills. The rectangular field faced Cerro Huanacaure, a mountain that rises out of the lake and surrounding plain (see Chap. 5, Fig. 5.1). This mountain was an important *apu* in Inka times and continues to be one today. To the northwest, two more *apus* are visible, the glaciers Chicón and Pitusiray (see Chap. 5, Fig. 5.2).

A hacienda overseer's house lay in ruins just beyond the road to Maras. I later learned that this house was built next to a natural spring that filled an "Inka bath." Unfortunately, the spring is now dry (due either to the water demands of the eucalyptus forest or the general desiccation of the Andes), and the stones of the basin have been used in modern construction. As a result, I will never be able to determine if this "Inka bath" might have actually been a Formative period well or basin, which is a likely possibility given that there is no Inka site nearby.

After my first visit to Yuthu, I was hooked on the beautiful and distinctive location. I hoped that the archaeological deposits below the surface were intact so that I could find out if the natural hill had been cut to create an artificial platform. I was also curious to learn what kinds of structures were built on top of this apparent platform. To investigate these questions, during the exploratory season in 2005 I excavated a 4 × 4 m unit (Unit A) that included part of the steep southeastern bank. I found two intriguing features—two stone-lined canals and a human burial—but the unit was too small to resolve my questions. I also excavated a 2 × 2 m test pit in the platform's center, but did not find any architectural elements or features.

Figure 4.1. The artificial platform in the Southern Sector is a striking feature on the landscape. Such flat areas are extremely rare in the Andes Mountains. This photo is a view from the northeast.

When I returned in 2006, I extended Unit A to 80 m². By excavating a larger area, I learned that the hill had, indeed, been cut off by Formative villagers to create a flat surface. In addition, the platform contained at least one structure with a sunken floor, stone and mortar retaining walls, stone-lined canals, a mud structure, and human burials.

The archaeological deposits from Unit A are described below, beginning with the earliest features excavated into geologic soil and the modification of the hill to create a platform. Each stratum was assigned a number after excavation based on its relative stratigraphic position. Figure 4.2 depicts the stratigraphic profile of Unit A.

Archaeological Deposits in the Southern Sector

Construction of Structure 1

After several weeks of digging along the platform's edge, we had not found any retaining walls or evidence of terracing. I began to doubt that there really was an artificial platform, despite the hill's odd shape. But then, our trowels began to scrape across very hard soil in the western half of the excavation and two parallel lines of stones appeared, running southeast to northwest—the same direction as the presumed artificial platform. We continued to dig, following the natural levels of soil deposited

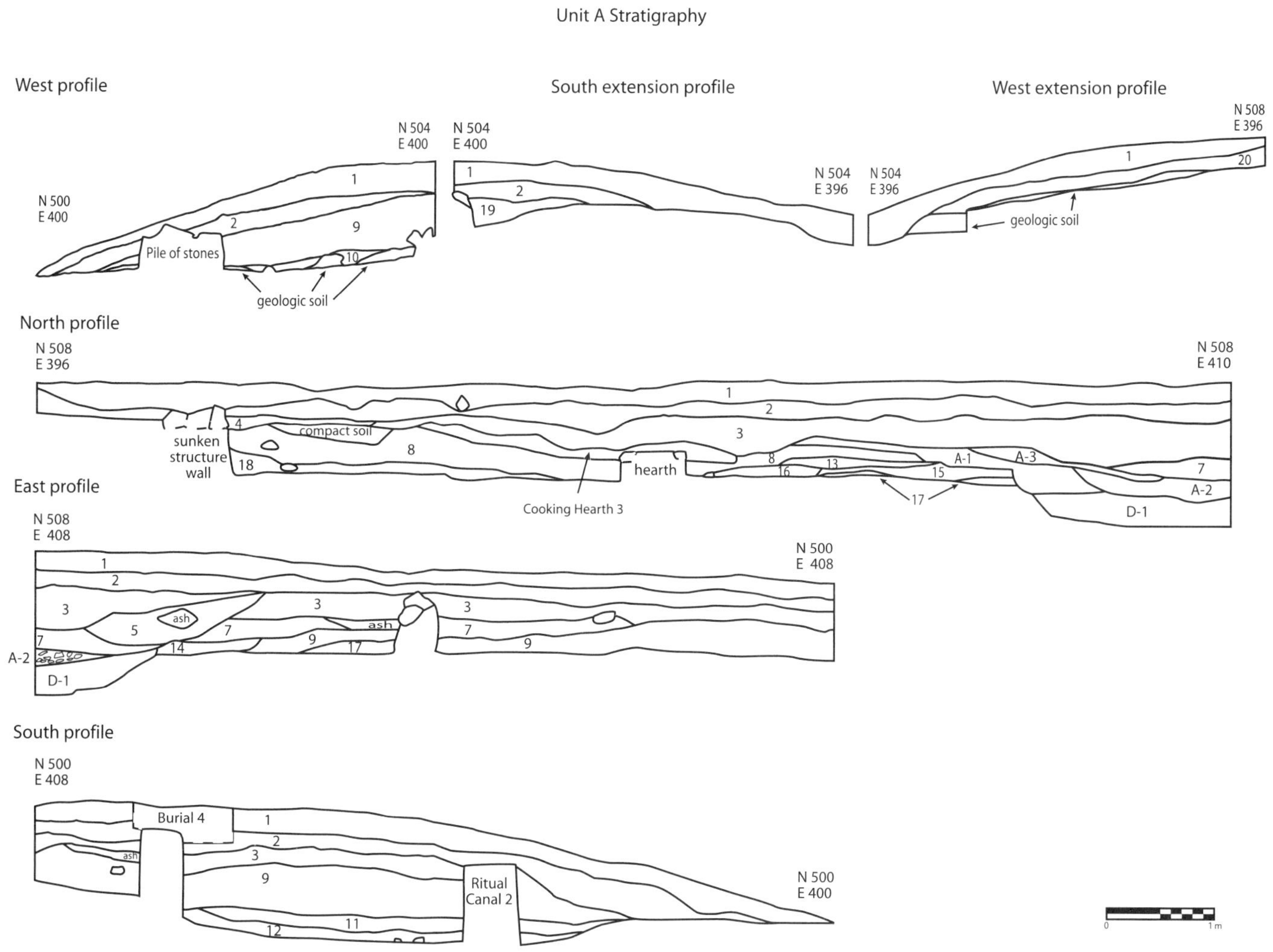

Figure 4.2. Stratigraphic profiles of Unit A. Note that the interior floor of Structure 1 was 60 cm lower than the surrounding ground surface in the north profile.

north of these stones, and we soon discovered that the lines of stones were the top row from the interior and exterior façades of a thick bench. The bench belonged to Structure 1, the largest and most carefully built structure that I found at Yuthu. It had a sunken floor that was 60 cm below the level of the surrounding ground surface. The bench, located along the southwestern edge, was at least partially responsible for the unusual shape of the hill—creating a straight southwestern edge and a flat top. Minor features included a retaining wall, stone-lined canals, and burials made during construction (Fig. 4.3).

To build Structure 1, an irregular-shaped hole, slightly larger than the desired size of the structure, was dug into bedrock. Then, a thick bench was built inside the hole, parallel to the edge of the platform. The bench was 7.8 m long and 1.05 m wide. A narrow gap divided it into two sections of about equal size. Each section was stone-faced and covered by a 5- to 7-cm-thick layer of very hard clay paving that gave it a smooth, flat surface. The two sections differed slightly—the western section was faced with stones set into clay, while the southeast section was not only faced with stones but also contained smaller rocks set into the interior mortar (Fig. 4.4).

Behind the western section, the excess space was filled with three human burials deposited in the construction fill used to restore the ground to the original surface level. A radiocarbon date from

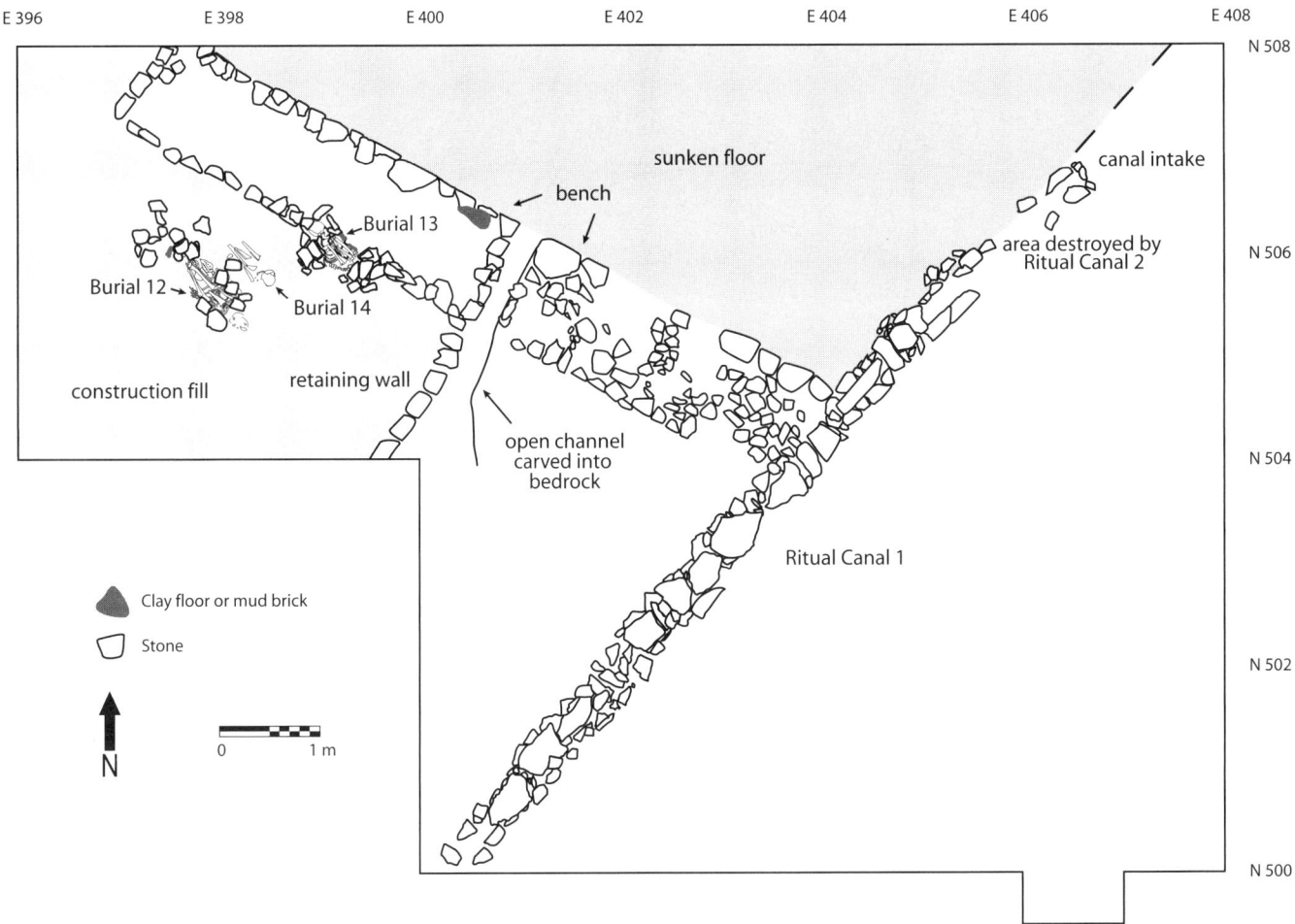

Figure 4.3. The earliest and most significant construction in Unit A was Structure 1, a sunken floor surrounded by a bench. An open channel cut into bedrock separated the east and west sections of the bench. Behind the west section of the bench, construction fill contained three secondary burials (Burials 12, 13, and 14) held in place by a retaining wall. In this part of the structure, the floor was 60 cm lower than the ground surface behind the west bench. East of the retaining wall, the interior and exterior of the structure were at the same level, so that Ritual Canal 1 was not buried. The structure may have been open toward the end of the artificial platform (located to the southeast).

the limit between the fill and geologic soil dates the creation of the structure to 417–209 BC.[1] The construction fill was held in place on the east by a simple retaining wall that ran perpendicular to the east end of the bench section (Fig. 4.5; Plate 4). Along the northern limit of Unit A, the west end of the bench formed a corner with a retaining wall or stone façade set into the natural geologic soil.

The eastern end of the bench abutted Ritual Canal 1, a stone-lined channel covered by stone slabs that ran northeast to southwest, approximately perpendicular to the bench. The canal carried water from the interior to the exterior of the structure. The intake was located about 2.5 m inside the bench, and the canal ended at the edge of the hill where the water would have spilled out over the steep slope. The interlocking stones in the bench and the canal show that they were built at the same time.

Although the area excavated was small, I can speculate about the overall form of Structure 1. Because we found no continuation of the wall to the southeast (for 4.3 m) beyond the canal, it is possible that this structure had no southeast wall and was "open" toward the end of the platform. While the interior may have been below the ground surface in the northwestern part, it was approximately equal with the leveled ground southeast of the retaining wall—leaving the stone-lined canal visible rather than buried. In addition, the "paving" of the bench and the lack of carbonized seeds from plants used for thatch suggest that the

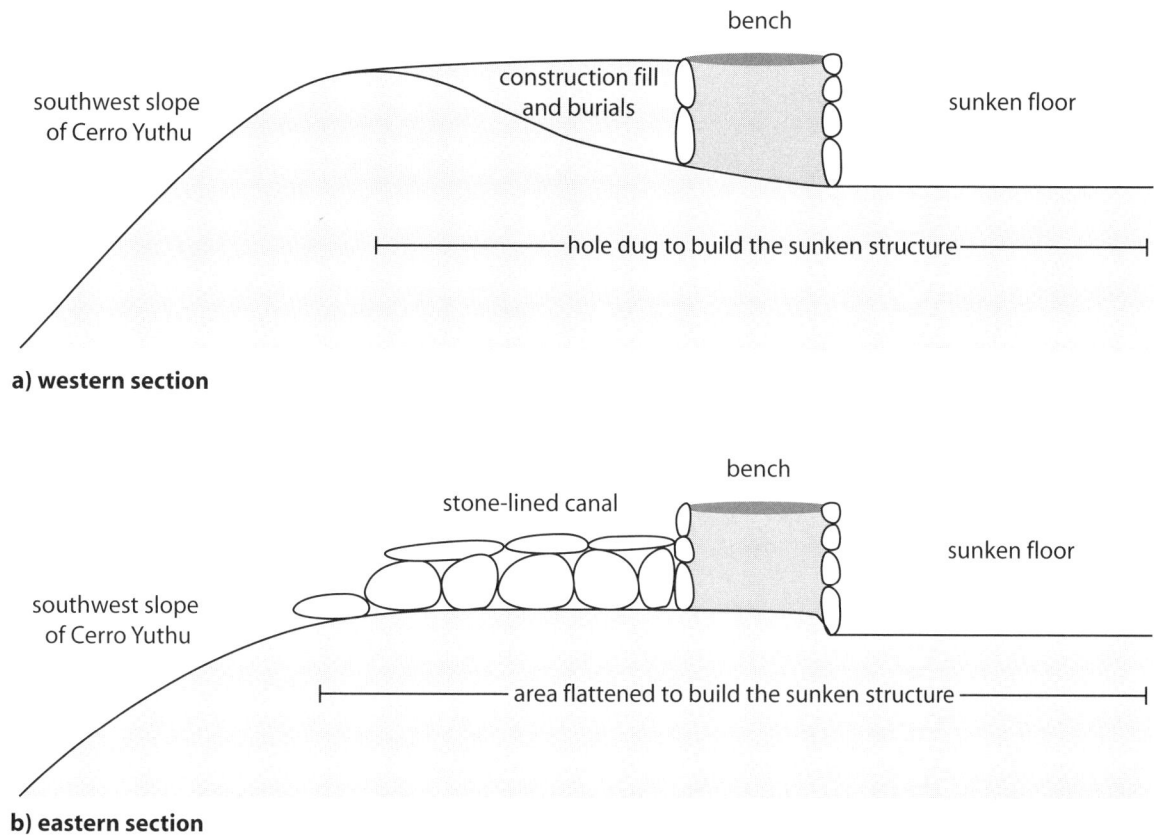

Figure 4.4. A schematic cross section of the western and eastern parts of Structure 1. The two parts were separated by a gap in the bench and a retaining wall. *a*, In order to build the western part, an irregular hole was dug into geologic soil that was 60 cm deep and the approximate size and shape of the structure to be built. Then the stone-faced bench was built and the excess space outside the structure was filled with soil and three secondary burials (Burials 12, 13 and 14). *b*, In order to build the eastern part, the hill was flattened to the level of the interior of the structure so that the exterior of the bench and the associated stone-lined canals would have been visible.

structure was unroofed. Unfortunately, we did not excavate a large enough area to determine whether the platform contained only one such structure or if there were several. Future excavations or geophysical survey will be necessary to determine this.

Burial 12

When Structure 1 was built, Burial 12, a 36- to 45-year-old man with tabular erect cranial modification, was buried behind the western section of the bench in a cavity cut into geologic soil. The body was in a flexed position on its back, surrounded by unworked field stones, with the head to the southwest (Fig. 4.6). There was evidence of scorching on the head and the lower left leg, suggesting that burning was part of the burial ritual. The grave contained an extra, nearly complete adult right hand with a notably different degree of preservation. The skeleton was 79% complete and in fair condition (Andrushko 2008). Despite the fact that this burial cut into geologic soil, it was very near the surface and had been disturbed by modern plowing. Although the disturbance makes it difficult to determine with certainty whether the burial was primary or secondary, the presence of an extra hand suggests that it was probably secondary (Burial Type 3).

This man had a massive healed fracture to the right tibia with ensuing chronic infection and an associated healed fracture to

Figure 4.5. The two parts of the bench were separated by a drain cut into bedrock and a retaining wall that extended out from the eastern end of the western section. In this photo, the construction fill and burials have already been excavated from behind the wall.

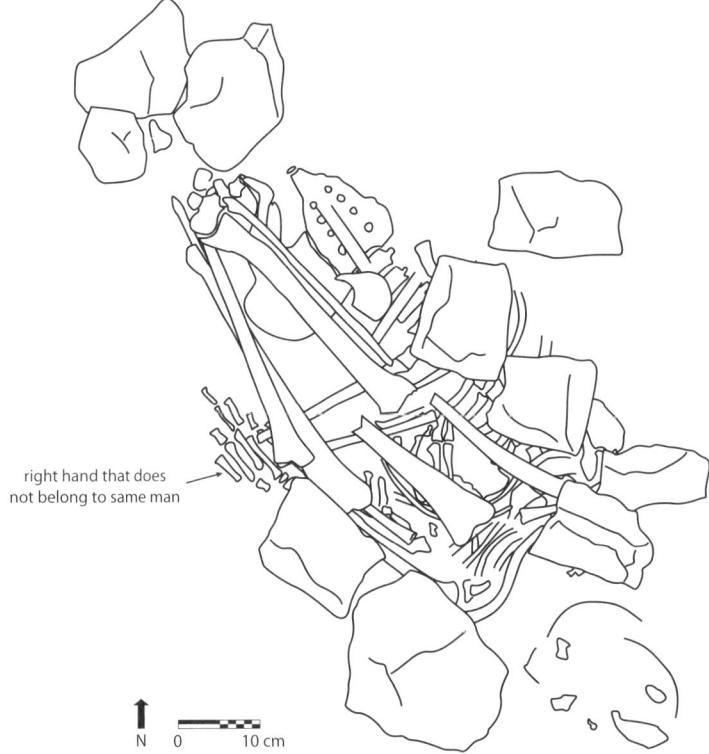

Figure 4.6. Burial 12 was the secondary burial of a 36- to 45-year-old man placed in the construction fill of Structure 1. It included a nearly complete hand that did not belong to the principal individual in the grave.

the right fibula. He had a fractured phalanx of the hand with an unhealed infection and spinal joint disease (Andrushko 2008).

Burial 13

Burial 13, a 26- to 45-year-old woman with tabular erect cranial modification (Andrushko 2008), was incorporated into the western section of the bench. Although the skeleton was only 14% complete and in poor condition, it closely approximated a flexed position with the woman resting on her left side facing the interior of the bench (Figs. 4.7, 4.8). The skeleton was aligned with the stones of the southern face so that the body formed part of a course of stones. There was scorching on the left side of the head (the part resting on the stones below). The body was covered with an additional row of stones and a line of mud brick; stone was placed in front of and around the body as well. The skeleton and stones were covered by the paving of the western section of the bench and by construction fill. This secondary burial was included as a dedicatory offering made during the construction of Structure 1 (Burial Type 3).

The woman suffered degenerative joint disease in her right wrist and hand and left hip, as well as chronic periostitis on the right tibia, indicating non-specific infection. She also had extreme antemortem tooth loss, leaving only one remaining tooth (Andrushko 2008).

Burial 14

Burial 14, a 26- to 45-year-old woman with tabular erect cranial modification, was buried in a cavity cut into geologic soil behind the western section of the bench. The body was only 7% complete and in poor condition, but the bones that were present were arranged as if the skeleton was in a flexed position facing up (Fig. 4.9). Some bones showed evidence of scorching and carnivore gnawing (Andrushko 2008), clearly indicating that this was a secondary burial made during the construction of Structure 1 (Burial Type 3).

Additions to Structure 1

After Structure 1 was built, several features were added including: (1) Burial 15 in the eastern part of the bench, (2) an intrusion in front of the intake of Ritual Canal 1, and (3) a white clay floor associated with a stone-lined circular cist. Outside Structure 1, an ovoid intrusion excavated into geologic soil was partially covered by compact pinkish-white soil. The intrusion was later covered by a 20-cm-thick stratum of soft green earth (Fig. 4.10).

Burial 15

Burial 15, a 36- to 45-year-old woman with tabular erect cranial modification, intruded into the mud mortar of the bench's eastern section (Fig. 4.10). In contrast with the other burials associated with Structure 1 that were dedicatory offerings made *during* construction (Burials 12, 13, and 14), Burial 15 was *added later*. It is not possible to determine exactly when the burial was placed in the bench, though it would have been after the original construction and before the structure was abandoned (see below).

The skeleton was facing up, in a flexed position with the head toward the interior of the structure (to the northeast). It was 86% complete and in fair condition, but the face (including most of the mandible), the right foot, the right clavicle, and all the thoracic vertebrae were absent (Andrushko 2008). The missing elements and the preservation of the bones indicate that this was a secondary burial (Burial Type 3).

This woman had a small depressed cranial fracture on the left anterior parietal. She suffered joint disease (enthesopathies) on the right and left patellae as well as spinal joint disease. Her left fibula shaft demonstrated periostitis (a mark of non-specific infection), and she had a button osteoma on the left parietal (new bone growth probably resulting from previous trauma or a tumor) (Andrushko 2008).

The Contents of Ritual Canal 1

I removed a slab from the top of Ritual Canal 1 to determine whether it was a canal or wall foundation (Fig. 4.11). Under the slab, I found an open space that contained four distinct strata. The top level was very loose soil. Below that, three more very compact layers easily "popped out" with the trowel. Each of these consisted of multiple thin laminar deposits of soil, full of small bits of charcoal and air pockets (Fig. 4.12). At the bottom, the channel had been cut into the limestone bedrock. Since laminar sediments are characteristic of soil deposited by flowing water, I concluded that this was a canal that carried water or another liquid. The slope of the canal would have conveyed water from the interior of Structure 1 to the exterior.

The presence of three compact sections of laminar deposits demonstrated that the canal was used in three distinct phases. Each phase consisted of dozens of instances in which the channel carried water (or other liquid) from inside the structure to the platform's edge. Unfortunately, I cannot determine whether each phase lasted for a season, a year, or multiple years, though this information would be crucial for understanding the rhythm and timing of rituals including water in Structure 1. It is clear, however, that the canal was not used for the entire life of the structure. In fact, it was replaced with Ritual Canal 2 (described below).

Each layer was taken as a flotation sample. The soil contained only carbonized quinoa and grasses, which were likely used for fuel when offerings were burned. In addition, it seems that at least one mouse crawled in the canal and died during the second phase of use. The deposits from the interior of the canal are described below, starting with the lowest layer.

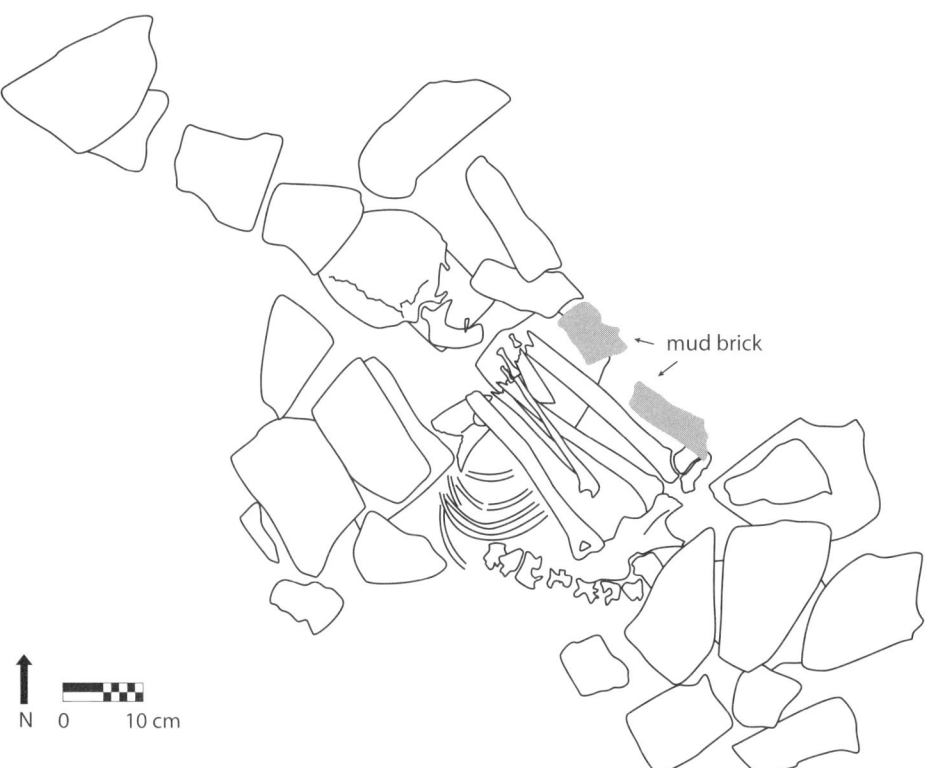

Figure 4.7. Burial 13 was a secondary burial of a 26- to 35-year-old woman that was incorporated into the western section of the bench in Structure 1. The burial was encased in stone and mud brick and was covered by the hard clay that "paved" the top of the bench.

Figure 4.8. Burial 13 was a secondary burial of a 26- to 35-year-old woman that was incorporated into the western section of the southwest bench.

Figure 4.9.
Burial 14 was the secondary burial of a 26- to 45-year-old woman in the construction fill of Structure 1.

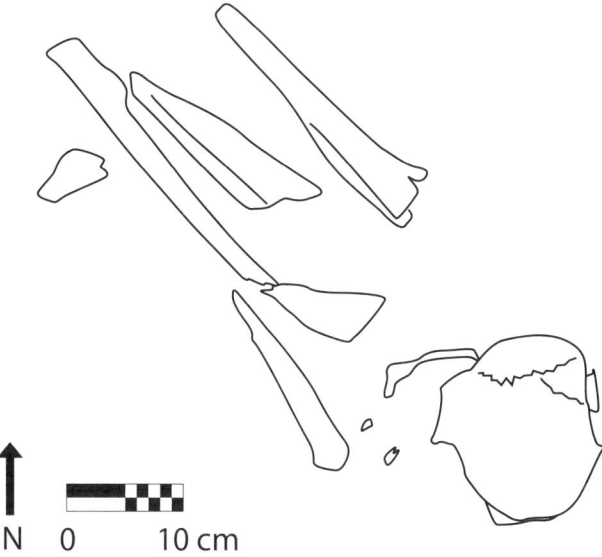

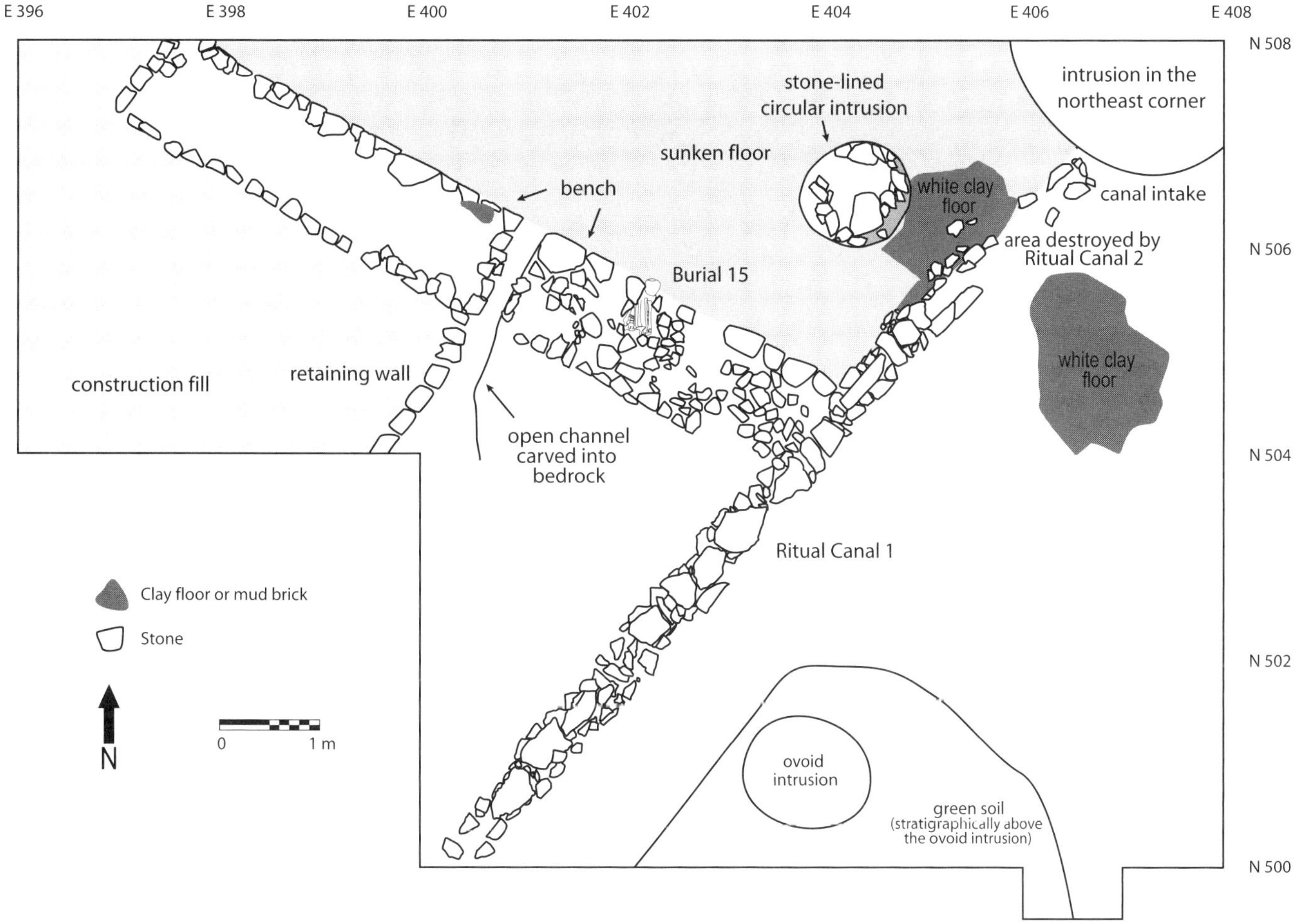

Figure 4.10. After Structure 1 was built, several features were added including: (1) Burial 15 in the eastern part of the bench, (2) an intrusion in front of the intake of Ritual Canal 1 in the northeast corner, and (3) a white clay floor associated with a stone-lined circular cist. Outside Structure 1, an ovoid intrusion excavated into geologic soil was partially covered by compact pinkish-white soil. The intrusion was later covered by a 20-cm-thick stratum of soft green earth.

Figure 4.11. When I removed a slab from the top of Ritual Canal 1, I found laminar deposits of soil typical of those deposited by water.

Canal 1: Level 1

Level 1 was at the base of the channel carved into bedrock. It was a 5-cm-thick layer of compact soil comprising very thin laminar deposits, charcoal bits, and air pockets.

Munsell color
   7.5 YR 4/3 brown

Botanical remains from flotation of 1.0 liter of soil (S-51)
   4 *Chenopodium quinoa* carbonized seeds
   2 Poaceae carbonized seeds

Animal bone (NISP)
   Mammals
      unidentified: 12 (all from flotation)

Canal 1: Level 2

Level 2 was a compact layer 6 cm thick. It was also made up of very thin laminar deposits of soil, charcoal bits, and air pockets (Fig. 4.12).

Munsell color
   7.5 YR 4/3 brown

Botanical remains from flotation of 2.3 liters of soil (S-50)
   15 *Chenopodium quinoa* carbonized seeds

Animal bone (NISP)
   Mammals
      field mouse (Muridae): 57 (all from flotation)

Figure 4.12. A section of Level 2 from the interior of Ritual Canal 1. Note the very fine laminar deposits, air pockets, and bits of charcoal indicating that burned organic matter mixed with water was carried through this channel.

Canal 1: Level 3

Level 3 was the last layer of compact soil with thin laminar deposits, charcoal bits, and air bubbles. It was 4 cm thick.

Munsell color
    7.5 YR 4/3 brown

Botanical remains from flotation of 0.7 liters of soil (S-49)
    1 *Chenopodium quinoa* carbonized seed

Animal bone (NISP)
    Mammals
        field mouse (Muridae): 1 (from flotation)
        unidentified: 35 (all from flotation)

Canal 1: Level 4

Level 4 was very loose dirt that was slightly darker in color. It was 9 cm thick. Unlike Levels 1–3, this layer was not deposited in laminar sheets; the soil probably accumulated after the canal was no longer used to carry water.

Munsell color
    7.5 YR 4/4 brown

Botanical remains from flotation of 3.4 liters of soil (S-48)
    10 *Chenopodium quinoa* carbonized seeds
    1 *Trifolium* sp. carbonized seed
    1 Poaceae carbonized seed

Animal bone (NISP)
    Mammals
        unidentified: 75 (all from flotation)

Strata That Accumulated Inside Structure 1

Several strata accumulated on top of the sunken floor during the use of Structure 1. A few of these deposits are particularly informative about how the structure was used. Compact brown soil accumulated inside Structure 1 on top of the original floor (Stratum 18). Most of the stratum was 8 cm thick, but the surface of this deposit sloped up at the southwestern edge of the floor so that it was 25 cm thick along the bench. A linear deposit of soil cut through this stratum, running from the interior of Structure 1, through the open channel cut into bedrock between the two sections of the bench, to the structure's exterior. The soil was probably deposited by water, but in contrast with Ritual Canal 1, the open channel did not contain laminar deposits. Unlike the covered canal, this feature's intake was lower than the level of the floor and it was occasionally cleaned out so that water could drain from the sunken floor of Structure 1. This drain was probably particularly important during the rainy season.

Two strata in the unit's eastern half help to clarify the form of Structure 1. A dark-brown layer of soil (Stratum 17) rested on bedrock in front of the intake of Ritual Canal 1. This stratum was located partially inside and partially outside the area enclosed by Ritual Canal 1 and the bench of Structure 1. This suggests that Structure 1 was open toward the northeast. In contrast, a deposit of compact reddish earth mixed with chunks of very compact soil (Stratum 14) did not extend beyond Ritual Canal 1 to the west, indicating that the canal did delimit the area in some way.

The contents of selected strata that accumulated during the use of Structure 1 are described below, starting with the earliest level. Most pottery fragments recovered were from restricted vessels with necks and open vessels made in a variety of wares. We found several reworked sherds, especially disc shapes. Very few botanical remains were recovered, and fauna included mostly camelid and bird bone, as well as some field mice. One deer bone was found in the drain; *cuy* was notably absent. The deposits contained a variety of chipped stone tools and a couple of small smooth stones that could be held between the fingers.

Stratum 18

Stratum 18 was compact brown soil 8–25 cm thick resting on the sunken floor of Structure 1. This soil accumulated during the use of the structure while the channel between the benches was cleaned periodically to drain the interior.

Munsell color
    7.5 YR 4/6 strong brown

Ceramic vessels
    Total sherds: 886
        Restricted vessels with a neck: 4 Chanapata redware, 28 plainware
        Open vessels: 2 Chanapata redware, 7 plainware
        Open vessels with a diameter greater than 30 cm: 2 Chanapata redware, 1 Chanapata blackware, 1 plainware
        Body sherds with diagnostic style: 26 Chanapata redware, 3 Chanapata blackware, 1 Chanapata incised, 3 pattern burnished

Reworked ceramic sherds
    Discs: 1 plainware, 1 with plastic application

Chipped stone
    Locally available stone (84.7% by count, 52.38% by wt)
        coarse grain quartzitic sandstone
            debitage: 5 proximal flakes (38.5 g), 1 fragment of flake shatter (4.9 g)
        fine grain quartzitic sandstone
            tool: 1 unimarginal flake tool (28.3 g)
            debitage: 1 proximal flake (3.1 g)
        quartzite
            debitage: 1 fragment of angular shatter (2.0 g)
        organic limestone
            tool: 1 unimarginal flake tool (6.6 g)
            debitage: 1 proximal flake (1.3 g)
    Regionally available stone (14.29% by count, 15.41% by weight)
        slate
            debitage: 1 proximal flake (< 0.1 g)
        rhyolite
            tool: 1 unimarginal flake tool (14.7 g)
            debitage: 1 proximal flake (1.7 g)
    Exotic stone (33.33% by count, 4.98% by weight)
        obsidian
            tools: 1 unimarginal flake tool (0.4 g), 1 bimarginal flake tool projectile point (2.7 g), 1 combination flake tool broken projectile point (0.8 g)
            debitage: 1 proximal flake (0.7 g), 1 fragment of flake shatter (0.2 g), 2 fragments of angular shatter (0.5 g)

Worked bone
    1 thin object with round cross section and pointed end

Groundstone
    Stone that could be pinched between the fingers with a flattened surface created by back and forth or circular strokes (Small Group 3, Type P). The length was unknown; it was 2.27 cm wide and 1.79 cm tall. The fragment weighed 10 g.
    Nondescript fragment of a grinding stone that weighed 60 g.

Botanical remains from flotation of 5.8 liters of soil (S-74)
    3 *Chenopodium quinoa* carbonized seeds

Animal bone (NISP)
    Mammals
        llama or alpaca (*Lama* sp.): 26 (6 from flotation)
        field mouse (Muridae): 9 (all from flotation)
        unidentified: 27 (15 from flotation)
    Birds
        unidentified: 1 (from flotation)

Contents of the Open Channel between the Two Sections of the Bench

Drain Level 1. The lowest level of soil in the drain was fine silt 14 cm thick.

Munsell color
    7.5 YR 4/3 brown

Ceramic vessels
    Total sherds: 113
    Restricted vessels without a neck: 4 plainware
    Open vessels: 3 Chanapata redware, 2 plainware
    Body sherds with diagnostic style: 5 Chanapata redware

Animal bone (NISP)
    Mammals
        llama or alpaca (*Lama* sp.): 8
        field mouse (Muridae): 4 (all from flotation)
    Birds
        unidentified: 4 (all from flotation)

Drain Level 2. A layer of compact dark brown soil mixed with lumps of very hard dirt rested on top of Drain Level 1.

Munsell color
    7.5 YR 4/4 brown

Ceramic vessels
    Total sherds: 239
    Restricted vessels with a neck: 3 Chanapata redware, 9 plainware
    Restricted vessels without a neck: 2 plainware
    Body sherds with diagnostic style: 18 Chanapata redware, 2 Chanapata blackware

Chipped stone
    Locally available stone (42.86% by count, 81.62% by wt)
        fine grain quartzitic sandstone
            tool: 1 multidirectional core (8.8 g)
            debitage: 1 proximal flake (1.3 g)
        organic limestone
            debitage: 1 unmodified manuport (20.1 g)

    Regionally available stone (28.57% by count, 15.41% by wt)
        diorite
            debitage: 1 fragment of flake shatter (3.4 g)
        rhyolite
            tool: 1 unimarginal flake tool (2.3 g)
    Exotic stone (28.57% by count, 2.97% by weight)
        obsidian
            tool: 1 unimarginal flake tool (0.7 g)
            debitage: 1 proximal flake (0.4 g)

Groundstone
    Small oval stone with no flat surface that may have been in an early phase of use (Small Group 2, Type N). The stone measured 3.9 × 2.78 × 2.35 cm; it weighed 30 g.

Animal bone (NISP)
    Mammals
        llama or alpaca (*Lama* sp.): 15
        white-tailed deer (*Odocoileus virginianus*): 1
        unidentified: 5

Stratum 17

Stratum 17 was a compact, dark-brown layer of soil resting on bedrock in front of the intake of Ritual Canal 1.

Munsell color
    7.5 YR 4/4 brown

Ceramic vessels
    Total sherds: 372
    Restricted vessels with a neck: 3 Chanapata redware, 17 plainware
    Restricted vessel without a neck: 1 plainware
    Open vessels: 1 Chanapata redware, 6 plainware, 1 indeterminate style
    Body sherds with diagnostic style: 9 Chanapata redware, 1 Chanapata incised, 3 pattern burnished
    Figurine: 1 plainware

Reworked ceramic sherd
    Non-disc: 1 plainware

Chipped stone
    Exotic stone (100% by count and weight)
        obsidian
            debitage: 1 proximal flake (0.4 g)

Animal bone (NISP)
    Mammals
        llama or alpaca (*Lama* sp.): 30
        unidentified: 6

Stratum 16

Stratum 16 covered a small area; it was dirt mixed with ash resting on geologic soil along the northern edge of Unit A. It was 10 cm thick, but because the area it covered was very small, this stratum was excavated along with Stratum 13.

Munsell color
    7.5 YR 5/3 brown

Stratum 15

Stratum 15 was semi-compact soil, 13 cm thick, resting partly on geologic soil and partly on Stratum 17.

Munsell color
    7.5 YR 4/6 strong brown

Ceramic vessels
    Total sherds: 166
    Restricted vessels with a neck: 1 Chanapata redware,
        1 pattern burnished, 7 plainware
    Open vessels: 2 Chanapata redware, 1 plainware
    Body sherds with diagnostic style: 4 Chanapata
        redware, 1 Chanapata incised, 3 pattern burnished

Animal bone (NISP)
    Mammals
        llama or alpaca (*Lama* sp.): 3
        unidentified: 3

Stratum 14

Stratum 14 was a compact reddish layer mixed with chunks of very compact soil. It was 12 cm thick. The stratum did not extend beyond Ritual Canal 1 to the west.

Munsell color
    7.5 YR 4/3 brown

Ceramic vessels
    Total sherds: 302
    Restricted vessels with a neck: 1 Chanapata redware,
        12 plainware
    Restricted vessels without a neck: 2 plainware
    Open vessels: 3 Chanapata redware, 7 plainware
    Open vessel with a diameter greater than 30 cm:
        1 plainware
    Body sherds with diagnostic style: 7 Chanapata
        redware, 1 Chanapata incised, 2 pattern burnished

Reworked ceramic sherds
    Disc: 1 plainware
    Non-discs: 1 Chanapata redware, 3 plainware

Chipped stone
    Locally available stone (66.67% by count, 72.33% by wt)
        fine grain quartzitic sandstone
            debitage: 2 fragments of angular shatter (15.5 g)
        quartzite
            debitage: 2 proximal flakes (7.5 g)
    Regionally available stone (16.67% by count, 21.70% by weight)
        rhyolite
            tool: 1 unimarginal flake tool (6.9 g)
    Unidentified (16.67% by count, 5.97% by weight)
        tool: 1 bimarginal flake tool (1.9 g)

Animal bone (NISP)
    Mammals
        llama or alpaca (*Lama* sp.): 1
        unidentified: 4

Intrusion in the Northeast Corner (Intrusion D)

A large intrusion was added in front of the intake of Ritual Canal 1 in the northeast corner (Fig. 4.13; Plate 4). It cut through Stratum 14 and Stratum 15 into geologic soil. The intrusion was 55 cm deep and had sloped walls and a flat base. The total size is not known because it extended beyond the northern and eastern limits of Unit A, but the excavated portion measured 2.2 m from east to west and 1.23 m from north to south.

The lowest level of soil and cultural material (Level D-1, 30 cm thick) did not extend beyond the limits of the intrusion. Therefore, it was probably deposited before Structure 1 was abandoned. This stratum contained food refuse (including quinoa, camelid, and *cuy*) as well as the remains of mice, which are drawn to organic materials. In addition, the stratum had a very high density of ceramic sherds. Most fragments were from restricted vessels with a neck, but several sherds were from restricted vessels without a neck and open vessels. Although most fragments were plainware, pattern burnished and redware pottery was also recovered. The intrusion contained a set of chipped stone tools—fairly large and flat on one side with straight cutting edges—that were made from locally and regionally available materials (including an unusual limestone tool) (Fig. 4.14; Plate 5). This deposit may be the remains of trash that was discarded after eating and/or cooking.

The soil and materials that accumulated during the use of the structure are described below. Three strata that filled the intrusion after Structure 1 was abandoned are described later in this chapter (see Levels A-1, A-2, and A-3).

Figure 4.13. There was a large semicircular intrusion in front of the intake of Ritual Canals 1 and 2 (Intrusion D).

Figure 4.14. Stone tools from Level D-1 in the base of the intrusion in the northwest corner: *a*, fine grain quartzitic sandstone unimarginal flake tool; *b*, organic limestone unimarginal flake tool; *c*, *d*, quartzite unimarginal flake tools; *e*, obsidian unimarginal flake tool.

Level D-1

Level D-1 was 30 cm of soil and refuse that filled the bottom of the intrusion in the northeast corner.

Munsell color
  7.5 YR 4/3 brown

Ceramic vessels
  Total sherds: 1775
  Restricted vessels with a neck: 4 Chanapata redware, 4 pattern burnished, 48 plainware
  Restricted vessels without a neck: 4 Chanapata redware, 1 pattern burnished, 30 plainware
  Open vessels: 3 Chanapata redware, 1 pattern burnished, 30 plainware
  Open vessel with a diameter greater than 30 cm: 1 plainware
  Lids: 1 Chanapata redware, 2 plainware
  Body sherds with diagnostic style: 14 Chanapata redware, 1 incised, 15 pattern burnished, 1 indeterminate style

Reworked ceramic sherds
  Discs: 5 plainware
  Non-discs: 5 plainware

Chipped stone (Fig. 4.14)
  Locally available stone (69.23% by count, 95% by wt)
    fine grain quartzitic sandstone
      tool: 1 unimarginal flake tool (14.7 g)
      debitage: 1 proximal flake (5.7 g)
    quartzite
      tools: 2 unimarginal flake tools (10.0 g), 1 multidirectional core (22.6 g)
      debitage: 1 proximal flake (3.3 g), 2 fragments of flake shatter (5.7 g), 7 fragments of angular shatter (51.6 g)
    organic limestone
      tool: 1 unimarginal flake tool (0.8 g)
      debitage: 1 proximal flake (139.0 g), 1 fragment of angular shatter (2.4 g)
  Regionally available stone (19.23% by count, 4.34% by wt)
    slate
      debitage: 1 fragment of angular shatter (0.2 g)
    andesite
      debitage: 3 proximal flakes (11.5 g)
    rhyolite
      tool: 1 unimarginal flake tool (0.8 g)
  Exotic stone (11.54% by count, 0.66% by weight)
    obsidian
      tools: 2 unimarginal flake tools (1.4 g), 1 multidirectional core (0.5 g)

Groundstone
  Fragment of a small oval stone with no flat surface that may have been in an early phase of use (Small Group 2, Type N). About 60% of the object was present. The length was unknown; it was 4.06 cm wide and 3.58 cm tall. The fragment weighed 70 g.

Botanical remains from flotation of 5.8 liters of soil (S-79)
  12 *Chenopodium quinoa* carbonized seeds

Animal bone (NISP)
  Mammals
    llama or alpaca (*Lama* sp.): 21 (3 from flotation)
    guinea pig (*Cavia porcellus*): 4
    field mouse (Muridae): 7 (all from flotation)
    unidentified: 34 (18 from flotation)

White Clay Floor

Two sections of floor made of white clay were built on either side of the intake of Ritual Canal 1. Each section measured 1.65 m from southwest to northeast. The eastern section was 1.4 m from southeast to northwest and rested on top of Stratum 14. The western part was 90 cm from southeast to northwest and rested on top of Stratum 13. It met the western edge of Ritual Canal 1 and, to the west, was associated with a stone-lined circular cist (see Intrusion C below). This floor was not excavated and no artifacts were recovered.

Munsell color
  7.5 YR 7/2 pinkish gray

Stone-Lined Circular Cist (Intrusion C)

A circular intrusion, associated with the white floor described above (Fig. 4.15; Plate 5), was 110 cm in diameter and 45 cm deep, cutting through Strata 13 and 16 into geologic soil. The walls of the intrusion were made of field stones set into hard red clay mortar. When we excavated the intrusion, we found that some of these stones had collapsed into the middle. Very loose dirt and air pockets surrounded them, suggesting that the intrusion was not filled in with soil when it was abandoned. The number and size of the rocks that we found inside the intrusion indicate that part of the walls may have originally extended above the surface of the floor.

The materials recovered included relatively few ceramic sherds, a broken bead, and a set of stone tools for punching and cutting made from locally available materials (Fig. 4.16). The pit was not filled with food waste. We recovered only 2 carbonized quinoa seeds and a few very small bits of bone. Given the location within a ceremonial structure, it is intriguing to consider whether ritual paraphernalia or mummy bundles were stored and

Figure 4.15. A stone-lined cist associated with a white clay floor was added to Structure 1 (Intrusion C). The walls of the intrusion were made of field stones set in red clay mortar.

Figure 4.16. Chipped stone tools for punching and cutting found in the circular cist (Intrusion C).

removed from this feature. It is likely that whatever was stored was used in rituals that included pouring water or other liquids mixed with burned materials into the mouth of the canal.

Munsell color
    7.5 YR 4/4 brown

Ceramic vessels
    Total sherds: 139
    Restricted vessels with a neck: 1 Chanapata blackware, 5 plainware
    Restricted vessel without a neck: 1 plainware
    Open vessels: 1 Chanapata redware, 1 plainware
    Body sherds with diagnostic style: 2 Chanapata redware, 1 pattern burnished

Chipped stone (Fig. 4.16)
    Locally available stone (80% by count, 95.78% by wt)
        coarse grain quartzitic sandstone
            tool: 1 bimarginal flake tool (1.0 g)
        fine grain quartzitic sandstone
            tool: 1 bimarginal flake tool (1.1 g)
        quartzite
            tools: 1 bimarginal flake tool (4.9 g), 1 multidirectional core (3.0 g)
            debitage: 1 proximal flake (< 0.1 g), 2 fragments of angular shatter (4.3 g)
        chert
            tool: 1 multidirectional core (1.6 g)
    Exotic stone (10% by count, 1.81% by weight)
        obsidian
            debitage: 1 fragment of angular shatter (0.3 g)
    Unidentified (10% by count, 2.41% by weight)
        debitage: 1 fragment of angular shatter (0.4 g)

Worked bone
    1 fragment of a tube-shaped, polished bone bead

Botanical remains from flotation of 6.0 liters of soil (S-73)
    2 *Chenopodium quinoa* carbonized seeds

Animal bone (NISP)
    Mammals
        llama or alpaca (*Lama* sp.): 4 (2 from flotation)
        guinea pig (*Cavia porcellus*): 1 (from flotation)
        field mouse (Muridae): 1 (from flotation)
        unidentified: 9 (all from flotation)

The Area South of Structure 1

An Ovoid Intrusion into Geological Soil (Intrusion B)

An ovoid intrusion 75 cm deep with a diameter of 1 to 1.5 m intruded into geologic soil outside Structure 1. It was filled with semi-compact soil mixed with gravel and many bits of charcoal. It also contained some loose stones at the base that showed evidence of having been burned. The fact that the intrusion was filled with a single stratum of soil indicates that it was filled quickly in a single action, not little by little over time. A hard pinkish-white deposit 4 cm thick covered the northern part of the soil that filled the ovoid intrusion. Radiocarbon dates indicate that this pit was filled after Structure 1 was built (384–205 BC) and stratigraphy shows that it was filled before Ritual Canal 2 was built.

The deposit contained a variety of items. Most ceramic fragments were from restricted vessels with a neck. Open vessels were second most common, followed by restricted vessels without a neck. The intrusion contained several reworked ceramic fragments shaped like discs and other forms. There were chipped stone flakes composed of a variety of materials, but only one formal tool. The pit contained at least one *qulluta* and a small grinding stone with pecking marks. Plant food was not an important part of the deposit. Carbonized botanical remains were low density and included only quinoa and wild brush or grass. The only bones from economically useful animals were from llama or alpaca.

One of the most exciting ritual objects from Yuthu was recovered from this pit. When we found a stone that had been carved and polished to resemble a potato with eyes (Fig. 4.17), my workmen were quick to explain that it was an *illa*, a stone potato used in offerings to ensure a good harvest. In my excavation notebook, archaeologist Vicentina Galiano Blanco, who grew up in a rural farming community, recorded that "las personas que producen papa utilizaban [*sic*] una *illa* o *rumin* para hacer sus pagos respectivos con la finalidad de buena cosecha de sus productos." Similarly, herders could use a stone *illa* or *iwayllu* in the shape of an animal as part of offerings made to request good productivity of herd or household domestic animals, such as sheep, llamas, and guinea pigs.

The workmen from Cruzpata, all committed potato enthusiasts and well-versed in sorting, planting, and eating a wide variety of tubers, were quick to offer speculations as to the variety of this "rock potato." *Qumpis* was the most popular suggestion, but there was some disagreement. We decided to record all the varieties of potatoes cultivated today in Cruzpata for further consideration as candidates (though potatoes that are no longer planted are also good possibilities). They included: *winiquta*, *imilla*, *qumpis*, *marida*, *yungay*, *wayk'uq qallun*, *qhachun waqachi*, *olomes*, and *sica*.

It is important to note that although there was little ethnobotanical evidence of any tuber at Yuthu, this *illa* demonstrates that potato farming was an important part of agriculture there.

Figure 4.17. A potato *illa* is a stone version of a potato used in offerings requesting more potatoes in the next harvest. This *illa* was found in a pit intruding into geologic soil (Intrusion B).

Munsell color
  7.5 YR 4/6 strong brown

Radiocarbon date
  AA84431/Yuthu RC-104, 2257 ± 36 uncalibrated radiocarbon years BP, 384–205 BC calibrated with sequential model (95.4% confidence)

Ceramic vessels
  Total sherds: 1344
  Restricted vessels with a neck: 11 Chanapata redware, 1 Chanapata blackware, 20 plainware
  Restricted vessels without a neck: 10 plainware
  Open vessels: 5 Chanapata redware, 2 Chanapata blackware, 9 plainware
  Open vessels with a diameter greater than 30 cm: 2 Chanapata redware, 1 plainware
  Lids: 3 Chanapata redware
  Body sherds with diagnostic style: 38 Chanapata redware, 3 Chanapata blackware, 4 Chanapata incised, 10 pattern burnished, 2 indeterminate style

Reworked ceramic sherds
  Discs: 5 plainware
  Non-discs: 2 plainware

Chipped stone
  Locally available stone (60.87% by count, 95.51% by wt)
    coarse grain quartzitic sandstone
      tool: 1 unimarginal flake tool (19.8 g)
      debitage: 4 proximal flakes (95.1 g), 2 fragments of angular shatter (27.6 g)
    fine grain quartzitic sandstone
      debitage: 2 proximal flakes (5.6 g)
    quartzite
      debitage: 3 proximal flakes (14.7 g), 1 fragment of angular shatter (0.2 g)
    organic limestone
      debitage: 1 fragment of angular shatter (19.8 g)
  Regionally available stone (4.35% by count, 3.71% by wt)
    andesite
      debitage: 1 fragment of angular shatter (7.1 g)
  Exotic stone (30.43% by count, 0.16% by weight)
    obsidian
      debitage: 6 proximal flakes (0.1 g), 1 fragment of flake shatter (0.2 g)
  Unidentified (4.35% by count, 0.63% by weight)
    debitage: 1 proximal flake (1.2 g)

Groundstone
  Fragment of a roughly spherical stone that fit into one hand with flattened surfaces created by grinding with back and forth or circular strokes (Group 1, Type A). About 40% of the object was present. The length was unknown; it was 6.56 cm wide and 3.13 cm tall. The fragment weighed 130 g.
  Stone that could be pinched between the fingers with a flattened surface created by back and forth or circular strokes (Small Group 3, Type P). The stone had pecking marks. It measured 3.58 × 3.19 × 2.28 cm; it weighed 30 g.
  Three nondescript fragments of groundstone that weighed 20 g, 20 g, and 79 g

Botanical remains from flotation of 5.5 liters of soil from higher in the intrusion (S-76)
  6 *Chenopodium quinoa* carbonized seeds
  1 *Ambrosia* sp. carbonized seed

Botanical remains from flotation of 5.2 liters of soil from lower in the intrusion (S-77)
  12 *Chenopodium quinoa* carbonized seeds
  4 Poaceae carbonized seeds
  1 unidentified carbonized seed

Animal bone (NISP)
  Mammals
    llama or alpaca (*Lama* sp.): 46 (4 from flotation)
    field mouse (Muridae): 4 (all from flotation)
    unidentified: 58 (56 from flotation)

Green Soil Outside Structure 1 (Stratum 11)

Stratum 11 was an unusual deposit of loose, green soil that contained many bits of charcoal. It was 20 cm thick and located along the southern edge of Unit A. The color of this stratum was striking when we excavated it, but it is not clear what caused this green hue. The large stratum contained a typical mix of stone tools and pottery and very little food rubbish.

Munsell color
  2.5 YR 4/2 light brownish gray

Ceramic vessels
  Total sherds: 1402
  Restricted vessels with a neck: 9 Chanapata redware,
    75 plainware, 2 indeterminate style
  Restricted vessels without a neck: 4 plainware,
    1 indeterminate style
  Open vessels: 9 Chanapata redware, 1 plainware,
    1 indeterminate style
  Open vessels with a diameter greater than 30 cm:
    9 Chanapata redware, 1 plainware
  Lids: 2 Chanapata redware, 1 plainware
  Body sherds with diagnostic style: 19 Chanapata
    redware, 4 Chanapata incised, 4 pattern burnished,
    7 indeterminate style

Reworked ceramic sherds
  Discs: 14 plainware
  Non-disc: 1 plainware

Chipped stone
  Locally available stone (48.28% by count, 62.56% by wt)
    coarse grain quartzitic sandstone
      tool: 1 bimarginal flake tool (21.9 g)
      debitage: 1 fragment of angular shatter (9.8 g)
    fine grain quartzitic sandstone
      debitage: 1 proximal flake (0.6 g), 1 fragment of
        flake shatter (4.3 g), 1 fragment of angular
        shatter (6.1 g)
    quartzite
      tool: 1 multidirectional core (20.1 g)
      debitage: 1 fragment of flake shatter (8.4 g),
        1 fragment of angular shatter (33.3 g)
    chert
      debitage: 1 proximal flake (0.3 g)
    organic limestone
      tool: 1 bimarginal flake tool (5.0 g)
      debitage: 1 proximal flake (26.8 g), 1 fragment of
        flake shatter (5.1 g), 2 fragments of angular
        shatter (33.4 g)
  Regionally available stone (20.69% by count, 28.15%
  by weight)
    andesite
      tool: 1 unimarginal flake tool (32.1 g)
      debitage: 3 proximal flakes (29.7 g), 1 unmodified
        manuport (6.7 g)
    rhyolite
      tool: 1 unimarginal flake tool (10.3 g)
  Exotic stone (27.59% by count, 0.54% by weight)
    obsidian
      tools: 1 unimarginal flake tool (0.2 g),
        1 multidirectional core (0.7 g)
      debitage: 5 proximal flakes (0.4 g), 1 fragment
        of angular shatter (0.2 g)
  Unidentified (3.45% by count, 8.75% by weight)
    debitage: 1 unmodified manuport (24.5 g)

Groundstone

Fragment of a grinding stone that fit in one hand with plano-convex cross section and flattened surfaces created by grinding with back and forth and rocking motions (Group 1, Type B). About 20% of the object was present. Length was unknown; it was 9.46 cm wide and 4.6 cm tall. The fragment weighed 300 g.

Fragment of an oval stone with rectangular cross section created by rocking the stone side to side along its edge (Group 2, Type D). About 50% of the object was present. The length was unknown; it was 8.85 cm wide and 4.12 cm tall. The fragment weighed 540 g.

Nondescript fragment of a grinding stone that weighed 20 g.

Special objects
  An odd white rock was found in this stratum. Although it does not appear to be carved, its unusual shape and color make it a likely candidate for having been brought to the site by humans.

Botanical remains from flotation of 6.5 liters of soil from higher in the stratum (S-71)
  5 *Chenopodium quinoa* carbonized seeds

Botanical remains from flotation of 5.1 liters of soil from lower in the stratum (S-72)
  6 *Chenopodium quinoa* carbonized seeds

Animal bone (NISP)
  Mammals
    llama or alpaca (*Lama* sp.): 23 (1 from flotation)
    white-tailed deer (*Odocoileus virginianus*): 1 (from
      flotation)
    unidentified: 32 (30 from flotation)

The Ritual Closing of Canals 1 and 3

Southeast of Structure 1, I found the remains of a stone-lined canal that curved around a large boulder and was similar in construction to Ritual Canals 1 and 2 (Figs. 4.18, 4.19). Unfortunately, the canal had been damaged by later construction and so it was not possible to determine its relationship to Structure 1. The canal rested on top of geologic soil and Stratum 12 and was fully buried by Stratum 9. From what little remained, it was possible to use stratigraphy to determine that the canal had been built after Structure 1, but destroyed before Ritual Canal 2 replaced Ritual Canal 1.

At some point, Ritual Canals 1 and 3 were no longer used. Several human burials were placed on the ground surface and offerings were burned before the canals and the burials were covered with a thick stratum of soil (Stratum 9) that effectively and symbolically "closed" these canals. In the case of Canal 3, Burial 9 "cut off" the southern end. The capstones of the northern end were removed, and the interior was filled with ash.

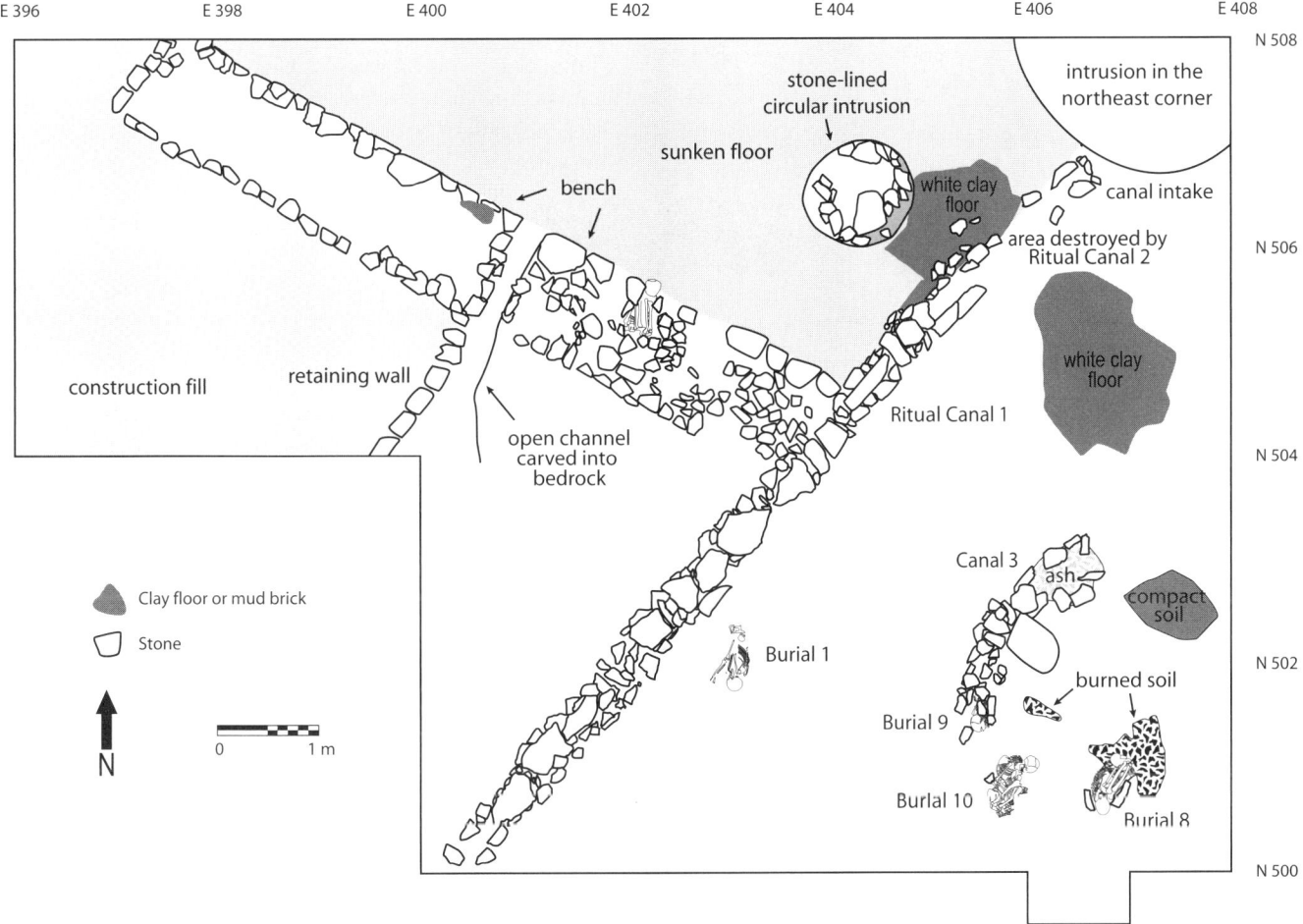

Figure 4.18. Canal 3 was built after Structure 1, but before Ritual Canal 2 replaced Ritual Canal 1. Because the canal was damaged by later construction, it was not possible to determine its relationship to Structure 1. At the south end, the canal was cut off by Burial 9 (a 1- to 2-year-old child). This burial, together with Burials 1 (a 12- to 13-year-old child), 8 (a 36- to 45-year-old woman), and 10 (an 18- to 25-year-old woman), was deposited in the matrix of Stratum 9, a 15- to 50-cm-thick layer of soil covering the entire area south of the bench.

Figure 4.19. Canal 3 was a stone-lined channel very similar to Ritual Canals 1 and 2. Because the canal was mostly destroyed, it is unclear how it related to Structure 1. The capstones of the canal were removed from the section in the foreground of this photograph and the interior was filled with ash when the canal was ritually closed.

Ash in the Northern End of Canal 3

The ash was 30 cm deep and nearly pure, but it did not contain a high density of botanical remains or other artifacts. Therefore, it was probably not a cooking hearth. It is more likely that this ash was the remains from a ritual associated with closing the canal.

Munsell color
 5 YR 4/1 dark gray

Ceramic vessels
 Total sherds: 243
 Restricted vessels with a neck: 2 Chanapata redware,
  1 Chanapata incised, 13 plainware
 Restricted vessel without a neck: 1 Chanapata redware
 Open vessels: 2 Chanapata redware, 1 plainware
 Open vessel with a diameter greater than 30 cm:
  1 plainware
 Body sherds with diagnostic style: 6 Chanapata redware

Reworked ceramic sherd
 Non-disc: 1 plainware

Botanical remains from flotation of 5.2 liters of soil (S-47)
 2 *Chenopodium quinoa* carbonized seeds

Burial 9

Burial 9, a 1- to 2-year-old child with tabular erect cranial modification, was placed at the south end of Canal 3. The skeleton was in a flexed position with the head to the south, or away from the canal. The child was surrounded by several small field stones, which were probably taken from Canal 3. In addition, a large fragment of an *olla* (a restricted vessel with a rim) was placed over the face and knees (Figs. 4.20, 4.21). This burial seems to have "cut off" Canal 3, symbolically and practically ending its use life. The skeleton was 100% complete and in good condition (Burial Type 1).

The child had deciduous carious lesions in 7 teeth. He or she also had non-specific stress indicators including unhealed cribra orbitalia and active periostitis on the internal surface of the occipital (Andrushko 2008).

Burial 1

Burial 1, a 12- to 13-year-old child with slight tabular erect cranial modification, was located at the base of Stratum 9 east of Ritual Canal 1. The skeleton was on its left side, bent at the waist with legs extended and arms folded over the chest, with the head facing south. The skeleton was 86% complete and in good condition (Burial Type 1).

The child had carious lesions on 4 teeth, enamel hypoplasias on 4 teeth, and slight to moderate calculus. He or she had non-specific stress indicators including delayed long bone growth and porosity on the internal surface of the right and left greater wings of the sphenoid (Andrushko 2008).

Burial 8

Burial 8, a 36- to 45-year-old woman with tabular erect cranial modification, was located in the southeast corner of Unit A. Her skeleton was in a tightly flexed position lying on its right side with the head toward the southwest. One large flat stone was placed behind the head and one in front of the knees and face (Fig. 4.22). The skeleton was 100% complete and in good condition (Burial Type 1).

The woman had antemortem loss of 9 teeth, carious lesions on 2 teeth, pulp exposure due to caries on 2 teeth, pulp exposure due to attrition on 1 tooth, four periapical abscesses, severe alveolar resorption, and heavy calculus. She had artificial abrasion with lingual attrition on the upper incisors, and distal attrition of the root of the lower right first molar. She also suffered from appendicular joint disease in the right and left hip joints. She had a small healed depressed cranial fracture and a healed fracture to one left middle rib from trauma experienced during her life. She exhibited osteitis in the right sphenoid with expansion of the lateral surface of the cranium, a marker of non-specific infection (Andrushko 2008).

Figure 4.20.
Burial 9, a 1- to 2-year-old child, cut off Canal 3, symbolically and ritually ending its use life.

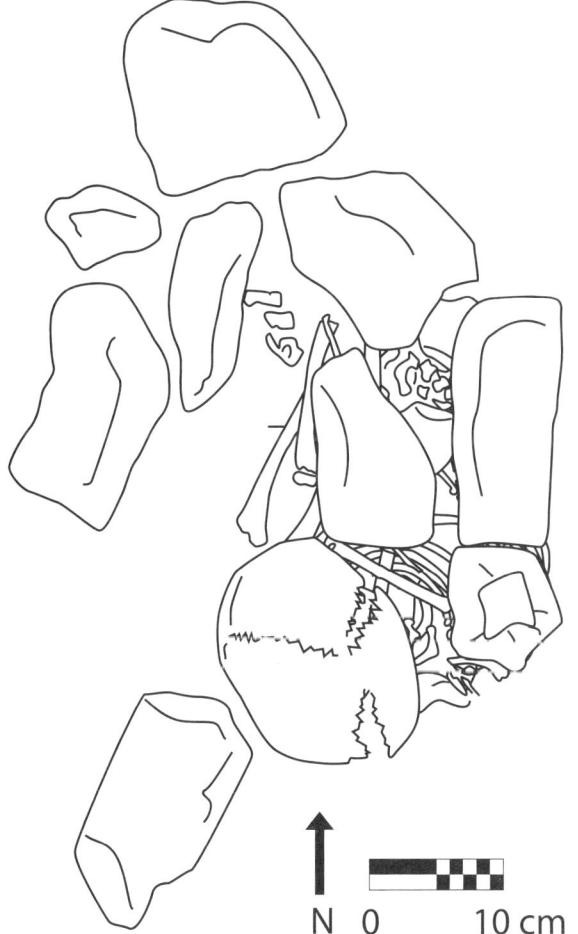

Figure 4.21. Burial 9 was a 1- to 2-year-old child included in Stratum 9 at the end of Canal 3.

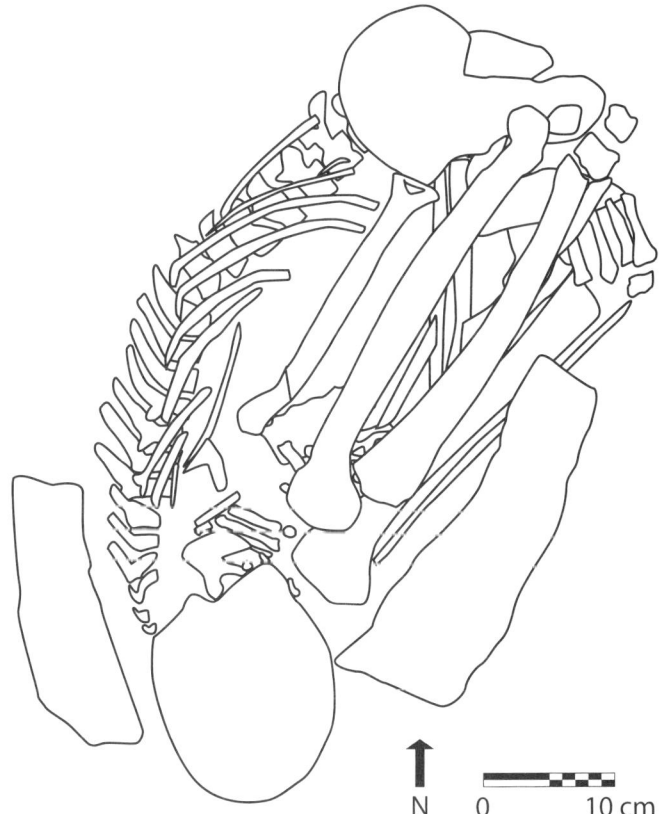

Figure 4.22. Burial 8 was a 36- to 45-year-old woman included in the matrix of Stratum 9.

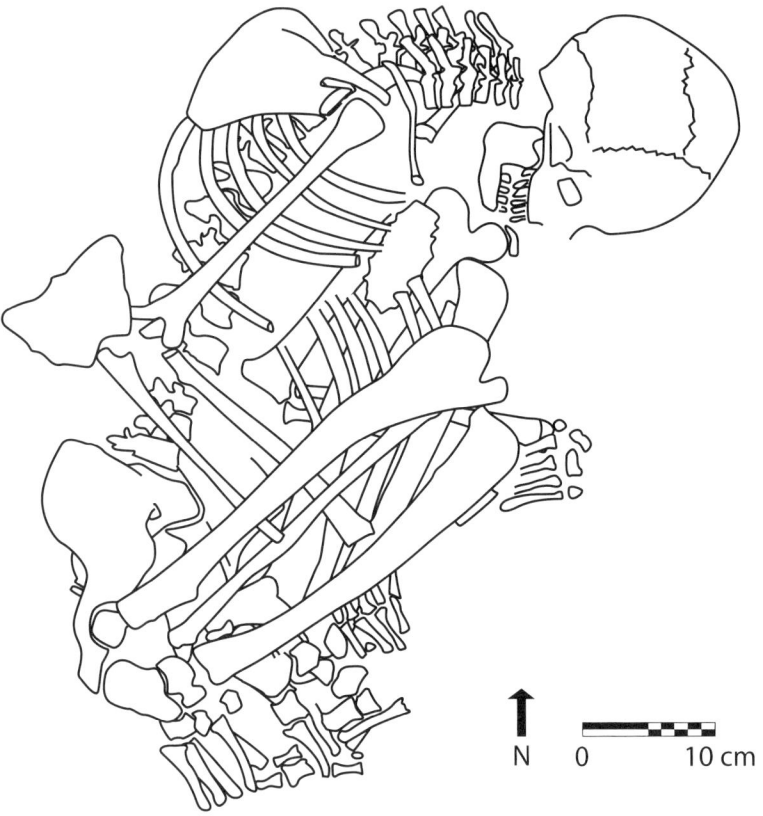

Figure 4.23. Burial 10 was an 18- to 25-year-old woman included in the matrix of Stratum 9. Scorching of parts of the left side of the skeleton indicates that burning an unknown material under the body was part of the burial ritual.

Burial 10

Burial 10 was a young woman 18 to 25 years old with tabular erect cranial modification. Her skeleton was in a flexed position on the left side with the head to the northeast. There was a small rock placed at her right elbow and some white soil, probably from the bedrock, on her chest (Fig. 4.23). Evidence of scorching or burning on several elements (including the left leg and pelvic bones) indicate burning of an unknown material under the body as part of the burial ritual. The skeleton was 100% complete and in good condition (Burial Type 1).

The woman had one periapical abscess, one periodontal abscess, calculus flecks, moderate alveolar resorption, and congenital absence of all third molars. She had a healed depressed cranial fracture, a healed fracture to the left nasal, and a healed greenstick fracture to the right middle rib.

Soil Covering the Ritual Canals and Burials

A thick deposit of compact, light-brown soil between 15 and 50 cm deep (Stratum 9) was deposited on top of Strata 10, 11, 12, and geologic soil, burying Ritual Canal 1 and Canal 3. Burials 1, 8, 9, and 10 were contained within the matrix of this stratum, not in cavities that intruded into it. Stratum 9 was intentionally laid down in order to bury and symbolically "close" some architectural features of Structure 1.

The Construction of Ritual Canal 2

Ritual Canal 2 was built on top of Stratum 9, replacing Ritual Canal 1. The intake of the new canal was in the same location as Ritual Canal 1, but whereas Ritual Canal 1 was straight, Ritual Canal 2 was curved so that its discharge was located about 3 m further east (Fig. 4.25; Plate 6).

Before the canal was built, Burial 11 (a secondary burial of a 2- to 3-year-old child) was placed in a cavity that intruded into Stratum 9. The cavity was located about 1.2 m southeast of the location where Ritual Canal 1 met the bench of Structure 1. Ritual Canal 2 was built over the top of this burial (Figs. 4.24, 4.26). Therefore, Burial 11 was probably an offering that guided the placement of the new canal as it was being built.

It is most likely that this construction took place as a single event that included the closing of Ritual Canal 1 and Canal 3, the interment of two women and two children, and the deposit of up to 50 cm of earth outside Structure 1 (Stratum 9). It is not possible, however, to determine with certainty that Ritual Canal 2 was not built later. A radiocarbon date from the matrix of Burial 11 indicates that this significant remodeling took place between 40 and 270 years after the original construction of Structure 1, with the median difference being about 150 years.

Burial 11

Burial 11, a 2- to 3-year-old child, was under Ritual Canal 2 in a cavity that intruded into Stratum 9 (Fig. 4.26). The intrusion was 20 cm deep with gently sloping sides; it measured 1 m from east to west and 1.6 m from north to south. The ashy remains of a burned offering were found at the eastern edge of the depression, and burned soil covered part of the cavity on the western side of the canal. The child's skeleton was only 57% complete and consisted primarily of the long bones of the legs and lower arms along with a rib fragment and a few fragments of lumbar vertebrae (Burial Type 3). The bones were oriented as if the body had been in a flexed position with the head to the northwest. No pathologies were noted.

Because the hole that was dug to make the burial included burned material and only a few human bones, it is likely that this feature was not simply an individual's grave, but was also an offering made during the construction of Ritual Canal 2. The high number of mouse bones suggests that significant

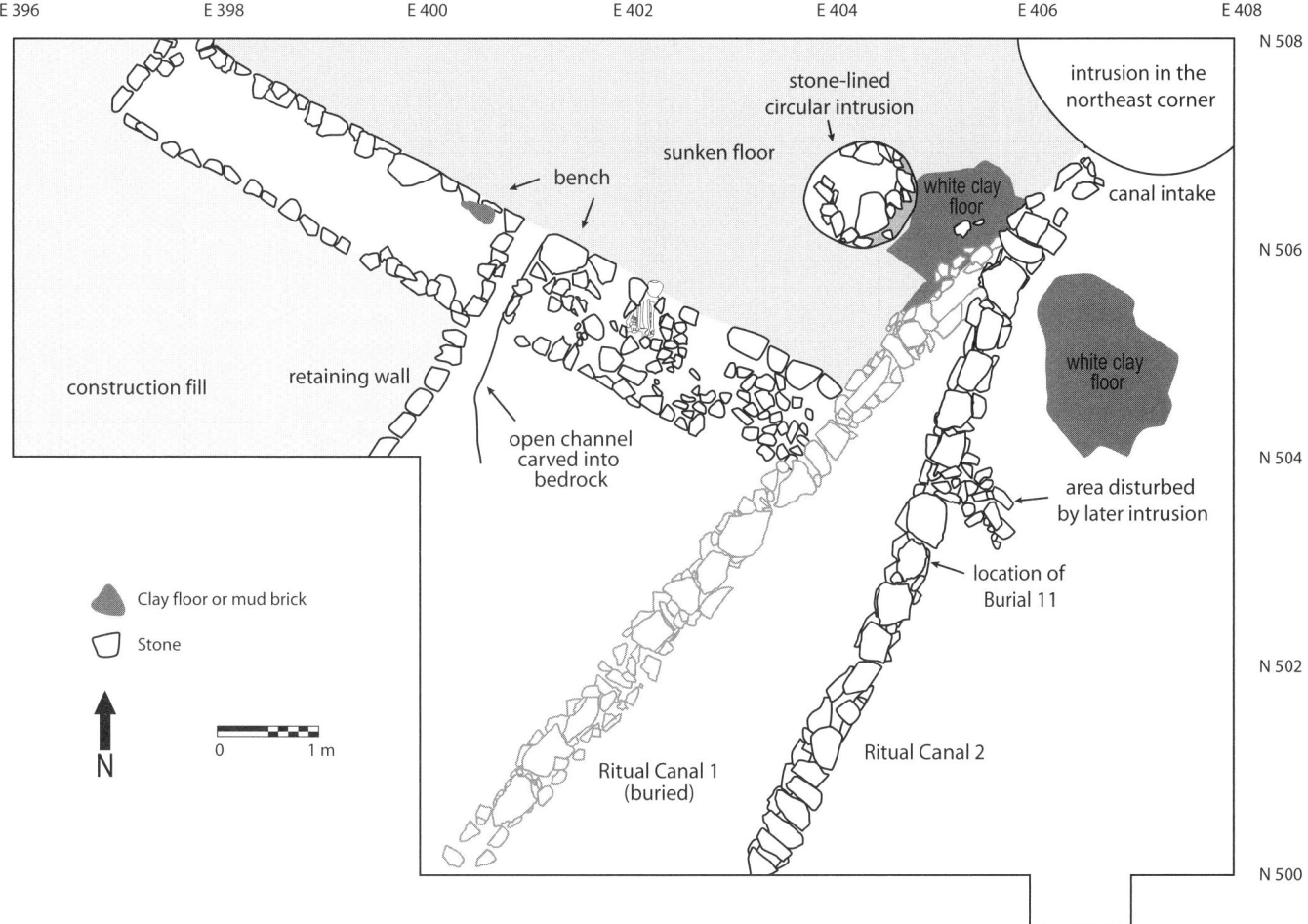

Figure 4.24. Stratum 9 buried Ritual Canal 1 and the villagers of Yuthu built Ritual Canal 2 to replace it. The new canal used the same intake as the old one, but it was curved so that it passed over Burial 11 and had a discharge about 3 m further east.

organic material was present in the offering, but no carbonized food remains were recovered. Instead, the combustion area held dense carbonized plant remains including quinoa, *Galium*, and an Asteraceae inflorescence. These are all plants with attractive flowers. It is possible that food remains were included in the offering, but only flowers were burned.

The Matrix of the Burial

The matrix of the burial was semi-compact, dark brown soil mixed with some ash.

Munsell color
   7.5 YR 4/3 brown

Radiocarbon date
   AA84432/Yuthu RC-109, 2226 ± 76 uncalibrated radiocarbon years BP, 376–144 BC calibrated with sequential model (95.4% confidence)

Ceramic vessels
   Total sherds: 111
   Restricted vessels with a neck: 3 Chanapata redware, 3 plainware
   Restricted vessels without a neck: 1 Chanapata redware, 3 plainware
   Open vessel: 1 plainware
   Body sherds with diagnostic style: 1 Chanapata redware, 1 Chanapata incised

Figure 4.25. Ritual Canal 2 cut off Ritual Canal 1. Both canals shared the same intake inside Structure 1.

Chipped stone
  Regionally available stone (25% by count, 92.38% by wt)
    andesite
      debitage: 1 proximal flake (9.7 g)
  Exotic stone (75% by count, 7.62% by weight)
    obsidian
      tool: 1 combination flake tool projectile point (0.8 g)
      debitage: 2 proximal flakes (< 0.1 g)

Botanical remains from flotation of 4.6 liters of soil west of Ritual Canal 2 (S-68)
  6 *Chenopodium quinoa* carbonized seeds

Botanical remains from flotation of approximately 6.0 liters of soil east of Ritual Canal 2 (S-69)
  10 *Chenopodium quinoa* carbonized seeds

Animal bone (NISP)
  Mammals
    llama or alpaca (*Lama* sp.): 8 (6 from flotation)
    field mouse (Muridae): 59 (55 from flotation)
    unidentified: 8

Combustion Area

At the eastern edge of Burial 11, there was a small concentration of ash with a high density of carbonized botanical remains.

Munsell color
  7.5 YR 3/2 dark brown

Ceramic vessels
  Total sherds: 98
    Restricted vessels with a neck: 1 Chanapata redware, 2 plainware

Figure 4.26. Burial 11 was a 2- to 3-year-old child buried in a cavity below Ritual Canal 2.

Restricted vessels without a neck: 3 pattern burnished,
 1 plainware
Lid: 1 plainware
Body sherds with diagnostic style: 2 Chanapata
 redware, 9 pattern burnished

Botanical remains from flotation of 4.6 liters of soil (S-66)
 50 *Chenopodium quinoa* carbonized seeds
 1 *Galium* sp. carbonized seed
 1 Asteraceae carbonized inflorescence

Burned Soil Covering Part of the Burial Cavity

A small area of burned soil located along the western edge of Ritual Canal 2 covered part of the burial cavity. It was 60 cm from northeast to southwest and 20 cm wide.

Munsell color
 2.5 YR 5/4 reddish brown

Ceramic vessels
 No pottery was found

Animal bone (NISP)
 Mammals
  llama or alpaca (*Lama* sp.): 2

Exploring the Interior of Ritual Canal 2

I removed one stone covering Ritual Canal 2. Unlike Ritual Canal 1, this canal did not contain laminar deposits of soil that are typical of having been laid down by water. Rather, the interior was filled with loose soil. Therefore, the use of this canal was less intense (either in frequency or duration) than that of the canal it replaced.

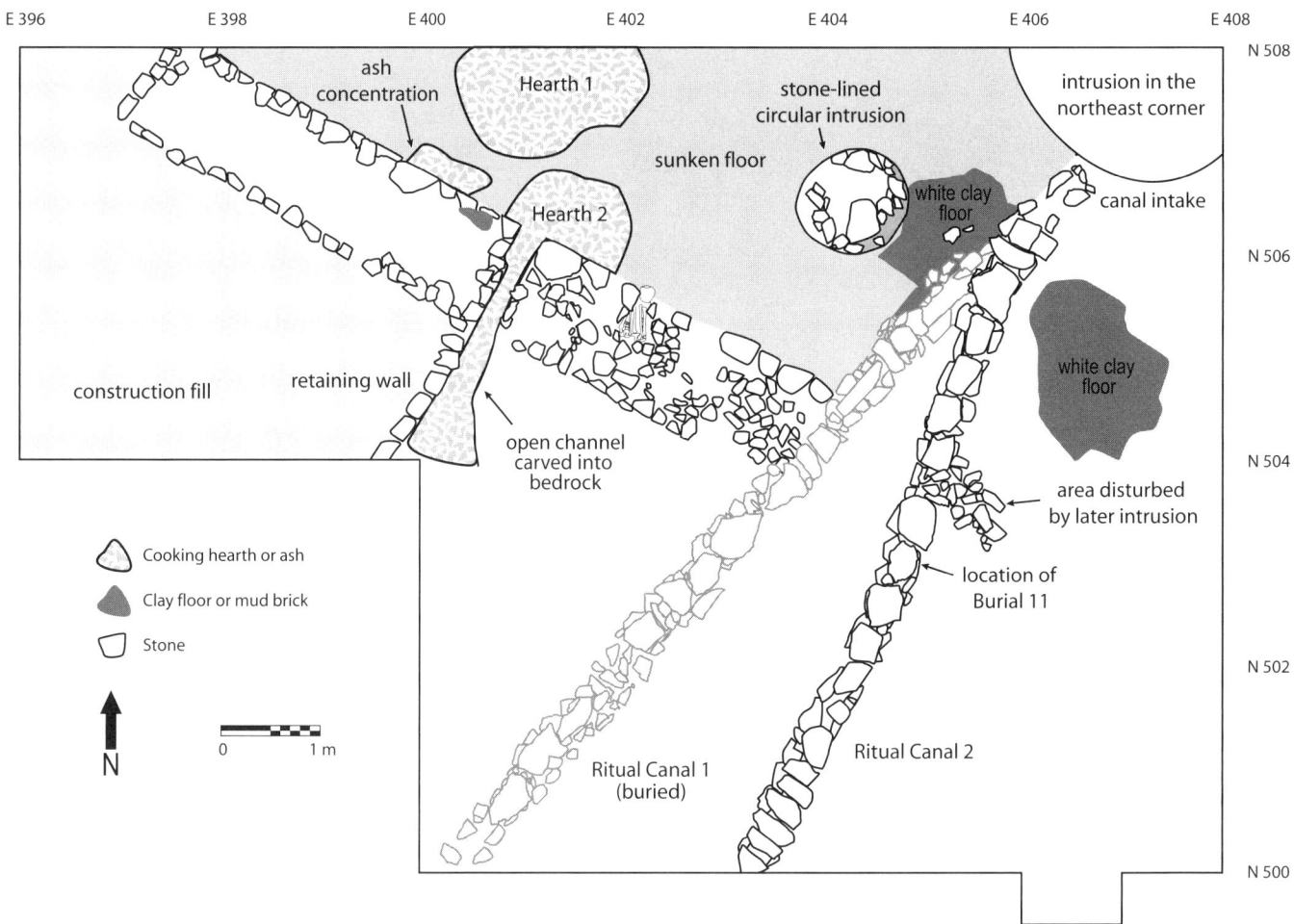

Figure 4.27. The last use of Structure 1 before it was abandoned and buried included two hearths and an ash concentration on the sunken floor.

The Final Use and Burial of Structure 1

Even after Structure 1 was significantly remodeled, the villagers of Yuthu eventually abandoned and buried it. The last activities inside the structure included food preparation and burning of other materials (Fig. 4.27). Based on stratigraphy, it is not possible to determine whether those activities were part of the rituals of interment, or whether they had happened earlier. Yet, considering that villagers had not previously built hearths inside the structure, it seems more likely that these activities took place as part of the closing rituals.

These hearths, the sunken floor, and the bench were covered with a layer of dirt mixed with ash (Stratum 8). This stratum was very thick (between 20 and 35 cm) and it was the first deposit we found both inside and outside Structure 1. Since the flat surface of the platform does not allow thick layers of soil to be deposited by erosion on the southeastern end (deflation is a more typical formation process), it seems likely that villagers intentionally brought this soil to bury Structure 1. After burial, a depressed surface remained so that the location of the Structure 1 would have been evident, but the stone-faced walls and flat sunken floor were hidden.

Hearth 1

An ash-filled depression was located on the sunken floor of Structure 1 about 2 m north of the bench. The full size of the feature is unknown because it extended beyond the northern limit of Unit A, but the excavated portion measured 1.7 m east to west, 1.5 m north to south, and 15 cm deep. The unusual contents of this hearth suggest that it may not have been used for meal preparation and consumption. Very few animal bones were recovered. The ashy soil contained a high density of carbonized quinoa, corn, and *Trifolium*. While two of these species may be eaten as food, all three are frequently used as fuel. We found equal numbers of restricted vessels with and without necks, but no serving vessels. Furthermore, we did not find any tools to suggest craft activities were carried out in this area.

In contrast with cooking hearths of similar size in the Northern Sector, this hearth was not a generalized activity area. We found no evidence of food consumption, and it is not clear whether food was prepared. Rather than being a cooking feature, this may have been an area where villagers burned an offering before burying the sunken structure.

Munsell color
   7.5 YR 5/3 brown

Ceramic vessels
   Total sherds: 232
   Restricted vessels with a neck: 1 Chanapata redware,
      1 pattern burnished, 11 plainware
   Restricted vessels without a neck: 1 pattern burnished,
      11 plainware
   Lid: 1 plainware
   Body sherds with diagnostic style: 1 Chanapata
      redware, 4 pattern burnished

Reworked ceramic sherds
   Discs: 3 plainware

Botanical remains from flotation of 6.0 liters of soil (S-60)
   35 *Chenopodium quinoa* carbonized seeds
   1 *Trifolium* sp. carbonized seed
   1 *Zea mays* carbonized cob fragment

Animal bone (NISP)
   Mammals
      llama or alpaca (*Lama* sp.): 7
      unidentified: 8 (all from flotation)

Hearth 2

A second concentration of ash (16 cm deep) was located on the sunken floor alongside the northern face of the bench, just to the east of the drain between the eastern and western sections. The densest concentration of ash was 1.4 m from east to west and 1 m from north to south, but ash from this area also extended through the drain. Soil samples held low densities of carbonized plants, yet we recovered many land snails and mice from this area. In other areas at Yuthu, these animals were drawn to concentrations of organic matter in hearths and storage pits. It is possible that non-carbonized plant or animal remains attracted them to this area.

Unlike Hearth 1, the contents of this feature were more typical of cooking hearths in other areas at Yuthu. The ceramic assemblage included common proportions of vessel forms (mostly restricted vessels with a neck, some restricted vessels without a neck, and a few open vessels). The hearth contained a variety of chipped stone tools and debitage from local, regional, and exotic sources. There were objects used for activities including two pinch grinders and a hand-held mortar that may have been used together and ceramic and stone discs. It is unclear why the two contemporary and nearby hearths were used for apparently different activities.

Munsell color
   7.5 YR 4/3 brown

Ceramic vessels
   Total sherds: 894
   Restricted vessels with a neck: 1 Chanapata incised,
      1 pattern burnished, 35 plainware, 1 indeterminate style
   Restricted vessels without a neck: 1 pattern burnished,
      13 plainware, 1 indeterminate style
   Open vessels: 2 Chanapata redware, 2 plainware,
      1 indeterminate style
   Open vessels with a diameter greater than 30 cm:
      2 Chanapata redware
   Lid: 1 plainware
   Body sherds with diagnostic style: 13 Chanapata
      redware, 2 Chanapata blackware, 1 Chanapata
      incised, 4 pattern burnished, 8 indeterminate style

Reworked ceramic sherds
   Discs: 2 Chanapata plainware

Chipped stone
   Locally available stone (10% by count, 8.42% by weight)
      quartzite
         debitage: 1 proximal flake (0.8 g)
   Regionally available stone (20% by count, 24.21% by wt)
      andesite
         debitage: 1 proximal flake (< 2.3 g)
      rhyolite
         debitage: 1 proximal flake (< 0.1 g)
   Exotic stone (70% by count, 67.37% by weight)
      obsidian
         tools: 1 unimarginal flake tool (4.2 g), 1 bimarginal
            flake tool (0.5 g), 1 bimarginal flake tool
            reutilized projectile point (0.4 g)
         debitage: 3 proximal flakes (0.8 g), 1 fragment of
            flake shatter (0.5 g)

Groundstone
   Roughly spherical stone that fit into one hand with flattened surfaces created by grinding with back and forth or circular strokes (Group 1, Type A). The stone had pecking marks. It measured 7.48 × 5.46 × 4.01 cm; it weighed 270 g.

Small oval stone with plano-convex cross section that could be held between the fingers (Small Group 2, Type O). The stone had pecking marks. It measured 7.58 × 3.45 × 4.17 cm; it weighed 100 g.

Stone that could be pinched between the fingers with a flattened surface created by back and forth or circular strokes (Small Group 3, Type P). The stone measured 3.35 × 2.79 × 2.50 cm; it weighed 20 g.

Palm-sized mortar (Type R) with evidence of pecking. About 70% of the object was present. It measured 12.55 × 10.35 × 3.65 cm; the fragment weighed 610 g.

A stone disc. About 50% of the object was present. The diameter was 4.88 cm; it was 1.21 cm tall. The fragment weighed 20 g.

Two nondescript fragments of grinding stones that weighed 280 g and 20 g.

Botanical remains from flotation of 5.8 liters of soil (S-45)
No identifiable plant remains were recovered from this sample

Botanical remains from flotation of 5.6 liters of soil (S-57)
7 *Chenopodium quinoa* carbonized seeds

Botanical remains from flotation of 5.6 liters of soil (S-75)
1 *Ambrosia* sp. carbonized seed

Animal bone (NISP)
Mammals
llama or alpaca (*Lama* sp.): 2
field mouse (Muridae): 17 (all from flotation)
unidentified: 24 (19 from flotation)

Use of the Depression Left by Structure 1 after It was Buried

After Structure 1 was buried, people continued to use the area on top of the platform. Within the excavated area, they prepared and consumed at least one meal and reused the intrusion that had been located in front of the intake of Ritual Canals 1 and 2. It is difficult to determine whether these activities took place as part of the ritual interment (immediately after soil was brought to cover the sunken structure) or whether more time passed between burial of the structure and reuse of this area.

Cooking Hearth 3

After Structure 1 was buried, a hearth was built in nearly the same place as Hearth 1. It contained pure ash 20 cm thick. The excavated portion of the feature measured 2 m (east to west) by 1.6 m (north to south), but the entire extent is not known because it extended beyond the northern limit of Unit A. The contents of this feature were typical of a cooking hearth in which people prepared and consumed food while carrying out other activities beside the fire. Stones were arranged to support a cooking pot at the deepest part of the intrusion. Fragments of ceramics included mostly restricted vessels with a neck, some restricted vessels without a neck, and a few open vessels. The hearth contained a high density of botanical remains including quinoa, corn, *Trifolium*, and *Ambrosia* (probably for fuel). Unlike the earlier hearths in this area, there were abundant animal bones including camelid and *cuy*. The hearth also held objects for other activities such as a variety of chipped stone items, an unusual large unhafted quartzitic sandstone biface, a worked bone object, a fragment of a groundstone axe, and a broken metal pin.

Because the feature intruded into the stratum that buried Structure 1 (Stratum 8), it is clear that this hearth was used after Structure 1 was buried. Unfortunately, it is not possible to determine whether it was used to prepare food immediately after people completed the task of burying this structure or whether it took place much later when people revisited the site. No stratified layers of ash or trampled surfaces indicate repeated or continuous use of the hearth.

Munsell color
7.5 YR 5/1 gray

Ceramic vessels
Total sherds: 709
Restricted vessels with a neck: 1 Chanapata redware, 1 Chanapata blackware, 1 pattern burnished, 23 plainware, 1 indeterminate style
Restricted vessels without a neck: 1 Chanapata incised, 1 pattern burnished, 16 plainware
Open vessels: 2 Chanapata redware, 5 plainware
Open vessels with a diameter greater than 30 cm: 2 Chanapata redware
Lids: 2 Chanapata redware
Body sherds with diagnostic style: 7 Chanapata redware, 3 Chanapata blackware, 1 Chanapata incised, 6 pattern burnished

Chipped stone
Locally available stone (66.67% by count, 98.19% by wt)
fine grain quartzitic sandstone
tools: 1 unhafted biface (23.6 g), 1 bimarginal flake tool (3.0 g)
debitage: 1 proximal flake (2.5 g)
quartzite
debitage: 1 proximal flake (41.3 g)
Exotic stone (33.33% by count, 1.81% by weight)
obsidian
tools: 1 bimarginal flake tool (< 0.1 g), 1 combination flake tool (1.3 g)

Worked bone
1 thin object with round cross section and pointed end

Groundstone

Fragment of a groundstone axe. About 50% of the object was present. The length was unknown; it was 3.25 cm wide and 2.22 cm tall. The fragment weighed 80 g.

Nondescript fragment of a grinding stone that weighed 10 g.

Metal

Part of a metal pin broken into 6 fragments was found near the stones arranged to hold a cooking pot. It had a round cross section about 3 mm in diameter; it weighed 1.0 g.

Botanical remains from flotation of 5.5 liters of soil surrounding the hearth stones (S-19)

18 *Chenopodium quinoa* carbonized seeds
1 *Trifolium* sp. carbonized seed
4 *Zea mays* carbonized cupule fragments

Botanical remains from flotation of 5.5 liters of soil stratigraphically higher than the hearth stones (S-17)

4 *Chenopodium quinoa* carbonized seeds
1 *Ambrosia* sp. carbonized seed

Animal bone (NISP)

Mammals
    llama or alpaca (*Lama* sp.): 50 (29 from flotation)
    guinea pig (*Cavia porcellus*): 1
    field mouse (Muridae): 3 (all from flotation)
    unidentified: 9 (5 from flotation)

Reuse of the Intrusion in the Northeast Corner (Intrusion A)

After ashy layers covered the sunken floor and bench of Structure 1, the intrusion in the northeast corner was filled with three more strata of soil. This may have happened within hours of the burial of Structure 1 or much later; it is not possible to determine the timing based on stratigraphy alone. The intrusion contained dense concentrations of pottery fragments, some ceramic discs, a variety of chipped stone tools, grinding stones, and llama and *cuy* bones.

Level A-1

Level A-1 filled the base of the intrusion and spread outside it to cover part of Stratum 8. The layer was semi-compact, dark brown earth mixed with ash 20 cm deep.

Munsell color

7.5 YR 4/6 brown

Ceramic vessels

Total sherds: 1203
Restricted vessels with a neck: 3 Chanapata redware, 1 Chanapata incised, 38 plainware
Restricted vessels without a neck: 1 Chanapata incised, 1 pattern burnished, 18 plainware
Open vessels: 4 Chanapata redware, 13 plainware
Lids: 2 Chanapata redware, 1 plainware
Body sherds with diagnostic style: 6 Chanapata redware, 1 Chanapata blackware, 2 Chanapata incised, 4 pattern burnished, 1 indeterminate style

Reworked ceramic sherds

Discs: 2 plainware
Non-discs: 4 plainware

Chipped stone

Locally available stone (57.14% by count, 93.49% by wt)
    quartzite
        debitage: 1 proximal flake (3.1 g)
    chert
        debitage: 1 proximal flake (0.4 g)
    organic limestone
        debitage: 1 unmodified manuport (33.8 g)
Regionally available stone (14.29% by count, 5.33% by wt)
    andesite
        tool: 1 unimarginal flake tool (2.7 g)
Exotic stone (28.57% by count, 1.18% by weight)
    obsidian
        tool: 1 unimarginal flake tool (0.3 g)
        debitage: 1 proximal flake (0.3 g)

Groundstone

Fragment of a grinding stone that fit in one hand with plano-convex cross section and flattened surfaces created by grinding with back and forth and rocking motions (Group 1, Type B). About 15% of the object was present. The length and width were unknown; it was 2.68 cm tall. The fragment weighed 100 g.

Stone that could be pinched between the fingers with a flattened surface created by back and forth or circular strokes (Small Group 3, Type P). The stone measured 3.86 × 2.35 × 2.01 cm; it weighed 20 g.

Special objects

Two rocks with unusual shapes and colors (one was black and one was orange) were found in Level A-1, just west of the intrusion. They had not been modified by humans.

Animal bone (NISP)

Mammals
    llama or alpaca (*Lama* sp.): 14
    guinea pig (*Cavia porcellus*): 2

Level A-2

Level A-2 was loose, light-brown soil that intruded into Level A-1. It was 20 cm deep and included many loose rocks and chunks of gypsum, the bedrock material in this area. The soil in the northeast corner was particularly hard and was filled with a high concentration of pottery.

Munsell color
   7.5 YR 4/3 brown

Ceramic vessels
   Total sherds: 934
   Restricted vessels with a neck: 7 pattern burnished, 38 plainware
   Restricted vessels without a neck: 2 pattern burnished, 13 plainware
   Open vessels: 2 Chanapata redware, 7 pattern burnished, 7 plainware
   Body sherds with diagnostic style: 4 Chanapata redware, 3 Chanapata blackware, 2 Chanapata incised, 5 pattern burnished

Reworked ceramic sherds
   Discs: 2 plainware
   Non-disc: 1 plainware

Chipped stone
   Locally available stone (56.25% by count, 74.35% by wt)
      coarse grain quartzitic sandstone
         debitage: 1 proximal flake (18.6 g)
      fine grain quartzitic sandstone
         tool: 1 multidirectional core (9.6 g)
         debitage: 2 proximal flakes (3.9 g), 1 fragment of angular shatter (10.1 g)
      chert
         tool: 1 multidirectional core (6.9 g)
      organic limestone
         debitage: 2 proximal flakes (15.7 g)
      schist
         debitage: 1 fragment of angular shatter (1.0 g)
   Regionally available stone (37.50% by count, 24.86% by weight)
      slate
         debitage: 1 fragment of angular shatter (0.7 g)
      andesite
         debitage: 1 proximal flake (0.5 g), 3 fragments of angular shatter (10.5 g)
      rhyolite
         tool: 1 unimarginal flake tool (10.3 g)
   Exotic stone (6.25% by count, 0.79% by weight)
      obsidian
         tool: 1 bimarginal flake tool (0.7 g)

Groundstone
   Roughly spherical stone that fit into one hand with flattened surfaces created by grinding with back and forth or circular strokes (Group 1, Type A). The stone had pecking marks. It measured 8.48 × 7.97 × 4.88 cm; it weighed 460 g.

Animal bone (NISP)
   Mammals
      llama or alpaca (*Lama* sp.): 13
      white-tailed deer (*Odocoileus virginianus*): 2
   Amphibians
      toad (*Bufo* sp.): 11

Level A-3

Level A-3 was a thin layer of compact earth between 5 and 10 cm thick located along the northern limit of Unit A. Because the layer was so thin, it was excavated together with Levels A-1 and A-2, the layers right below it. No artifacts were recovered.

Munsell color
   7.5 YR 4/3 brown

Compact Deposits of Clay and Ash Concentrations

Stratum 7 was a layer of loose, brown soil mixed with ash and burned earth (18 cm thick). This stratum was associated with several cultural features. Two linear deposits of very compact clay 8 cm tall ran northwest to southeast, approximately parallel to the bench of Structure 1. The western section was 70 cm long by 35 cm wide, and the eastern section was 100 cm long by 50 cm wide. These features were similar to the foundation of the mud structure (described below). They were associated with many loose or roughly aligned stones and an ash concentration 13 cm deep on the western edge of the excavation unit. Because I found these features in a very disturbed state, it was not possible to determine what kind of structure or activity they represented. Based on stratigraphy, these features were built after Structure 1 had been buried.

The Mud Structure

During excavation, we noticed a line of red soil about 15 cm wide running from northwest to southeast. We began to refer to this mysterious feature as the "*mancha roja*," or "red stain," but it was several days before we discovered what it was. Since the feature was marked only by its unusual color and slightly more compact texture, we proceeded with caution, and soon discovered a corner at the eastern end of the line. I began to look for the limits of what seemed to be a rectangular structure, made not of stone or adobe, but of hardened mud. Eventually, we traced out wall foundations 10 cm high on three sides (Figs. 4.28, 4.29). The structure was open to the southwest (or toward the outside of the platform); a round deposit of hardened mud about 15 cm in diameter may have been a base for a post on that side. The east and west wall foundations had interior niches whose purpose was not clear. This foundation probably supported a perishable superstructure made of poles, cane, or thatch.

Although I did not realize it at the time, I soon learned that this structure shared the same alignment as the buried bench of Structure 1, the earliest ceremonial structure in this area. In fact, the mud structure was located in nearly the same place as the eastern section of the bench, though its northern wall was about 30 cm further north than the interior façade of the earlier building. It may be difficult to imagine how villagers could have achieved such a similar orientation and location, given that Structure 1 was buried, but the features inside the mud structure provide a clue as to how this might have been accomplished. A single large stone that had been part of the interior bench façade was incorporated as a significant feature of the interior of the mud structure. It was located next to a small circular stone hearth (Fig. 4.29). We found a concentration of bones and pottery south of the hearth and burned soil along the north wall. Outside the structure, a semicircular formation of loose stones was located at the northwest corner. The soil inside and outside of these stones was the same and no artifacts were found in situ inside the ring. Therefore, it is difficult to determine the purpose of these stones.

The construction techniques and shape of the mud structure do not resemble the simple houses that we found in Unit D. Furthermore, the interior hearth was not like the large open cooking hearths that held high concentrations of carbonized botanical remains. Instead, it closely resembled a circular hearth associated with the burials from the final phase in Unit D. Considering these features along with the location and alignment shared with ceremonial Structure 1, it is clear that the mud structure, though it was of simple construction, had a ritual purpose that was related to, but evolved from, the earlier ceremonial system. A radiocarbon date from the lowest level of the hearth dates the use of the mud structure to 361–62 BC—no more than 455 years after Structure 1 was built, and probably less (Structure 1 was built between 417 and 209 BC, 95.4% confidence).

The Circular Stone Hearth

The circular stone hearth was 25 cm in diameter and 7 cm deep. It was filled with two levels of ash. Each level was taken as a flotation sample. The low density of plant remains recovered indicates that this feature was probably not used to cook food.

Circular Stone Hearth: Level A

The lowest level of the hearth was 4 cm thick. It was less ashy than Level B.

Munsell color
7.5 YR 4/4 brown

Radiocarbon date
AA84430/Yuthu RC-61, 2213 ± 61 uncalibrated radiocarbon years BP, 361–62 BC calibrated with sequential model (95.4% confidence)

Ceramic vessels
Two non-diagnostic body sherds with a diameter less than 2.5 cm

Botanical remains from flotation of 1.8 liters of soil (S-52)
No identifiable plant remains were recovered from this sample

Circular Stone Hearth: Level B

The upper level in the hearth was ashy soil 3 cm thick.

Munsell color
7.5 YR 5/2 brown

Ceramic vessels
No pottery was found in this soil

Botanical remains from flotation of 1.1 liters of soil (S-54)
1 *Chenopodium quinoa* carbonized seed

Concentration of Animal Bones and Reworked Pottery

There was a small concentration of burned llama or alpaca bone and reworked pottery fragments just south of the circular stone hearth.

Munsell color
7.5 YR 4/3 brown

Reworked ceramic sherds
Non-discs: 3 plainware

Botanical remains from flotation of 5.8 liters of soil (S-36)
2 *Oxalis* sp. carbonized seeds

Animal bone (NISP)
Mammals
  llama or alpaca (*Lama* sp.): 11
  unidentified: 11 (7 from flotation)

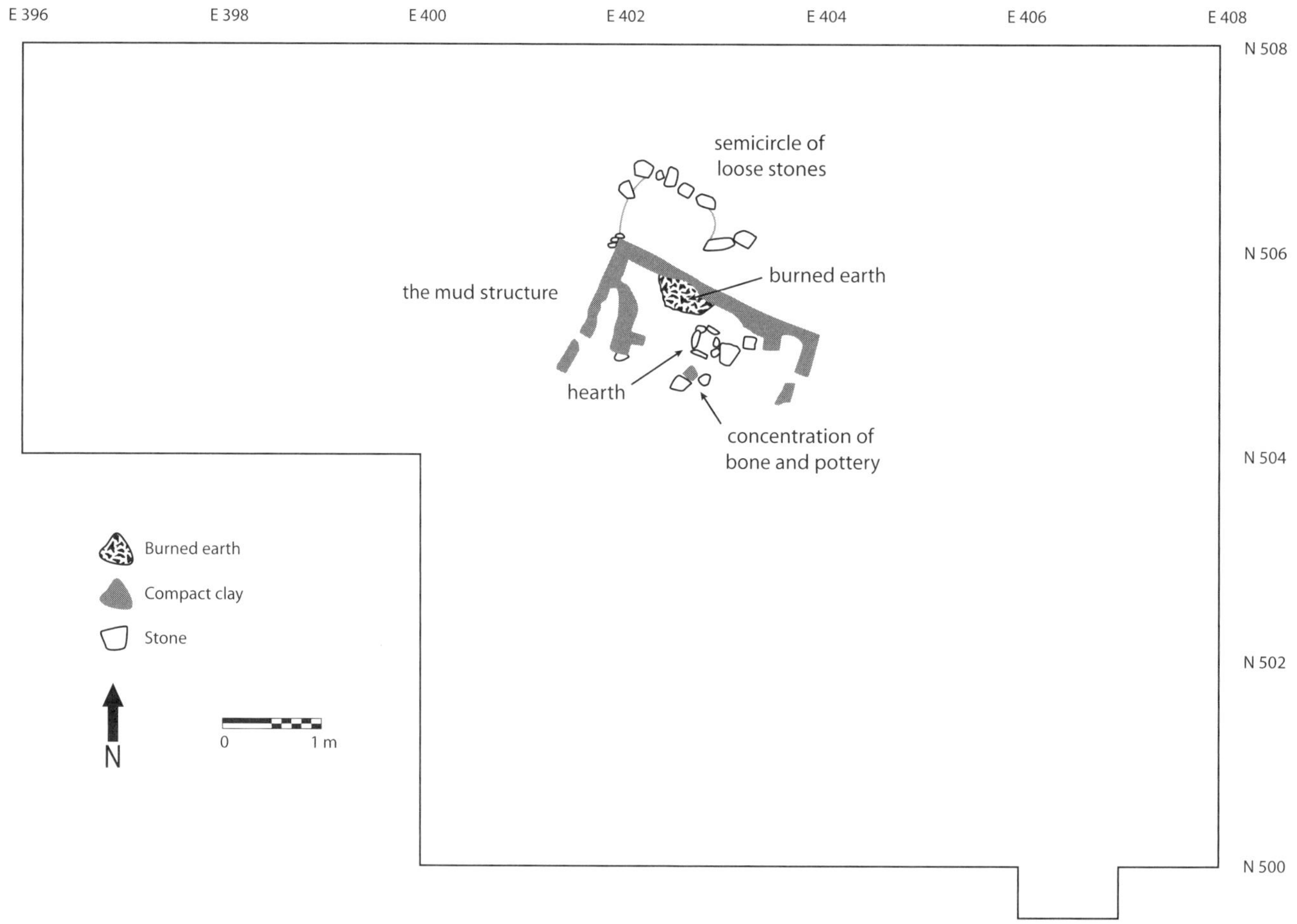

Figure 4.28. The mud structure had three walls and was open to the southwest. The 10-cm-high foundation was made of compact red clay. Inside the structure, there was a small circular stone hearth, a concentration of bone and pottery, and an area of burned earth. North of the structure, there was a semicircle of loose stones.

Figure 4.29. The mud structure. The large stone next to the circular hearth was part of the northern façade of the bench of Structure 1.

The Final Use of the Southern Sector: Human Burials and Stone Alignments

The latest cultural stratum in Unit A was a layer of semi-compact dark brown soil between 16 and 46 cm deep that buried the mud structure. This stratum (Stratum 3) held human burials and stone alignments. Other than mortuary rituals, no other significant human activities took place during this phase. We found no buildings, pits, or floors. Although many flotation samples from this deposit were analyzed, carbonized plant remains were either completely absent or were present in very low numbers, indicating that no cooking took place at this time.

Human burials were the most notable features in this stratum. A cluster of five burials, found in the southeast corner of Unit A, included one young man who had been stored as a mummy before being buried at Yuthu, a group burial of three children, and an older woman (Fig. 4.30). Separate from this cluster, the only formal tomb at Yuthu held the remains of a man who was the only person we found without cranial deformation. This man also had the highest number of injuries typical of violent interactions. Each burial is described in detail below.

In addition to the burials, four stone alignments one-course high and three circular piles of stone were seated on top of Stratum 3. The lines of rocks shared the orientation of Structure 1 and the mud structure; that is, they were oriented according to the long and short axes of the platform. It is unlikely that these stones served as foundations for superstructures of adobe, cane, or another perishable material. I found no evidence of adobes and no seeds from plants that may have been used for thatch. Furthermore, most alignments were isolated features. The only two that formed a corner (as might be expected of a structure foundation) did so at the location of Burial 5. These alignments were probably the remains of ritual activities associated with the burials. One intriguing possibility is that they were similar to miniature houses and enclosures that people build at shrines today (see Aldenderfer 1991 for similar comparison at Asana).

Two objects found in this stratum merit description, though they were not found in meaningful cultural contexts: (1) a block

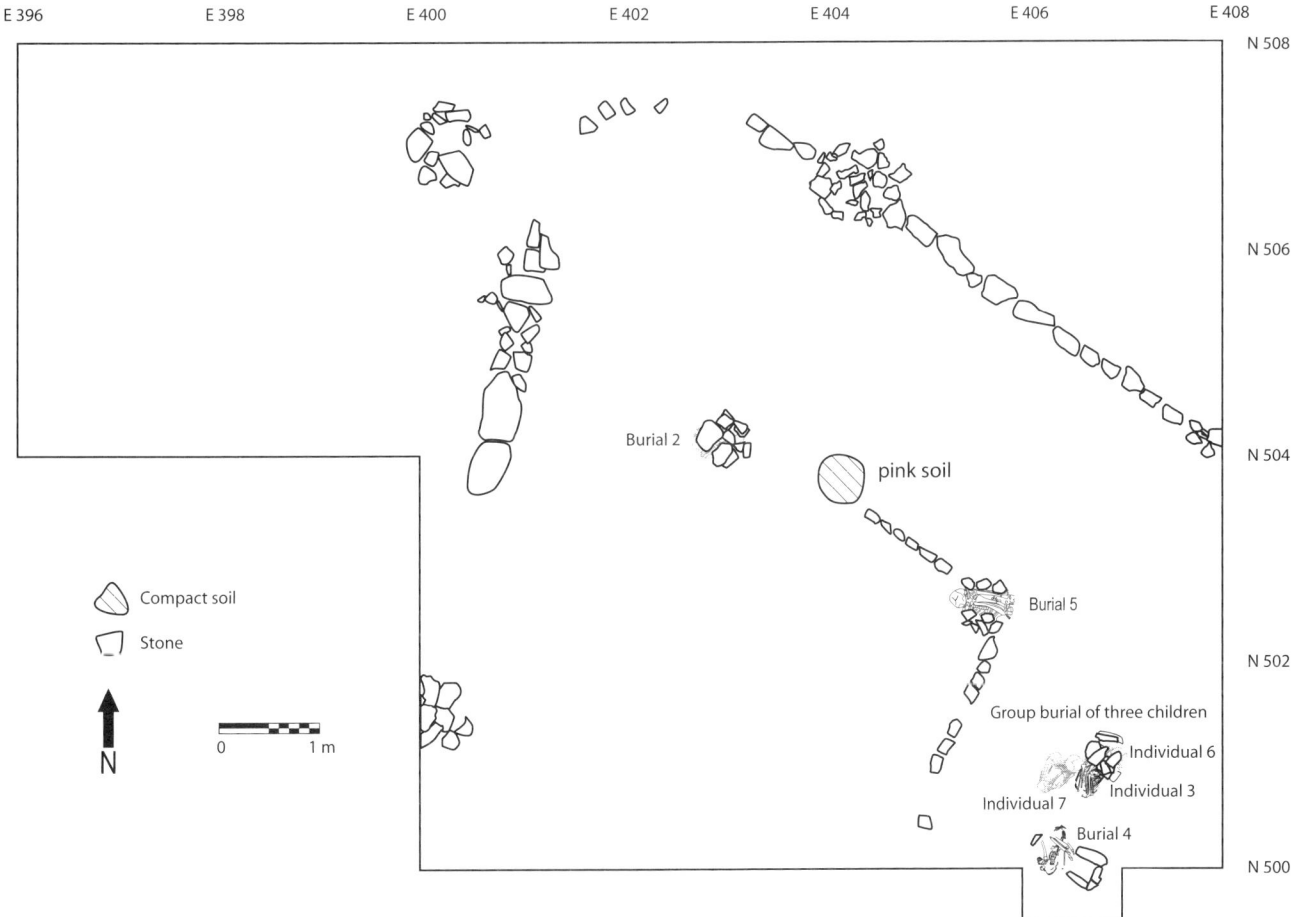

Figure 4.30. The final use of Unit A included human burials and several alignments and circular piles of stones that were one course high. A cluster of burials in the southeast corner included an 18- to 25-year-old man who had been stored as a mummy before being buried at Yuthu (Burial 4); a group burial of three children (Individual 3 [7–8 years old], Individual 6 [11–12 years old], and Individual 7 [1–2 years old]); and possibly Burial 5, an older woman (46+ years). Burial 2 was a 26- to 35-year-old man who was buried in a tomb capped with clay and stone.

of sandstone shaped like a pyramid with a flat top may have been an *illa*, or stone representation of a mountain; and (2) we found a stone figurine carved into the shape of a person in a seated and flexed position. This pose was very similar to that of nearly all the individuals buried at Yuthu. The hat, eyes, nose, and part of the body were painted red. We found the figurine snapped in two at the neck (see Fig. 5.4). The role of these objects in the ritual system is discussed further in Chapter 5.

A Cluster of Burials in the Southeast Corner

Burial 4

Burial 4 was an 18- to 25-year-old man buried in a flexed seated position with a multidirectional core of fine grain quartzitic sandstone in his lap. At shoulder height, a three-sided stone box was located on his right side and a single rock on his left (Fig. 4.31). We recovered *Chenopodium*, *Galium*, and *Oxalis* seeds from the flotation sample of the box's contents. Because this burial was located close to the modern ground surface, modern plowing had broken the knees. The skeleton was only 29% complete and in fair condition.

Like Burial 19, the cranium was absent from this burial, and the cervical vertebrae and the mandible were present, yet there was no evidence of cut marks on the mandible or vertebrae. Unlike Burial 19, however, this grave had been disturbed by modern plowing. If the cranium had been removed by a tractor or plow, fragments of cranial bones would have remained in or around the grave. No such bones were present. Therefore, like Burials 19 and 16, this man had been stored in an above-ground location until the soft tissue had decayed enough to remove the cranium before burying the rest of the mummy bundle in the Southern Sector (Burial Type 4). I found no evidence of how or where the cranium might have been used.

The man had carious lesions on 3 teeth, slight to moderate calculus, and rotation of the lower canines due to crowding (Andrushko 2008).

Botanical remains from flotation of 6.0 liters of soil in the stone box of Burial 4 (S-33)
  2 *Chenopodium quinoa* carbonized seeds
  1 *Galium* sp. carbonized seed
  1 *Oxalis* sp. carbonized seed

Chipped stone
  Locally available stone (100% by count and weight)
    fine grain quartzitic sandstone
      tool: 1 multidirectional core (63.4 g) (found resting in the man's lap)
    chert
      tool: 1 unimarginal flake tool (0.5 g)

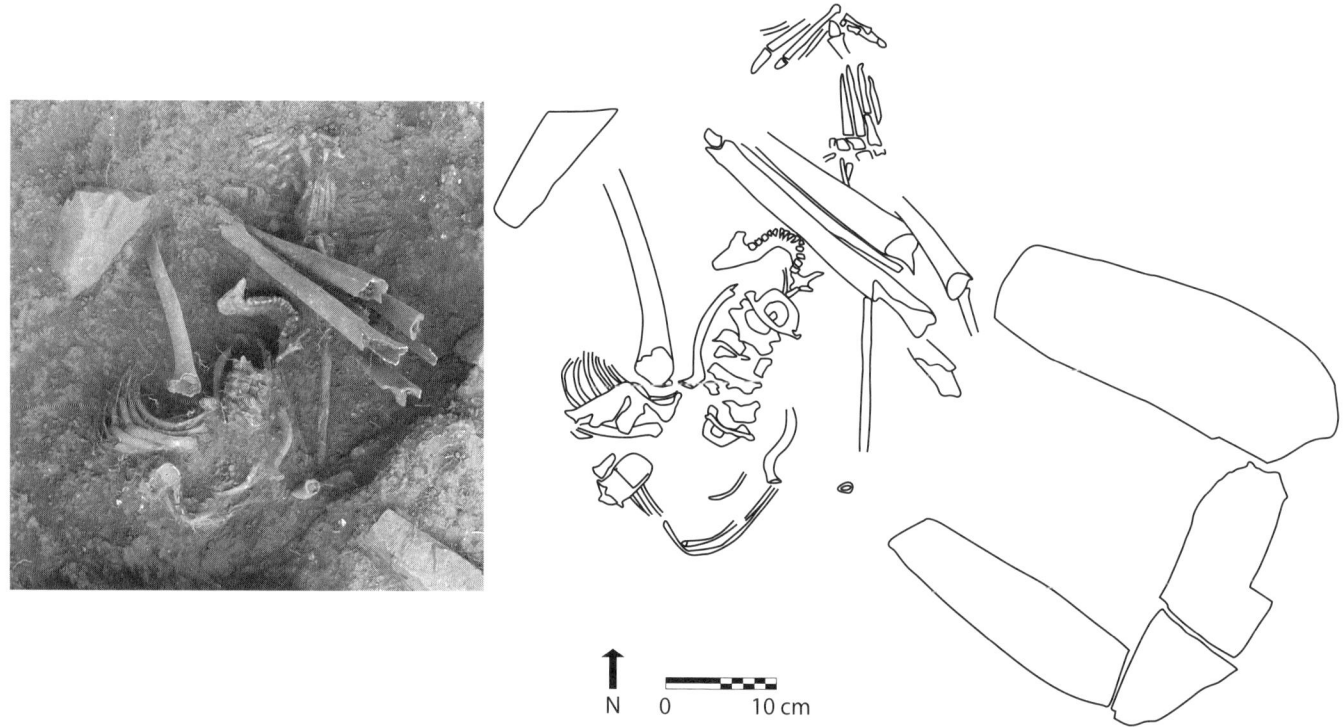

Figure 4.31. Burial 4 was an 18- to 25-year-old man. The cranium was missing from the grave. Note that the vertebrae of the neck and the mandible were found in correct anatomical position and did not have cut marks. This man was probably stored above ground as a mummy before being buried at Yuthu.

Group Burial of Three Children

North of Burial 4, three children were buried together in a single grave shortly after death (Burial Type 1). The individual at the center of the grave was an 11- to 12-year-old child who had been killed by a blow to the skull (Individual 6). Relative to this person, a 1- to 2-year-old child was buried at the feet (Individual 7), and a 7- to 8-year-old child above the head (Individual 3). The 7- to 8-year old was buried without his or her head and neck, and a fragment of an adult right ilium was placed over the feet of the 1- to 2-year old (Figs. 4.32, 4.33). The inclusion of this bone is significant because a right pelvis was taken from Burial 16, a 26- to 35-year-old man who had been stored above ground

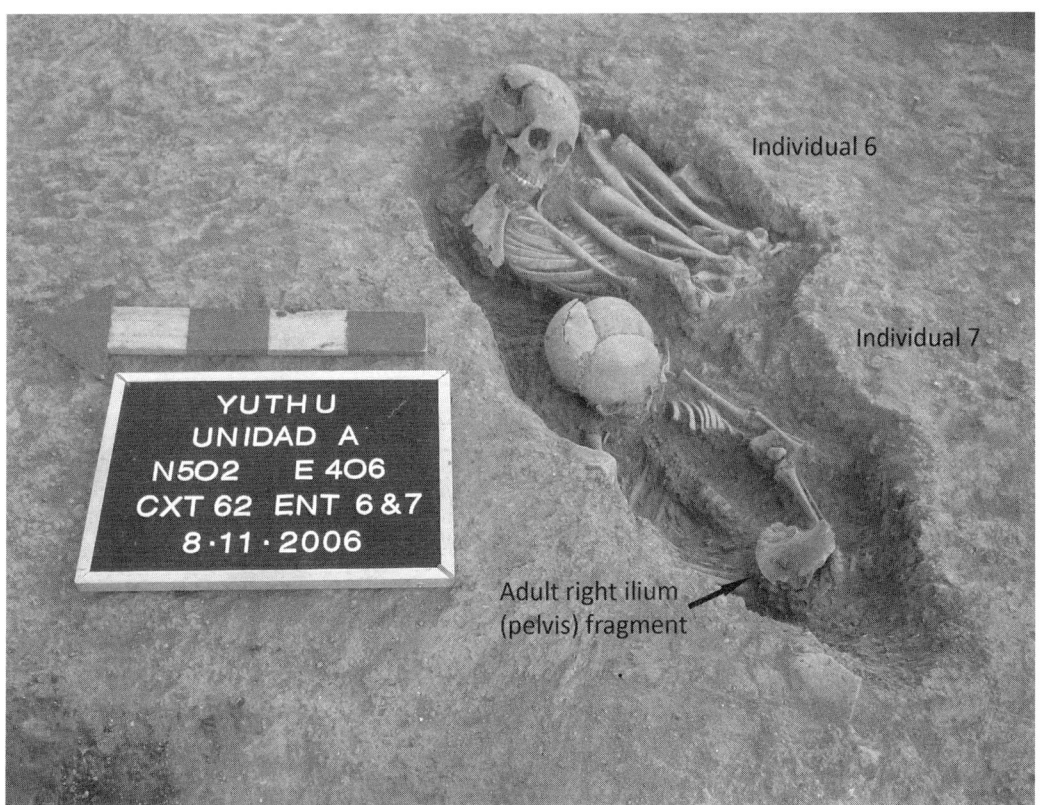

Figure 4.32. An 11- to 12-year-old child (Individual 6) and a 1- to 2-year-old child (Individual 7) were stratigraphically lowest in the group burial of children. Note the adult right ilium fragment placed over the feet of the youngest child.

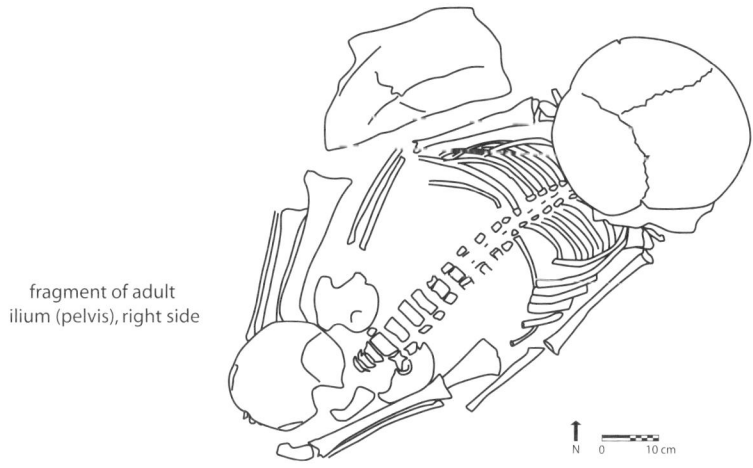

Figure 4.33. Individual 7 was a 1- to 2-year-old child. A fragment of an adult pelvis was placed over this child's feet.

as a mummy before he was buried in the Northern Sector during the last phase of use in that area (see Chap. 3). There is no way to know if this pelvis fragment belonged to that man, but the important thing to note is that, at least in one case, a bone that had been saved from an adult mummy was eventually buried with children who experienced violent deaths.

A textile fragment made of plant fiber was found under the youngest child, indicating that the children were originally wrapped in a textile or were wearing clothing. Each individual is described in detail below, in stratigraphic order from lowest to highest.

Individual 7. Individual 7 was a 1- to 2-year-old child of indeterminate sex with tabular erect cranial modification. The child was buried in a flexed position on his or her back. The skeleton was in good condition and 100% complete. He or she had an unhealed periostitis on the eleventh right rib shaft (external surface), a marker of non-specific infection (Andrushko 2008).

Individual 6. Individual 6 was an 11- to 12-year-old child of indeterminate sex with tabular erect cranial modification. The body was in a flexed position on the left side (Fig. 4.34). The child had unhealed cribra orbitalia, a non-specific stress indicator. In addition, a perimortem depressed skull fracture with open fracture lines was located above the right eye. This wound almost certainly caused the child's death. The skeleton was 100% complete and in good condition.

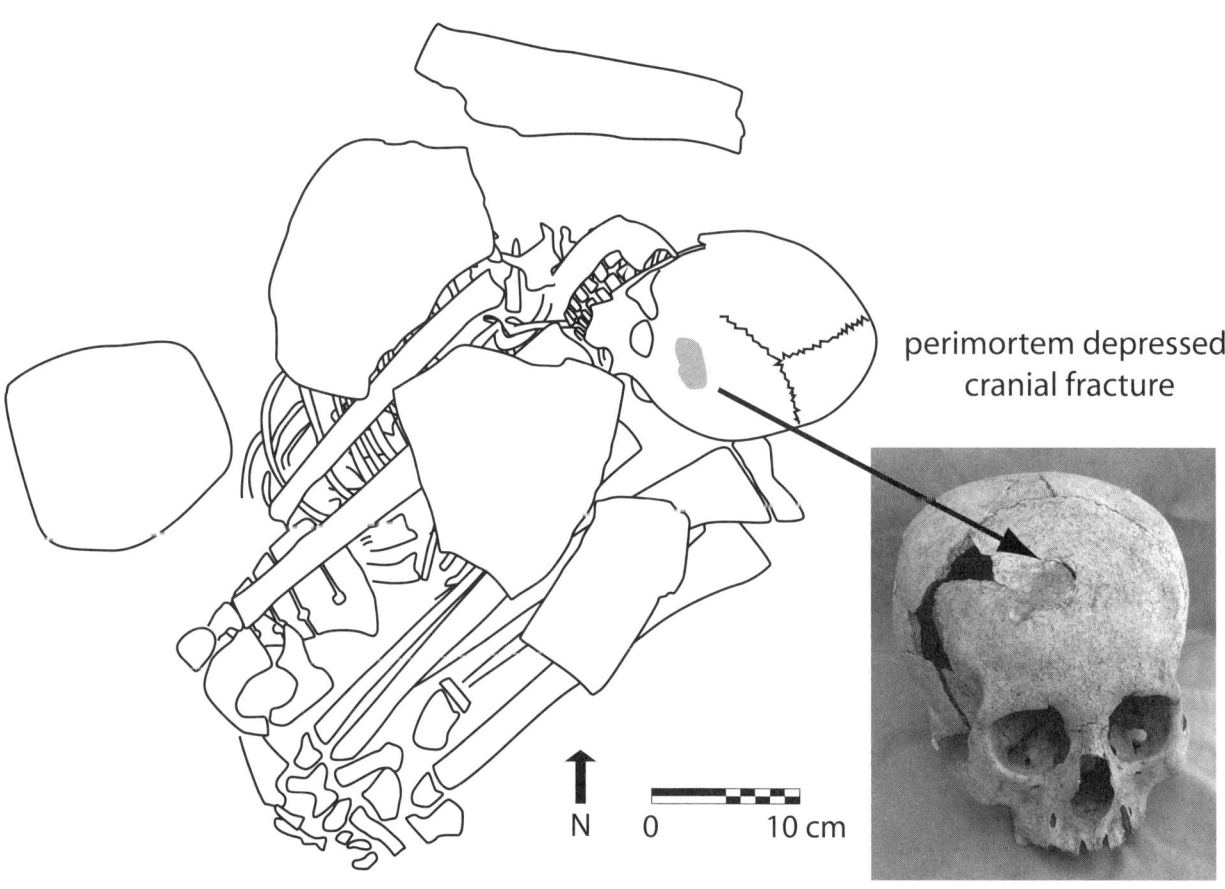

Figure 4.34. Individual 6 (an 11- to 12-year-old child) was probably killed by the blow that left the perimortem depressed cranial fracture with open fracture lines above the right eye. Photo courtesy of Valerie Andrushko.

Individual 3. Individual 3 was a 7- to 8-year-old child of indeterminate sex buried in a flexed position on the right side directly above Individual 6 (Fig. 4.35). The skeleton was in good condition, but only 86% complete. The entire head and neck of the child was missing—including the cranium, mandible, and vertebrae of the neck (except for a very small fragment of the left mandibular condyle). No cut marks were noted on the vertebrae (Andrushko 2008). Four rocks were arranged where this child's head would have been located and above the head of Individual 6.

It is not clear when or how the head was removed, but it seems likely that it was removed intentionally during the Formative period. Though the burial was relatively close to the modern ground surface, if the bones had been removed by a tractor or plow, shattered fragments would have been left in or around the grave.

Burial 5

Burial 5 was an older woman (over 46 years old) with tabular erect cranial modification. She was buried in a flexed position on her back and encircled by stones (Fig. 4.36). In addition, her burial was located where two stone alignments met to form a corner (see Fig. 4.30). Evidence of burning was found on her face and lower legs, indicating that an offering was burned on top of the body during the burial ritual. The skeleton was in fair condition and 79% complete (Burial Type 3).

The woman had appendicular joint disease in the right and left hip and knee joints. She also had antemortem loss of 1 tooth, one periapical abscess, one periodontal abscess, pulp exposure due to attrition (3 teeth), moderate to severe calculus, and congenital absence of the lower left third molar (Andrushko 2008).

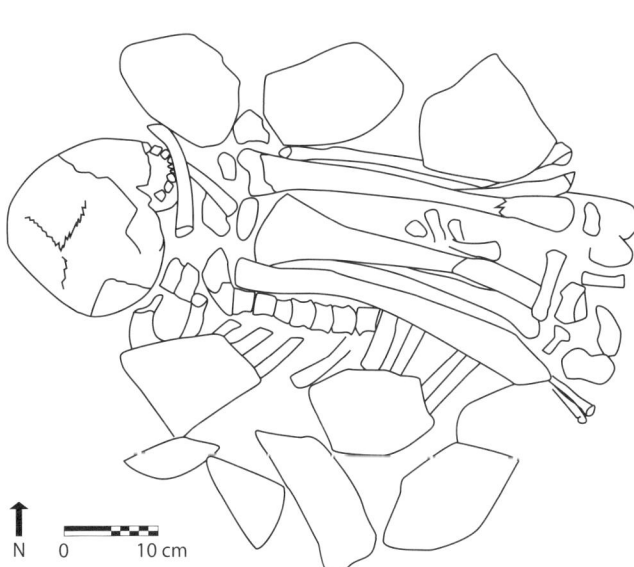

Figure 4.35. Individual 3 (a 7- to 8-year-old child) was stratigraphically highest in the group burial. The entire head and neck of this child were removed before burial, and four rocks were placed where the head should have been.

Figure 4.36. Burial 5 was an older woman (over 46 years of age). An offering was burned on top of her face and lower legs as part of the burial ritual.

Burial 2

Burial 2 was a 26- to 35-year-old man with unique burial treatment and unusual physical characteristics. He was the only person buried in a circular pit with straight walls and a flat bottom that was covered with a clay and stone cap. The pit was 120 cm in diameter and 40 cm deep. His body was in a seated, flexed position, and he had slick red clay under his ribs and a bird bone in his mouth (Fig. 4.37). The skeleton was 100% complete and in good condition (Burial Type 1).

This man was the only individual without cranial modification who was buried at Yuthu. In addition, he had many healed traumas that reflect involvement in interpersonal fighting, including healed facial fractures to the right frontal along the supraorbital ridge, the right zygomatic and maxilla on the lower orbital rim, the right and left nasal bones, and the left maxilla. He had a massive right tibia fracture with healed infection, a healed fracture to the left fourth metacarpal, and at least eight healed rib fractures. Artificial abrasion on the lower left central incisor resulted in lingual wear down to the tooth root (Andrushko 2008).

He also bore several marks of stress. He had active and healed periostitis on the left tibia (a mark of non-specific infection), spinal joint disease, appendicular joint disease in the right and left hip joints, and a small button osteoma on the left parietal. He had carious lesions on 2 teeth, two periapical abscesses, one periodontal abscess, pulp exposure due to caries on 1 tooth, pulp exposure due to attrition on 3 teeth, calculus flecks, and moderate alveolar resorption (Andrushko 2008).

Contents of the Burial Matrix

The tomb was filled with semi-compact light brown soil.

Munsell color
    7.5 YR 4/4 brown

Ceramic vessels
    Total sherds: 46
    Restricted vessels with a neck: 2 Chanapata redware, 1 plainware
    Body sherds with diagnostic style:
        3 Chanapata redware, 1 Chanapata blackware

Chipped stone
    Regionally available stone (50% by count, 92.86% by weight)
        debitage: 1 proximal flake (3.9 g)
    Exotic stone (50% by count, 7.14% by wt)
        obsidian
            tool: 1 unimarginal flake tool (0.3 g)

Tomb Cap

The cap of the tomb was composed of hard clay covering five stones and the cranium of the man.

Munsell color
    7.5 YR 4/4 brown

Ceramic vessels
    Total sherds: 1 (non-diagnostic)

Botanical remains from flotation of 5.3 liters of soil (S-39)
    No identifiable plant remains were recovered from this sample

Animal bone (NISP)
    Mammals
        unidentified: 12 (all from flotation)

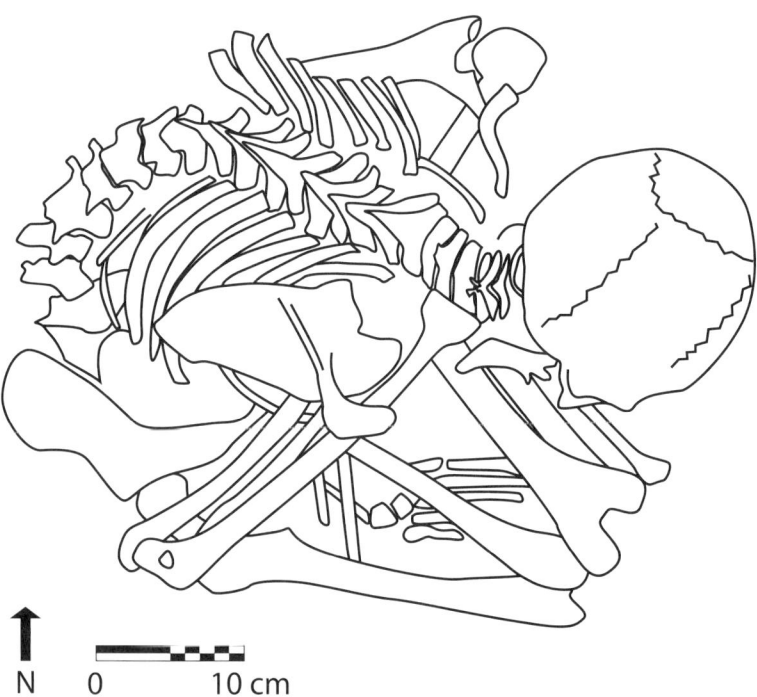

Figure 4.37. Burial 2 was a 26- to 35-year-old man who had unique burial treatment and physical characteristics. He was the only individual at Yuthu without cranial modification. In addition, he had many healed traumas and stress markers indicative of being involved in raiding or warfare. He was buried in a circular pit with a clay and stone cap. A bird bone was placed in his mouth.

Discussion of the Deposits and Features in the Southern Sector

I was first drawn to the Southern Sector because of its unusually flat, rectangular shape and the high density of broken pottery on the surface. It was unlike the Northern Sector or any other contemporary settlement that I had visited. I wanted to know if Formative period villagers had modified the shape of the hill, and if so, for what purpose? Was the platform a terrace for an elite house? Did it support ceremonial architecture, such as a single temple or multiple ritual structures? Perhaps it held a large, open plaza for community events. Each of these possibilities excited me because any one of them would help me to understand the social organization of the village—whether politics were managed by a powerful chief, an exclusive council, multiple lineage heads, or inclusive community gatherings.

After excavating units in both the Northern and Southern Sectors, it is clear that before the final use of Yuthu as a cemetery, there were significant differences between the constructions and activities, which suggest very different uses of the space. The most striking difference was in the type of architecture present in each area (see Fig. 4.38, a final view of excavations; Plate 7).

The first structures in the Northern Sector were pit houses excavated into sterile soil. The shape of these houses remains unknown because they were only partially exposed, but based on the excavated portion, they were probably elongated ovals, possibly with a truncated end that served as an entryway. They were roofed with thatch and sometimes had interior hearths. Although these structures were simple and could be built quickly, the presence of superimposed floors indicates that they were used for fairly long periods. The small structures had little interior space and were associated with exterior storage pits and a hearth. Therefore, most activities probably took place outdoors. Two of these structures were found in the Northern Sector, one dating to 383–118 BC and the other to 366–96 BC (calibrated, 95.4% confidence).

An adobe or mud house with a simple stone foundation was built on the surface of the ground. Repeated use created superimposed trampled surfaces inside the house. Unfortunately, the structure was disturbed by later agricultural activity and its total size and form are unknown, but the straight northwest wall and the shape of the interior floor indicate that it was probably rectangular or trapezoidal. This structure was contemporary with a very large outdoor cooking hearth that also had many superimposed trampled surfaces indicating continual use. As was the case for the earlier pit houses, it seems that most domestic activities took place in outdoor areas. This house was stratigraphically above the pit houses and dated to 409–209 BC.

The earliest construction in the Southern Sector was very different from that of the Northern Sector. The natural hill was leveled to create a platform overlooking Lake Huaypo. Because only a small part of the platform was excavated, the total number and layout of structures remain unknown. Excavations did uncover part of an unroofed sunken structure on the platform's southwestern edge. The southern wall was a stone-faced bench with a paved top and clean clay mortar divided into two sections. At the western end, the bench met a single-faced retaining wall at approximately a right angle. The eastern edge of the western section of the bench abutted another retaining wall that extended outside the structure. The section of the structure behind this retaining wall would have been surrounded by a ground surface higher than the interior floor. In contrast, the eastern section of the bench would have been visible from inside and outside the structure (Fig. 4.39). The eastern part of the bench ended where it met a stone-lined canal that carried water from the interior to the platform's edge. Beyond the canal, we found no additional walls or benches, so it is possible that this structure may have been open to the southeast (or toward the end of the platform facing Lake Huaypo and Cerro Huanacaure).

Unfortunately, I was not able to excavate a large enough portion of the platform to determine with certainty how many structures there were, or even the entire shape and size of Structure 1. It may have been one of many similar sunken courts located on the platform, or it may have been the corner of a single large structure. And, there are many other possibilities.

During the use of Structure 1, features were added or changed over time. A prepared white clay floor was placed on either side of the canal. The western end of this floor was associated with a stone-lined cist. An oval pit was dug outside the eastern section of the bench and a large pit was excavated in front of the canal intake. Over time, the canal filled with layers of soil mixed with flecks of charcoal that were deposited by water or another flowing liquid. Eventually, this canal was replaced by a new one that shared the same intake but was curved so that the discharge was offset to the east. This canal did not contain soil deposited by liquids. It seems that shortly after it was built, the whole structure was covered with soil and abandoned.

After the sunken structure was buried, some time passed and several strata of soil accumulated over the platform. Later, a three-sided structure with mud foundations was built in nearly the same place as the eastern section of the bench of Structure 1. It had a small circular stone hearth. It is difficult to determine what the purpose of the structure might have been, though the small size and lack of a fourth wall make it unlikely it was a permanent residence.

What Accounts for the Differences between the Northern and Southern Sectors?

The striking differences between the sectors cannot be explained by change over time. All radiocarbon dates from both sectors overlap within a 95.4% probability range (Fig. 4.40). Even so, up to about 300 years may have passed from the first occupation of the site to its conversion to a cemetery. Unfortunately, a relative chronology for structures in both sectors cannot be established by stratigraphy because the sectors are far apart and separated by a gully. The chronology of the two areas can

Final view of Unit A, Southern Sector

Final view of Unit D, Northern Sector

Figure 4.38. The final view of excavations in Units A and D highlight the drastic differences in architecture between the Northern and Southern Sectors.

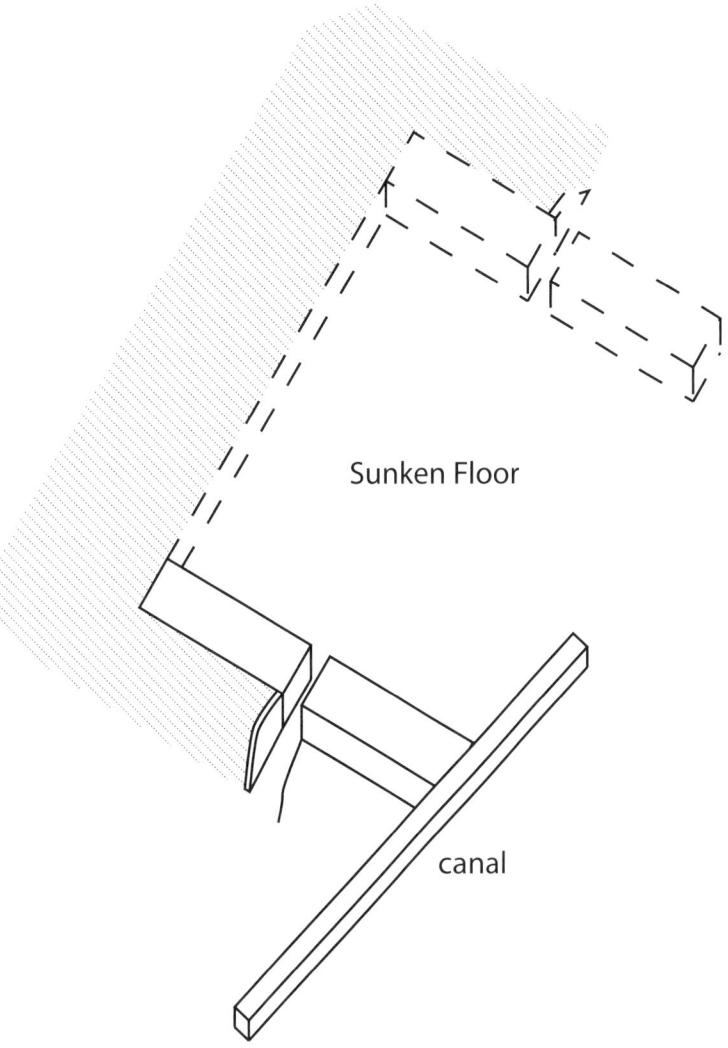

Figure 4.39. Simplified sketch of what the original construction of Structure 1 might have looked like based on the excavated section (indicated with solid black outline). The dotted lines are speculations of what the rest of the structure might have looked like if it were basically symmetrical and rectangular. Only additional excavation will be able to determine the true layout.

only be compared based on radiocarbon dates, which are not sufficiently fine-grained to place building events in chronological order. Future refinements in ceramic chronology may help to better define the sequence of building events in the village, but I doubt that temporal factors could ever explain the vast differences between the two sectors.

It is more likely that the differences reflect distinct uses rather than changes over time in architectural style and building techniques. I would suggest that the Northern Sector was used for everyday domestic activities while the Southern Sector was used for periodic ceremonial practices. This interpretation is based on comparisons with contemporary Formative domestic[2] and ceremonial architecture from other parts of highland Peru, and on comparisons of the artifacts and features recovered from both sectors to characterize the activities carried out in each area.

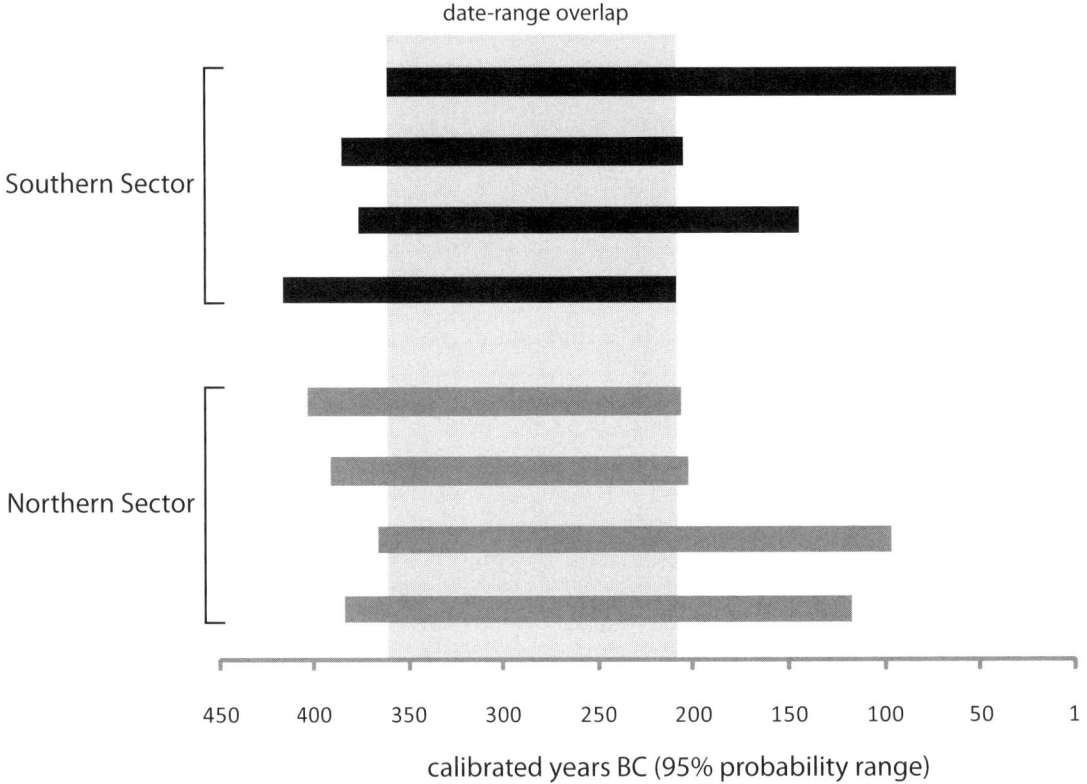

Figure 4.40. All radiocarbon dates from the Northern and Southern Sectors of Yuthu overlap within the 95.4% probability range. Therefore, the chronology cannot be refined sufficiently to assess to what extent those differences may be due to time.

Activities in the Northern and Southern Sectors

The following section examines the distribution of artifacts such as pottery, stone tools, and food remains to determine whether the practices carried out in and around the apparently ceremonial architecture of the Southern Sector were consistent with what archaeologists would expect to see in public or ritual spaces and whether the activities that took place near the simple architecture of the Northern Sector were typical of daily domestic life.

To establish which activities took place in each sector, I examine artifact distributions on two levels. First, I compare the overall trends in artifact distribution, considering all materials recovered from contexts that were not disturbed by modern agricultural activities. Given that the two sectors are separated by a gully, it is likely that the refuse that accumulated in each area came from activities carried out nearby. I feel confident that this assumption is valid for most deposits, with the possible exception of the layer of soil that covered the walls of Structure 1; it may have been brought from elsewhere to deliberately bury the structure. After establishing overall patterns, I compare similar features in both sectors, including hearths, refuse in pits, and floors.

Overall Trends

Differences in the remains of food preparation are particularly informative. When considering only bones recovered from heavy fractions of flotation, the mean density was significantly higher in the south than the north.[3,4] However, the ratio of all bones recovered to pottery fragments was similar in both. Taking into account only the food animals with more than two elements recovered (birds, deer, guinea pig, and camelids), the Southern Sector yielded much more camelid bone and less bird, deer, and guinea pig compared with the Northern Sector.

The density of carbonized botanical remains in the Northern

Sector was more than twice that of the Southern Sector, but there were no significant differences between plants present. In Peru, corn is often a special or ceremonial food (Hastorf 2003). At Yuthu, corn remains were much denser in the domestic sector than in the ceremonial sector. The lower density of corn in the Southern Sector does not rule out the possibility that it was a special food at Yuthu (especially if it was consumed as mush or corn beer), but it was probably not prepared and cooked in the ceremonial areas.

Overall, contrasting densities of carbonized plant remains probably indicate that more cooking took place in the Northern Sector. The more even distribution of faunal remains may indicate that eating and discard took place equally in both sectors with the main difference being that more camelids were eaten in the Southern Sector.

If more food preparation took place in the north, one might expect grinding stones to be more common or varied in that area. In fact, the densities of one- or two-handed grinding stones do not vary much. Large mortars were located in the domestic sector, but the distribution of hand stone types was similar in both areas. There were no significant differences in the distribution of stones used with back and forth versus rocker motions or stones held with one versus two hands. The only notable difference was in the ratio of small pulverizing or polishing stones that were held between the fingers to pottery, which was 3.2 times higher in the north than the south.

Pottery vessels can also provide information about food preparation and serving. Overall, relatively more plainware and cooking vessels with necks were found in the domestic area while more open serving bowls and painted redware were recovered from the ceremonial sector. This pattern indicates that although food preparation and serving took place in both areas, relatively more serving in fancier pottery took place in the Southern Sector.

It is more difficult to attribute specific functions to stone tools without very detailed analyses, but the types and materials of chipped stone recorded at Yuthu do yield interesting patterns. The overall density of chipped stone tools and debitage recovered from flotation was more than twice as high in the Northern Sector. When comparing the distribution of tools and debitage, relatively more tools were found in the Southern Sector.

The presence of local, regional and exotic stone materials varied between sectors (considering only materials collected in flotation). By count, more exotic high-quality stone (obsidian) was found in the Southern Sector and more locally available low-quality sedimentary and metamorphic stones were found in the Northern Sector. By weight, high-quality regionally available materials were more common in the Southern Sector. There was no significant difference in the mean weight of tools or debitage collected from flotation. This may indicate more intense or frequent activities using stone tools in the Northern Sector, and more selective use of high-quality tools for less frequent activities in the Southern Sector.

Some tools are difficult to assign specific functions. Bone tools were highly variable and difficult to compare by type, but the ratio of bone tools to pottery sherds was 2.5 times greater in the Northern Sector. Reworked ceramic sherds were classified as either disc or non-disc shapes. Discs were more common in the Southern Sector while other shapes occurred more frequently in the Northern Sector.

Other classes of artifacts were too rare to consider with statistical comparisons. Five out of seven pieces of quartz crystal were found in the Southern Sector. Five out of six beads were found in the Northern Sector. Six out of nine metal objects were from the Northern Sector. More stone and pottery figurines and carved stones were found in the Southern Sector including anthropomorphic figures, a painted circular stone, a pyramid-shaped stone, a human figurine, a polished stone human head, a painted white rock, a double-headed figurine in bone, and a rock shaped like a potato. In the Northern Sector, there were two figurines, both in the shape of animals (a bird and possibly a llama or alpaca), and a carved antler.

Overall, the most notable differences between the sectors were in density and quality of objects recovered. This indicates that activities were more frequent and varied in the Northern Sector in houses and outdoor activity areas, as would be typical of daily life. In contrast, fewer activities were carried out in and around the ceremonial architecture of the Southern Sector. This may result from a smaller set of proscribed activities that were considered appropriate and were carried out only during periodic rituals.

Refuse in Pits

The pits considered include: one stone-lined cist and two large oval intrusions in the Southern Sector and six storage pits from the Northern Sector. Although the primary use of these features varied, it is likely that the secondary use of each was to be filled with refuse. The pits from the Northern Sector were probably filled with domestic trash discarded during the use of the pit houses while the intrusions in the Southern Sector were filled with refuse during the use of Structure 1.

The density of botanical remains did not vary significantly between sectors, though the mean number of carbonized botanical remains per liter was nearly twice as high in the Northern Sector. The Northern Sector yielded a much wider variety of plant remains including weeds (amaranth), fuel plants (ambrosia and quinoa), forage and thatch plants (Poaceae, *Scirpus*, *Trifolium*, quinoa), food (maize, quinoa), dye (*Galium*), and medicine (*Verbena*). In contrast, the Southern Sector had a much more limited set of plants including fuel (ambrosia, quinoa), forage and thatch plants (Poaceae), and one possible food plant (quinoa).

The number of bones recovered from pits was too small to yield statistically significant results, but there were interesting differences in the most common animals in each sector. Birds, guinea pigs, deer, llama, and mice were found in pits in the Northern Sector. All of these animals except birds were found in the south. When mice were excluded in order to consider only potential food species, camelids comprised the majority of food remains from both sectors, though they were slightly more common in the Southern Sector. When only food species were used to calculate the ratio of faunal remains to sherds, the estimated density of faunal remains was higher in the Northern Sector.

Field mice made up a very large proportion of faunal remains recovered from the Northern Sector (north = 70.63%; south = 9.73%). Given that mice are attracted to food refuse, the high number of these animals suggests that more food waste was deposited in pits around houses in the Northern Sector. This interpretation is consistent with the higher density of carbonized plants and animal bones in these contexts.

Slightly more plainware was found in the Northern Sector and more painted and pattern burnished pottery was found in the Southern Sector. Restricted vessels with a neck were more common in the Northern Sector while open vessels and restricted vessels without a neck were more common in the Southern Sector. Both of these patterns are consistent with the overall trends. There were no clear patterns in terms of tools used for food preparation, and no differences in chipped stone tool types, the proportion of tools versus debitage, or the source of material used to make chipped stone tools. No bone tools were found in refuse pits in the Southern Sector, but two short polished tubes and one carved bone were found in the Northern Sector. Likewise, no special objects were recovered from the pits in the Northern Sector, but the potato-shaped stone *illa* was found in the intrusion outside the sunken structure and two oddly shaped stones were recovered from the stone-lined cist in the Southern Sector.

The patterns from the pits follow the overall trends established in the previous section. Materials were much more dense and diverse in the Northern Sector, indicating more varied and frequent daily activities. Finer serving wares, figurines, and higher quality chipped stone materials were found in the Southern Sector.

Hearth Contents

This section considers the contents of (1) two hearths in the Southern Sector located inside the sunken structure and (2) seven outdoor hearths and two indoor hearths in the Northern Sector. Unlike the analysis of pits, the contents of hearths did not follow all of the overall trends. There was no significant difference in the mean density of carbonized botanical remains between the two sectors, though it was higher in the north than in the south. A much greater variety of plants was found in the Northern Sector, including plants for fuel (ambrosia and quinoa), food (quinoa, maize, *Solanum*, *Oxalis*, *Brassica*, Fabaceae), weeds (amaranth), dye (*Galium*), forage or thatch (Poaceae), and thatch or basketry (*Scirpus*). In contrast, hearths in the Southern Sector contained only fuel species (ambrosia and quinoa), food (maize and quinoa), and forage plants (*Trifolium*).

The distribution of faunal remains followed a similar pattern with greater diversity in the north than in the south. Camelids, guinea pigs, and some birds were recovered from hearths in each sector, but fish, most bird species, and deer were present only in the Northern Sector.

The diversity of plant and animal remains followed the overall trends, but the density of remains breaks from earlier patterns. Unlike in other contexts, the mean density of faunal remains was higher in the Southern Sector, and there were no significant differences in pottery wares present. Plainware and decorated pottery occurred in similar proportions. There were more restricted vessels without a neck in the south and more restricted vessels with a neck in the north, but unlike the patterns found in pits and overall, there were fewer open serving vessels in hearths in the Southern Sector compared with the Northern Sector. Hearths in the Southern Sector had a higher proportion of plain cooking vessels than hearths in the Northern Sector. In addition, there were relatively more grinding stones used for food preparation in the south (though diversity of grinding stone forms was higher in the north).

Considering tools that may have been used for non-food processing activities, the mean density of chipped stone was higher in the north than in the south. By count, there was no significant difference in the quality or availability of raw materials used to make chipped stone tools or the proportion of debitage to tools. By weight, however, there was more high-quality obsidian and regionally available material in the Southern Sector and more poor-quality local material in the Northern Sector.

The trend of greater diversity in tools held for worked bone. The only worked bone object recovered from a hearth in the Southern Sector was a long pointed tool. In contrast, a wide variety of worked bone was found in higher density in the Northern Sector, including eight broad, flat pointed tools; one broad, flat rounded tool; a scapula spatula; a tool made from a carnivore maxilla; and a tubular polished bead.

It seems that in the Northern Sector, hearths were general activity areas where people not only prepared food but also gathered to engage in many other daily tasks. In contrast, the hearths in the Southern Sector were used only for cooking a more limited set of foods (especially camelid). The lack of serving wares in southern hearths and the abundance of fancy serving wares in refuse pits nearby suggest that, in the ceremonial sector, serving and eating took place away from the preparation area. In contrast, in the domestic sector, food preparation included a greater variety of dishes, and craft production and eating took place in the same space.

Floors

There were small prepared clay floors in both sectors, but trampled surfaces (or areas that had become compacted from foot traffic) were present only in the Northern Sector. This indicates more intense and continuous use of that area compared with the Southern Sector. Very few artifacts were recovered from the surfaces of floors in either sector and many artifacts incorporated into the trampled surfaces were deposited as part of the stratum below, so no comparisons were made between materials recovered from floor contexts.

Ceremonial Architecture at Yuthu in a Regional Perspective

The ceremonial architecture of Yuthu was part of a larger highland Andean tradition. In particular, two aspects were similar to ceremonial constructions found at contemporary sites. Sunken rectangular structures are best known from the altiplano surrounding Lake Titicaca, though they have been found as far north as Cajamarca. In addition, canals were associated with a variety of ceremonial architecture traditions from the Titicaca Basin to Cajamarca.

Rectangular Sunken Structures with Stone-Faced Walls

The "cult of the sunken court" has been identified as part of a larger tradition of raising and lowering areas that was important in ceremonial architecture dating from the Preceramic period to the Middle Horizon on the Andean coast and in the highlands (Moseley 1985). The earliest sunken courts were circular and were most common on the coast (Williams 1985). This discussion is limited to rectangular sunken structures that were built and used in the highlands at about the same time as Structure 1 at Yuthu.

Sunken rectangular structures were an important part of Titicaca Basin ceremonial architecture, especially at Middle Formative period sites that were roughly contemporary with Yuthu (800–250 BC; see Table 4.1) (Bandy 2006; Beck 2004a; Hastorf 2005, 2008; Janusek 2004; Stanish 2003). These structures were usually made by cutting a depression into sterile soil or bedrock and lining it with unworked field stones. Less often, the interior walls were covered with plaster. On the Taraco Peninsula, where a great deal of research on this period has been carried out, sunken structures have a long history. The earliest and simplest was the Choquehuanca enclosure at Chiripa that dates to 1000–800 BC. However, most sunken rectangular structures at Chiripa and other sites were built and used in the Middle Formative period (800–100 BC) (Bandy and Hastorf 2007; Chávez 1988; Chávez and Chávez 1997). At Kala Uyuni, a pair of sunken courts was built on a raised area. The lower court near the front of the platform was not completely subterranean, but had one wall that was visible on both sides (Cohen and Roddick 2007).

In Cusco, much less research has been carried out, but it seems that sunken rectangular structures may have been equally important. During the first excavations at a Formative period site, Rowe found the retaining wall of a subterranean structure. Unfortunately, excavations were too limited to determine its shape or size (Rowe 1944). More recently, Zapata excavated two large Formative period sites with sunken courts. At Muyu Orqo in the Cusco Valley, a sunken rectangular plaza atop a stepped platform was associated with Chanapata-derived-style pottery. It had benches for the northeast and southwest walls, an altar in the center, and offerings of buried llamas on the interior (Zapata 1998). At Batan Urqo, located 40 km east of Cusco along the route to the Titicaca area, retaining walls of a sunken structure were associated with Chanapata pottery, but the entire structure was not excavated.

Further north, sunken rectangular courts were built and used during the Formative period, but they were incorporated as one element of much larger monumental ceremonial complexes. In Cajamarca, at Kuntur Wasi, sunken courts were part of a larger complex with platforms, circular courts, stairways, and terraces (800–300 BC) (Kato 1993). At Chavín de Huántar, a sunken rectangular court was built in front of the Black and White

Table 4.1. Dimensions of sunken rectangular structures from the southern Andes.

Location	Dimensions	Date	Source
Muyu Orqo (Cusco)	16.8 × 12.6 m 1.2 m deep	600 BC–AD 200	Zapata 1998
Choquehuanca enclosure, Chiripa (Titicaca)	13 × 13 m depth not reported	1000–800 BC	Bandy 2001
Santiago enclosure, Chiripa (Titicaca)	14 × 14 m depth not reported	1000–800 BC	Dean and Kojan 1999
Llusco enclosure, Chiripa (Titicaca)	13.5 × 11.5 m 0.7 m deep	800–400 BC	Paz Soría 1999
Lower court, Kala Uyuni (Titicaca)	18 × 18 m at least 1 m deep	800–100 BC	Cohen and Roddick 2007
Upper court, Kala Uyuni (Titicaca)	18 × 15 m 0.6 m deep	800–100 BC	Cohen and Roddick 2007
Ch'isi (Titicaca)	14 × 14 m depth not reported	220–10 BC	Chávez and Chávez 1997

Portal of the New Temple. This construction dated to 400–200 BC according to traditional chronologies (Burger 1984, 1992; Lumbreras 1989). More recent studies date its construction and use to 900–500 BC (Kembel 2008). In either case, the sunken rectangular structure was added to an already large and diverse ceremonial complex with subterranean galleries, U-shaped constructions, and a sunken circular court.

Structure 1 was more similar to sunken rectangular courts from the Titicaca Basin. Each of these structures was rectangular or trapezoidal in shape. Most were semi-subterranean on all four sides, but there was a precedent for structures that were partly visible from both sides at Kala Uyuni. Zapata has already proposed that sunken courts in Cusco were linked to the traditions of the altiplano, though there were important differences between the two areas (Zapata 1998). I would agree the ceremonial architecture at Yuthu is part of a larger tradition in the southern highlands.

Canals

Sacred waterways were widespread elements of ceremonial architecture at early sites in the Andes (Moseley 1985). Water manipulation was a significant part of ritual among the Inka and continues to be important in many parts of the Andes today. During the Formative period, canals associated with ceremonial architecture were common from the Titicaca Basin to Cajamarca. These canals may have been used for rituals involving water. Alternatively, they may have served as drains, especially during the rainy season when daily precipitation would have flooded semi-subterranean structures.

On the Taraco Peninsula in the Titicaca Basin, canals were associated with both above-ground and semi-subterranean ritual structures of the Middle Formative period (800–400 BC). Excavators rarely discuss the function of these canals, but at the Llusco enclosure at Chiripa, a stone-lined canal was found with its intake located at the lowest point in the northwest corner of a sunken court. This canal served as a drain that emptied into a nearby stream (Paz Soría 1999). At Alto Pukara, a canal was located outside the northwest corner of an above-ground ritual structure (Beck 2004b). This canal did not drain the structure, but the excavator did not suggest another function.

At Huaricoto in the Callejón de Huaylas, Ancash, the earliest canal was built during the late Huaricoto phase associated with ceremonial architecture consisting of circular structures with fire pits and subterranean flues atop a terraced mound. During the later Capilla phase (700–200 BC), the ceremonial architecture was elaborated to include a sunken circular plaza and megalithic stone walls. At that time, canals were added that emptied into the original canal (Burger and Salazar-Burger 1980, 1985). The excavators recognized the possibility that the structures served as drains, but because drainage was very good on the platform, they suggested that the canals had a "nonutilitarian function related to that of the adjacent ceremonial hearths" (Burger and Salazar-Burger 1985:129).

Nearby at Chavín de Huántar, a large system of stone-lined canals ran through and beneath the galleries and temple structure (900–400 BC in the old chronology; 1200–800 in the new chronology) (Bustamante and Crousillat 1974). Lumbreras et al. (1976) have suggested that the extent and elaboration of the canal system exceeded practical drainage needs and would have provided acoustic effects for ceremonies within and around the temple (though this interpretation remains controversial). In this area, canals were not used as simple drains, but were incorporated as elements of ceremonial practice.

Many canals have been found in the Cajamarca area at Huacaloma, Layzón, and Kuntur Wasi. At Huacaloma, canals were built during three separate phases. The earliest stone-lined canal was associated with ceremonial architecture consisting of three platforms, stairways, small rectangular rooms with painted polychrome murals, and retaining walls dating between 1000 and 500 BC (Matsumoto 1993; Ōnuki et al. 1985; Terada 1985). Because this canal was on the highest platform where there was no water source and drainage was good, authors have suggested that it was used for ritual activities (Ōnuki et al. 1985). After these ceremonial structures were buried and no longer used, a pair of canals sharing the same intake (one straight and one serpentine in form, very similar to the canals at Yuthu) was built near a large hearth on the mound (500–200 BC). The serpentine canal still had soot, stuck to the interior wall, that probably came from fire in the hearth (Terada 1985). In this case, the authors suggest that these canals were used to carry burned offerings. Even later, when there was no longer ceremonial architecture at the site (after 200 BC), some structures located in a low area off the platform were associated with subterranean canals. In that area, drainage was poor and scholars maintain that these canals probably served as drains (Ōnuki et al. 1985).

At Layzón, two stone canals were associated with the elaborate ceremonial architecture consisting of platforms and structures (250–50 BC). Although both canals pass under or beside similar circular platforms, they suggest that the simpler one (which was a channel cut into bedrock) served as a drain, and that the other stone-lined canal was too large to be a drain and may have served a ritual purpose (Kato and Seki 1985; Seki 1993).

At Kuntur Wasi around 700–250 BC, an extensive canal network included subterranean stone-lined canals under rectangular sunken courts that linked with above-ground canals located in passageways that expelled water off the side of the large artificial platform (Kato 1993; Ōnuki 1995). These canals certainly would have drained the ceremonial architecture, but the dramatic way in which the water would have jetted out of the retaining walls indicates that they were built with more than functional purposes in mind.

Throughout highland Peru, canals were integrated into ceremonial architecture. When they were associated with low areas and closed sunken courts, these structures have been interpreted as functional drains that were necessary to maintain the integrity of the architecture and to keep the area dry so that it could be used for ceremonial activities. When canals were located on top of mounds or artificial platforms, they have more often been interpreted as architectural features that were used to carry out rituals associated with water. In at least one case, these rituals also included burning materials in a nearby hearth.

At Yuthu, the slope of the canals carried water away from the interior of Structure 1, yet it seems unlikely that they were built only to drain water. A sunken floor certainly might have filled with water during the rainy season, but other features of the structure were sufficient to drain it. For example, a channel carved into bedrock ran through the gap between the two sections of the bench. Loose soil deposited in this area indicates that water flowed through this gap and that the drain was occasionally cleaned. In addition, the structure might have been open beyond the canal to the southeast. If that were the case, the three-sided building would not have required elaborate drainage located at the open end. The intake of the canals was delimited by stones placed above the level of the original floor, and the soil inside the canal was deposited by flowing liquids and contained flecks of charcoal. Therefore, it is most likely that the canals in the Southern Sector of Yuthu carried offerings of poured water or other liquids mixed with burned materials.

Ceremonial and Domestic Spaces

When I began excavating, I knew almost nothing about ceremonial or domestic architecture in Formative period Cusco. When I began to find thick stone benches and short, yet well-made canals, I knew that this architecture was special, but I was not sure exactly what purpose it served. When I compared the features of Unit A with the Northern Sector, however, it became clear that what I found was not simply an elaborate house. The Northern Sector had small structures and large outdoor activity areas that were used for diverse daily activities. The presence of trampled surfaces in structures and hearths as well as the accumulation of fine strata indicate that the area was used continuously. In contrast, the Southern Sector had more elaborate architecture and a smaller set of activities took place there. Furthermore, the thicker strata and lack of trampled surfaces indicate that the space was used less frequently. Infrequent use for a proscribed set of activities is typical of ceremonial or public areas. Therefore, the most likely explanation for the differences between the two sectors is that the Northern Sector was used for domestic activities and the Southern Sector was an area for ceremonial practices.

Although each of these areas has been designated as "domestic" or "ceremonial," it is not true that domestic activities occurred only in the north or that ritual practices took place exclusively in the south. Cooking did take place in the Southern Sector, though it was probably food preparation for special meals. In addition, there were several tools for quotidian tasks found in that sector. Likewise, ritual activities took place in both areas. For example, bird-focused rituals took place in the Northern Sector, as evidenced by the burial of an eagle hawk and the recovery of a bird figurine from one of the pit houses. In addition, human burials were common in both sectors, beginning with the earliest houses in the north and the construction of the platform and sunken structure in the south (north, $n = 7$; south, $n = 16$).

The community created distinct spaces for quotidian activities and ceremonial practices, which indicates that creating and maintaining a community-level group identity through ritual was important to villagers at Yuthu. How was that identity conceptualized and enacted? People built a ceremonial structure that incorporated a sunken rectangular structure and canals—two features that were common throughout the Andean highlands. Yet, the simple architecture clearly lacked many of the features that were characteristic of better known Formative traditions. For example, constructions were never as large and did not integrate as many different buildings as the ceremonial complexes located further north in Ancash and Cajamarca. So far, no pottery or stone sculpture with elaborate iconography has been found at any Formative period site in Cusco. In contrast, rich and easily recognizable art styles were typical of other religious traditions. Chavín de Huántar is famous for its widespread art style, stone sculpture, and ritual paraphernalia such as conch shell trumpets. Likewise, the Yaya-Mama religious tradition of the altiplano had its own unique iconography, stone monoliths, and characteristic ceramic "trumpets" (which were probably not instruments).

Unlike these areas north and south of Cusco, the material culture at Yuthu was very simple. The most elaborate objects were large bowls with painted interior rims and a few figurines in the shapes of humans, animals, or crops. Chapter 5 considers the features of the Southern Sector, the surrounding terrain, and burial data to demonstrate that community members understood their shared identity and territorial rights as established by ancestors and conceptualized through relationships with the living features of the landscape.

Notes

1. Radiocarbon date: AA84433/Yuthu RC-110, 2369 ± 36 uncalibrated radiocarbon years BP, 417–209 BC calibrated with sequential model (95.4% confidence).

2. See Chapter 3 for regional comparisons of domestic architecture.

3. Because the volume of excavated soil was not recorded in the field, density was calculated in two ways: (1) when quantities were sufficient, I calculated density using only objects collected in flotation samples, and (2) when too few items were recovered from flotation to use this method, I approximated density by calculating the ratio of objects to the total number of ceramic sherds from the same contexts. Although this measure is not ideal, total sherd count should be a reasonable proxy for total soil excavated.

4. See Davis 2010 for detailed statistical analyses.

—5—

Group Identity, the Sacred System, and Politics

The construction of special non-domestic space in the Southern Sector demonstrates that—from the moment people moved to Yuthu to establish a village—creating and maintaining group identity above the level of the household was important. Ethnographic and ethnohistoric sources describe group identity in the Andean highlands that was expressed in terms of kinship and conceptualized through relationships with the living landscape and ancestors. These systems tied together politics and economics because they established rights to territory and resources for living descendants. In addition, nested levels of group identities created a segmentary social structure that could be mobilized and reformulated to suit new political circumstances.

Other scholars have argued that elements of similar ritual and political systems existed in the highlands and on the coast during the late Formative period in the Central and South-Central Andes (about 800–200 BC) (Dulanto 2002a, 2002b; Hastorf 2003). In this chapter, I use the ceremonial architecture of the Southern Sector and multiphase burials described in Chapter 4 to argue that the first villagers at Yuthu similarly understood their shared identity and territorial rights as related to a sacred landscape. Later, mummy centered rituals shifted the focal point of ceremonial life from the village level to factions within the community, most likely families. Understanding the ritual and political system of the village allows us to appreciate the context for negotiating access to resources and other political actions in the area.

Andean Social Groups

The following description of how people constructed and understood shared identity in modern and colonial period Andean communities provides a frame for interpreting the material remains of ritual and mortuary practices at Yuthu. The discussion outlines the role that ritual focused on ancestors and the sacred landscape played in the formation and maintenance of social group identity, briefly reviews general trends that were widespread in the highlands, and highlights the ways that territoriality, agricultural productivity, and politics intertwined with an overtly ritual system (for more detailed discussions, see Doyle 1988; Gose 1993; Salomon 1995; Sherbondy 1992).

This discussion includes both ethnographic and ethnohistoric examples, though there are risks associated with drawing on each as a source for analogy. Colonial accounts of ancestor veneration were recorded closer in time to a prehispanic past, but they have frequently been skewed by the interests of chroniclers or Spanish bureaucrats who tried to understand Inka statecraft for their own benefit. Even if Inka practices were accurately recorded, they came from an imperial context unlike the social environment we would expect to find in an early village. In addition, by the time priests began to record religious customs in the interest of eliminating them, many people had begun to shift to more secretive practices.

Ethnographic accounts include the richest level of detail, but they vary widely from place to place. They are also more distant in time from the Formative period, and the societies represented have undergone further social and political changes such as Spanish conquest and the restructuring of group identity that accompanied forced resettlement during *reducción*. Modern Andean religious belief and practices are thoroughly intertwined with Christian (especially Catholic) traditions. In addition, politics and power are no longer understood in indigenous terms, but are negotiated within modern capitalist states. In some ways, ethnographic examples may have an advantage because the politics of empire are removed from traditional understandings of social groups within small villages. Overall, however, the significant transformations make direct analogy a dangerous endeavor. Even so, recurring general themes that have endured 500 years of significant political change in many regions of the highlands may have existed in earlier times and are worth exploring using the archaeological record.

Geographical place and genealogical descent were two key aspects of shared group identity. Both of these concepts were included in origin stories, which recounted journeys made by ancestors in mythical time. The journeys began when ancestors emerged from places that were usually sources of water, such as the sea, a lake, or a glacial peak (Doyle 1988; Sherbondy 1992). After that, in some colonial and modern accounts, ancestors traveled in water, oftentimes in underground channels (Allen 2002; Sherbondy 1992), though some Inka ancestors walked at least part of the way (Sillar 2002). In either case, they completed the journey by emerging from places such as caves or springs to claim the surrounding territory and resources for their descendants. The places that these ancestors passed along the way were often seen as the limits of the territory or as important shrines for lineages to venerate during pilgrimages (Doyle 1988).

The descent groups that shared origins and rights were not necessarily entire villages, but were often large corporate kin groups within them, or *ayllus*. In ethnohistoric documents, some towns were composed of two groups with their own origin stories—herders whose ancestors emerged from Lake Titicaca and agriculturalists whose forebearers emerged from the sea. Both traveled independently to the location of the community to claim it for their descendants (Doyle 1988).

In contrast with mythical ancestors that claimed group rights to large territories, real ancestors remembered by name legitimated rights to resources for certain families within the Inka state (e.g., Dillehay 2007; Rowe 1946; Salomon 1995). Most famously, the mummies of Inka kings could own estates that included fields, flocks, irrigation systems, and servants. In fact, according to stories recorded by the Spaniards, a later ruler complained that the mummies of earlier kings were taking up too much land. In reaction, he redistributed rights to the *ayllus* and used a system of lines on the landscape marked with sacred places (the *ceque* [*ziqi* in Quechua] system) to encode the new distribution of resources (Bauer 1998; Farrington 1992; Sherbondy 1992).

In practice, shared identity was reinforced through storytelling and rituals of integration focused on material objects. Mummies, such as those venerated by the Inka nobility, were the most straightforward material representation of shared descent. They were often claimed by families or lineages. Outside the heartland of the empire, a particularly ancient mummy could serve as a focal point for rituals of integration for multi-village social groups, but most large groups rallied around a sacred living mountain (Salomon 1995).

Even though mythical ancestors emerged from and traveled through the natural world, they cannot be conceived of as distinct from it. In fact, most Andean world views do not strictly separate the natural from the cultural (Acuto 2005). The relationships between supernatural figures and between those figures and humans were understood in terms of kinship (Martínez 1983). Inequality was encoded in this scheme. Progenitors and older siblings were of higher status and had broader influence. Children were of lower rank, were influential within smaller territories, and had authority in a more limited set of matters. During the colonial period, the hierarchy of *ayllus* in the central Andes was understood in terms of kin relationships between the ancestors, which created social differences between groups including unequal access to political power (Doyle 1988).

The sacred landscape recognized by people in myth and ritual was localized and included features that were visible from a village. Mountains were often arranged in a hierarchy based on distance and grandeur. Far away but large features were responsible for the general well-being of the surrounding land and people while the closest bodies of water and mountains were responsible for the productivity of the immediate land and resources (Flannery et al. 1989; Gow et al. 1976). In many cases, mummified ancestors were considered children of sacred mountains and were able to influence local productivity of fields and herds (Allen 2002; Mariño Ferro 1989; Salomon 1995).

This nested and hierarchical social structure meant that any person or nuclear family could identify with several groups defined at different levels of the mythical or real ancestral family tree. This formulation is typical of a segmentary social structure, like that described most famously for the Nucr (see Evans-Pritchard 1967; Gose 1993; Nielsen 2006). Andean societies could activate shared group affiliation at increasingly inclusive levels by focusing on different ancestors or landscape features. For example, in the 1970s, Ausangate, the largest and most imposing glacier visible from the village of Ocongote, was a rallying point and protector in the war with Chile. In contrast, the "children" of Ausangate (the smaller nearby mountains) were called upon to ensure productivity of fields, good weather, and abundant potato crops (Gow et al. 1976).

Given the close relationship between the livelihood of people and the landscape that surrounds them, it is not surprising that group membership was closely related to territorial rights and agricultural productivity. For example, colonial period origin stories described mythical ancestors who introduced important crops and agricultural techniques when they ended their journeys and founded their *ayllus*. In colonial and modern contexts, local or nearby mountains were often understood as being the ultimate owners of alpaca and llama herds (Doyle 1988; Flannery et al. 1989; Martínez 1983).

One of the most often cited relationships between ancestors and fertility relates to managing water needed for farming. In the highlands, six months a year pass without rain. The growing season depends on water, from precipitation and melting glaciers, that flows from springs and in streams from November through May. Andean ethnohydrology conceives of all water as being part of a large sea beneath and surrounding the earth. Lakes are places where the water rises to the surface. Mountains are often considered water sources because of their association with lakes, snow-capped peaks that feed streams, and springs on their slopes. These sources of water feed rivers that cycle back into the sea (Allen 2002; Bastien 1978; Gelles 2000; Sherbondy 1992).

In at least one ethnographic case in Arequipa, the mountain that was the focal point of community ritual was the true source of water used to irrigate the fields (Gelles 2000). But that was not necessarily the case. For example, in a modern community in Bolivia, a mountain associated with two lakes that were imagined to be united underground was the focus. In that case, villagers believed that an underground river constructed by the "Inka" (in this case meaning ancestral people living in another time) carried water from the *puna* to fields in subterranean tunnels (Martínez 1983). Furthermore, ancestors were credited with building the first irrigation canals in some colonial period communities (Doyle 1988). The belief that mountains were sources of water justified conducting water rituals related to mountains. The reality of the source of local irrigation water was less important.

Mountains, water, and ancestors could influence many other aspects of life as well. They could be beneficent or malevolent depending on the kinds of offering they received from their living descendants (Gow et al. 1976; Mariño Ferro 1989; Martínez 1983; Sillar 1992). Colonial documents describe interactions between descendants and mummified ancestral remains (*mallkikuna*), which included dressing, feeding, and wrapping the person, as well as processions through the streets calling out to the deceased. In general, funerary treatments for a deceased person took place in two phases. Similar rituals took place shortly after death and one year later, when the ancestor made the final transition from living society to ancestral status. Once ancestral status was achieved, the person could be consulted for protection during travel, naming children, curing illness, recommending marriage partners, and other general life cycle events. Mummies received sacrifices and were consulted through ministers. Community-wide rituals often took place near planting and harvest time and involved sacrifices to request agricultural productivity (Doyle 1988; Salomon 1995).

Modern ethnographers have recorded more detailed descriptions of rituals, but for the most part, these practices were focused exclusively on mountains because mummies were no longer created. Many aspects of ritual were related to the reciprocal relationship of care between people and supernatural figures. Local mountains were called upon most often in rituals (Kuznar 2001), which may suggest that they had taken on some of the roles of mummified ancestors in modern communities. They became hungry and thirsty and needed to be fed (Allen 2002). This was often accomplished by burning offerings like chicha, llama, guinea pig, or other items (Kuznar 2001). In some cases, archaeological sites were considered to be dwelling places of ancestors who labored in fields and kept herds just like their living descendants.

The overtly mythical and ritual system described above was inextricably linked to politics (Gose 1993; Meddens 1994). Shortly after conquest, political influence within communities was related primarily to mummified ancestors. Although people perceived authority as being held by ancestors, living individuals decided and expressed their wants and needs. Authority was depersonalized as long as listeners were willing to believe that influence was held not by the speaker, but by the ancestor (Nielsen 2006). The male or female minister in charge of mummies in a particular *ayllu* could influence the community, accrue fees, and build status through this ritual post (Doyle 1988; Salomon 1995).

In addition, people who were nearing death could "borrow" from the status they would soon have as an ancestor in order to influence village politics directly (Salomon 1995). Yet after death, not every person would be equally powerful. Those who were more influential in life or whose families became more prominent after their death were thought to remain close to the village and to continue to participate in local politics while less powerful ancestors eventually returned to the origin place of the *ayllu* and disappeared from the affairs of the living (Gose 1993). As Salomon (1995) pointed out, ancestor cult did not follow strict rules, but was an interaction of rules and current circumstance. As a result, this system was a venue for status negotiation and political action.

The same ideology could be exploited by political systems that incorporated many different villages situated in diverse landscapes. The Inka reconfigured local sacred geography and ancestry so that their own ethnic group would be positioned at the highest level of the nested segmentary social organization. They reworked origin stories by adding a deity who directed other ancestors. After destroying an earlier race of humanity, Wiraqucha created a new people from stone who called the ancestors of all the *ayllus* to emerge from their origin places and directed their journeys to the locations where they would found their kin groups (Doyle 1988). This revision legitimized empire in a segmentary society. Since the ancestors of the Inka emerged first, they had the highest status in the system. Furthermore, the Inka kings acquired an additional special ancestor, the sun, to legitimize their rule (Doyle 1988).

The Inka also revised conceptions of hydrology. As mentioned above, Andean people believed that the ultimate source of water was Lake Titicaca or the sea though it emerged from locally visible locations (that may or may not have been the true source of the water). In reality, most people in the highlands could control all the water they needed for farming from within their local territory by diverting streams and springs. Yet, the Inka took advantage of the idea that the ultimate source of water was far away and that it traveled in underground waterways. By equating the empire with the control point closest to the source of the mythical irrigation system, they placed themselves at the highest level and highest status of the segmentary social structure (Gose 1993; Sherbondy 1992).

For the Inka, the sacred mountains and lakes were tools for structuring the empire and replicating icons of power in each conquered territory. The Inka captured sacred objects (*wakakuna*) of conquered people, built new Cuscos, and modified local sacred mountains (for a detailed discussion see Acuto 2005). In most parts of the pre-Hispanic Andes, the highest status ancestors were those who existed in separate mythical primordial time. In contrast, living Inka royalty could become the highest status ancestors after death (Doyle 1988).

One important ritual that reinforced the restructuring of sacred space was tied to the transition of a living Inka king to the new status as a mummy or ancestor. When the king died, an empire-wide cycle of ritual began (called the *qhapaq hucha*, or "great obligation"). On mountaintops, shrines were built and offerings were made. Elite children and some women who were chosen for beauty or perfect qualities were selected and called to travel to the capital from their homes. After preparation in Cusco, they were sent out to locations throughout the provinces to be sacrificed atop local sacred mountains. In some situations, statues of humans made from gold or silver could stand in for children (Benson 2001; Ceruti 2004). Through this ritual performance, the Inka imposed hierarchy and claimed to be part of the local past through actions that were visible to people throughout the kingdom (Acuto 2005; Ceruti 2004; Cornejo 1995; Gelles 2000; Reinhard 1985).

Archaeological Expectations

The preceding discussion includes rich descriptions that are available only from myth, storytelling, and observation of living people. This level of detail will never be available to prehistoric archaeologists, but it can be used to identify materials that might be found in the archaeological record. Based on the discussion above, archaeologists can investigate whether ancestors and the landscape might have been features of a sacred system that existed in some form in the more distant past.

Ancestor Veneration

The preserved human body (*mallki*) was the most common object of ancestor veneration (Doyle 1988; Nielsen 2006; Salomon 1995). Therefore, finding preserved mummies would be a strong indication that a system of ancestor veneration existed in the past. Mummies were often wrapped in textiles. Most commonly, they were in a seated position, sometimes with hands raised to the mouth. We know relatively little about how mummies were made, though the topic has long been of interest to many scholars. Based on ethnohistoric documents and some investigations of preserved mummies, it is likely that the majority of mummies were made naturally through a process of freeze-drying in the highlands, but that the Inka kings underwent an artificial embalming (Penna 1909). Since embalming was reserved for royalty, it seems unlikely that such elaborate practices were common in early villages.

Ancient mummies would be difficult to find in the highlands where the rainy environment can lead to decomposition of organic materials. In addition, looting of tombs has been common for a very long time. In the absence of mummies, some archaeologists have focused on architecture where the remains could have been kept accessible for offerings and consultation, and from which they might occasionally have been taken out for processions or changing their wrappings. Human remains are rarely found in such structures, though some contain a few scattered and disarticulated human bones indicating that bodies were moved in and out of them (e.g., Dulanto 2002a; Isbell 1997; Mantha 2009). When human skeletal remains are recovered, a taphonomic approach to human burials can be used to infer multiple phases of funerary treatment from the final burial (see Chap. 2). Such ongoing interaction may indicate ancestor veneration, but not every multiphase burial does. Human remains can also be moved to be incorporated as offerings (Blom and Janusek 2004; Verano 1995). Alternatively, captives can be sacrificed and their remains processed in multiple steps (Verano 2008).

Sacred Landscape

Despite the fact that many scholars readily acknowledge the importance of the sacred landscape in Andean culture, most are hesitant to study this tradition due to the dearth of satisfactory empirical methods. Some authors suggest that an "unusual" feature is more likely to be a sacred place (e.g., van de Guchte 1999), but it would be difficult to define what ancient people might have found "unusual." From any location in the Andes, dozens of impressive mountains, several sources of water, and at least a few peculiar rocky outcrops are visible. Without some archaeological evidence it would be impossible to determine which parts of the landscape were important in prehistory. The obstacles to identifying sacred places were made clear in Bauer's (1998) study of the sacred landscape of Inka Cusco. Even with detailed ethnohistoric descriptions of the shrines of the *ceque* (*ziqi*) system, many could be identified only tentatively and some could not be identified at all.

In the case of sacred mountains, the mountain itself rarely has archaeological remains on the summit. In fact, the few mountaintop sanctuaries that have been found are Inka constructions, which are more common in the southern part of the empire (Castro and Aldunate 2003; Reinhard 1985). Because building these shrines was part of an imperial strategy of conquest, it is unlikely that we would find such shrines associated with early villages.

When a sacred mountain has not been modified in any way, special architecture can demonstrate that visible features were important. An ethnoarchaeological study by Kuznar (2001) found that sacred places were often marked by alignments. The Inka used architecture and lines of sight to highlight distant elements of the landscape by mimicking their form or by framing them with windows or passageways (Niles 1987, 1992; Von Hagen and Morris 1998). In addition, archaeologists have found that the windows of Late Intermediate period and Inka *chullpas* (above-ground mortuary structures) faced mountains and that modern chapels and churches are oriented to revered hills (Castro and Aldunate 2003). Castro and Aldunate (2003) have rightly noted that archaeologists often miss these details because they record orientation in cardinal directions that cannot detect such patterns. Ideally, archaeologists working in the Andes should record orientations of graves, buildings, and other structures in relation to the landscape that surrounds them.

Ritual Practice

Ritual practices associated with veneration of ancestors or the sacred landscape may help strengthen the identification of such systems in the past. Manipulating flowing water or pouring liquids were common activities. Occasionally, these rituals involved cleaning utilitarian canals in fields (e.g., Gelles 2000). Alternatively, they were sometimes associated with special architecture. It was common to pour liquids through objects such as mortars with holes in the bottom or ritual channels (Nielsen 2006). In addition, Inka fountains have been found at many sites (Niles 1987, 1992). At Cacha (modern Raqchi), the Inka used canals to bring water from springs located at the base of a revered volcano to create a small sacred lake (Sillar 2002).

Certain kinds of offerings often accompanied ancestor veneration rituals, though they were rarely made exclusively in that context. In some cases, small stone receptacles or certain types of pottery vessels were used to receive offerings to ancestors (Nielsen 2006). Burning was the most common method by which supernatural beings were perceived to receive the essence of sacrificed items (Kuznar 2001). *Illas* or *conopas* (figurines that represented crops or livestock) were often used in places where ancestor veneration occurred in both ethnographic and ethnohistoric contexts (Doyle 1988; Gow et al. 1976; Lau 2008; Salomon 1995). *Mullu*, or Spondylus shells, were commonly associated with water ritual (Cornejo 1995; Doyle 1988; Reinhard 1985). This brief discussion has highlighted only a few of the most common objects. For a more thorough inventory of all possible items, see Kuznar's (2001) ethnoarchaeological study of Andean religion.

Identifying and Interpreting Change

Even if we found all of these material correlates, it would not mean that a ritual and political system exactly like any of those described above emerged at a single point in time and endured unchanged until the present. Even within 500 years, changes in the system have occurred according to circumstance.

Scholars generally agree that a sacred system that integrated mountains, water, and ancestor veneration was not spread by the Inka, but that these elements already existed as part of widespread Andean beliefs (Acuto 2005; Doyle 1988; Reinhard 1985; Sherbondy 1992). In fact, this would have been a precondition that allowed the Inka to use these beliefs as a basis for imperial expansion. Rituals like the *qhapaq hucha* marked changes in the distribution of provincial power and added a level to the ancestral family tree of each local group. We do not know very much about the role that local ancestors and sacred mountains continued to play within the empire (Nielsen 2006), but the sacred status of each mountain was not static. In fact, an Inka official was in charge of deciding and tracking which places had lost that status (van de Guchte 1999). During Inka rule, a new political organization changed which mountains were important and what they meant in the context of an expanding empire.

After conquest, the Spanish colonial administration initially took advantage of the existing *ayllu* segmentary social system when creating *encomiendas*, but eventually the system was broken down as communities were resettled into new administrative units or *reducciones*. Ancestor cults were actively persecuted and people were relocated to new villages far away from the landscape and ancestral tombs that were central to group identity (Doyle 1988; Salomon 1995). As a result, the focus of rituals shifted from mummies to mountains and inconspicuous objects that could be kept secretively within homes. Overt political action based on ancestral authority declined.

In some modern communities, mountain gods were associated with ancestors from a newly invented ancient time, the time of the "Inka" (Martínez 1983). These figures continue to participate in reciprocal relationships of care and are particularly important for rituals focused on agricultural or pastoral productivity. Status and power, however, are more likely to be negotiated through new institutions like the *cargo* system (which is related to Andean catholic festivals) or to financial success in capitalist market systems (Van den Berghe 1978).

Great variability exists in how modern and historic Andean peoples relate water, mountains, ancestors, productivity, and ownership. This discussion has demonstrated that an apparently ritual system intertwined with politics and economics in many times and places. Studying the changes in such a system in prehistory will be just as important to understanding ancient social structures as identifying it in the first place.

Ancestor Veneration and Sacred Landscapes before the Inka

Some scholars have argued that the sacred landscape concept was more central for the Inka than for pre-Inka societies. For example, van de Guchte (1999) proposed that in contrast with the Wari, who imposed architectural features and installations with an aesthetic of order and little regard for the natural landscape, the Inka incorporated the landscape into constructions, as instruments for collective memory, and as tools for the creation of the empire. More recently, however, archaeologists have argued that the Wari were also concerned with sacred geography (Glowacki and Malpass 2003; Williams and Nash 2006).

Archaeologists have noted that, even before the Wari, doorways, platforms, or buildings were aligned with distant mountain peaks in the Formative period in Ancash (Burger and Salazar-Burger 1986) and the Titicaca Basin (Beck 2004b; Hastorf 2008). But, they rarely explore the implications of this architectural layout in ritual or politics. With further research, we may learn that these alignments are artifacts of a widespread and ancient conception of sacred landscape.

Ancestor veneration has been detected in several pre-Inka societies in the Andes. Isbell (1997) has argued that it emerged with Andean states when people began to build above-ground stone mortuary monuments that remain visible on the landscape today, but subsequent research has shown that ancestor veneration is a much older Andean tradition that existed in earlier, pre-state societies. Two examples of ancestor veneration tied to the sacred landscape that are roughly contemporary with the occupation of Yuthu are particularly relevant to the current study.

In Formative period Pampa Chica (700–200 BC), Dulanto (2002a, 2002b) identified ancestor veneration by comparing the archaeological remains of the ongoing manipulation of human skeletons in a ceremonial structure with expectations for material remains of ancestor veneration inferred from practices described in sixteenth-century ethnohistoric documents. Although the two periods are very distant in time, these practices proved remarkably similar. Within the most secluded and enclosed areas of a ceremonial complex, located at least 1 km from residential sites, bodies underwent multiphase burial treatment before being moved somewhere else. This treatment was mostly for males and involved movements between pits, small rooms, and an open sunken patio before remains were taken ultimately to another undetermined site. Dulanto stressed that Pampa Chica occupied a unique location between many different resource zones and that these practices were closely tied to the landscape and linked to concerns about resource rights. He also noted the importance of ancestor veneration to community identity and politics. When many groups in the Lurín Valley ceased to get along, some communities used rituals of ancestor veneration as a means to strengthen their own social group and to compete with others.

In Formative period highland Bolivia at the site of Chiripa, evidence for ancestor worship included: tombs of women, located in an enclosure, that were reopened to access their remains and present them with offerings (1500–1000 BC); a later niche in a semi-subterranean structure that was presumably used for displaying the dead (1000–800 BC); a new type of ritual architecture, independent lineage houses, that may have been associated with the dead (800–400 BC); and, finally, community authorized houses for the "official lineages" that held burials, niches for display of sacred objects, and antechambers that may have held ancestral remains and that were constructed around a large community ritual space (400–250 BC) (Hastorf 2003). Hastorf stresses that practices of ancestor veneration were not static; rather, they reflected the social structure of the people who carried them out. In each phase, ancestor veneration created a community identity that was strongly tied to a place or territory. Over time, the community identity shifted from (1) communal to (2) independent lineages to (3) lineages structured by some greater community power.

During the Formative period outside Cusco, ancestor veneration was tied to group identity, sacred landscape, and territoriality. Both Hastorf and Dulanto independently emphasize three key aspects of ancestor veneration that may guide archaeological study. Dulanto outlined these dimensions explicitly (drawing heavily on Salomon 1995):

> (1) the *landscape* that was imagined as a complex of sacred objects, spaces, and natural forces originating in the actions of ancestral heroes;
> (2) the *public spaces* within this complex where the communities gathered periodically to add their recent dead to the heroic dead and to venerate their ancestors; and
> (3) the *mummified bodies* of the recent dead, which were intentionally preserved and frequently manipulated and moved within and between such public spaces. [Dulanto 2002a:98]

By examining these three aspects, it should be possible to identify a similar ritual system in Formative period Cusco. Because the material remains of the landscape and ceremonial architecture are inseparable, I first consider these two dimensions together. Second, I present the evidence for ongoing interaction with ancestral remains.

Ceremonial Architecture in the Local Landscape

During most of the occupation of the Yuthu, major ceremonial activities took place in a space that was constructed to emphasize important mountains, springs, and lakes in the local landscape. The Southern Sector was a prominent artificial platform that faced Cerro Huanacaure,[1] a mountain that rises out of the plain on the opposite shore of Lake Huaypo (about 1.5 km to the southeast) (Fig. 5.1). An unroofed structure with a sunken floor built on top of the platform (Structure 1) also faced Huanacaure (Fig. 5.2). A spring was located directly behind the platform to the northeast, though today it has dried up.

Some of the most intriguing features of Structure 1 were ritual canals that carried water from the inside to discharge it off the platform's edge. Each of these canals was aligned with glacial peaks visible to the west (Fig. 5.3). Canal 1 pointed to Pitusiray, a glacier about 25 km to the northeast above the modern town of Calca on the other side of the Sacred Valley. The flecks of carbon in the deposits inside this canal indicate that the liquid that passed through it carried burned materials. It may be that bits of items burned nearby were inadvertently picked up by water being poured into the mouth of the canal. Alternatively, ash or other burned items may have been intentionally put into the intake and rinsed away. Or, burned material may have been mixed with water that was then poured into the canal.

Figure 5.1. The platform in the Southern Sector faced Cerro Huanacaure.

Regardless of the specific activity that created these deposits, the mixture of water and charcoal bits indicates that some of the rituals performed in the Southern Sector involved burned offerings and libations of water or other liquids. Based on analogy with ethnohistoric and ethnographic accounts, it seems likely that this ritual practice was related to the conceptual association between glacial peaks and water, even though the distant peaks could not have been the true source of water for the fields around Yuthu.

During the use of Structure 1, Ritual Canal 1 was replaced by a new canal that shared the same intake but was curved so that the discharge was offset to the east (Ritual Canal 2). Therefore, the new canal no longer pointed to Pitusiray, but to Chicón, another glacier located 20 km northeast of Yuthu above the modern town of Urubamba (about 9 km southwest of Pitusiray). In contrast with Ritual Canal 1, Ritual Canal 2 did not have such thick deposits of soil deposited by water. This indicates that Ritual Canal 1 was used either more frequently or for a longer time than Ritual Canal 2. It seems that shortly after the replacement, the whole structure was covered with soil and abandoned.

Offerings or burials of human remains were included in canal renovations. Canal 3 was similar to Ritual Canals 1 and 2, but it is impossible to determine its purpose because most of it was demolished during the replacement of Ritual Canal 1 with Ritual Canal 2. When Canal 3 was destroyed, material was burned in the eastern portion and the body of a 1- to 2-year-old child was positioned to cut off the discharge end, ritually closing the canal (Burial 9). This interment and three others were covered with a thick stratum of soil that buried Ritual Canal 1 and Canal 3. The other burials included a 12- to 13-year-old child (Burial 1), an 18- to 25-year-old woman (Burial 8), and a 36- to 45-year-old woman (Burial 10). A secondary burial of a 2- to 3-year-old child was placed in a small depression cut into that stratum of soil (Burial 11), and an offering that included flowers was burned inside the depression before it was buried and covered with Ritual Canal 2.

These burials indicate that young children were closely associated with water and glaciers through ritual practice that involved canals. These activities may have been related to concerns about having sufficient water for growing crops. An *illa*, or stone potato, found in this area supports the proposition that productivity was a major concern. The *illa* was probably used in offerings made to request a good potato harvest (Fig. 5.4; Plate 8).

Although it is possible that some other explanation may account, at least in part, for the placement of ceremonial architecture, the location of the ceremonial sector between a spring and a lake, the use of canals for offerings of water, and the orientation of the platform and structure indicate that the ritual system was closely tied to a sacred landscape in which mountains and water were prominent features. Within this context, it may be possible

Ceremonial architecture and the local landscape

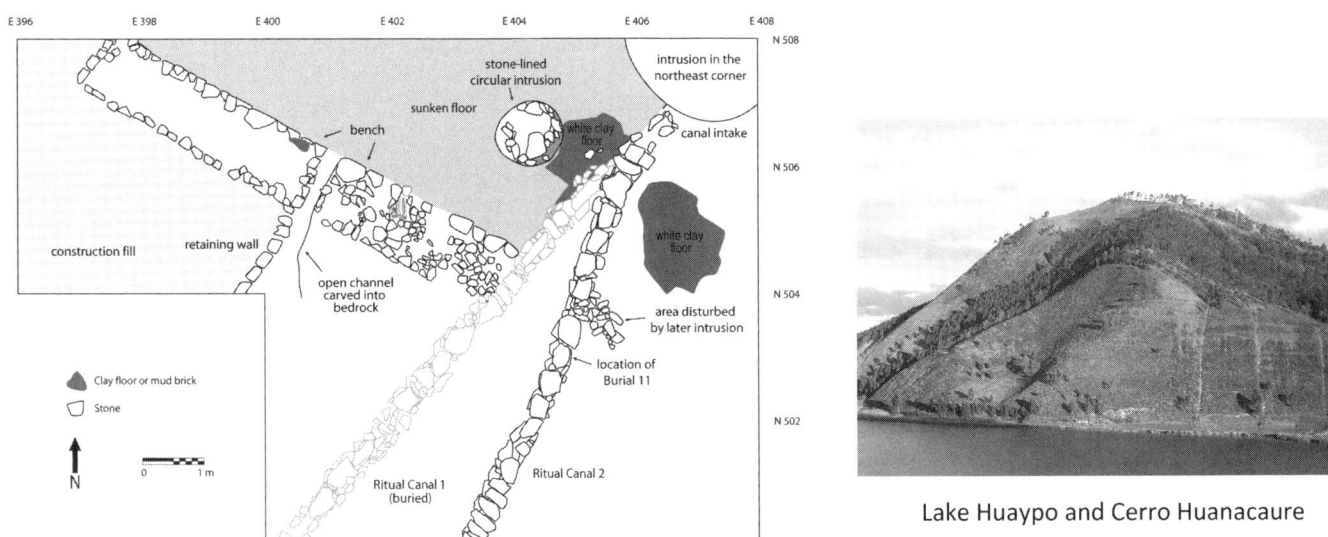

Figure 5.2. The platform and Structure 1 in the Southern Sector faced Lake Huaypo and Cerro Huanacaure. Ritual Canal 1 was built to face the glacier Pitusiray. The replacement, Ritual Canal 2, was built to align with the glacier Chicón.

to interpret a pyramid-shaped stone from this sector as a representation of a mountain, though it is not possible to determine this with any certainty (Fig. 5.4; Plate 8).

Unfortunately, because only a small part of the platform has been excavated, it is impossible to determine whether there might be additional sunken structures. If there were no similar structures, it would indicate that group identity was shared by the entire village. If there were, it would suggest that group identity was constructed for divisions within the village such as moieties or lineages. Only further excavation will be able to determine the level of group identity that was conceptualized in terms of the sacred landscape and constructed during periodic rituals.

Multiphase Burial and Ancestor Veneration

At Yuthu, some burials were the last step in multiphase mortuary treatment while others were primary interments made immediately or relatively soon after the individual's death. In all cases, the burials were not accessed or disturbed later in prehistory. Changes in the locations and types of multiphase burials at Yuthu can be used to trace the emergence and evolution of ancestor veneration in the region. Multiphase burials were common at Yuthu (10 out of 23 burials and 14 out of 27 individuals, Types 2–4 as defined in Chap. 2). They were located in both the Northern and Southern Sectors, starting with the earliest constructions in each area.

In the Northern Sector, the earliest pit houses were associated with two burials that included the deteriorated bones of multiple individuals that were burned in situ before being buried (Type 2). Burial 20 contained an adult woman at least 25 years old and a 3-month-old infant. Burial 21 included 4 individuals: 2 infants around 3 months old, a 5- to 6-year-old child, and an adult of indeterminate sex more than 25 years old. In many ways, these contexts were more like "offerings" than graves. The oldest pit

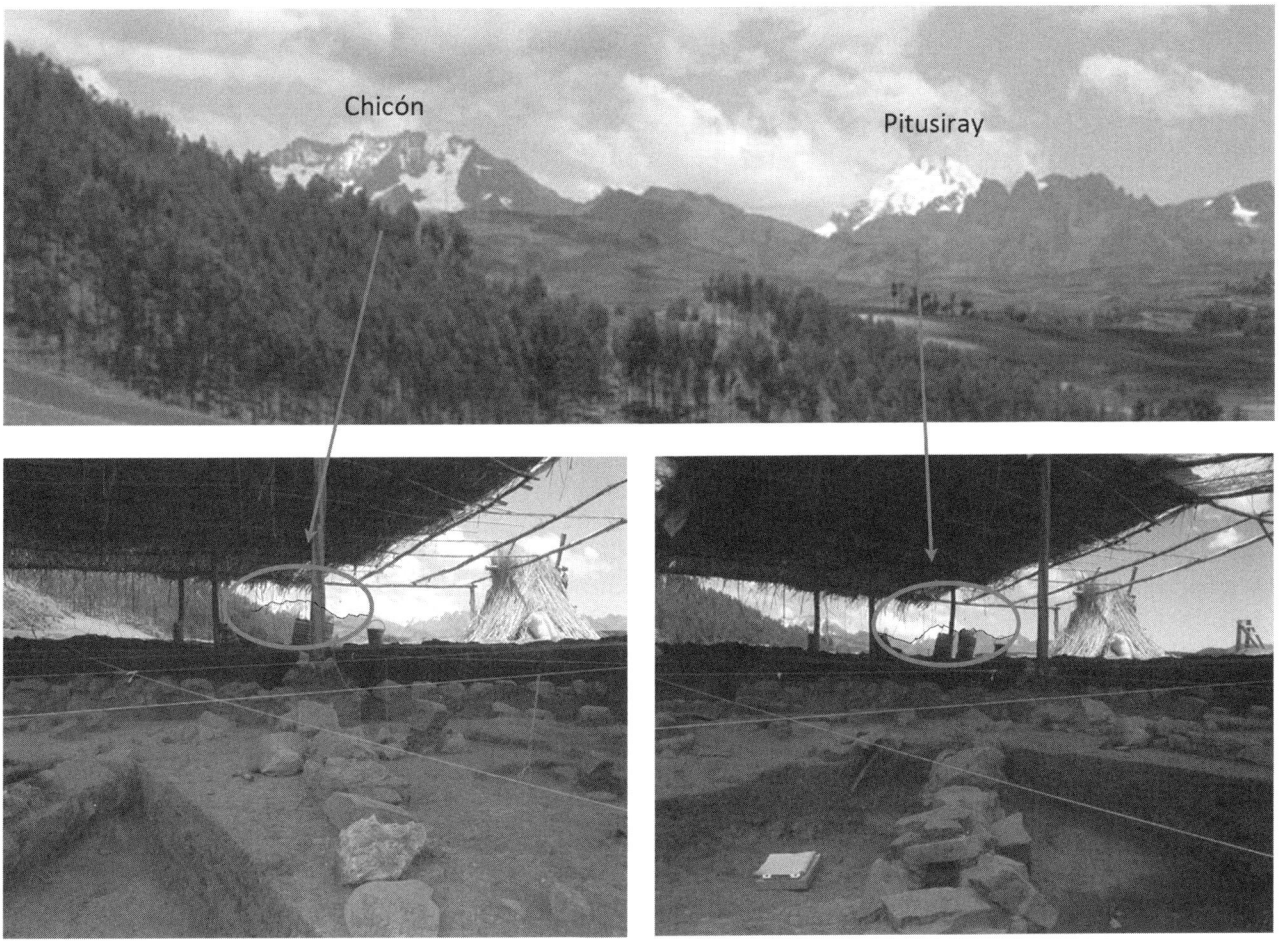

Figure 5.3. The ritual canals in the Southern Sector were built to align with distant glacial peaks.

house was also associated with the primary interment of an infant under a small mound that would have been visible to passersby.

Secondary burials of a single individual (Burial Type 3) were never found in the domestic sector. In contrast, in the ceremonial sector, when Structure 1 was built, three such burials were included in the construction fill. They included a 36- to 45-year-old man who had an extra adult right hand buried with him (Burial 12), a 26- to 35-year-old woman incorporated into the southern face of the bench and with scorching on her face where it was lying on the course of stones (Burial 13), and a 26- to 45-year-old woman with scorching on some bones (Burial 14). After initial construction, a similar burial of a 36- to 45-year-old woman was placed within the eastern section of the bench (Burial 15).

Later, when the structure was remodeled, primary burials of women and children were included in a stratum used to close Ritual Canal 1 and Canal 3. A secondary burial of a 2- to 3-year-old child was placed below the new canal construction. No human burials were associated with the covering and abandonment of the Structure 1.

While Structure 1 was still in use, a new mortuary tradition emerged. "Mummies" were human bodies that were stored in empty or accessible locations with desiccated soft tissue restraining the movement of bones that would otherwise occur as a part of natural decomposition. This preservation was probably achieved through a process of freeze-drying. After the soft tissues had decayed sufficiently so that single bones could be detached without cutting, the cranium or pelvis was removed and the individual was buried (Burial Type 4). The earliest mummy at Yuthu was a 12- to 16-year-old adolescent of unknown sex whose skeleton was found in a tightly flexed, articulated position with all bones present except the cranium (Burial 19). The individual was buried directly above Burials 21 and 22 and was associated with the latest domestic structure found at Yuthu.

Figure 5.4. Objects found in the Southern Sector (*from left to right*): An *illa* of a potato may have been related to rituals requesting agricultural fertility. A pyramid-shaped rock may have represented a mountain or platform. A human figurine in a flexed pose similar to burial positions at Yuthu may be related to ancestor veneration; note that the head has been snapped off the body.

The rest of the burials at Yuthu were made after Structure 1 and all houses had been abandoned and buried. Flotation samples recovered from the associated strata contained no or very few carbonized plants, indicating that no cooking took place at that time. The final use of the site (in both the Northern and Southern Sectors) was exclusively as a cemetery. Individuals would have been brought there from other villages for burial at that time. Dense surface scatters of human bone in both sectors suggest that the cemetery was extensive.

At this time, two men who had been kept as mummies elsewhere were buried at the former village. The right half of the pelvis of a 26- to 35-year-old man (Burial 16) was removed before he was buried in a shallow pit in the Northern Sector near primary interments of two young women and an infant. All of these individuals surrounded a small stone hearth that contained ashy soil but almost no carbonized plant remains or animal bones.

In the Southern Sector, an 18- to 25-year-old man was buried in a seated upright position with a three-sided stone box—which contained carbonized quinoa, *Oxalis*, and *Galium* seeds—at his right shoulder (Burial 4). Four individuals were buried nearby, including the secondary burial of a woman over 46 years old who was given burial treatment like that of earlier women in this area (Burial Type 3). Nearby, a primary group burial included three children. The oldest child was killed by blunt force to the head (Individual 6, 11–12 years old). A 1- to 2-year old was at that child's feet (Individual 7). A 7- to 8-year old missing his or her head and neck was located above the older child's head (Individual 3). The right half of an adult pelvis was placed over the feet of the 1- to 2-year old.

Although very little representational iconography has been found at Yuthu, a single anthropomorphic stone figurine was found in the Southern Sector in a stratum that was contemporary with the final burials (Fig. 5.4; Plate 8). This figurine was an individual in a seated flexed position. The forehead and nose were painted with red pigment and the head had been snapped off at the neck. Considering that the figurine was found near the burial of a male mummy whose head had been similarly removed, it seems probable that this figurine is a mummy image that was used in ancestor veneration rituals. Ongoing interaction with human remains was an important part of ritual life starting with the original settlement at Yuthu, but the tradition of mummy veneration that emphasized ongoing interaction with an intact and portable mummy, which retained the individual identity of the deceased, developed late within domestic contexts and endured after the village was abandoned.

Why Mummies?

A key dimension of ancestor veneration is ongoing interaction with ancestral remains. The earliest burials in the Northern Sector were the final step in a multiphase process that eventually ended when bones from more than one individual were mixed in an offering pit. At the same time, burials associated with the ceremonial structure were individuals whose identities were kept intact until their bodies were moved to a new burial place. In both cases, since these bodies were allowed to decay, they could not have been moved without loss of bones and soft tissue. Therefore, interaction with living people was limited to moments of burial or placement in an ossuary, visits to that location, removal, and final burial.

Compared to these earlier multiphase burial treatments, mummies were available for much longer and probably more intense interaction with living people. Mummies must have been maintained by the living for a significant amount of time in order for the bodies to decay enough to remove the cranium or pelvis. During that time, the mummies remained in open structures, accessible to family members, and possibly to others. The preserved bundles could have been transported and displayed many times without loss of bones or soft tissue. It is likely that these mummies were dressed, fed, carried in processions, or otherwise integrated into rituals. It is not clear if the cranium or pelvis was removed as part of ongoing rituals or immediately before final burial. And, there is little evidence as to what happened to the curated skeletal elements, though in one case an adult right pelvis was buried in a new grave with children.

The nature and duration of interaction between the living and mummies differed from earlier multiphase burials. Unfortunately, it is impossible to determine how long the bodies were stored as mummies before final burial, but I can suggest two possibilities based on ethnohistoric accounts: (1) deceased persons may have transitioned to "ancestral" status one year after death, or (2) this transition may have occurred when the individual identity was "forgotten," usually after about three generations (Salomon 1995). By attributing influence to a mummy during this long transition time after death, authority could be depersonalized. That is, it could be displaced from the living speaker to the deceased. If mummies were family figures, this ideological shift could break an egalitarian ethic and allow inheritance of influence or wealth, either for a relatively short one-year transition period or for up to several generations after an individual's death. Such inheritance along family lines would have been at odds with rights to resources and territory established at the group level through rituals in the ceremonial sector. In fact, Structure 1 was eventually abandoned while mummy veneration continued. For some time, however, large group ritual and lineage-focused ancestor veneration were two potentially conflicting practices that existed alongside each other.

Even in the Formative period, Andean ancestor veneration was part of a larger sacred system in which group identity was constructed and territorial claims were legitimized through rituals associated with a sacred landscape. Politics, especially related to ritual authority and territorial rights, played out within this context. The role of this system in the origins of inequality and the development of a multi-village polity are further discussed in Chapter 6.

Social Groups and Change

Internal and external factors may have triggered or facilitated transformations in community organization that are visible to archaeologists through changes in ritual practice at Yuthu. Competition surrounding the selection of deceased individuals for ritual and political activities may have led to a shift from a ceremonial system promoting group identity to one focused on family groups. Drought and regional processes of political consolidation may have been related to transferring ritual focus from one glacier to another.

Group identity above the level of the household was important to the earliest villagers at Yuthu. In the ceremonial sector, it was established, revised, and expressed in relationship to the local sacred landscape. Rituals carried out within the ceremonial sector were related to agricultural and pastoral fertility. Human burials made during the use of Structure 1 included both primary interments and multiphase burials. In either case, maintaining the recognizable identity of each individual seems to have been a priority. Most people buried in this area during the use of the ceremonial structure were women and children, though one man was buried on the platform at this time. Even though early rituals in the ceremonial sector focused on integration, they could have been venues for competition between groups who wanted their relatives or representatives to be buried in the shared space.

In contrast, the earliest burials in the Northern Sector contained bones from multiple women and children that were burned in situ. The burned offerings were close to houses and probably included the remains of several family members brought to this new place from their original location in a burial ground or ossuary. In these cases, the association of ancestral bones with the family group was more important than individual identity.

Mummies were never associated with Structure 1 (which was related to group identity above the level of the household). Like multiple secondary burials, it seems most likely they were affiliated with families. The earliest mummy was buried next to a house. Later, one man was associated with two women and an infant buried around a small stone hearth. The other man was buried in close association with the secondary burial of an adult woman and three children who died violent deaths. A plausible explanation for this arrangement is that when the family was killed in a single event, there was no longer anyone left to care for their family or lineage mummy. Another possibility is that the children were buried with ancestral caretakers (a mummified man and a secondary burial of a woman). In either case, these funerary arrangements mimic family structures.

Competition between families at Yuthu may have led to this abandonment of village-level integrative ceremonial practice and a shift in focus to family-level mortuary ritual. This transition took place in the context of external change. The replacement of the original canal with one that faced a different snow-capped peak suggests that the relationship between villagers and more distant mountains was reconceived within less than 300 years while the relationship with nearby Cerro Huanacaure and Lake Huaypo (materialized in the orientation of the platform and ceremonial structures built on top of it) remained the same. Based on analogy with ethnographic and historic accounts, I can suggest two plausible explanations.

(1) A drought that occurred near the end of the occupation may have caused people to lose trust in the ability of the first glacier to provide water. Snail species recovered at Yuthu reveal a transition from a cooler and wetter climate to a drier climate during the use of the site. *Gastrocopta* sp., gastropods that thrive in drier environments, were found only in Stratum 3 of Unit A. *Charopidae*, which live in cool and wet climates, were found in

lower strata in both sectors (Stratum 7 and below in Unit A and Stratum 4 and below in Unit D) (Vásquez Sánchez and Rosales Tham 2009). This climatic shift coincides with the abandonment of the village and its conversion to a cemetery.

(2) The change in ritual focus from one glacier to another may also indicate a realignment of political alliances as a multi-village polity was forming for the first time. A settlement pattern shift from many small villages of roughly the same size to a site-size hierarchy with one large village hints that this process may have taken place during the Formative period. In either case, the renovation occurred just before the structure was abandoned along with the related group-level ritual system.

While it is true that a ritual system that shared several elements with Andean traditions known from ethnohistory and ethnography existed at Yuthu, the specific practices at the early village were particular to the social, political, and environmental context of Formative period Cusco. Furthermore, the role of the dead and of each feature of the landscape changed over time. At first, family-related ancestor veneration did not prioritize individual identity, though it was important in group-level ritual. Later, as the climate became drier, water ritual shifted from one distant glacier to another. Eventually, family-level ceremonial practice focused on portable mummies that maintained individual identity emerged and endured, even after group-level ritual associated with the structure and glaciers was abandoned.

Note

1. This is not the same Cerro Huanacaure where the founding ancestor Ayar Uchu turned to stone in the Inka origin story. That mountain is located south of the modern city of Cusco. There are, however, important Inka myths that cite this mountain as the source of irrigation water in this area and recount how ethnic groups and polities in this area were incorporated into the empire. See Sherbondy 1992:59 for further discussion.

— 6 —

Conclusions

When I began this project, very little was known about daily life, ritual, or politics in early villages in Cusco, Peru. Because of the dearth of information, I decided to employ a community approach that is particularly suitable for excavation of a single small village site when little is known and great variability in social configuration, economics, and ritual practice is possible. As defined in the introduction, a community approach has five aspects: (1) the unit of analysis should be a single village with a variety of people and institutions, (2) the study should be holistic, (3) it should examine social institutions above the level of the village as they are experienced within it, (4) it should include the study of divisions within the community and mechanisms that can result in change, and (5) it should balance historical and comparative inquiry.

The ideal village for community study should be neither the largest nor smallest in the area, but it should be big enough to include the activity areas and architectural remains of a wide variety of practices such as household activities and public rituals. I selected Yuthu because it was a moderately sized site with a visible platform and two separate scatters of artifacts. Surface remains suggested that a variety of activities took place in distinct spaces. Indeed, this village contained one sector of domestic houses and associated outdoor activity areas as well as a ceremonial sector where community members participated in activities above the level of the household. The presence of these two kinds of sectors allowed me to study daily life as well as social and political institutions within a single village.

Yuthu was situated on the shore of a spring-fed lake located on a high rolling plain northwest of the modern city of Cusco (3600 masl). The residents of the village were herders and farmers; wild foods made up a very minimal part of the diet. Therefore, farming and herding filled many hours of daily life and also served as a frame to schedule other activities throughout the year. Tending to flocks of llamas and alpacas required daily attention by at least some family members. Guinea pigs were kept in households and required little work other than daily feeding of kitchen scraps. Farming, in contrast, would have required group labor for planting, tending, and harvesting plants. The two most demanding moments with the highest labor input would have been at the beginning of the rainy season, when the ground was prepared and planted, and during harvest time. Quinoa, *kiwicha*, potatoes, and tubers could be grown in fields near the village. Corn and early crops of potatoes could have been grown in the nearby valley where the growing season was longer.

Many other daily tasks took place alongside these subsistence practices. People prepared food, gathered fuel, and cared for family members. As need arose, they crafted several kinds of items like bone tools, pottery, woven garments, and chipped stone tools. They hunted or trapped wild animals only occasionally and used herbs and wild plants to practice medicine. While performing these tasks, mothers or other caretakers probably carried their babies in a way that created a distinct head shape that was common throughout Formative period Cusco. When a loved one died, they did not immediately disappear from social life.

Family members and others continued to interact with deceased individuals through multiphase mortuary rituals. Yet relationships between people were not always peaceful and amicable. The rates of interpersonal violence were high at Yuthu, showing that conflict was a significant part of social life at this time.

With each added detail, it becomes easier to imagine what life might have been like in this small village. People spent most of their time out of doors under the warm mountain sun with the exception of the star-filled nights when they entered small simple houses to retreat from the cold or to escape a storm during the rainy season. Groups might have gathered around smoky campfires to gossip and tell stories while cooking, shaping stone tools, or winnowing quinoa. During planting or harvest, work groups shared food and drink during breaks from difficult work. And each day, lone individuals may have minded herds outside the village, without even a dog for company. If a woman accompanied flocks, perhaps she spun yarn; if a child were the shepherd, he or she might have practiced aiming a slingshot. Imagining life in this way provides the context necessary to understand politics, ideology, and economics that are more typically the focus of anthropological archaeology.

Taking a community approach allows investigation of social institutions that crosscut many villages or existed at a level above the single settlement by considering how those institutions were experienced by local people. Based on previous studies in the Andes, I chose to investigate three types of institutions above the local level: (1) participation in long-distance trade networks, (2) integration into a set of vertical communities, and (3) incorporation into a multi-village polity.

Villagers participated in long-distance trade that was probably facilitated by llama caravans. Obsidian stone tools were the most visible remains of this network. This raw material has no known local source and would have been imported from distant regions of the highlands such as Arequipa or Ayacucho (Glascock et al. 2007). Other exotic items were very rare at Yuthu, but included a macaw beak and half of a fish bone from the jungle. This dearth of imports may indicate either that trade consisted primarily of perishable items like textiles, feathers, and coca, or that nearly all items used for subsistence and ritual came from the local environment. The lack of marine shell and the low quantity of items from the jungle indicate that trade networks were focused on the highlands. Future studies that identify the source of the obsidian at Yuthu will help to determine the true extent of this principally highland trading network.

It is impossible to know for sure at this time whether the inhabitants of Yuthu were part of a multi-village community that spanned several ecological zones, but it seems that this village obtained most of its resources nearby. Quinoa, the most common crop, grows very well in fields surrounding the village and llamas and alpacas can graze happily in this area year-round. As long as pasture and farm fields could be managed so that llamas would not eat young plants, both the agricultural and pastoral systems could coexist successfully in this area.

The significant presence of maize (nearly 9% of all carbonized plant remains) challenges the notion that villagers could have exclusively exploited the ecological zone in which they lived. It is true that some corn can grow around the edge of Lake Huaypo, but maize cobs are considerably larger and the corn is tastier in the Sacred Valley, which is only a half-day walk from Yuthu. Because the Sacred Valley has no large Formative settlements, I would suggest that farmers living at Yuthu and other nearby villages directly exploited both the plain and the nearby valley. As a result, not only did they have access to more diverse crops, but they were able to manage risk and schedule labor to maximize the number of fields that workers could tend. There is no evidence that Yuthu was part of a vertically integrated community that included multiple settlements or that inhabitants practiced seasonal transhumance, though it is difficult to say for sure without further study. It is most likely that villagers chose to live in a location where they could directly exploit two distinct resource zones.

A community approach should pay particular attention to the presence of factions within a single village and the potential role of competition in social change. At Yuthu, a sacred and political system that included the landscape, ancestors, and territorial rights structured society. This institution can be considered in terms of its potential to crosscut multiple settlements, but it is equally intriguing because of the potential role that competition within this venue may have played in the transformation of the village.

When I began this study, I knew that many aspects of indigenous Andean cosmology and religion focused on or integrated the dramatic mountain landscape. I also knew that studying such a system in the distant past was notoriously difficult for archaeologists. I never expected to be able to discuss this aspect of life at Yuthu, but the presence of special architecture including a platform, sunken structure, and ritual canals designed to align with prominent mountains has allowed me to demonstrate that a system focused on the landscape was important for establishing and maintaining group identity above the level of the household in this village. Practices associated with this collective identity focused on water and agricultural fertility. Therefore, group membership involved shared rights to territory and resources.

Unfortunately, I was not able to excavate the entire platform in the Southern Sector. Knowing the total number and layout of structures would have allowed me to determine whether shared identity was conceived of at a lineage, moiety, or community level depending on whether there were many similar structures, only two, or just one on the platform.

Reports from as far north as Cajamarca and as far south as the Titicaca Basin describe public or ceremonial architecture that was oriented toward mountain peaks. Though the implications have not been discussed in detail, similar traditions may have been present throughout the Andean highlands at this time. Therefore, although this institution has been studied primarily within the village of Yuthu, it has the potential to have crosscut multiple villages or to have united people living in several settlements.

For example, if the structures were used to maintain corporate kin groups, it may be true that members of these groups lived in several settlements. Such a system also had the potential to be exploited by an emerging multi-village polity, which could have reconfigured the system, requiring veneration of a new sacred mountain that was considered higher ranking and more powerful than the local one. This may have been an ideological expression of the loss of village autonomy. Future research will be necessary to understand this fundamental aspect of social organization.

A complementary, but sometimes conflicting, tradition of ancestor veneration changed significantly over time at Yuthu. Early practices that incorporated the remains of ancestors into offerings or structures differed between sectors. In the domestic Northern Sector, the bones of several individuals were used to establish family ties to a new house. Individual identity was not a priority in household mortuary ritual at this time. In contrast, in the ceremonial Southern Sector, which was created to integrate large social groups, the opposite was true. Individual identity was always maintained, even in secondary burials. This suggests that status negotiation took place in this venue even though it was overtly tied to group unity. Competition may have occurred between individuals (who were usually women) before their death, but given that most interments in this sector were secondary burials brought from other places after significant decomposition of the body, it seems more likely that surviving family members carried out the most important status negotiations after the death of the individual.

Living people had limited access to these dead who were buried in enclosed spaces or environments that would allow significant decay. Interaction would have been limited to moments of primary burial, visits to the interment location, removal, and reburial in individual or group graves. In contrast, a new tradition emerged, which allowed ongoing interaction between the living and the dead who had been preserved as portable mummies in open spaces for some time before final burial. Like the earlier offerings that incorporated many individuals, mummies were related to family groups. An important contrast with earlier family mortuary ritual is that individual identity was now highly prioritized in the same way that it had been in the ceremonial sector, suggesting that the individual could be used in status negotiation and competition.

When I first identified these mummies, I immediately thought of the implications of this type of mortuary tradition for the creation and maintenance of inequalities. Preserving and interacting with the mummy of a lineage head who was a high-status person in life could have been a way for families to inherit status, influence, territory, and wealth for the first time in a formerly egalitarian village. Attributing power and authority to a dead ancestor would effectively break the egalitarian ethic and allow inheritance across generations within families.

The reality of the data, however, has challenged this interpretation. If the described scenario were accurate, we would expect that families would have selected people who had the qualities of leaders, who had earned status in life, and who had descendants. In fact, two of the three individuals were adult males. One was 26 to 35 years old, with several healed fractures on the head, face, and neck. The other was 18 to 25 years old. No evidence of trauma was recorded for this man, but the head (where most healed traumas were located for the other man) was missing from this burial. These individuals would fit the above expectations if men who earned status at least partially through violent conflict also held rights to important resources or wealth—for example, if families were interested in controlling agricultural fields, and land was inherited through the male line.

The third and earliest mummified individual, a 12- to 16-year-old adolescent, does not fit this model. This teen was very young to have gained much respect or influence. He or she had no healed injuries and was certainly too young to be the father or mother of a large number of children. Why would this person have been kept as a mummy? At this point, it is unclear whether this was a unique occurrence or a larger social pattern. If it were a common practice, I can only speculate as to the motivation. At the time that this person was buried in the domestic sector next to a house, burials of children were important in the ceremonial sector as well—especially in association with rituals that related to water and glacial peaks. It could be that children were considered best able to communicate with supernatural deities after their death and, therefore, they were regarded as suitable "spokespersons" for the living. This was true for some later groups in the Andes (Benson 2001).

If that were the case, the earliest mummies may have not have been the focus of ancestor veneration. Rather, the mummy could have served as a medium between the living and the supernatural. It may be that this system evolved only later into a mechanism that facilitated inheritance and broke the egalitarian ethic. This transition would have occurred when the caliber of the spokesperson became tied to his or her status, achievements, and wealth accrued during life. Of course, with the available data we cannot know for sure. Excavations at Yuthu on a much larger scale could reveal whether there was a large-scale shift from child to adult male mummies.

Although this exciting new tradition of mummy veneration involved men and children, it is important to note that the older tradition of secondary burial of individuals who were not stored as mummies continued for individual adult females. Ancestral women continued to play an important role in the community even as this new tradition emerged.

Mummy veneration was a regional institution that extended beyond the limits of the local village. Two of the mummies, a secondary burial of a woman, and several primary interments of women, men, and children at Yuthu were made when the site was used exclusively as a cemetery. Families would have had to bring the dead from other villages to be buried there. Therefore, some kind of social institution that valued this location existed beyond the limits of this single place.

By incorporating many aspects of village life to build a holistic picture of this early community, I have been able to learn many new things about the Formative period in Cusco. Based on models of chiefdoms, archaeologists had predicted that between 500 BC and AD 200, we would find sumptuary goods, elite burials, variation in household status, craft specialization, and significant public works projects in Formative villages. From 400 to 100 BC at Yuthu, however, we see no preserved sumptuary goods or rich burials of high-status people. Most craft production took place around outdoor hearths in generalized activity areas, and public works were limited to ceremonial spaces for group rituals. The three houses excavated so far were very simple with no variation in elaboration. With such a small sample, however, it is possible that economic inequalities could not be perceived.

It is possible that all the aspects of the chiefdom model could be discovered with further excavation or that they could have appeared quickly only at the end of the period when people no longer lived at Yuthu (between 100 BC and AD 200). But, it is also possible that the social and political changes during the Formative period in this area were not like those anticipated by previous scholars.

The Emergence of Inherited Rank in Cusco

The social structures and the economics of early Cusco might have created unique opportunities for inequality. Certainly, mummy focused ancestor veneration was an institution that could have allowed wealth and status to be transferred across generations. Yet typical archaeological indicators of inherited status have not been found at Yuthu. Houses did not vary in quality or elaboration and health did not vary between groups. Even though the village participated in long-distance trade networks, exotic items were not used as prestige goods that might have indicated high-status burials or differences in household wealth.

It is possible that all prestige goods were perishable items, like textiles or colorful feathers from the jungle, which would not be recovered archaeologically. In that case, influence may have been tied to economic wealth measured in prestige goods as was predicted. Alternatively, wealth may have been measured by large herds or better agricultural fields. Another possibility is that access to labor for working fields, leveling platforms, or other tasks was more important than access to prestige goods. This scenario is intriguing because later highland Andean states valued labor service more highly than tribute in finished products. It is also possible that inequalities were not overtly economic. Given that status and politics were negotiated within a ritual system, inequalities may have been linked to perceived influence with supernatural beings.

Taphonomy and non-economic status are certainly important considerations, yet it is dangerous to explain the absence of data that fit anthropological expectations by simply asserting that material correlates will be impossible to find. Given that the adult mummies were created and cared for by people living in other villages after Yuthu was abandoned, mummies may have begun to serve as mechanisms for inheritance only after Yuthu was abandoned. If that were the case, this ideological shift was present in Yuthu, but significant inequalities were not.

It is possible that future excavation at later villages will never recover indications of significant individual inequalities, suggesting that society was similar to the "group oriented chiefdoms" described by Renfrew (1974). In this type of society, prestige goods were uncommon and solidarity was associated with group activities. This type of social organization contrasts with "individualizing chiefdoms" in which leaders were identifiable by rich burials or prominent residences (expectations that closely resemble those outlined for the Cusco Formative period by previous scholars).

Increasingly, scholars working in the Andes use the model of corporate societies. In this type of organization, power is held by groups rather than by individuals and hierarchies rank groups such as families instead of individuals. Public ceremonies and rituals stress the importance of shared identity and egalitarian principles. Conspicuous consumption and glorification of the elite is often lacking even when real inequalities exist (Nielsen 2006). This type of social organization is a distinct possibility at Yuthu where authority was purposely depersonalized by displacing it from the speaker to the dead. If that were the case, personal wealth may not have been common or appropriate even if inequalities were very real.

The Role of Social Institutions in the Emergence of Multi-Village Polities

Settlement patterns that include sites from at least an 800-year time span suggest that multi-village polities may have developed in the Late Formative period in many subregions of Cusco including the area northwest of the modern city. Excavations at Yuthu have found that conditions were consistent with those that anthropologists expect to see in contexts where the loss of village autonomy occurs. The population was increasing on the plain. Despite the fact that the agropastoral system seems to have been well suited to the environment, skeletal data have shown that these villagers were under rather high degrees of stress as a result of poor nutrition, difficult work, disease, or other factors. It seems that the subsistence regime was not adequate to support the population.

This problem may have been exacerbated by a shift from a cool and wet environment to a drier climate toward the end of the Formative period. Regionally, this change appears by AD 100 in pollen data from Lake Marcacocha near Ollantaytambo (Chepstow-Lusty et al. 1998). At Yuthu, gastropods that inhabit drier climates were present only after the village was abandoned and the site was converted to a cemetery. In the Andes, climatic cooling can have serious effects on the local ecology, creating a drier environment and shifting the limits of where certain crops can grow lower in elevation (Seltzer and Hastorf 1990). This might have had a real effect on the productivity of land around Yuthu, resulting in changes in: (1) which crops were grown, (2) what agricultural technologies were used, and/or (3) where people farmed.

As a result, there may have been increasing competition between communities or families that sought to expand their own access to land or other resources, perhaps at the expense of others. These efforts probably motivated at least some of the conflict that was prevalent at Yuthu. It is possible that violence occurred during village raids though no other evidence of inter-village raiding, such as palisades, defensible site locations, or burned temples or houses, has been found.

These conditions are known to be a hotbed for the formation of multi-village polities cross-culturally. Yet, without excavations at additional sites, it is very difficult to understand the relationships between Yuthu and other villages. For example, the ceramic chronology is not sufficiently refined to determine whether the largest site was occupied at the same time as Yuthu and other smaller settlements. In addition, it is unclear if any political institutions crosscut multiple villages. At Yuthu, politics were tied to rituals related to ancestors and the sacred landscape. During future excavations at other Formative period sites, we may look for shared maximal sacred mountains as evidence for a multi-village polity. At Yuthu, for example, there was a shift from veneration of the glacial peak Pitusiray to Chicón. If we find a similar shift at several villages from diverse glacial peaks as objects of veneration to a single shared sacred mountain, it may indicate the emergence of a shared identity that was related to polity formation.

Implications for Comparative Study of Early Villages

This study suggests that archaeologists who study the origins of inequality should not focus exclusively on economic indicators. Ideological changes that allow inequalities may be identifiable *before* economic indicators. Findings also suggest that corporate social organization must be considered as a possible scenario for the emergence of inequality and multi-village polities. The study also highlights that in early villages, ritual and politics cannot be analyzed independently. They are not only linked, but are often a single system.

Concluding Remarks

Knowing what life was like in early villages, how inequality was first established, and what institutions were used to achieve political control has important implications for understanding the long-term history of Cusco. Lack of earlier research on this time period has led to uninformed speculation, especially regarding the antiquity of certain practices recorded in ethnohistoric documents describing the Inka. Many scholarly articles have one of two tendencies. Some presume that Inka practices that were uncommon outside the heartland emerged with this late empire. Others attempt to investigate the antiquity of widespread Andean traditions. Yet, the lack of research on early villages often leads scholars to conclude that traditions emerged with earlier states—often the Wari, less often Tiwanaku. I suggest that this has less to do with the realities of history and more to do with the bias of research toward states.

This study has shown that some traditions that were widespread in the colonial and modern Andes were not practiced by early villagers in Cusco. For example, the village was not part of a vertically integrated spatially dispersed community such as the vertical archipelago described by Murra (1968, 1972, 1985a, 1985b), who suggested that the tradition was probably very ancient and called on archaeologists to investigate it.

Other traditions have been identified in this early village. For example, many scholars who study how the Inka used the conception of a hierarchically ranked sacred landscape to legitimize their rule often note that the belief system must have been ancient for this strategy of incorporation to work. Indeed, this study has shown that at least in Cusco, this tradition extends back about 2000 years before Inka imperial expansion.

Many scholars are also interested in the role that ancestor veneration played in the Inka empire. Some have suggested that mummy veneration emerged as a political strategy of earlier Andean states (Isbell 1997). Others suggest that the Wari specifically introduced this tradition to Cusco (McEwan 2005). We can now dismiss the suggestions that mummy veneration emerged as a tool of statecraft or that it was a practice that the Inka learned from other groups. In fact, mummy veneration was an indigenous development in Cusco that emerged in early villages. This local practice continued and was modified and utilized much later by the Inka and other groups.

Several scholars have also suggested that the Wari first established the precursor to the famous Inka road system as a tool for state administration (Isbell 1978; Isbell and Schreiber 1978; Lumbreras 1974; McEwan 2005). Yet, the road that forms the northern limit of Yuthu and the location of Formative period sites along some known Inka routes (see also Kendall 2000) demonstrate that roads existed in Cusco by at least 400 BC. At that early time, roads were more likely to have developed as long-distance trade routes rather than as tools of political administration.

Overall, this study highlights the fact that knowledge of long-term local history will allow us to give credit to indigenous developments that contributed to the Inka state. Extensive excavation of early villages is the only way to build such a detailed local history. Moving forward, the best way to proceed will be to build a collection of similar studies that employ a holistic approach to the investigation of village life so that we can appreciate the similarities and differences among Formative period settlements. Through this kind of research, we will be able to identify the institutions and cultural traditions that will help us to understand *how* broad sociopolitical changes occurred in the Andes.

Appendix

Radiocarbon Date Calibration

All radiocarbon dates from Yuthu were processed by the Arizona Radiocarbon Lab and were calibrated using OxCal 4.1 software and the ShCal 04 calibration curve for the southern hemisphere (see Table A). The four radiocarbon dates from Unit A were calibrated using an Analysis Model that considered the stratigraphy of the unit (the "Sequence Feature" of OxCal software package). This kind of probability modeling effectively reduces the two sigma possible range of dates. Because the samples taken from Unit D came from features that were not stratigraphically superimposed, no modeling was used for those dates.

I calibrated all of the published Formative period dates from the Cusco area without modeling. Those dates are listed in Table B with the associated pottery, starting with the earliest style. The dates that had no information about associated pottery style are included at the end of the table as "not specified." Overall, Marcavalle pottery was associated with dates from about 1200 to 400 BC, Chanapata pottery was associated with dates from 700 BC to 50 AD, and Chanapata-derived pottery was associated with dates from 400 BC to AD 200. The fact that these dates overlap may be due to several factors, including radiocarbon error range, non-standardized reporting of pottery styles, or the possibility that these styles were used at the same time during transition periods, either within a single site or in different sites. Overall, however, these dates support the general ceramic chronology of Rowe (1943) that placed Marcavalle pottery as the earliest Formative period style, followed by Chanapata pottery, and finally Chanapata-derived (sometimes including Pacallamoqo style when found near Maras).

The site of Yuthu was one of the earlier sites with Chanapata-derived pottery, dating to between 400 and 100 BC.

Table A. Radiocarbon date calibration for samples from Unit A. This output was created by OxCal 4.1 using a sequential model on September 8, 2009.

Name	Unmodeled (BC/AD)			Modeled (BC/AD)			Indices A_{model} 110.5 $A_{overall}$ 111.5				
	from	to	%	from	to	%	A_{comb}	A	L	P	C
Curve ShCal04											
Sequence											
Boundary Start 1				-709	-211	95.4					97.1
Sequence 1											
R_Date AA84430 Yuthu RC-61	-376	-51	95.4	-361	-62	95.4		106.2			98.2
R_Date AA84431 Yuthu RC-104	-385	-171	95.4	-384	-205	95.4		101.3			99.4
R_Date AA84432 Yuthu RC-109	-393	-43	95.4	-376	-144	95.4		114.3			98.7
R_Date AA84433 Yuthu RC-110	-509	-209	95.4	-417	-209	95.4		101.1			99.6
Boundary End 1				371	166	95.4					95.4

Table B. List of Cusco area Formative period dates.

Ceramic Style	Radiocarbon Years BP	Calibrated Date	Site	Source or Sample Number
Marcavalle	2916 ± 55	1258 to 896 BC, 95.4%	Marcavalle	Lawn 1971
Marcavalle	2860 ± 47	1114 to 834 BC, 95.4%	Marcavalle	Lawn 1971
Marcavalle	2685 ± 49	913 to 561 BC, 95.3%	Marcavalle	Lawn 1971
Marcavalle	2661 ± 46	896 to 548 BC, 95.3%	Marcavalle	Lawn 1971
Marcavalle	2645 ± 115	976 to 403 BC, 95.4%	Marcavalle	Lawn 1971
Marcavalle	2571 ± 45	798 to 417 BC, 95.4%	Marcavalle	Lawn 1971
Marcavalle	695 BC ± 115	insufficient information	Marcavalle	Patterson 1967
Marcavalle	650 BC ± 150	insufficient information	Chanapata	Patterson 1967
Chanapata	2380 ± 70	750 to 199 BC, 95.5%	Huillca Raccay	Burleigh 1983
Chanapata	2190 ± 60	373 to 3 BC, 95.4%	Chokepukio	McEwan et al. 1995
Chanapata	2130 ± 70	350 BC to AD 57, 95.4%	Chokepukio	McEwan et al. 1995
Chanapata-derived	2131 ± 55	356 BC to AD 73, 95.4%	Marcavalle	Lawn 1971
Chanapata-derived	2096 ± 51	193 BC to AD 69, 95.4%	Marcavalle	Lawn 1971
Chanapata-derived	2073 ± 29	151 BC to AD 68, 95.4%	Batan Urqo	Zapata 1998
Chanapata-derived	2525 ± 39	764 to 413 BC, 95.4%	Wat'a	Kosiba 2010
Chanapata-derived	2495 ± 39	755 to 405 BC, 95.4%	Wat'a	Kosiba 2010
Chanapata-derived	2005 ± 38	49 BC to AD 134, 95.4%	Wat'a	Kosiba 2010
Chanapata-derived	1985 ± 42	41 BC to AD 212, 95.4%	Peqokaypata	Bauer and Jones 2003
Chanapata-derived	1881 ± 42	AD 77 to 325, 95.4%	Peqokaypata	Bauer and Jones 2003
Chanapata-derived	2213 ± 61	361 to 62 BC, 95.4%	Yuthu	AA84430\Yuthu RC-61
Chanapata-derived	2257 ± 36	384 to 205 BC, 95.4%	Yuthu	AA84431\Yuthu RC-104
Chanapata-derived	2226 ± 76	376 to 144 BC, 95.4%	Yuthu	AA84432\Yuthu RC-109
Chanapata-derived	2369 ± 36	417 to 209 BC, 95.4%	Yuthu	AA84433\Yuthu RC-110
Chanapata-derived	2329 ± 37	403 to 206 BC, 95.4%	Yuthu	AA84434\Yuthu RC-214
Chanapata-derived	2295 ± 38	391 to 203 BC, 95.4%	Yuthu	AA84435\Yuthu RC-216
Chanapata-derived	2223 ± 36	366 to 96 BC, 95.4%	Yuthu	AA84436\Yuthu RC-251
Chanapata-derived	2243 ± 36	383 to 118 BC, 95.4%	Yuthu	AA84437\Yuthu RC-255
not specified	2520 ± 150	907 to 204 BC, 95.4%	Chanapata	Yamasaki et al. 1966
not specified	2360 ± 760	2486 BC to AD 1148, 95.4%	Chanapata	Yamasaki et al. 1966
not specified	3330 ± 240	2200 to 934 BC, 95.4%	Chanapata	Krueger and Weeks 1966

Glossary

(Quechua and Spanish)

allachu: an agricultural tool that has a blade that attaches at an angle to the handle in order to cut soil horizontally

ayllu: corporate kin group

apu: mountain spirit or deity

ceque: the more common Spanish spelling of the Quechua term *ziqi*, which means "a line"

ch'arki: freeze-dried meat

ch'uñu: freeze-dried potatoes

chaki taklla: foot plow

chakra: agricultural field

Cheq'oq: an Inka period site near Yuthu and the modern city of Maras

chullpa: above-ground mortuary monument

conopa: a popular Spanish spelling for *qunupa*, a stone effigy of something (usually an agricultural product) used in offerings; should be more properly referred to as an *illa*

cuy: common Spanish spelling for *quwi* (guinea pig)

escudilla: flaring rim bowl

herranza: a traditional ceremony in which herders decorate camelids and sheep

illa: a stone effigy of something (usually an agricultural product) used in offerings, sometimes called *qunupa* or *conopa* in Spanish, or simply *rumin* (meaning stone)

imilla: a variety of potato

iwayllu: a stone effigy in the shape of an animal used in offerings *k'allawa:* a weaving sword for a belt

kiwicha: the grain amaranth

k'utuna: rocker grinding stone, also called *tunaw*

mallki: mummy

maran: grinding slab, also called *qhuna*

marida: a variety of potato

markhu: Ambrosia arborescens, a woody shrub often used for fuel

maway: early potato crop cycle

minikuna: a bobbin

miskha: early corn crop cycle

muña: Minthostachys mollis, a plant made into tea to treat stomach ache and to serve as an aphrodisiac; also used to flavor soups and stews; the leaves can be used to line storage pits to discourage the growth of fungi, bacteria, and larva

olomes: a variety of potato (Spanish)

olla: restricted vessel with a rim

p'irka: Bidens andicola var. *andicola*, a plant used to make tea to treat pneumonia

pallana: pick-up sticks for weaving

pisqu sisaq: Galium weberbaueri, a plant used to make tea or cold drinks; it may also be used as medicine, also called *rata rata*

puna: high-altitude grassland

qachi: a tool made of deer antler, used to harvest potatoes

qhachun waqachi: a variety of potato

qhapaq hucha: literally "great obligation," it was the cycle of ritual that took place when the Inka king died; the ritual famously included sacrifice of children and some women

qhuna: grinding slab, also called *maran*

quechua: the ecological zone between 2300 and 3500 masl that includes very productive agricultural land; this zone is the upper limit of maize cultivation

qulluta: a hand-sized grinding stone

qumpis: a variety of potato

qunupa: a stone effigy of something (usually an agricultural product) used in offerings, should be more properly referred to as an *illa*; *conopa* is a popular Spanish spelling

quwi: a guinea pig, also *cuy* in Spanish

rata rata: Galium weberbaueri, a plant used to make tea or cold drinks; it may also be used as medicine, also called *pisq'u sisaq*

ruk'i: a beater for weaving, also called *wich'uña*

rumin: stone

sica: a variety of potato (Spanish)

tunaw: rocker grinding stone, also called *k'utuna*

wakakuna: sacred objects (singular: *waka*)

wakatay: a condiment from the mustard family

warmiq p'ananan: an agricultural tool to break clumps of soil, also called *wini*

wathiya: earth oven for cooking potatoes

wayk'uq qallun: a variety of potato

wich'uña: a beater for weaving, also called *ruk'i*

wini: an agricultural tool to break clumps of soil, also called *warmiq p'ananan*

winiquta: a variety of potato

Wiraqucha: an Inka deity

yungay: a variety of potato

yuthu: tinamou, or Andean partridge

ziqi: line; the Spanish spelling *ceque* is more commonly used

Bibliography

Acuto, F. A.
2005 The materiality of Inka domination: Landscape, spectacle, memory, and ancestors. In *Global Archaeological Theory: Contextual Voices and Contemporary Thoughts*, edited by P. P. Funari, A. Zarankin, and E. Stovel, pp. 211–35. Kluwer Academic, New York.

Aldenderfer, M. S.
1991 Continuity and change in ceremonial structures at Late Preceramic Asana, southern Peru. *Latin American Antiquity* 2(3):227–58.

Allen, C. J.
1982 Body and soul in Quechua thought. *Journal of Latin American Lore* 8:179–96.
2002 [1988] *The Hold Life Has: Coca and Cultural Identity in an Andean Community*, 2nd ed. Smithsonian Institution Press, Washington, D.C.

Allison, M. J., E. Gerszten, J. Munizaga, C. Santoro, and G. Focacci
1981 La Práctica de la Deformación Craneana entre los Pueblos Andinos Precolombinos. *Chungará* 7:238–60.

Anderson, B. R.
2006 [1983] *Imagined Communities: Reflections on the Origin and Spread of Nationalism*, rev. ed. Verso, London.

Andrefsky, W. J.
2005 *Lithics: Macroscopic Approaches to Analysis*, 2nd ed. Cambridge Manuals in Archaeology. Cambridge University Press, New York.

Andrushko, V.
2008 *Yuthu Complete Burial Summaries*. Report available from author.

Arensberg, C. M.
1954 The community study method. *American Journal of Sociology* 60:109–27.
1961 The community as object and as sample. *American Anthropologist* 63:241–64.

Arensberg, C. M., and S. T. Kimball
1965 *Culture and Community*. Harcourt, Brace, and World, New York.
1968 Community study: Retrospect and prospect. *The American Journal of Sociology* 73(6):691–705.

Arroyo, P., and G. Choque
1992 Mamaqolla y la Ocupación Inka del Área de la Laguna de Muyna. Licenciatura thesis, Ciencias Sociales, Universidad Nacional San Antonio Abad del Cuzco, Cuzco.

Babić, S.
2005 Status identity and archaeology. In *The Archaeology of Identity: Approaches to Gender, Age, Status, Ethnicity and Religion*, edited by M. Díaz-Andreu, S. Lucy, S. Babić, and D. N. Edwards, pp. 67–86. Routledge, London.

Bandy, M. S.
2001 Population and History in the Ancient Titicaca Basin. PhD dissertation, Anthropology, University of California, Berkeley. University Microfilms, Ann Arbor.
2004 Fissioning, scalar stress, and social evolution in early village societies. *American Anthropologist* 106(2):322–33.
2005 Trade and social power in the southern Titicaca Basin Formative. *Archaeological Papers of the American Anthropological Association* 14:91–111.
2006 Early village society in the Formative period in the southern Lake Titicaca Basin. In *Andean Archaeology III: North and South*, edited by W. H. Isbell and H. Silverman, pp. 210–36. Springer, Boston.

Bandy, M. S., and C. A. Hastorf
2007 An introduction to Kala Uyuni and the Taraco Peninsula polity. In *Kala Uyuni: An Early Political Center in the Southern Lake Titicaca Basin: 2003 Excavations of the Taraco Archaeological Project*, edited by M. S. Bandy and C. A. Hastorf, pp. 1–12. Contributions of the Archaeological Research Facility 64. Archaeological Research Facility, University of California Berkeley, Berkeley.

Banning, E. B.
2002 *Archaeological Survey*. Manuals in Archaeological Method, Theory, and Technique Series. Kluwer Academic/Plenum Publishers, New York.

Bastien, J. W.
1978 *Mountain of the Condor*. West Publishing, St. Paul.

Bauer, B. S.
1992 *The Development of the Inca State*. University of Texas Press, Austin.
1998 *The Sacred Landscape of the Inca: The Cusco Ceque System*. University of Texas Press, Austin.
1999 *The Early Ceramics of the Inca Heartland*. Fieldiana Anthropology, n.s. 31. Field Museum of Natural History, Chicago.
2002 *Las Antiguas Tradiciones Alfareras de la Región del Cuzco*. Centro de Estudios Regionales Andinos Bartolomé de las Casas, Cuzco.
2004 *Ancient Cuzco, Heartland of the Inca*. University of Texas Press, Austin.

Bauer, B. S., and B. M. Jones
2003 *Early Intermediate and Middle Horizon Ceramic Styles of the Cuzco Valley*. Fieldiana Anthropology, n.s. 34. Field Museum of Natural History, Chicago.

Beck, C. M.
1979 Ancient Roads on the North Coast of Peru. PhD dissertation, Anthropology, University of California, Berkeley. University Microfilms, Ann Arbor.

Beck, R. A., Jr.
2004a Architecture and polity in the Formative Lake Titicaca Basin, Bolivia. *Latin American Antiquity* 15(3):323–43.
2004b Platforms of Power: House, Community, and Social Change in the Formative Lake Titicaca Basin. PhD dissertation, Anthropology, Northwestern University. University Microfilms, Ann Arbor.

Bello, S., and P. Andrews
2006 The intrinsic pattern of preservation of human skeletons and its influence on the interpretation of funerary behaviors. In *Social Archaeology of Funerary Remains*, edited by R. Gowland and C. J. Knüsel, pp. 1–13. Oxbow Books, Oxford.

Benson, E. P.
2001 Why sacrifice? In *Ritual Sacrifice in Ancient Peru*, edited by E. P. Benson and A. G. Cook, pp. 1–20. University of Texas Press, Austin.

Bermann, M.
1994 *Lukurmata: Household Archaeology in Prehispanic Bolivia*. Princeton University Press, Princeton.

Bermann, M., and J. Estévez Castillo
1995 Domestic artifact assemblages and ritual activities in the Bolivian Formative. *Journal of Field Archaeology* 22(4):389–98.

Berreman, G. D.
1981 Social inequality: A cross-cultural analysis. In *Social Inequality: Comparative and Developmental Approaches*, edited by G. D. Berreman and K. M. Zaretsky, pp. 3–40. Academic Press, New York.

Binford, L. R.
1972 Mortuary practices: Their study and their potential. In *An Archaeological Perspective*, edited by L. R. Binford, pp. 208–43. Seminar Press, New York.

Blom, D. E.
2005 Embodying borders: Human body modification and diversity in Tiwanaku society. *Journal of Anthropological Archaeology* 24(1):1–24.

Blom, D. E., and J. W. Janusek
2004 Making place: Humans as dedications in Tiwanaku. *World Archaeology* 36(1):123–41.

Bonavia, D.
2008 *The South American Camelids*. Cotsen Institute of Archaeology, University of California, Los Angeles.

Bourdieu, P.
1972 *Outline of a Theory of Practice*, translated by R. Nice. Cambridge University Press, Cambridge.

Browman, D. L.
1975 Trade patterns in the central highlands of Peru in the first millennium B.C. *World Archaeology* 6(3):322–29.
1977 External relationships of the Early Horizon ceramic style from the Jauja-Huancayo Basin, Junín. *El Dorado* 11(1):1–16.

Brush, S.
1976 Man's use of an Andean ecosystem. *Human Ecology* 4(2):147–66.

Burger, R. L.
1984 *The Prehistoric Occupation of Chavín de Huántar, Peru*. University of California Publications in Archaeology 14. University of California Press, Berkeley.
1992 *Chavín and the Origins of Andean Civilization*. Thames and Hudson, New York.
1998 *Excavaciones en Chavín de Huántar*. Pontificia Universidad Católica del Perú, Fondo Editorial, Perú.

Burger, R. L., K. L. M. Chávez, and S. J. Chávez
2000 Through the glass darkly: Prehispanic obsidian procurement and exchange in southern Peru and northern Bolivia. *Journal of World Prehistory* 14(3):267–362.

Burger, R. L., and R. Matos Mendieta
2002 Atalla: A center on the periphery of the Chavín Horizon. *Latin American Antiquity* 13(2):153–77.

Burger, R. L., and L. Salazar-Burger
1980 Ritual and religion at Huaricoto. *Archaeology* 33(6):26–32.
1985 The early ceremonial center of Huaricoto. In *Early Ceremonial Architecture in the Andes: A Conference at Dumbarton Oaks, 8th to 10th October 1982*, edited by C. B. Donnan, pp. 111–38. Dumbarton Oaks Research Library and Collection, Washington, D.C.
1986 Early organizational diversity in the Peruvian highlands: Huaricoto and Kotosh. In *Andean Archaeology: Papers in Memory of Clifford Evans*, edited by R. Matos Mendieta, S. Turpin, and H. Eling, pp. 65–82. Vol. 27. UCLA Monographs in Anthropology, Los Angeles.

Burleigh, R., J. Ambers, and K. Matthews
1983 British Museum natural radiocarbon measurements XVI. *Radiocarbon* 25(1):39–58.

Bustamante, J., and E. Crousillat
1974 Análisis Hidráulico del Sitio Arqueológico de Chavín de Huántar. Licenciatura thesis, Programa Académico de Ingeniería Civil, Universidad Nacional de Ingeniería, Lima.

Callañaupa Alvarez, N.
2007 *Weaving in the Peruvian Highlands: Dreaming Patterns, Weaving Memories*. Centro de Textiles Tradicionales del Cusco, Cusco.

Canuto, M. A., and J. Yaeger (editors)
2000 *The Archaeology of Communities: A New World Perspective*. Routledge, New York.

Carneiro, R.
1981 The chiefdom: Precursor of the state. In *The Transition to Statehood in the New World*, edited by G. D. Jones and R. R. Kautz, pp. 37–79. Cambridge University Press, Cambridge.

Castro, V., and C. Aldunate
2003 Sacred mountains in the highlands of the south-central Andes. *Mountain Research and Development* 23(1):73–79.

Ceruti, C.
2004 Human bodies as objects of dedication at Inca mountain shrines (north-western Argentina). *World Archaeology* 36(1):103–22.

Chávez, K. L. M.
1977 Marcavalle: The Ceramics from an Early Horizon Site in the Valley of Cusco, Peru, and Implications for South Highland Socio-Economic Interaction. PhD dissertation, Department of Anthropology, University of Pennsylvania. University Microfilms, Ann Arbor.
1980 The archaeology of Marcavalle, an Early Horizon site in the Valley of Cuzco, Peru: Part I. *Baessler-Archiv* n.f. 28(2):203–329.
1981a The archaeology of Marcavalle, an Early Horizon site in the Valley of Cuzco, Peru. Part II. *Baessler-Archiv* n.f. 29(1):107–25.
1981b The archaeology of Marcavalle, an Early Horizon site in the Valley of Cuzco, Peru. Part III (decorated ceramics). *Baessler-Archiv* n.f. 29(1):241–386.
1982 Resumen de los Trabajos en Marcavalle. In *Arqueología de Cuzco*, edited by R. Oberti, pp. 1–8. Instituto Nacional de Cultura, Cuzco.
1988 The significance of Chiripa in Lake Titicaca Basin developments. *Expedition* 30(3):17–26.

Chávez, K. L. M., and S. J. Chávez
1997 The Yaya-Mama archaeological project, Bolivia. *Willay* 44:5–7.

Chepstow-Lusty, A. J., B. S. Bauer, and M. Frogley
2004 Human impact and environmental history of the Cuzco region. In *Ancient Cuzco, Heartland of the Inca*, edited by B. S. Bauer. University of Texas Press, Austin.

Chepstow-Lusty, A. J., K. D. Bennett, J. Fjeldså, A. Kendall, W. Galiano, and A. Tupayachi Herrera
1998 Tracing 4,000 years of environmental history in the Cuzco area, Peru, from the pollen record. *Mountain Research and Development* 18(2):159–72.

Cobo, B.
1990 [1653] *Inca Religion and Customs*, translated by R. Hamilton. University of Texas Press, Austin.

Cohen, A. B., and A. Roddick
2007 Excavations in the AC (Achachi Coa Kkollu) sector. In *Kala Uyuni: An Early Political Center in the Southern Lake Titicaca Basin: 2003 Excavations of the Taraco Archaeological Project*, edited by M. S. Bandy and C. A. Hastorf, pp. 41–65. Contributions of the Archaeological Research Facility 64. Archaeological Research Facility, University of California Berkeley, Berkeley.

Cornejo, M.
1995 Arqueología de Santuarios Inkas en la Guaranga de Sisicaya, Valle de Lurín. *Tawantinsuyu* 1:18–28.

Coupland, G.
1985 Household variability and status differentiation at Kitselas Canyon. *Canadian Journal of Archaeology* 9:39–56.

Davis, A. R.
2010 Excavations at Yuthu: A Community Study of an Early Village in Cusco, Peru (400–100 BC). PhD dissertation, Department of Anthropology, University of Michigan, Ann Arbor.

Davis, A. R., and R. A. Covey
2007 A Possible Early "Vertical Archipelago?" Patterns of Landscape Use on the Xaquixaguana Plain, Cusco, Peru (2200 BC–AD 200). Paper presented at the Annual Meeting of the Society for American Archaeology, Austin, Texas.

Dean, E., and D. Kojan
1999 Santiago. In *Early Settlement at Chiripa, Bolivia: Research of the Taraco Archaeological Project*, edited by Christine A. Hastorf, pp. 37–49. Vol. 57. Archaeological Research Facility, University of California at Berkeley, Berkeley.

de las Casas, B.
1875 [1561] *Historia de las Indias*. Imprenta de Miguel Ginesta, Madrid.

deFrance, S. D.
2007 Faunal remains from the site of Kasapata. In *Kasapata and the Archaic Period of the Cuzco Valley*, edited by B. S. Bauer, pp. 111–17. Cotsen Institute of Archaeology, University of California at Los Angeles.

Díaz-Andreu, M.
2005 Gender identity. In *The Archaeology of Identity: Approaches to Gender, Age, Status, Ethnicity and Religion*, edited by M. Díaz-Andreu, S. Lucy, S. Babić, and D. N. Edwards, pp. 13–42. Routledge, London.

Dillehay, T. D.
2007 *Monuments, Empires, and Resistance: The Araucanian Polity and Ritual Narratives*. Cambridge University Press, Cambridge.

Dillehay, T. D., and A. Lautaro Núñez
1988 Camelids, caravans and complex societies in the south-central Andes. In *Recent Studies in Pre-Colombian Archaeology*, edited by N. Saunders and O. de Montmollin, pp. 603–34. Vol. 421. BAR International Series. British Archaeological Reports, Oxford.

Doyle, M. E.
1988 The Ancestor Cult and Burial Ritual in Seventeenth and Eighteenth Century Central Peru. PhD dissertation, Department of Anthropology, University of California, Los Angeles. University Microfilms, Ann Arbor.

Drennan, R. D., and C. E. Peterson
2006 Patterned variation in prehistoric chiefdoms. *Proceedings of the National Academy of Sciences of the United States of America* 103(11):3960–67.

Duday, H.
2006 L'Archéothanatologie ou l'Archéologie de la Mort (Archaeothanatology or the archaeology of death). In *Social Archaeology of Funerary Remains*, edited by R. Gowland and C. J. Knüsel, translated by C. J. Knüsel, pp. 30–56. Oxbow Books, Oxford.
2009 *The Archaeology of the Dead: Lectures in Archaeothanatology*, translated by A. M. Cipriani and J. Pearce. Lezioni di Archeotanatologia. Oxbow Books, Oxford.

Duday, H., and M. Guillon
2006 Understanding the circumstances of decomposition when the body is skeletonized. In *Forensic Anthropology and Medicine: Complementary Sciences from Recovery to Cause of Death*, edited by A. Schmitt, E. Cunha, and J. Pinheiro. Humana Press, Totowa, NJ.

Dulanto, J.
2002a The archaeological study of ancestor cult practices: The case of Pampa Chica, a Late Initial period site on the central coast of Peru. In *The Space and Place of Death*, edited by H. Silverman and D. B. Small, pp. 97–117. Vol. 11. Archaeological Papers of the American Anthropological Association. Washington, D.C.
2002b Pampa Chica: Prácticas de Culto a los Ancestros en la Costa Central del Perú. *Gaceta Arqueológica Andina* 26:37–68.

Earle, T. K.
1977 A reappraisal of redistribution: Complex Hawaiian chiefdoms. In *Exchange Systems in Prehistory*, edited by T. K. Earle and J. Ericson, pp. 213–29. Academic Press, New York.
1987 Chiefdoms in archaeological and ethnohistorical perspective. *Annual Review of Anthropology* 16(1):279–308.

Evans-Pritchard, E. E.
1967 *The Nuer: A Description of the Modes of Livelihood and Political Institutions of a Nilotic People*. Clarendon Press, Oxford.

Farrington, I. S.
1992 Ritual geography, settlement patterns and the characterization of the provinces of the Inka heartland. *World Archaeology* 23(3):368–85.

Feinman, G. M., and J. Neitzel
1984 Too many types: An overview of prestate societies in the Americas. In *Advances in Archaeological Method and Theory*, Vol. 7, edited by M. B. Schiffer. Academic Press, Orlando.

Fester, G. A.
1953 Einige Farbstoffe Südamerikanischer Kulturvolker. *Isis* 44:13–16.

Fioravanti-Molinié, A.
1982 Multi-leveled Andean society and market exchange: The case of Yucay (Peru). In *Ecology and Exchange in the Andes*, edited by D. Lehmann, translated by D. Lehmann, pp. 211–30. Cambridge University Press, Cambridge.

Flannery, K. V.
1976 *The Early Mesoamerican Village*. Academic Press, New York.
1995 Prehistoric social evolution. In *Research Frontiers in Anthropology*, edited by C. R. Ember and M. Ember, pp. 1–26. Prentice Hall, Englewood Cliffs, NJ.

Flannery, K. V., J. Marcus, and R. G. Reynolds
1989 *The Flocks of the Wamani: A Study of Llama Herders on the Punas of Ayacucho, Peru*. Academic Press, San Diego.

Flores Ochoa, J. A.
1979 [1967] *Pastoralists of the Andes: The Alpaca Herders of Paratía*, translated by R. Bolton. Institute for the Study of Human Issues, Philadelphia.
1985 Interaction and complementarity in three zones of Cusco. In *Andean Ecology and Civilization*, edited by S. Masuda, I. Shimada, and C. Morris, pp. 251–76. University of Tokyo Press, Tokyo.

Franquemont, C., T. Plowman, E. Franquemont, S. R. King, C. Niezgoda, W. Davis, and C. R. Sperling
1990 Ethnobotany of Chinchero, an Andean community in southern Peru. *Fieldiana* 24:126.

Gade, D. W.
1975 *Plants, Man and the Land in the Vilcanota Valley of Peru*. W. Junk, The Hague.

Gelles, P. H.
2000 *Water and Power in Highland Peru: The Cultural Politics of Irrigation and Development*. Rutgers University Press, New Brunswick, NJ.

Gerszten, P. C.
1993 Investigation into the practice of cranial deformation among the pre-Columbian peoples of northern Chile. *International Journal of Osteoarchaeology* 3(2):87–98.

Giddens, A.
1984 *The Constitution of Society: Outline of the Theory of Structuration*. University of California Press, Berkeley.

Glascock, M. D., R. J. Speakman, and R. L. Burger
2007 Sources of archaeological obsidian in Peru: Descriptions and geochemistry. In *Archaeological Chemistry: Analytical Techniques and Archaeological Interpretation*, edited by M. D. Glascock, R. J. Speakman, and R. S. Popelka-Filcoff, pp. 522–52. Vol. 968. ACS Symposium Series. American Chemical Society, Washington, D.C.

Glowacki, M., and M. Malpass
2003 Water, huacas, and ancestor worship: Traces of a sacred Wari landscape. *Latin American Antiquity* 14(4):431–49.

Goldstein, M. C., and D. A. Messerschmidt
1980 The significance of latitudinality in Himalayan mountain ecosystems. *Human Ecology* 8(2):117–34.

Gose, P.
1993 Segmentary state formation and the ritual control of water under the Incas. *Comparative Studies in Society and History* 35(3):480–514.

Gow, R., B. Condori, and D. D. Gow
1976 *Kay Pacha*. Biblioteca de la Tradición Oral Andina 1. Centro de Estudios Rurales Andinos "Bartolomé de las Casas," Cuzco.

Greer, S. A.
1955 *Social Organization*. Studies in Sociology. Random House, New York.

Guillet, D.
1981 Land tenure, ecological zone, and agricultural regime in the central Andes. *American Ethnologist* 8(1):139–56.

Hastorf, C. A.
2003 Community with the ancestors: Ceremonies and social memory in the Middle Formative at Chiripa, Bolivia. *Journal of Anthropological Archaeology* 22:305–32.
2005 The Upper (Middle and Late) Formative in the Titicaca region. In *Advances in Titicaca Basin Archaeology-1*, edited by C. Stanish, A. B. Cohen, and M. S. Aldenderfer, pp. 65–94. Cotsen Institute of Archaeology, University of California, Los Angeles.
2008 The Formative period in the Titicaca Basin. In *The Handbook of South American Archaeology*, edited by H. Silverman and W. H. Isbell, pp. 545–61. Springer, New York.

Hawkes, J. G.
1990 *The Potato: Evolution, Biodiversity and Genetic Resources*. Smithsonian Institution Press, Washington, D.C.

Helms, M. W.
1998 *Access to Origins: Affines, Ancestors, and Aristocrats*. University of Texas Press, Austin.

Hey, G.
1984 Early occupation on the Huillca Raccay Promontory site, Cusichaca: The archaeological evidence. In *Current Archaeological Projects in the Central Andes*, edited by A. Kendall, pp. 291–304. Vol. 210. BAR International Series. British Archaeological Reports, Oxford.

Hoshower, L. M., J. E. Buikstra, P. S. Goldstein, and A. D. Webster
1995 Artificial cranial deformation at the Omo M10 site: A Tiwanaku complex from the Moquegua Valley, Peru. *Latin American Antiquity* 6(2):145–64.

Hyslop, J.
1984 *The Inka Road System*. Studies in Archaeology. Academic Press, Orlando.

Isbell, W. H.
1978 Environmental perturbations and the origin of the Andean state. In *Social Archaeology: Beyond Subsistence and Dating*, edited by C. L. Redman, M. Berman, E. Curtin, W. Langhorne, N. J. Versaggi, and J. Wasner, pp. 303–13. Academic Press, New York.
1997 *Mummies and Mortuary Monuments: A Postprocessual Prehistory of Central Andean Social Organization*. University of Texas Press, Austin.
2000 What we should be studying: The "imagined community" and the "natural community." In *The Archaeology of Communities: A New World Perspective*, edited by M. A. Canuto and J. Yaeger, pp. 243–66. Routledge, New York.

Isbell, W. H., and K. J. Schreiber
1978 Was Huari a state? *American Antiquity* 43(3):372–89.

Janusek, J. W.
2004 Tiwanaku and its precursors: Recent research and emerging perspectives. *Journal of Archaeological Research* 12(2):121–83.

Johnson, G. A.
1980 Rank-size convexity and system integration. *Economic Geography* 56:234–47.

Kaplan, L.
1980 Variation in the cultivated beans. In *Guitarrero Cave: Early Man in the Andes*, edited by T. F. Lynch, pp. 145–48. Academic Press, New York.

Kato, Y.
1993 Resultados de las Excavaciones en Kuntur Wasi, Cajamarca. In *El Mundo Ceremonial Andino*, edited by L. Millones and Y. Ōnuki, pp. 203–28. Vol. 37. Senri Ethnological Studies. National Museum of Ethnology, Osaka, Japan.

Kato, Y., and Y. Seki
1985 Excavations at Layzón. In *The Formative Period in the Cajamarca Basin, Peru: Excavations at Huacaloma and Layzón, 1982*, edited by K. Terada and Y. Ōnuki, pp. 183–264. University of Tokyo Press, Tokyo.

Kelly, R. C.
2000 *Warless Societies and the Origin of War*. University of Michigan Press, Ann Arbor.

Kembel, S. R.
2008 The architecture at the monumental center of Chavín de Huántar: Sequence, transformations, and chronology. In *Chavín: Art, Architecture, and Culture*, edited by W. J. Conklin and J. Quilter, pp. 35–81. Cotsen Institute of Archaeology, University of California, Los Angeles.

Kendall, A.
1973 *Everyday Life of the Incas*. Everyday Life Series. Batsford, London.
1976 Preliminary report on ceramic data and the pre-Inca architectural remains of the (Lower) Urubamba Valley, Cuzco. *Baessler-Archiv* n.f. 24:41–159.
1994 Proyecto Arqueológico Cusichaca, Cuzco. In *Investigaciones Arqueológicas y de Rehabilitación Agrícola*. Southern Peru Copper Corporation, Lima.
2000 Red de Caminos Prehispánicos: Rutas de Comercio en el Distrito de Ollantaytambo, Cuzco, Perú. In *Caminos Precolombinos: Las Vías, los Ingenieros y los Viajeros*, edited by L. Herrera and M. Cardale de Schrimpff, pp. 221–42. Instituto Colombiano de Antropología e Historia, Ministerio de Cultura, Bogotá.

Kent, J. D.
1982 The Domestication and Exploitation of the South American Camelids: Methods of Analysis and their Application to Circum-lacustrine Archaeological Sites in Bolivia and Peru. PhD dissertation, Anthropology, Washington University, St. Louis. University Microfilms, Ann Arbor.
1988 Del Cazador al Pastor en los Andes Centrales. In *Rituales y Fiestas de las Américas* (first published in: *Memoria 45 Congreso Internacional de Americanistas: Patrones Cognitivos*), edited by E. Reichel D., pp. 127–45. Ediciones Uniandes, Bogotá.

Kimura, H.
2000 La Tierra sin Mano de Obra no Tiene Valor: Tierra y Labor en la Agroganadería Cuzqueña. *Senri Ethnological Reports of the National Museum of Ethnology (Osaka, Japan)* 19:295–315.

Knapp, A. B.
2003 The archaeology of community on Bronze Age Cyprus: Politiko "Phorades" in context. *American Journal of Archaeology* 107(4):559–80.

Koepcke, M.
1970 *The Birds of the Department of Lima, Peru*. Livingston Publishing Co., Wynnewood, PA.

Kosiba, S. B.
2010 Becoming Inka: The Transformation of Political Place and Practice during Inka State Formation (Cusco, Peru). PhD dissertation, Anthropology, University of Chicago, Chicago. University Microfilms, Ann Arbor.

Krueger, H. W., and C. F. Weeks
1966 Geochron Laboratories, Inc., radiocarbon measurements II. *Radiocarbon* 8:142–60.

Kuznar, L. A.
2001 An introduction to Andean religious ethnoarchaeology: Preliminary results and future directions. In *Ethnoarchaeology of Andean South America: Contributions to Archaeological Method and Theory*, edited by L. A. Kuznar, pp. 38–66. International Monographs in Prehistory, Ann Arbor.

Lau, G. F.
2008 Ancestor images in the Andes. In *The Handbook of South American Archaeology*, edited by H. Silverman and W. H. Isbell, pp. 1027–45. Springer, New York.

Lawn, B.
1971 University of Pennsylvania radiocarbon dates XIV. *Radiocarbon* 13(2):363–77.

LeBlanc, S. A.
1971 Computerized Conjunctive Archaeology and the Near Eastern Halafian. PhD dissertation, Anthropology, Washington University, St. Louis. University Microfilms, Ann Arbor.

Lessa, A., and S. Mendonça de Souza
2004 Violence in the Atacama Desert during the Tiwanaku period: Social tension? *International Journal of Osteoarchaeology* 14(5):374–88.

Lesure, R. G., and M. Blake
2002 Interpretive challenges in the study of early complexity: Economy, ritual, and architecture at Paso de la Amada, Mexico. *Journal of Anthropological Archaeology* 21:1–24.

Liu, L.
1999 Who were the ancestors? The origins of Chinese ancestral cult and racial myths. *Antiquity* 73(281):602–12.

Logan, M. H., C. S. Sparks, and R. L. Jantz
2003 Cranial modification among 19th century Osages: Admixture and loss of an ethnic marker. *Plains Anthropologist* 48(187):209–24.

Lumbreras, L. G.
1974 *The Peoples and Cultures of Ancient Peru*, translated by B. J. Meggers. Smithsonian Institution Press, Washington, D.C.

1989 *Chavín de Huántar en el Nacimiento de la Civilización Andina*. Ediciones INDEA, Instituto Andino de Estudios Arqueológicos, Lima.

Lumbreras, L. G., C. González, and B. Lietaer
1976 Acerca de la función del sistema hidráulico de Chavín. In *Investigaciones de campo No. 2*. Museo Nacional de Antropología y Arqueología, Lima.

MacNeish, R. S.
1983 *Prehistory of the Ayacucho Basin, Peru*. Vol. 3, *Nonceramic Artifacts*. University of Michigan Press, Ann Arbor.

Mannheim, B.
1991 *The Language of the Inka since the European Invasion*. Texas Linguistics Series. University of Texas Press, Austin.

Mantha, A.
2009 Territoriality, social boundaries and ancestor veneration in the central Andes of Peru. *Journal of Anthropological Archaeology* 28(2):158–76.

Marcus, J.
1976 *Emblem and State in the Classic Maya Lowlands: An Epigraphic Approach to Territorial Organization*. Dumbarton Oaks, Washington, D.C.
2000 Toward an archaeology of communities. In *The Archaeology of Communities: A New World Perspective*, edited by M. A. Canuto and J. Yaeger, pp. 231–42. Routledge, New York.
2008 The archaeological evidence for social evolution. *Annual Review of Anthropology* 37(1):251–66.

Marcus, J., and K. V. Flannery
1996 *Zapotec Civilization*. Thames and Hudson, New York.

Mariño Ferro, X. R.
1989 *Muerte, Religión y Símbolos en una Comunidad Quechua*. Universidad de Santiago de Compostela, Servicio de Publicaciones e Intercambio Científico, Santiago de Compostela.

Marroquín, J.
1944 El Cráneo Deformado de los Antiguos Aimaras. *Revista del Museo Nacional* 13(1):1–14.

Martínez, G
1983 Los Dioses de los Cerros en los Andes. *Journal de la Société des Américanistes* 69:85–115.

Matsumoto, R.
1993 Dos Modos de Proceso Socio-cultural: El Horizonte Temprano y el Período Intermedio Temprano en el Valle de Cajamarca. In *El Mundo Ceremonial Andino*, edited by L. Millones and Y. Ōnuki, pp. 169–202. Vol. 37. Senri Ethnological Studies. National Museum of Ethnology, Osaka.

McAnany, P. A.
1995 *Living with the Ancestors: Kinship and Kingship in Ancient Maya Society*. University of Texas Press, Austin.

McEwan, G. F.
2005 *Pikillacta: The Wari Empire in Cuzco*. University of Iowa Press, Iowa City.

McEwan, G. F., A. Gibaja, and M. Chatfield
1995 Archaeology at the Chokepukio site: An investigation of the origins of the Inca civilization in the Valley of Cuzco, Peru. A report on the 1994 field season. *Tawantinsuyu* 1:11–17.

Meddens, F.
1994 Mountains, miniatures, ancestors, and fertility: The meaning of Late Horizon offerings at a Middle Horizon structure in Peru. *Bulletin of the Institute of Archaeology* 31:127–50.

Miller, G. R.
1979 An Introduction to the Ethnoarchaeology of the Andean Camelids. PhD dissertation, University of California, Berkeley. University Microfilms, Ann Arbor.

Miller, G. R., and R. L. Burger
2000 Ch'arki at Chavín: Ethnographic models and archaeological data. *American Antiquity* 65(3):573–76.

Minar, D. W., and S. Greer
1969a *The Concept of Community: Readings with Interpretations*. Aldine, Chicago.
1969b Introduction: The concept of community. In *The Concept of Community: Readings with Interpretations*, edited by D. W. Minar and S. Greer, pp. ix–xii. Aldine, Chicago.

Mohr, K. L.
1969 Excavations in the Cuzco-Puno area of southern highland Peru. *Expedition* 2:48–51.

Moseley, M. E.
1985 The exploration and explanation of early monumental architecture in the Andes. In *Early Ceremonial Architecture in the Andes: A Conference at Dumbarton Oaks, 8th to 10th October 1982*, edited by C. B. Donnan, pp. 29–58. Dumbarton Oaks Research Library and Collection, Washington, D.C.

Mujica, E. J., M. A. Rivera, and T. F. Lynch
1983 Proyecto de Estudio sobre la Complementaridad Económica Tiwanaku en los Valles Occidentales del Centro-Sur Andino. *Chungará* 11:85–109.

Murdock, G. P.
1949 *Social Structure*. Macmillan, New York.

Murdock, G. P., C. S. Ford, A. E. Hudson, R. Kennedy, L. W. Simmons, and J. W. M. Whiting
1945 *Outline of Cultural Materials*. Yale Anthropological Studies. Yale University Press, New Haven.

Murra, J. V.
1968 An Aymara kingdom in 1567. *Ethnohistory* 15(2):115–51.
1972 El "Control Vertical" de un Máximo de Pisos Ecológicos en la Economía de las Sociedades Andinas. In *Visita de la Provincia de León de Huánuco en 1562*, Vol. II, edited by J. V. Murra, pp. 427–76. Universidad Hermilio Valdizán, Huánuco.
1975 *Formaciones Económicas y Políticas del Mundo Andino*. Instituto de Estudios Peruanos, Lima.
1980 *The Economic Organization of the Inca State*. JAI Press, Greenwich, CT.
1985a "El archipiélago vertical" revisited. In *Andean Ecology and Civilization*, edited by S. Masuda, I. Shimada, and C. Morris, pp. 3–13. University of Tokyo Press, Tokyo.

1985b The limits and limitations of the "vertical archipelago" in the Andes. In *Andean Ecology and Civilization*, edited by S. Masuda, I. Shimada, and C. Morris, pp. 15–20. University of Tokyo Press, Tokyo.

Nash, D.
2009 Household archaeology in the Andes. *Journal of Archaeological Research* 17(3):205–61.

Nielsen, A. E.
2006 Plazas para los Antepasados: Descentralización y Poder Corporativo en las Formaciones Políticas Preincaicas de los Andes Circumpuneños. *Estudios Atacameños* 31:63–89.

Niles, S. A.
1987 *Callachaca: Style and Status in an Inca Community*. University of Iowa Press, Iowa City.
1992 Inca architecture and sacred landscape. In *The Ancient Americas: Art from Sacred Landscapes*, edited by R. Townsend, pp. 346–57. The Art Institute of Chicago, Chicago.

Nilsson Stutz, L.
2003 *Embodied Rituals & Ritualized Bodies: Tracing Ritual Practices in Late Mesolithic Burials*. Acta Archaeologica Lundensia. Almqvist & Wiksell International, Stockholm.

O'Shea, J.
1996 *Villagers of the Maros*. Plenum Press, New York.

Ōnuki, Y. (editor)
1995 *Kuntur Wasi y Cerro Blanco: Dos Sitios del Formativo en el Norte del Perú*. Hokusen-sha, Tokyo.

Ōnuki, Y., T. Ushino, and Y. Seki
1985 Excavations at Huacaloma. In *The Formative Period in the Cajamarca Basin, Peru: Excavations at Huacaloma and Layzón, 1982*, edited by K. Terada and Y. Ōnuki, pp. 1–182. University of Tokyo Press, Tokyo.

Owoc, M.
2005 From the ground up: Agency, practice, and community in the southwestern British Bronze Age. *Journal of Archaeological Method and Theory* 12(4):257–81.

Parsons, J.
1972 Archaeological settlement patterns. *Annual Review of Anthropology* 1:127–50.

Patterson, T. C.
1967 Current research, highland South America. *American Antiquity* 32(I):143–44.

Paz Soría, J. L.
1999 Excavations in the Llusco area. In *Early Settlement at Chiripa, Bolivia: Research of the Taraco Archaeological Project*, edited by C. A. Hastorf, pp. 30–41. Vol. 57. Archaeological Research Facility, University of California Berkeley, Berkeley.

Pearsall, D. M.
2008 Plant domestication and the shift to agriculture in the Andes. In *The Handbook of South American Archaeology*, edited by H. Silverman and W. H. Isbell, pp. 105–20. Springer, New York.

Peebles, C. S., and S. M. Kus
1977 Some archaeological correlates of ranked societies. *American Antiquity* 42(3):421–48.

Penna, J.
1909 Costumbres Funerarias en el Imperio de los Inca. *Crónica Médica* 36(495–96):290–95, 301–12.

Pérez, S. I.
2007 Artificial cranial deformation in South America: A geometric morphometrics approximation. *Journal of Archaeological Science* 34(10):1649–58.

Perry, L., D. H. Sandweiss, D. R. Piperno, K. Rademaker, M. A. Malpass, A. Umire, and P. de la Vera
2006 Early maize agriculture and interzonal interaction in southern Peru. *Nature* 440(2):76–79.

Peterson, C. E., and R. D. Drennan
2005 Communities, settlements, sites, and surveys: Regional-scale analysis of prehistoric human interaction. *American Antiquity* 70(1):5–30.

Plog, S.
1976 Measurement of prehistoric interaction between communities. In *The Early Mesoamerican Village*, edited by K. V. Flannery, pp. 255–72. Academic Press, New York.

Pomeroy, E., J. T. Stock, S. R. Zakrzewski, and M. Mirazón Lahr
2009 A metric study of three types of artificial cranial modification from north-central Peru. *International Journal of Osteoarchaeology* 20(3):317–34.

Puig, S., and S. Monge
1983 Determinación de la Edad en Lama guanicoe (Müller). *Deserta* 7:246–70.

Redfield, R.
1955 *The Little Community: Viewpoints for the Study of a Human Whole*. University of Chicago Press, Chicago.

Reinhard, J.
1985 Sacred mountains: An ethno-archaeological study of high Andean ruins. *Mountain Research and Development* 5(4):299–317.

Renfrew, C.
1974 Beyond a subsistence economy: The evolution of social organization in prehistoric Europe. In *Reconstructing Complex Societies: An Archaeological Colloquium*, edited by C. B. Moore, pp. 69–95. Supplement to the Bulletin of the American Schools of Oriental Research, Vol. 20. Ann Arbor.
1975 Trade as action at a distance: Questions of integration and communication. In *Ancient Civilization and Trade*, edited by J. A. Sabloff and C. Lamberg-Karlovsky, pp. 3–59. University of New Mexico Press, Albuquerque.

Rhoades, R. E., and S. I. Thompson
1975 Adaptive strategies in alpine environments: Beyond ecological particularism. *American Ethnologist* 2(3):535–51.

Rivero Luque, V.
2005 *Herramientas Agrícolas de Perú Antiguo*. Centro Bartolomé de las Casas, Cusco.

Rose, C. E.
2001 Household and Community Organization of a Formative Period, Bolivian Settlement. PhD dissertation, Department of Anthropology, University of Pittsburgh. University Microfilms, Ann Arbor.

Rowe, J. H.
1943 Chanapata: La Cultura Pre-Incaica del Cuzco. *Tupac Amaru (Cuzco)* 2(2/3):41–43.
1944 An introduction to the archaeology of Cuzco. In *Papers of the Peabody Museum of American Archaeology and Ethnology*, Vol. 27, pp. 10–23. Harvard University, Cambridge.
1946 Inca culture at the time of the Spanish Conquest. In *Handbook of South American Indians*, Vol. 2, pp. 183–330. Bureau of American Ethnology, Washington, D.C.

Sahlins, M.
1963 Poor man, rich man, big man, chief. *Comparative Studies in Society and History* 5:285–302.

Salomon, F.
1995 "Beautiful grandparents": Andean ancestor shrines and mortuary ritual as seen through colonial records. In *Tombs for the Living: Andean Mortuary Practices, a Symposium at Dumbarton Oaks, 12th and 13th October 1991*, edited by T. D. Dillehay, pp. 315–53. Dumbarton Oaks Research Library and Collection, Washington, D.C.

Saxe, A. A.
1970 Social Dimensions of Mortuary Practices. PhD dissertation, Department of Anthropology, University of Michigan, Ann Arbor. University Microfilms, Ann Arbor.

Schulenberg, T. S.
2007 *Field Guide to the Birds of Peru*. Christopher Helm, London.

Seki, Y.
1993 La Transformación de los Centros Ceremoniales del Período Formativo en la Cuenca de Cajamarca, Perú. In *El Mundo Ceremonial Andino*, edited by L. Millones and Y. Ōnuki, pp. 203–28. Vol. 37. Senri Ethnological Studies. National Museum of Ethnology, Osaka.

Seltzer, G. O., and C. A. Hastorf
1990 Climatic change and its effect on prehispanic agriculture in the central Peruvian Andes. *Journal of Field Archaeology* 17:397–414.

Sherbondy, J. E.
1992 Water ideology in Inca ethnogenesis. In *Andean Cosmologies through Time: Persistence and Emergence*, edited by R. V. H. Dover, K. E. Seibold, and J. H. McDowell, pp. 46–66. Indiana University Press, Bloomington.

Shimada, M.
1982 Zooarchaeology of Huacaloma: Behavioral and cultural implications. In *Excavations at Huacaloma in the Cajamarca Valley, Peru, 1979*, edited by K. Terada and Y. Ōnuki, pp. 303–36. University of Tokyo Press, Tokyo.

1985 Continuities and changes in patterns of faunal resource utilization: Formative through Cajamarca periods. In *The Formative Period in the Cajamarca Basin, Peru: Excavations at Huacaloma and Layzón, 1982*, edited by K. Terada and Y. Ōnuki, pp. 289–310. University of Tokyo Press, Tokyo.

Sillar, B.
1992 The social life of the Andean dead. *Archaeological Review from Cambridge* 11(1):107–23.
1996 The dead and the drying. *Journal of Material Culture* 1(3):259–89.
2002 Caminando a Través del Tiempo: Geografías Sagradas en Cacha/Raqchi, Departamento del Cuzco (Perú). *Revista Andina* 35:221–46.

Song-Nai, R., and C. Mong-Lyong
1992 Emergence of complex society in prehistoric Korea. *Journal of World Prehistory* 6(1):51–95.

Spencer, C. S.
1990 On the tempo and mode of state formation: Neoevolutionism reconsidered. *Journal of Anthropological Archaeology* 9:1–30.

Stahl, P. W.
2008 Animal domestication in South America. In *The Handbook of South American Archaeology*, edited by H. Silverman and W. H. Isbell, pp. 121–30. Springer, New York.

Stanish, C.
1989 Household archeology: Testing models of zonal complementarity in the south central Andes. *American Anthropologist* 91(1):7–14.
2003 *Ancient Titicaca: The Evolution of Complex Society in Southern Peru and Northern Bolivia*. University of California Press, Berkeley.

Steward, J. H.
1956 *Area Research, Theory and Practice*. Bulletin 63. Social Science Research Council, New York.

Tainter, J. A.
1977 Modeling change in prehistoric social systems. In *For Theory Building in Archaeology*, edited by L. R. Binford, pp. 327–52. Academic Press, New York.

Terada, K.
1985 Early ceremonial architecture in the Cajamarca Valley. In *Early Ceremonial Architecture in the Andes: A Conference at Dumbarton Oaks, 8th to 10th October 1982*, edited by C. B. Donnan, pp. 191–208. Dumbarton Oaks Research Library and Collection, Washington, D.C.

Torres-Rouff, C.
2002 Cranial vault modification and ethnicity in Middle Horizon San Pedro de Atacama, Chile. *Current Anthropology* 43(1):163–71.

Torres-Rouff, C., and L. T. Yablonsky
2005 Cranial vault modification as a cultural artifact: A comparison of the Eurasian steppes and the Andes. *HOMO—Journal of Comparative Human Biology* 56(1):1–16.

Ugent, D., and C. M. Ochoa
2006 *La Etnobotánica del Perú*. CONCYTEC, Lima.

Valdez Cárdenas, L. M.
1988 Los Camélidos en la Subsistencia Nasca: El Caso de Kawachi. *Boletín de Lima* 57:31–35.
2000 On ch'arki consumption in the ancient central Andes: A cautionary note. *American Antiquity* 65(3):567–72.

Valdez Cárdenas, L. M., and J. E. Valdez
1997 Reconsidering the archaeological rarity of guinea pig bones in the central Andes. *Current Anthropology* 38(5):896–98.

Van Buren, M.
1996 Rethinking the vertical archipelago: Ethnicity, exchange, and history in the south central Andes. *American Anthropologist* n.s. 98(2):338–51.

van de Guchte, M.
1999 The Inca cognition of landscape: Archaeology, ethnohistory, and the aesthetic of alterity. In *Archaeologies of Landscape*, edited by W. Ashmore and A. B. Knapp, pp. 149–68. Blackwell, Malden, MA.

Van den Berghe, P. L.
1978 El Cargo de las Animas: Mortuary rituals and the cargo system in highland Peru. *Anthropological Quarterly* 51(2):129–36.

Vásquez Sánchez, V. F., and T. E. Rosales Tham
2008 *Análisis de Restos de Fauna y Vegetales del Sitio Wat'a*. Centro de Investigaciones Arqueobiológicas y Paleoecológicas Andinas, Trujillo, Peru. Report submitted to Steven J. Kosiba.
2009 *Análisis de Restos de Fauna y Vegetales del Sitio Yuthu*. Centro de Investigaciones Arqueobiológicas y Paleoecológicas Andinas, Trujillo, Peru. Report submitted to Allison R. Davis.

Vaughn, K. J.
2004 Households, crafts, and feasting in the ancient Andes: The village context of Early Nasca craft consumption. *Latin American Antiquity* 15(1):61–88.

Verano, J. W.
1995 Where do they rest? The treatment of human offerings and trophies in ancient Peru. In *Tombs for the Living: Andean Mortuary Practices, a Symposium at Dumbarton Oaks, 12th and 13th October 1991*, edited by T. D. Dillehay, pp. 189–228. Dumbarton Oaks Research Library and Collection, Washington, D.C.
1997 Advances in the paleopathology of Andean South America. *Journal of World Prehistory* 11(2):237–68.
2008 Trophy head-taking and human sacrifice in Andean South America. In *The Handbook of South American Archaeology*, edited by H. Silverman and W. H. Isbell, pp. 1047–60. Springer, New York.

Von Hagen, A., and C. Morris
1998 *The Cities of the Ancient Andes*. Thames and Hudson, New York.

Waldron, T.
1987 The relative survival of the human skeleton: Implications for paleopathology. In *Death, Decay, and Reconstruction: Approaches to Archaeology and Forensic Science*, edited by A. Boddington, A. N. Garland, and R. Janaway, pp. 55–64. Manchester University Press, Manchester.

Walker, P. L.
2001 A bioarchaeological perspective on the history of violence. *Annual Review of Anthropology* 30:573–96.

Wason, P. K.
1994 *The Archaeology of Rank*. New Studies in Archaeology. Cambridge University Press, Cambridge.

Webster, S.
1971 An indigenous Quechua community in exploitation of multiple ecological zones. *Revista del Museo Nacional* 37:176–83.
1972 The Social Organization of a Native Andean Community. PhD dissertation, Anthropology, University of Washington. University Microfilms, Ann Arbor.

Welch, P. D., and C. M. Scarry
1995 Status-related variation in foodways in the Moundville chiefdom. *American Antiquity* 60(3):397–419.

Wernke, S. A.
2007 Negotiating community and landscape in the Peruvian Andes: A transconquest view. *American Anthropologist* 109(1):130–52.

Wheeler, J. C.
1982 Aging llamas and alpacas by their teeth. *Llama World* 1:12–17.
1993 Evolution of high Andean puna ecosystems: Environment, climate, and culture change over the last 12,000 years in the central Andes. *Mountain Research and Development* 13(2):145–56.

Wheeler, J. C., A. J. F. Russel, and H. Redden
1995 Llamas and alpacas: Pre-conquest breeds and post-conquest hybrids. *Journal of Archaeological Science* 22:833–40.

Wheeler Pires-Ferreira, J., E. Pires-Ferreira, and P. Kaulicke
1976 Preceramic animal utilization in the central Peruvian Andes. *Science* 194:483–90.

Wiessner, P.
2002 The vines of complexity: Egalitarian structures and the institutionalization of inequality among the Enga. *Current Anthropology* 43(2):233–69.

Williams, C.
1985 A scheme for early monumental architecture of the central coast of Peru. In *Early Ceremonial Architecture in the Andes: A Conference at Dumbarton Oaks, 8th to 10th October 1982*, edited by C. B. Donnan, pp. 227–39. Dumbarton Oaks Research Library and Collection, Washington, D.C.

Williams, P. R., and D. J. Nash
2006 Sighting the Apu: A GIS analysis of Wari imperialism and the worship of mountain peaks. *World Archaeology* 38(3):455–68.

Winter, M. C., and J. W. Pires-Ferreira
1976   Distribution of obsidian among households in two Oaxacan villages. In *The Early Mesoamerican Village*, edited by K. V. Flannery, pp. 306–11. Academic Press, New York.

Wobst, H. M.
1977   Stylistic behavior and information exchange. In *Papers for the Director: Research Essays in Honor of J. B. Griffin, 1977*, edited by C. Cleland. Anthropological Papers, no. 61. Museum of Anthropology, University of Michigan, Ann Arbor.
1999   Style in archaeology or archaeologists in style. In *Material Meanings: Critical Approaches to the Interpretation of Material Culture*, edited by E. Chilton, pp. 118–32. University of Utah Press, Salt Lake City.

Wright, H. T.
2000   Modeling tributary economies and hierarchical polities: A prologue. In *Cultural Evolution: Contemporary Viewpoints*, edited by G. M. Feinman and L. Manzanilla, pp. 197–213. Kluwer Academic/Plenum Publishers, New York.

Wylie, A.
2002   *Thinking from Things: Essays in the Philosophy of Archaeology*. University of California Press, Berkeley.

Yábar Moreno, J.
1959   La Cultura Pre-Incaica de Chanapata. *Revista del Museo e Instituto Arqueológico* 18:93–100.
1972   Época Pre-Inca de Chanapata. *Revista Saqsaywaman* 2:211–33.
1982   Figurillas de la Cultura Pre-Inka del Cuzco. In *Arqueología de Cuzco*, edited by I. O. Rodríguez. Instituto Nacional de Cultura, Cuzco.

Yaeger, J.
2000   The social construction of communities in the Classic Maya countryside: Strategies of affiliation in western Belize. In *The Archaeology of Communities: A New World Perspective*, edited by M. A. Canuto and J. Yaeger, pp. 123–42. Routledge, New York.

Yamasaki, F., T. Hamada, and C. Fujiyama
1966   RIKEN natural radiocarbon measurements II. *Radiocarbon* 8:324–39.

Zapata, J.
1998   Los Cerros Sagrados: Panorama del Período Formativo en la Cuenca del Vilcanota, Cuzco. In *Perspectivas Regionales del Período Formativo en el Perú*, pp. 307–36. Vol. 2. Boletín Arqueología PUCP. Pontificia Universidad Católica del Perú, Lima.

Index

adobe brick, 33, 70, 81, 133
agriculture: practice of, 8–10, 14–15, 155, 158–59; tools for, 15, 54–55, 155–56
Alto Pukara, 140
ancestor veneration: Formative period architecture and, 10, 148; material remains of, 144, 146, 150–52; multi-village polities and, 144–45, 157, 159; politics and, 11, 143, 145, 147–48; practice of, 10, 144–45; and status negotiation, 145–46, 157
ancestors: agricultural productivity and, 143–45; in origin stories, 10, 144–45; resource rights and, 10, 144, 152–53, 156; in relation to the landscape, 10, 144; segmentary social structure and, 143–45, 147; shared identity and, 10, 141, 143–45, 153
Anthropologie de terrain, 35
apu, 93
Arensberg, C. M., 6–8
ayllu, 144–45, 147

Batan Urqo, 5, 33, 92, 139
Bauer, B. S., 4–5, 11
beans, domestication of, 13–14
Big Man society, 5, 11
birds: burial of, 60–61; exploitation of, 13, 25, 136, 138; ritual related to, 13, 37–38, 132
bone tools: manufacture, 29, 155; production areas, 73, 75, 79; types, 28, 137–38

burials, human: in a cemetery, 82, 88–91, 127–33, 152; associated with ceremonial architecture, 93–101, 113–19, 150–53; associated with domestic structures, 50, 56–57, 73–74, 91, 150–53; evidence for inequality in, 3, 35, 158; associated with water ritual, 149, 157. *See also* mortuary practice; mummies
burned offerings, 88, 91, 140–41, 145, 147, 149, 153

camelids: age estimation of, 16–17; butchery of, 16, 26; cooking of, 22, 136–38; domestication of, 13–14; herd maintenance of, 16, 18; species identification of, 16–17
canals: aligned with glaciers, 148–51; in ceremonial architecture, 93–94, 96, 99–103, 107, 119, 133, 139, 140–41, 148–50, 156; construction of, 33, 96–97, 116, 118; human burials associated with, 113–19, 149; used for poured offerings, 99–103, 119, 140–41, 147–49; ritual closing of, 113–16, 148
caravan, llama, 38, 156
ceque system, 144, 146
Ch'isi, 139
Chanapata: archaeological site, 33; pottery style, 29–31, 38, 139
Chavín de Huantar, 38, 92, 139–41
Chicón, 93, 149–51, 159
chiefdom, 5, 158
Chiripa: ancestor veneration at, 148; ceremonial architecture at, 139–40, 148; trade at, 38
Choquepukio, 33

climate change, 153–54, 158
collecting wild plants, 26
community: approach to research, 5–8, 155–56; imagined, 5–7; natural, 5–7; shared identity in, 7, 141
cooking: of camelid meat, 22, 136, 138; carried out inside a house, 22, 46, 66, 73; carried out in outdoor hearths, 22, 49, 62, 73, 121–22; practice of, 22, 136–37
corn: consumption of, 137; cooking of, 22; domestication of, 13; farming of, 15, 18, 155–56
Covey, R. A., 1
cranial modification, 23–25, 155
cuy. *See* guinea pig

deer: antler of, 15, 67, 137; cooking of, 22, 136, 138; exploitation of, 13, 25
domestic structures: above ground, 64–72, 81–82, 91, 133; and economic inequality, 3, 158; outside Cusco during the Formative period, 92; semi-subterranean, 33, 42–50, 54–55, 91, 133, 150
Dulanto, J., 148
dye, plants for making, 26, 28–29

egalitarian villages, 5, 11, 157
ethnography, 143–46
ethnohistory, 1, 143–46

farming. *See* agriculture
figurine: bird, 137; human, 128, 137, 152; pyramid-shaped, 128, 137, 150, 152; zoomorphic, 137. *See also* illa
fish, 25, 138
floors: made of prepared clay, 60–61, 91, 101, 108, 133, 138; trampled surfaces associated with hearths, 49–50, 58, 61–64, 73, 77, 79–81, 91, 138; trampled surfaces in houses, 44–45, 48, 54, 66–70, 91, 133, 138
fuel, gathering, 21–22, 155

glaciers: and agricultural productivity, 144, 149; and group identity, 144; and multi-village polities, 159; in the sacred landscape, 144, 148–51; and water ritual, 149, 151. *See also* Chicón; Pitusiray
Greer, S. A., 6
grinding stones, 20–21, 137–38
group identity: and ancestors, 10, 141, 143–44, 148, 153; and kinship, 143–44; and the landscape, 9–10, 141, 143–44, 150, 153, 156; and mummy veneration, 144, 152–53; and resource rights, 10, 141, 143–44, 148, 153, 156; ritual related to, 141, 144, 148
guinea pig: cooking of, 22, 136; domestication of, 13–14; raising of, 20, 46, 48, 155

Hastorf, C., 148
hearth: for indoor cooking, 66, 91, 133, 138; as outdoor activity area, 13, 49, 52, 59, 61–65, 73–81, 91, 121–22, 133, 138, 158; for ritual, 82, 88–89, 91, 120–21, 125–26, 133, 139, 152

herding, 15–16, 155–56
houses. *See* domestic structures
Huacaloma, 140
Huanacaure, Cerro, 30, 93, 133, 148, 150, 153–54
Huaricoto, 140
Huaypo, Lake: location of, 41, 93, 133; as a natural resource, 25, 156; in the sacred landscape, 148, 150, 153
hunting, 25, 155

illa, 110–11, 128, 138, 147, 149, 152
inequality: economic, 158; hereditary, 1–4, 152–53, 157–58; ideology legitimating, 153, 157–58; kinship metaphor for, 144
Inka: ancestor veneration of, 143–46, 159; ancestors in origin stories of, 144–46, 153; architecture of, 146–47; cranial modification by, 23; in Cusco, 1–2; inheritance practices of, 144; mummies of, 144–46, 159; roads of, 38; sacred landscape of, 93, 145–47, 159; water ritual of, 140, 147
Isbell, W. H., 7, 148

Junín, 92

Kala Uyuni, 139–40
Kimball, S. T., 6–7
kinship: and group identity, 143–44; and inequality, 144
Kuntur Wasi, 139–40

Layzón, 140
Lukurmata, 54, 92

maize. *See* corn
mallki, 145, 146. *See also* mummies
Marcavalle: archaeological site, 4–5, 33; pottery style, 4; subsistence at, 15–16, 25
maway, 18–20. *See also* potato: farming of
medicine, 26, 59, 62, 155
miskha, 18–20. *See also* corn: farming of
mortuary practice: and ancestor veneration, 146, 148, 150–53, 157; and ongoing interaction with the dead, 152–53, 156–57; primary burial, 35, 50, 64, 90–91, 114–16, 129–32, 151–52; secondary burial of an individual, 35–37, 91, 97–101, 116–19, 131, 151, 157; secondary burial including multiple individuals, 35, 56–57, 64, 150; types at Yuthu, 35–37. *See also* burials, human; mummies
mountains: ecology of, 8–10, 16–20, 158; and group identity, 144, 156; in the sacred landscape, 144, 156
multi-village polity, 1–5, 154–59
mummies: burials at Yuthu of, 37, 64–66, 73–74, 82, 90–91, 127–29, 151–53; creation of inequality using, 11, 144, 153, 157; and inheritance, 144, 153; of Inka king, 144, 146; and politics, 144–45; production by freeze-drying of, 37, 146, 151; ritual focused on, 144–46; and shared identity, 144, 148, 153
Murdock, G. P., 6–7
Murra, J. V., 9–10, 159
Muyu Orqo, 5–6, 33, 139

ornaments, personal, 23, 137

Pampa Chica, 148
pastoralism. *See* herding
pit house. *See* domestic structure: semi-subterranean
Pitusiray, 93, 148–51, 159
platform, 1, 33, 93–94, 133, 139–40, 148–50, 155–56
potato: cooking of, 22; domestication of, 13; farming of, 14, 18, 19, 110, 155; illa of, 110–11, 138, 149, 152; ritual related to, 110–11
pottery: Chanapata style, 29–31; forms, 19, 29–30, 137–38; Marcavalle style, 4; Paqallamoqo style, 29; production of, 29, 155

qhapaq hucha, 146–47
quinoa: cooking of, 22; domestication of, 13; farming of, 14, 19, 155

rank, inherited, 2–4, 158. *See also* inequality
Redfield, R., 6, 8
refuse in pits, 22, 51–52, 59, 81–84, 106, 110–12, 123, 137–38
ritual: related to agricultural productivity, 145, 153; related to birds, 92; domestic, 92; spatial distribution of, 13; related to water, 140, 145, 147–49. *See also* mortuary practice
ritual structure, made of mud, 94, 124–26, 133
roads, 38–39, 159
Rowe, J. H., 29, 139

sacred landscape: and agricultural productivity, 143–45, 147, 156; and architecture, 146–48; and ceremonial architecture at Yuthu, 148–50, 156; local to Yuthu, 148–50; material evidence for, 146–47; and multi-village polities, 9–10, 145, 156–57, 159; and politics, 143, 145, 156; and segmentary social structure, 143–45, 147
Sacred Valley, agriculture in, 15–16, 18, 156
scheduling agropastoral activities, 13, 16–18, 156
segmentary social organization, 143–45, 147
site-size hierarchy: and Chanapata pottery, 4–5, 38, 158; and political organization, 4
settlement patterns, 4
stone tools: chipped, 29–32, 137–38, 155; production areas, 46, 49, 59, 73; projectile points, 30, 32, 62, 73, 76; raw materials for, 30, 32, 137–38. *See also* grinding stones
storage pits: in the domestic sector, 22, 44–45, 48, 50–52, 54–55, 59, 81, 91, 133; in the ceremonial sector, 101, 108–10
sunken structures: construction of, 95–97; rectangular ceremonial, 94, 133, 135, 139–40, 148, 156; ritual interment of, 120–22
survey, systematic archaeological, 4

terracing, 33
textiles: dyeing of, 28–29, 52, 59, 62, 73; production of, 26–29, 155; remains at Yuthu of, 130
thatch roofs, 26, 33, 44–45, 66, 91
Titicaca Basin: ceremonial architecture in, 139–40, 148, 156; domestic architecture in, 92

Tiwanaku, 159
trade, 38, 46, 156, 158
tubers, domestication of, 13. *See also* potato

Urubamba Valley. *See* Sacred Valley

vertical archipelago, 9–10, 159
verticality: community organization and, 8–10, 156; as a production strategy, 9–10, 16–20, 156
violence, 34–35, 127, 129–30, 132, 152, 157–58

Wari: 24–25, 147–48, 159
Wat'a, 16
water: children and ritual related to, 149, 157; glaciers as a source of, 145; in origin myths, 144; ritual involving, 140, 145, 147–49
Wimpillay, 5–6. *See also* Muyu Orqo

Xaquixaguana Plain Archaeological Survey, 1, 16, 18, 38, 93

Yaya-mama religious tradition, 141

Zapata, J., 33, 139–40

Plate 1

Objects used for personal adornment included: beads made of bone (*a*), shell (*b*), and stone (*c, d*); and clothing pins made of bone (*e*) and metal (*f*).

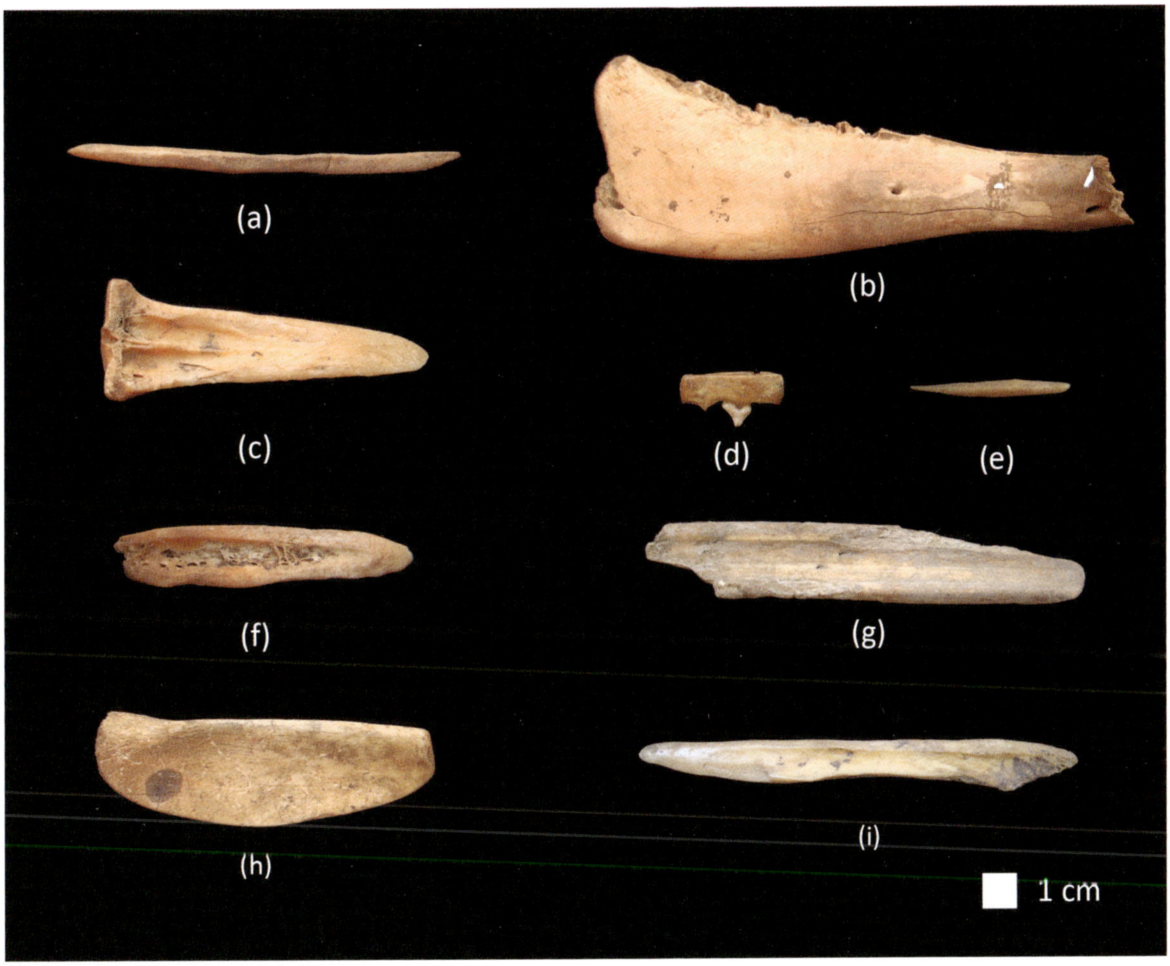

Examples of bone tools from Yuthu: *a*, a thin pointed object; *b*, a camelid mandible spatula; *c*, a *ruk'i* or bone awl; *d*, a polished jaw fragment with tooth; *e*, a small needle; *f*, a long bone shaft fragment with smooth rounded tip; *g*, a long bone shaft fragment with square tip; *h*, a camelid scapula scraper; *i*, a long bone shaft fragment with pointed tips.

Plate 2

Chanapata sub-styles identified at Yuthu: *a*, Chanapata plainware; *b*, Chanapata pattern burnished; *c*, Chanapata redware; *d*, Chanapata blackware; *e*, Chanapata painted and incised; *f*, Chanapata incised. Molded decorations (*g*) were applied to the body or rim of pottery of many different styles.

Plate 3

Exterior and interior views of a modern semi-subterranean thatched structure excavated into a hillside. Note that the simple roof was built directly on the ground surface. This structure is similar to the early pit houses in the Northern Sector of Yuthu.

Several obsidian tools were found in Ashy Intrusion 2 in the northwest corner of Unit D. It is likely that they were used for craft production of some kind.

A carved antler found on the first trampled surface of the above-ground house in the southeast corner of Unit D.

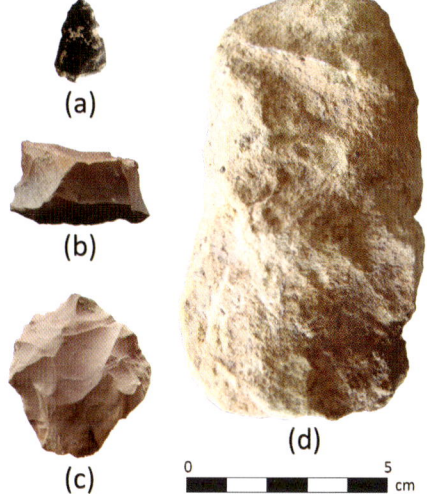

Chipped stone tools found in the hearth inside the above-ground house in Unit D: *a*, obsidian hafted biface projectile point (Level F-1); *b*, quartzite unidirectional core tool (Level F-2); *c*, quartzite multidirectional core tool (Level F-3); *d*, coarse grain quartzitic sandstone bimarginal flake tool (Level F-3).

Several chipped stone tools were in Level E-7 of the hearth in the southwest corner of Unit D (*left to right starting at the top*): obsidian unimarginal flake tool, obsidian combination flake tool, obsidian bimarginal flake tool projectile point, obsidian multidirectional core tool, obsidian unimarginal flake tool reutilized projectile point, chert combination flake tool, quartzite unidirectional core, quartzite multidirectional core, quartzite bimarginal flake tool, laminar andesite bimarginal flake tool.

Plate 4

The artificial platform in the Southern Sector is a striking feature on the landscape. Such flat areas are extremely rare in the Andes Mountains. This photo is a view from the northeast.

The two parts of the southwestern bench of Structure 1 in Unit A were separated by a drain cut into bedrock and a retaining wall that extended out from the eastern end of the western section. In this photo, the construction fill and burials have already been excavated from behind the wall.

There was a large semicircular intrusion in front of the intake of Ritual Canals 1 and 2 (Unit A, Intrusion D).

Plate 5

Stone tools from Level D-1 in the base of the intrusion in the northeast corner of Unit A: *a*, fine grain quartzitic sandstone unimarginal flake tool; *b*, organic limestone unimarginal flake tool; *c, d*, quartzite unimarginal flake tools; *e*, obsidian unimarginal flake tool.

A stone-lined cist associated with a white clay floor was added to Structure 1 (Unit A, Intrusion C). The walls of the intrusion were made of field stones set in red clay mortar.

Plate 6

Ritual Canal 2 cut off Ritual Canal 1. Both canals shared the same intake inside Structure 1 in Unit A.

Plate 7

The final view of excavations in Units A and D highlight the drastic differences in architecture between the Northern and Southern Sectors.

Plate 8

Objects found in the Southern Sector (*from left to right*): An *illa* of a potato may have been related to rituals requesting agricultural fertility. A pyramid-shaped rock may have represented a mountain or platform. A human figurine in a flexed pose similar to burial positions at Yuthu may be related to ancestor veneration; note that the head has been snapped off the body.